Human–Computer Interaction Series

Editors-in-Chief

Desney Tan
Microsoft Research, Redmond, WA, USA

Jean Vanderdonckt
Louvain School of Management, Université catholique de Louvain,
Louvain-La-Neuve, Belgium

The Human–Computer Interaction Series, launched in 2004, publishes books that advance the science and technology of developing systems which are effective and satisfying for people in a wide variety of contexts. Titles focus on theoretical perspectives (such as formal approaches drawn from a variety of behavioural sciences), practical approaches (such as techniques for effectively integrating user needs in system development), and social issues (such as the determinants of utility, usability and acceptability).

HCI is a multidisciplinary field and focuses on the human aspects in the development of computer technology. As technology becomes increasingly more pervasive the need to take a human-centred approach in the design and development of computer-based systems becomes ever more important.

Titles published within the Human–Computer Interaction Series are included in Thomson Reuters' Book Citation Index, The DBLP Computer Science Bibliography and The HCI Bibliography.

More information about this series at http://www.springer.com/series/6033

Martin Schmettow

New Statistics for Design Researchers

A Bayesian Workflow in Tidy R

 Springer

Martin Schmettow
Cognition, Data & Education
University of Twente
Enschede, The Netherlands

ISSN 1571-5035   ISSN 2524-4477 (electronic)
Human–Computer Interaction Series
ISBN 978-3-030-46382-3   ISBN 978-3-030-46380-9 (eBook)
https://doi.org/10.1007/978-3-030-46380-9

This Springer imprint is published by the registered company Springer Nature Switzerland AG
The registered company address is: Gewerbestrasse 11, 6330 Cham, Switzerland

This book is dedicated to my father,
Dr. Walter Schmettow, with love.
Ask me and I will read it to you.

And to my daughter, Eli, with all my love.
Your songs are another book.

Contents

Part I
Preparations

Chapter 1
Introduction

1.1 Whom This Book Is For

Are you a design researcher? Is your work about improving computer software, cars, medical devices, services or trainings? Are you using data for your work, in order to measure or compare how well a design works? Welcome to the club!

Of course, I have no idea who you are, personally, but I figure you as one of the following types:

You are a Human Factors researcher, 33 years old, leading a small team in the center for research of a German car manufacturer. Your task is to evaluate emerging technologies, like augmented reality, car-to-car communication and smart light. Downstream research relies on your competent assessment of what is feasible. For example, you have just been asked to evaluate whether blue light can make for safer driving: Blue light makes people wake up easier. Could this also be used to let car drivers not fall asleep? You are working together with two engineers and a student of industrial design. Your plan is to put a light color device into a prototype car. Two workstations are stuffed into the boot of the car for record physiological signals and driving performance. All this is very expensive and someone is paying for it. Your skin is in the game.

Or, you are a young academic and just got a cum laude master's degree in computer science. For your thesis, you developed and implemented an animated avatar for a digital assistant. A professor from the social psychology department has read your thesis. She just got funding for a project on mass emergency communication using projected virtual characters. Being afraid that a psychologist researcher would not be up to the technical part of the project and found you. But, you ask yourself, am I up to the task of running experimental studies and do the statistics?

Or, you are a student in some applied field of Psychology and your thesis project is about evaluating a design, or a training, or a therapeutic intervention, or making this world a better place in any other way. From your bachelor studies, you already have a background in Statistics, but it occurs to you, the basics won't do it for what you have in mind.

© Springer Nature Switzerland AG 2021
M. Schmettow, *New Statistics for Design Researchers,*
Human–Computer Interaction Series,
https://doi.org/10.1007/978-3-030-46380-9_1

Finally, perhaps you are an experimentalist. Are you doing research with people, but your research question addresses the human mind, in general, and the answers you seek are far from being applicable to anything in sight? You are not a design researcher, but don't put this book away too fast! The only difference between a design experiment and a psychological lab experiment is, in the different stakes, not the research design and structure of data. In cognitive experiments, a drop in reaction time can mean that some priming or learning has occurred, which can either strengthen or defeat a certain theory on human cognition. In a design experiment, if users can work faster with one interface compared to another, that is usually a good thing. For a statistical model, intentions don't matter. Chances are good that you will be able to read through the ephemeral details of the design research cases I present and apply the same methods to your own research situations.

1.2   Quantitative Design Research

A *design* is the structure of an artifact (or a process) that someone conceived for a purpose. This definition is extremely broad as it covers everything, tea kettles, software, cockpits, training programs and complex human-machine systems. The only exception I can think of is art, which is not design, because purposefulness is a requirement. Quantitative design research simply is about measuring to what extent a design, a class of designs or a design feature fulfills its purposes. We all have purposes and most of the time it is quite a job to get there. Getting there typically requires resources and often we have to strike some sort of balance. The two basic questions in *quantitative design research* are

1. To what extent does a design fulfill its purpose?
2. What are the costs for the design?

A good design simply fulfills its purpose enough to justify the costs. The methods and examples in this book all deal with the first question. Quantitative design research practically always is an *evaluation* of some sort. This evaluation can either be very specific, such as the effect of a new or changed feature in A/B testing, or generic, such as the uncanny effect of human-likeness of robot faces on the feelings of people. Broadly, the purpose of specific design study is to evaluate the fitness of a single design before it enters the next development stage (or is rolled out to the users). In contrast, generic design studies have the purpose to inform future designs of a class. In both cases, something is at stake, immediately or in the future, and this is why quantification is required.

Quantification happens on two levels: the research questions and measures. In most research, a process called measurement produces numbers. This can be as simple as the reaction time to a signal, or as advanced as a trained neural network that judges the emotional content of tweets.

For calling a study *quantitative research*, it is required to ask *quantitative research questions*. In the real world, decisions are (or should be) based on benefits and rational allocation of resources. Changing the background color of a website might just be a switch (and can have undesired effects as users hate change), but restructuring an intranet site can be very costly. In industrial design research, there usually is someone who wants to know whether this or that redesign is worth it, and that requires to ask research questions like the following examples:

- By how much does reaction time degrade with age and is it safe that people beyond 80 still drive?
- Does design B reduce the required number of steps by a third, at least?
- What proportion of users prefers red over yellow? All websites better go red?

Sadly, in much existing research, the quantitative perspective is frequently lost along the way and conclusions read more like

- Older people have longer reaction times in traffic situations ($p \leq 0.05$).
- People find information more easily with design A, compared to B ($p \leq 0.05$).
- Chinese people on average prefer red color schemes over yellow ($p \leq 0.001$).

There simply is no numbers in these statements (except for the notorious p-values, which I will briefly discuss in Chap. 3). The statistical methods introduced in this book do a terrific job at drawing quantitative conclusions. Every regression model features a so-called *outcome*, which must be a measure (rather than a category).

Modern designs tend to be very complex and so are research questions, potentially. The options for designing just your personal homepage are myriad and there is considerable uncertainty about which features, or rather which configuration of features works best. Consider every option, say font type, font size, color, background color, position of menu and a potential impact factor on how pleasant the page is to read. At the same time, these features are not independent. For a simple example, readability of a website depends on font size and contrast, which means you can trade in one for the other. Perhaps, someone should once and for all figure out the optimal configuration. Such a study would require that as many as possible impact factors are represented in a single study and evaluated by a single comprehensive statistical model. The models introduced in this book handle such complexity with grace. There is theoretically no limit for the number of impact factors or *predictors*.

The central peculiarity in all behavioral research is that measures are extremely *noisy*, with the consequence that we can never draw totally firm conclusions. In Chap. 3, the concept of uncertainty will be elaborated upon, but for now it suffices to understand that no statistical models can make fully certain predictions. Imagine a simple test for cognitive processing speed. Participants wait for a signal and react to it. Although the task is the same every time, the measures most likely will be scattered, like 900, 1080 and 1110 ms. Imagine further this were an ability test in a training for, say, astronauts. To be admissioned to the space program, the applicant needs a score of less than 1000 ms. Would you dare to decide on the career of a young person based on these three observations? Hardly so. Uncertainty can be reduced by taking more measures, but 100% certainty can never be reached. The approach presented in this book addresses the uncertainty problem by making the level of uncertainty transparent.

In contrast, consider measuring a person's waist length for the purpose of tailoring a suit. By using a meter, the tailor measures 990 mm, and would be perfectly fine with that. Why did the tailor not take a second and a third measure? Well, experience tells that meters are pretty precise measures and waist length shows relatively little variation (under constant habits). Say the two measures were 995 and 989 mm. Such small deviations have practically no influence on cutting the linen.

> Our minds are not run as top-down dictatorships; they are rambunctious parliaments, populated by squabbling factions and caucuses, with much more going on beneath the surface than our conscious awareness ever accesses.

> Carroll, Sean. The Big Picture (Kindle Locations 5029-5031). Oneworld Publications. Kindle Edition.

Vast fluctuations of measures are common in design research, simply for the fact that human behavior is involved. Every magnitude we derive from a study is uncertain to some degree. Uncertainty makes that at any moment, we can rely on a quantitative result only to some extent, which influences how we take risks. New Statistics solves this problem by attaching a degree of uncertainty to every effect. Section 3.1 gives some reasoning and examples, how to operate rationally under uncertainty, and drives you right into the arms of Bayesian statistics.

When you have no greater goal in mind than proving your design is of quality, *user studies* are effective and quick means. In the easiest case, you want to put your design against a fixed benchmark. For example, in the design of automotives, media devices in the cockpit may not distract the driver for more than 1.5 s at times. If you want to prove that a design complies with this rule, you will have to plug some advanced eye tracking gear into a prototype car and send people on the test drive. But once the data is in, things get really simple. The saccade measures directly represent what you were out for: the length of episodes of visual attention on the media display. In web design, it is common to compare two or more designs in order to make the best choice. An e-commerce company can put a potential future design on the test drive, delivering it to a customer sample. Performance is measured as hard currency, which is as close to the purpose as it can get.

A user study solves the momentary problem of comparing a local design to a benchmark (which can be another design). In the long run, design configurations are too manyfold to be compared in a one-by-one manner. It is inevitable that we try to trace some general patterns and apply our knowledge to a whole class of designs at once. Our research design just got one step more complex. Instead of just checking whether a smaller font size creates problems on a single website, the researcher reaches out to comparing the combined effect of aging and font size on reading time, in general. This is what I call a *design experiment*.

Design experiments allow for much broader conclusions, if done right, but there are some issues:

1. The design features under scrutiny must be under control of the researcher. It does not suffice to collect some websites with varying font sizes, but every website needs to undergo the test at various font sizes.

2. The design feature must undergo a full range of manipulations. You will not find the laws of readability by just comparing 10 pt versus 12 pt.
3. Design features usually do not stand on their own. Readability is influenced by other factors, such as contrast and comprehensibility. Deriving a model from just one design will only generalize to this one design. Hence, the researcher must run the experiment on a sample of designs, with one of two strategies (or a mix of both): the *randomization strategy* takes a representative sample of designs, hoping that other impact factors average out. As we will see in Sect. 5.4, this is a daring assumption. Therefore, the preferred way is *statistical control*, where potential impact factors are recorded and added as control variables to the regression model.

The parameters for decision-making vary with the purpose. In an admission test for astronaut training, a decision is raised on individuals. Also, there is only this one shot, figuratively and literally, and the costs are enormous. Down on earth, many designs affect many people at once, sometimes in the billions, if just a little bit. Consider any commercial or informational website. If you decide, for aesthetic reasons, to shrink the font size, it is not unlikely that you just start loosing all visitors from the e-senior generation. Or, if your content is really good, they may swallow the bitter pill and start using looking glasses on their O-pads. As a researcher, you can approach any of these problems by a specific user study or a generic design experiment.

Effective design research hinges on many methodological considerations, such as selection of valid measures, efficient experimental designs and sampling schemes. To keep this confined in a textbook on statistical models, I will briefly address measures in the following chapter. Experimental design will not be explicitly addressed, but all real case studies used in this book have been carefully designed and I am confident to offer them as templates for your own research.

1.3 What Is New Statistics?

New Statistics is neither novel, nor are the contained methods truly bleeding edge. The term has been coined by [1] and it is new in two respects: first, what can be subsumed as Classic Statistics is a zoo of crude tools from the first half of the twentieth century. Second, NewStats and ClassicStats take different perspectives. ClassicStats emphasizes the approach of testing hypotheses that were derived from theories, which is known as *null hypothesis significance testing (NHST)*. New Statistics is about quantification of impact factors.

The difference is best illustrated by seeing how in either one the results are reported. A classic analysis report has the following structure:

1. Recollect the hypothesis: *Participants in the control condition are faster.*
2. Descriptive statistics: *The difference of means in the sample is* 217.
3. State the null hypothesis: $H_0 : (M_{exp} - M_{control}) = 0$.
4. Test the assumptions of ANOVA:

    a. Homogeneity of variance;

    b. Normal distribution of residuals.

5. If assumptions are not violated, continue with ANOVA, otherwise with a non-parametric test.
6. Report *p*-values: *The chance that a difference of* 217 ms *happens, when the null hypothesis is true, is* $p \leq 0.05$.
7. ... proceeding to the next research question and repeat the cycle.

A New Statistics report has the following structure:

1. Collect all research questions: *Participants in the experimental condition are 10% faster* and *Older participants are slower*.
2. Explorative figures: *The boxplot shows that participants with the novel design are faster by around 200 s on average,* and *the scatterplot shows a positive trend with age*.
3. Reasoning about the measures and shape of randomness: *Response times are strictly positive and frequently left-skewed*.
4. Building one model: *We use a model on response time with two predictors, condition and age, with Exponential-Gaussian distributed responses*.
5. Reporting quantities with uncertainty: *The novel design leads to faster reaction times, with the best guess of 205 ms difference. With 95% certainty, the true difference is at least 172 ms*.

The first to note is that in NewStats, *research questions are quantitative*. For the design researcher, it is essential to know how large an improvement is, because design always takes place in a web of trade-offs. Let's take the example of putting blue light into cars, to keep drivers awake. It is one thing to test that on a test drive or a simulator, it is another to kick it off into development and produce a car series. That means that applied or industrial researchers eventually have to report their results to decision makers and the data must ascertain not only that there is an improvement but also that the improvement justifies the costs.

In New Statistics, we have a much *higher flexibility in designing statistical models*. Classic models are like a zoo, where most animals cannot interbreed. You can find an animal that is furry, another one that has green color and a third one that can swim. But, you cannot cross them into one animal that does it all. New Statistics is like modern genetics, where properties of animals are encoded on basic building blocks. Theoretically, once you understand the basic building blocks, you can assemble the animal you want. In our favor, the building blocks of statistical models have long been understood and they are just a few. This book covers the family of *Generalized Linear Multi-level Models*, which consists of the following building blocks:

1. A *linear relation* describes the basic quantitative relationship between a metric predictor and a metric outcome.
2. By *dummy coding*, categorical (i.e. non-metric) predictors can be used, as well.
3. By *linear combination*, the simultaneous effect of multiple predictors can be modeled.

4. *Random effects* apply for categorical variables, where the levels represent members of one population.
5. *Multi-level* modeling allows the simultaneous estimations on population level and participant level.
6. *Link functions* linearize the predictor-outcome relationship for outcomes which have boundaries (which they all do).
7. *Error distributions* adjust the shape of randomness to the type of outcome variable.

The power NewStats model lies in the combinatorics explosion arising from the full interoperability of its building blocks. The most powerful building block is the combination of linear terms. A linear model for the effect of blue light would be written as RT ~ Light. To simultaneously address the age effect, we had to write just RT ~ Light + age. In New Statistics, statistical models are not pulled off the shelf but are designed in a thoughtful manner, based on an analysis of the *data-generating process*.

I wouldn't go so far as to say, we are only scratching the surface with the family of Generalized Linear Multi-level Models GLMM, but there definitely are more building blocks that further expand the family of models, for example, also allowing non-linear relationships (see Sects. 5.5 and 7.2.1.2). New Statistics does not require the GLMM family per se; it only requires that models have a *quantitative interpretation*. That includes the whole set of models commonly referred to as *parametric models*, of which GLMM is one class.

If there are parametric models, what about *non-parametric models*? In ClassicStats, non-parametric tests are routinely used as a fallback for when none of the few available parametric models sits well. Non-parametric methods are banned from NewStats, for two reasons: first, they don't give quantitative answers. Second, they are not needed. When reaction times are not "distributed Normal", the researcher can simply swap the building block that defines the shape of randomness. Or even better: the researcher knows that reaction times are not Normal and selects an appropriate response distribution right away. Infamously in ClassicStats, non-parametric tests are often misused to check the assumptions of a model, like the Normality assumption. New Statistics does not require such crude tricks. The process of assumption checking (and being screwed if any are violated) is simply replaced by a top-down *knowledge-driven model design*.

Finally, ClassicStats and NewStats models differ in what pops out of them. The very reason to run a statistical model, rather than pulling the answers from descriptive statistics, like group averages, is that data obtained from a sample is never a complete picture but is always tainted by some *degree of uncertainty*. In ClassicStats, questions are posed as binary (Yes/No), following the traditional method of null hypothesis significance testing: Is there a difference, or not? Awkwardly, the way a null hypothesis is posed does not seem to focus on the difference, but on the opposite: Imagine, there really was no difference. How likely would the observed data be? If we were to repeat the experiment a hundred times, how often would we see such a result? If this blurs your mind, you are not alone. Where do all these experiments come from?

In fact, the p-value is just a clever mathematical trick to extrapolate from the data at hand, to what would happen with an infinite number of replications. While we could view the so-called alpha error as a continuous measure of certainty, it is not a measure of how strong an effect is. Instead, the p-value is a convolution of effect size, noise level and sample size. That makes it very difficult to interpret, which is most apparent with the mal-practice of non-parametric tests for assumptions checking: If the data set is small, even large deviations from, say Normality, will not be detected. On large data sets, the opposite happens: minor deviations lead to the rejection of a reasonable approximation. In practice, the p-value is not even used as a continuous measure, but is further simplified by a social norm: If the p-value is smaller than 5%, the null hypothesis is rejected, if it is not, we are in the limbo.

New Statistics asks quantitative questions and our models produce quantitative answers, together with levels of uncertainty. These answers come as parameter estimates, like the difference between two groups. Estimates are uncertain and it is common to express the level of uncertainty as intervals that contain the true value with a probability of 95%. This can be customized in various ways, which is immensely useful in decision-making situations.

In this book, I am advocating the *Bayesian approach* for doing New Statistics. That does not mean you cannot use classic tools, such as the method of maximum likelihood estimation or bootstrapping, to estimate parameters and certainty intervals. However, the Bayesian approach has a number of advantages that make it a perfect match for New Statistics:

1. The Bayesian school of thinking does not require you to imagine infinite series of replications. Parameters and uncertainty have a *straightforward interpretation*: There is the best guess for the true value and there is an interval within which it lies with a given certainty. Even stronger, Bayesian models produce posterior distributions, which contain the full information on uncertainty and can be used in multiple ways. That means we can practically always create an certainty statement that precisely matches whatever is at stake.
2. In classic models, the level of uncertainty is only given for a subset of parameters, called population-level coefficients. A Bayesian model generates information on *uncertainty for every parameter* in the model. As a result, Bayesian models can be used to compare variance parameters between groups, or individuals within a group (so-called random effects), and even correlations between individual traits. This may sound unusual and complicated, but we will see several examples of when this is very useful.
3. The classic p-value also is a trick in the sense of you can only pull it a number of times. Null hypothesis tests are available only for a very limited class of models. Bayesian tools cover a *much broader class of models*. For example, modeling reaction times correctly requires a response distribution that is skewed and has an offset. Classic tools have few options for skewed response distributions, but not with an offset. Modern Bayesian engines even give you the choice out of three such distributions (such as the Ex Gaussian; see Sect. 7.3.2.)

4. Sometimes, it is fully legit to ask Yes/No questions, such as does an effect contribute to making predictions, or not? Modern Bayesian Statistics has developed a powerful toolset for what is called *model selection* (Sect. 8.2.4). This can either be used to test hypotheses, or to harness the shear variety of models that can be built.

1.4 How to Use This Book

Section 1.2 introduces a framework for quantitative design research. It carves out the basic elements of empirical design research, such as users, designs and performance and links them to typical research problems. Then the idea of design as decision-making under uncertainty is developed at the example of two case studies.

Chapter 3 introduces the basic idea of Bayesian statistics, which boils down to three remarkably intuitive conjectures:

1. uncertainty is the rule;
2. you gain more certainty by observations;
3. your present knowledge about the world is composed of what you learned from data and what you knew before.

The same chapter goes on with introducing basic terms of statistical thinking. Finally, an overview on common statistical distributions serves as a vehicle to make the reader familiar with data-generating processes. I am confident that this chapter serves newbies and classically trained researchers with all tools they need to understand Bayesian statistics. Arguably, for the formally trained reader this is more of a bedtime reading.

Chapter 2 is a minimal introduction to R, this marvelous programming language that has quickly become the Lingua Franca of statistical computing. Readers with some programming experience can work through this in just one day, and they will get everything they need to get started with the book. Readers with prior R experience still may get a lot out of this chapter, as it introduces the *tidy* paradigm of R programming. Tidy R is best thought of as a set of standard libraries 2.0 that all follow the same regiment and are therefore highly interoperable. New tidy packages are arriving at an accelerating pace in the R world, and coding tidy is usually much briefer, easier to read and less error-prone than "classic" R. While this chapter can only serve as a stepping stone, the reader will encounter countless code examples throughout the book, which can serve as exercises (Sect. 1.4.3) and templates alike.

The second part of the book starts with three chapters that are strictly built on each other. The first Chap. 4 introduces basic elements of linear models, which are factors, covariates and interaction effects. A number of additional sections cover under-the-hood concepts, such as dummy variables or contrasts. Working through this chapter is essential for beginners as it develops the jargon.

However, for most readers, the first chapter is not sufficient to get to do some real work, as it does not cover models for more complex research designs, such as repeated measures. This is treated extensively in Chap. 6. It proceeds from simple repeated measure designs to complex designs, where human and multiple non-human populations encounter each other. It culminates in a rebuild of psychometric models, consisting entirely of GLMM building blocks. The chapter ends with a completely novel, yet over-due, definition of designometrics, statistical models for comparing designs (not humans).

The third Chap. 7 opens up a plethora of possibilities to analyze all kinds of performance variables that are usually considered "non-Normal" in Classic Statistics. In fact, the first part of the chapter is dedicated to convince the reader that there is no such thing as a Normal distribution in reality. Standard models are introduced to deal with counts, chances, temporal variables and rating scales. It is also meant as an eye opener for researchers who routinely resorted to non-parametric procedures. After working through this chapter, I would consider anyone a sincere data analyst.

1.4.1   Routes

If you use this book for self-study, two considerations play a role for finding the optimal route through this book. What is your *background in Statistics?* For using this book, effectively, you need a little bit of understanding of probabilities and basic statistics, most of which is high-school math. As such, it may be a while ago and a refresher is in order. Section 3.1 is a quick-read, if you are feeling confident. If you lack any background in statistics, Chap. 3 should be studied, first. If your background is Social Sciences, then you probably know quite something about probabilities and Statistics. If you wonder what all this new "Bayesian" is all about and how compatible it is to you, Sect. 3.4.4 is a small bridge.

The precondition for using this book effectively is the skill of *coding in R.* If you have basic skills in another programming language, studying Chap. 2 will do. If you are very experienced in programming, but not yet in R, feel confident to skip that chapter and return to it only when you have a strange encounter. Sections 2.2.8–2.2.12 explain programming techniques, where R differs the most from general-purpose languages. If this is the first time, you learn a programming language, and your mileage may vary. Chapter 2 can at least provide you with an overview of all that you have to know, but some other books provide a more gentle and detailed introduction to R. In any case, learning your first programming language by one book alone may turn out difficult.

All of Chaps. 4 through 7 have a similar structure. The first half adds a few essential techniques, whereas the remaining sections explore the depths and possibilities. If you read this book to get an overview at the first read, the recommended route is as follows:

1. Section 4.1 introduces the regression engine and basic reporting techniques, such as coefficient tables.

2. Section 4.3.1 introduces the principles of factorial models, just enough to analyze data from an experimental design comparison.
3. Section 6.3 introduces just enough multi-level thinking to get you started.
4. Section 7.1 explains the three limitations of linear models, and introduces link functions and choice of random distribution.
5. Section 3.5.2.4 introduces Poisson distribution as one common shape of randomness that many people have not yet heard of.
6. Section 7.2.1 puts Poisson distribution and link function to practical use on the response variable deviations.

Readers approaching this book with a specific class of problems in mind can also drill into it, like in the following examples.

Experimenters in Cognitive Psychology often use reaction time measures to test their hypotheses. The suggested vertical route matches the above up to Sect. 7.1. Then, Sect. 7.3 introduces Exponential-Gaussian distribution as plug-in-and-use alternative to the "Normal" error term. Sections 8.2.4 and 8.2.6 in particular show how hypothesis testing (and more) can be done in a Bayesian framework.

User Experience researchers (and Social Psychologists) make abundant use of rating scales. The vertical route in such a case is

1. Sections 4.1, 4.3.1 and 6.3.
2. Section 6.5 introduces items of a rating scale as non-human populations.
3. Section 6.8 shows how basic psychometric analysis can be done by using multi-level models.
4. Section 7.4 elaborates on the randomness pattern of rating scales and suggests Beta regression (Sect. 7.4.2).

That being said, if you are in the process of *developing a design-oriented rating scale*, start by reading the last paragraph of Sect. 6.8.4!

There can also be reasons to take a more horizontal route. For example, market research often involves an insane amount of possible predictors (for when and why someone is buying a product or using a service). Chapter 5 and Sect. 5.4 explore a broad set of multi-predictor models. Section 8.2.4 introduces techniques to find just-the-right set of predictors. Experimentalists, in turn, can learn more efficient ways of designing their studies by working through Chap. 6, entirely. Researchers in Human Factors routinely collect multiple performance variables, such as time-on-task, number of errors and cognitive workload ratings. All these measures deserve their special way of being treated, which is emphasized in Chap. 7.

1.4.2 In the Classroom

Content-wise, this book covers roughly 200% of a typical Social Sciences Statistics curriculum. At least at my university, students roughly learn the equivalent of the first 50% of Chaps. 3, 4, 6, 7 and 8, before they graduate. However, only occasionally have I been in the situation myself, to teach a whole statistics curriculum to a cohort of students. Instead, this book emerged from statistics workshops, which I have given inside and outside universities, for professionals, colleagues and groups of master students.

If you are a docent in the *Social Sciences*, this book certainly can back an entry-level Statistics course. However, you should be aware that the approach in this book is not yet common ground. While you yourself may find the approach of Bayesian parameter estimation compellingly intuitive, your colleagues may not like the idea that future generations of students perceive their work as outdated. Another consideration is that this book is only useful for students with the capacity to learn just a little bit of programming. But, do not underestimate your students on this. I have seen it happen at my home university, that cohorts of Psychology students first started learning SPSS syntax, and now learn R and also Python. Still, using this book in the classroom poses the challenge to teach some programming that puts you into the situation of teaching Programming. Chapter 2 has served me well to push Psychology students over the first hurdles.

To my personal observations, there is an increasing demand to teach social science research methods to *engineering* students. If that is your situation, this book is particularly well-suited to make a course. Not only will programming in R not be a major hurdle but also is this book free of outdated customs that actually have never been appropriate for an engineering context, especially the approach of null hypothesis significance testing. Engineers, as I know them, are interested in quantification of design effects, rather than falsifying theories. In addition, the case studies in this book convey knowledge about effective research designs and validity of measures.

In both of the above cases, if I were asked to develop a full course on the matter, I would make it a series of workshops. The most effective method for a *workshop* is to have students get acquainted with the matter by studying selected parts of the book, in advance, and let them work on assignments during tutored workshops. I have made good experience with tutored pair-programming, where two students work together, while the teacher stays in the background, most of the time. During each workshop, students are given a data set with a brief story to it and an assignment, like the following example:

Some novel augmented reality (AR) side-view car mirrors have been designed and the benefits for driving performance need to be assessed. An experiment has been conducted, where the AR mirrors were compared to the classic side-view mirrors. Participants have been classified in low and high driving experience, and age was recorded. Every participant completed a set of eight tasks under the following conditions:

- AR mirrors versus classic mirrors;
- day ride versus night ride.

The following measures were taken:

- time-on-task (seconds);
- steering reversal rate (counts, lower is better);
- cognitive workload (rating scale, 0–1).

Assignment:

1. Conceive one or more research questions, e.g.

   - The AR design creates less workload.
   - The AR design improves performance especially at night.

2. Read and clean the data set.
3. Produce summary tables and graphs that reflect the research question.
4. Build a model and interpret the parameter estimates.

   a. Start with a linear model that reflects your research question. Use Sects. 5.3, 5.2 and 5.4.3.
   b. Select a GLM family that matches your chosen response variable. Use Sects. 7.3.2, 7.2.1 or 7.4.2.
   c. Build a multi-level model. Use Sects. 6.3, 6.1 and 6.2.

If you use this book for teaching, it means you will have to come up with some data sets. Unless you are a seasoned researcher who can pull data out of the drawer, this might be a problem. Generalized Linear Models a solution is to simulate data, like I have done multiple times in this book. While I haven't gone to the lengths of systematically introducing data simulation, the code for all simulated data can be found in electronic resources accompanying this book.

During my workshops, I often use the method of *live programming*. This is best pictured as think-aloud live demonstration—you talk while you are writing the code. This requires that you speak R natively, such that you can write valid code, while you talk and think. An important element of live programming is that students type the code as they see it on the presentation screen. Encouraging your students to type along keeps them in an action-feedback loop, from head to the finger tips, Sect. 1.4.3.

Examination is the other part of teaching and here is what I do in my courses: During my workshops, students get to work on a case study and for examination they get to do a data analysis on a similar case. If you prefer written exams, I advise against letting students produce code on paper. Rather, I would construct questions that focus reading code, or the understanding of concepts, such as

- Interpret the following coefficient table.
- What is the difference between saturation and amplification effects?
- In which situation is it better to use an ordinal factor model, rather than a linear regression?
- Customer waiting times have been measured in several customer service hotlines. What would be an appropriate distribution family?

1.4.3 The Stone of Rosetta

Next to my favorite hobby of writing books on Statistics, I am giving programming courses to Psychology students. Long have I held the belief that the skill of coding grounds on abstract thinking (similar to learning math) and computer enthusiasm. Being a formal thinker and a nerd are not the first things that come to mind for psychology students. Almost surprisingly, almost all of them can learn this skill within 3 months.

Shortly after I started working in the Netherlands, a Dutch teacher wasted my time by explaining Dutch language in English words. Only recently, a study revealed that learning a programming language is just that learning a second language [2]. If that is true, the best way to learn it is to create a closed feedback loop. Taken to the extreme, that means every moment a programming teacher distracts a student from writing and reading code is lost.

You learn a language by being exposed to it, and that is what I will do to you in this book. Following the brief introduction to the programming language R, I will show to you every single line of code that I used to produce data, statistical models, tables and graphics. Some may find this a bit repetitive to see code for producing, say a boxplot, over and over again. I beg to differ: for learning a language, repetition is essential.

Before I came to the Netherlands, I lived for about 10 years in the southern part of Germany where many people speak a strong dialect, Bayrisch. Surprisingly, I am better at speaking Dutch than I ever were at this dialect. Maybe, this is because Dutch people react cheerful when you try in their language, whereas people from Bayern hate it, when you imitate their way of speaking. (The trick I found most useful for doing a half-way acceptable imitation is to imagine a native-speaking friend and how he would say it.) When learning R, no one will laugh at you when you struggle to express yourself. And the same trick works here, too: If you want to produce or express a certain result, just flip through the pages of this book and you may find a piece of code where I "said" something similar. Cutting-and-pasting is a basic form of a fundamental principle of good coding: maximizing reuse.

The importance of closed-loop interaction holds even stronger, if the skill to be learned is a language. This book is written in three languages: English, R and here and there a little bit of math. Precise description of a chain of data processing is difficult to do in a fuzzy natural language, like English (or Dutch). R, like math, is a formal language, and every piece of code will always produce the exact same result. The difference between math and R is that math is purely descriptive (or rather, imaginative), whereas R is not just productive but is also interactive. You can specify a Gaussian distributed variable in math, by saying:

$$\mu = 7$$
$$\sigma = 3$$
$$Y \sim \text{Gauss}(\mu, \sigma)$$

Or, you can *produce* such a variable in R:

```
Data_gaus <- tibble(y = rnorm(n = 1000, mean = 3, sd = 5))
```

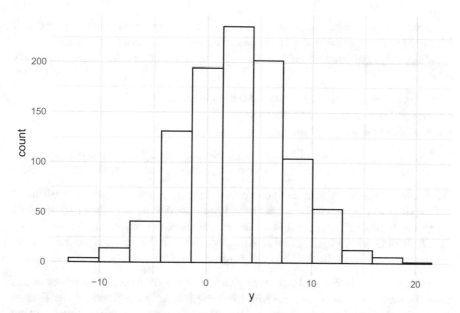

Fig. 1.1 A Gaussian distribution

The math expression requires that the recipient of the message can imagine how a Gaussian distribution looks like. In R, you can simply show how it looks like (Fig. 1.1):

```
Data_gaus %>%
  ggplot(aes(x = y)) +
  geom_histogram(bins = 12)
```

In many other books on statistics, math is used to precisely specify a model or any other data transformation. Specifying how data has been processed is essential for *transparency of research*. In the ideal case, data processing is given as a recipe so precise that every other researcher would obtain the exact same results. That is called *re-producability*. Math notation lives up to the principle of transparency, but most people do not have the skills to produce something from math notation. Speaking for myself, if someone would ask me for the formula of Gaussian distributions from the top of my head, I would be in trouble:

$$P(x) = \frac{1}{\sigma\sqrt{2\pi}}e^{-(x-\mu)^2/2\sigma^2}$$

Because math is such an inaccessible language, in practice, math notation is hardly reproducable, whereas R code is. If anyone gives me their R code and the data, I can expect to get the exact same results. If I apply the code to my own data, I am

doing an exact replication of a study. On top of that, I will always be able to check
the validity of every single step in the analysis, as I will demonstrate below.

The principle of transparency in scientific reports requires the author to specify
all

- transformations that have been acted out on the data;
- tables and figures that are presented;
- assumptions of statistical models.

Traditionally, specification of figures and tables is done by putting text in captions.
While English texts may please a lot of readers, this has disadvantages:

1. A table or figure is the result of complex data transformations, which are difficult
   to put in words, precisely. Sometimes, important details are given in other parts
   of the document, or are just lost. An example is outlier removal.
2. Describing what a figure or table shows does not put the readers into the position
   to reproduce or replicate the table or figure.

For these reasons, I decided to spare any caption texts on figures and tables in this
book. Instead, all results presented in this book are fully specified by the R code
that produces them. From a didactic point of view, I am deliberately taking away the
convenience that may come with natural language, for putting my readers' brains
into an action-feedback loop. All R code in this book has been crafted to specifically
serve this purpose. In particular, all code snippets are written as data processing
chains, with one operation per line. The best way to understand the code at first is to
run it starting at the top, examine what the first transformation did and then include
the next step:

```
set.seed(47)
tibble(y = rnorm(n = 20, mean = 2, sd = 5)) %>%
  as_tbl_obs()

set.seed(47)
tibble(y = rnorm(n = 20, mean = 2, sd = 5)) %>%
  as_tbl_obs() %>%
  filter(y > 0)


set.seed(47)
tibble(y = rnorm(n = 20, mean = 2, sd = 5)) %>%
  as_tbl_obs() %>%
  filter(y > 0) %>%
  ggplot(aes(x = y))


set.seed(47)
tibble(y = rnorm(n = 20, mean = 2, sd = 5)) %>%
  as_tbl_obs() %>%
  filter(y > 0) %>%
```

Table 1.1 Data set with 2 variables, showing 8 of 20 observations

Obs	y
1	11.97
5	2.54
8	2.08
10	−5.33
14	−7.14
16	5.35
19	−1.52
20	1.80

```
ggplot(aes(x = y)) +
geom_histogram(binwidth = 2)
```

It is almost obvious that changing `mean = 2` changes the mean (Table 1.1) of the distribution ß, and that `filter(y > 0)` removes non-positive values (Table 1.2). The real fun starts when the ggplot graphics engine is loaded with data. In Fig. 1.2 you only see an empty coordinate system. In Fig. 1.3, a so-called geometry is added, creating a histogram.

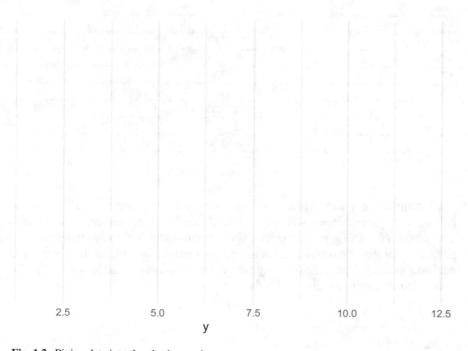

Fig. 1.2 Piping data into the plotting engine

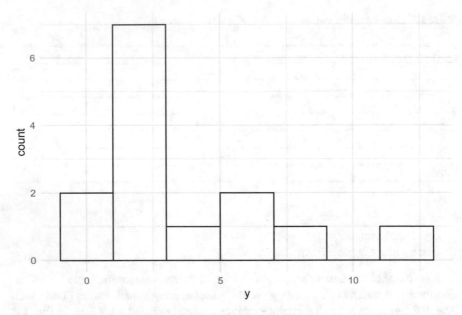

Fig. 1.3 Plotting a histogram

Table 1.2 Data set with 2 variables, showing 8 of 14 observations

Obs	y
1	11.97
3	2.93
5	2.54
12	2.20
13	4.47
16	5.35
18	8.32
20	1.80

And this is not the end of the story. Rather, it is the beginning of another phase in learning to programming, where you start working with existing code and modify it to your needs. The ggplot graphics engine in particular is easy to learn and, yet, provides almost endless possibilities to express yourself in a report. It is also very well documented. With some googling you will quickly find a recipe to add a properly scaled density line to the plot (Fig. 1.4):

```
set.seed(47)
tibble(y = rnorm(n = 20, mean = 2, sd = 5)) %>%
  filter(y > 0) %>%
  ggplot(aes(x = y)) +
```

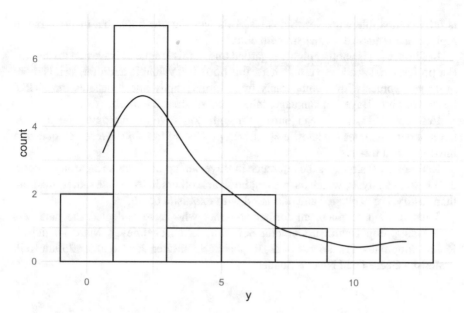

Fig. 1.4 Adding another layer

```
geom_histogram(binwidth = 2) +
geom_density(aes(y = 2 * ..count..))
```

In contrast to math notation, R is productive and that opens new ways for learning statistics. Several chapters will make use of a technique best described as generation-and-recovery, where a data-generating process is expressed as a simulation function and the result is recovered by a matching model. Loop closed!

1.5 Thank You and Supplementary Readings

To keep the book lean, I refrained to use citations a lot. That does not mean I was independent. The opposite is the case and the following authors greatly influenced my way of thinking, and I certainly copy-catted more than I am aware of. Thank them for the inspiration!

Reference [3] is the oldest Statistics textbook I still have in use. Not only was it the first one of its kind to promote the programming language R, but it also develops a similar framework of models and already introduces a few Bayesian

Reference [4] is targeted at statistical users, who are so deeply stuck in the Classic Statistics paradigm that they need a proper therapy. In an informal language, it covers theoretical and philosophical issues of Bayesian Statistics at a great of a depth and is fully compatible with New Statistics. This was the one book that inspired me to replace mathematical formalism with code.

Reference [5] is another highly regarded one in this league of Bayesian textbooks. For professional academic researchers, this book is a valuable addition, as it is more profound, comes with a comparably huge bibliography and translates the NHST framework into Bayesian language, rather than dismiss it entirely.

Reference [6] is a Bayesian journey through Cognitive Psychology. Like no other book, it demonstrates the knowledge-driven process of translating research question into statistical models.

Reference [7] simply is the reference in Bayesian applied statistics. Many aspects of Bayesian analysis, which the present book and others in its league rather illustrate than justify, are explained and discussed with exquisite detail.

Then, I want to thank all former students who have collected the data sets I am using: Jop Havinga, Cornelia Schmidt, Lea Echelmeyer, Marc Danielski, Robin Koopmans, Frauke van Beek, Raphaela Schnittker, Jan Sommer, Julian Keil, Franziska Geesen and Nicolas Sander.

References

1. Cumming G (2013) Understanding the new statistics. Routledge. Accessed 19 June 2013. https://doi.org/10.4324/9780203807002
2. Prat CS, et al. (2020) Relating natural language aptitude to individual differences in learning programming languages. In: Scientific Reports 10.1. Accessed 2 March 2020. https://doi.org/10.1038/s41598-020-60661-8
3. Andrew G, Jennifer H (2006) Data analysis using regression and multilevel/hierarchical models. https://doi.org/10.1017/cbo9780511790942
4. McElreath R (2018) Statistical rethinking. Chapman and Hall/CRC, New York. Accessed 3 Jan 2018. https://doi.org/10.1201/9781315372495
5. Analysis Doing Bayesian Data (2015) Elsevier, Amsterdam. https://doi.org/10.1016/c2012-0-00477-2
6. Michael DL, Wagenmakers E-J (2009) Bayesian cognitive modeling. Cambridge University Press, Cambridge. https://doi.org/10.1017/cbo9781139087759
7. Gelman A, et al. (2013) Bayesian data analysis. Chapman and Hall/CRC, New York. Accessed 27 Nov 2013. https://doi.org/10.1201/b16018

Chapter 2
Getting Started with R

In this book, we will be using the statistical computing environment R. R at its core is a programming language that specializes in statistics and data analysis. Like all modern programming languages, R comes with a compiler or interpreter that translates human-writable formal statements into something a computer understands and can execute. But there is much more: R comes with a complete set of *standard packages* that cover common routines in statistical analysis, for example, functions to compute mean and variance, table-like data structures and the t-test. Also regression analysis and plotting are included in R. Finally, packaged with R comes a rudimentary programming environment, including a console, a simple editor and a help system.

Most of what comes packaged with R, we will set aside. R is basically a brilliantly designed programming language for the task, but many of the standard packages are an inconsistent and outdated mess. For example, R comes with a set of commands to import data from various formats (SPSS, CSV, etc.). Some of these commands produce objects called data.frames, whereas others return lists of lists. Although one can convert lists into data frames, it is easier and prevents confusion if all import functions simply create data frames. As another example, to sort a data frame by participant number, one has to write the following syntax soup:

```
D[order(D$Part),]
```

In the past few years, a single person, Hadley Wickham, has started an initiative known as the *tidyverse*. Tidyverse first of all is a set of ground rules for dealing with data. For example, one ground rule is that all data processing routines take a data frame as input and give their results as a data frame. That may sound trivial, but it is not. Many legacy routines in R take matrices as input (or output). Matrices and data frames are both rectangular, but while you can convert all matrices to data frames, the opposite is not true.

The result of the dogma is a fast-growing collection of libraries that all ground on a coherent and powerful set of principles for data management, and are therefore highly interoperable. One of the core tidyverse packages is *dplyr* and it introduces

© Springer Nature Switzerland AG 2021
M. Schmettow, *New Statistics for Design Researchers*,
Human–Computer Interaction Series,
https://doi.org/10.1007/978-3-030-46380-9_2

a rich, yet rather generic, set of commands for data manipulation. The sorting of a data frame mentioned above would be written as

```
D %>% arrange(Part)
```

One of Wickham's first and well-known contributions is the *ggplot* system for graphics. Think of R's legacy graphics system as a zoo of individual routines, one for boxplots, another one for scatterplots asf. Like animals in a zoo, they live in different habitats with practically no interaction. Ggplot implements a rather abstract framework for data plots, where all pieces can be combined in a myriad of ways, using a simple and consistent syntax.

Where to get these gems? R is an open-source system and has spawned an open ecosystem for statistical computing. Thousands of extensions for R have been made available by data scientists for data scientists. The majority of these packages is available through the *comprehensive R archive network (CRAN)*. For the common user, it suffices to think of CRAN as a repository of packages that can be searched and where desired packages can be downloaded from and installed in an instance.

Finally, R comes with a very rudimentary programming environment that carries the questionable charm of the early 1990s. While several alternatives exist, most R users will feel most comfortable with the R programming environment RStudio. At the time of writing, it is the most user-friendly and feature-rich software to program in R. The next sections describe how you can set up a fully functional environment and verify that it works. Subsequently, we will get to know the basics of programming in R.

2.1   Setting up the R Environment

First, we have to make sure that you have the two essential applications R and RStudio downloaded and installed on your computer. The two programs can be retrieved from the addresses below. Make sure to select the version fit for your operating system.

- R
- RStudio

If you fully own the computer you are working with, meaning that you have administrator rights, just do the usual downloading and running of the setup. If everything is fine, you'll find R and RStudio installed under c\Programs\ and both are in your computer's Start menu. You can directly proceed to the installation of packages.

In corporate environments, two issues can arise with the installation: first, a user may not have administrator rights to install programs to the common path c:\programs\. Second, the home directory may reside on a network drive, which is likely to cause trouble when installing packages.

If you have no administrator rights, you must choose your home directory during the setup. If that is a local directory, (c:/Users/YourName/), this should work fine and you can proceed with the installation of packages.

If your home directory (i.e. My Documents) is located on a network drive, this is likely to cause trouble. In such a case, you must install R and RStudio to a local directory (on your computer's hard drive), where you have full read/write access. In the following, it is assumed that this directory is D:/Users/YourName/:

1. Create a directory D:/Users/YourName/R/. This is where both programs, as well as packages, will reside.
2. Create a subdirectory Rlibrary where all additional packages reside (R comes with a pack of standard packages, which are in a read-only system directory).
3. Start RStudio.
4. Create a regular text file File -> New File -> Text file.
5. Copy and paste code from the box below.
6. Save the file as .Rprofile in D:/Users/YourName/R/.
7. Open the menu and go to Tools -> Global options -> General -> Default working directory. Select D:/Users/YourName/R/.

```
## .Rprofile

options(stringsAsFactors = FALSE)

.First <- function() {
  RHOME <<- getwd()
  cat(''\nLoading .Rprofile in'', getwd(), ''\n'')
  .libPaths(c(paste0(RHOME, ''Rlibrary''), .libPaths()))
}


.Last <- function() {
  cat(''\nGoodbye at '', date(), ''\n'')
}
```

With the above steps, you have created a customized start-up profile for R. The profile primarily sets the library path to point to a directory on the computer's drive. As you are owning this directory, R can install the packages without admin rights. In the second part, you configure RStudio's default path, which is where R, invoked from RStudio, searches for the .Rprofile.

After closing and reopening RStudio, you should see a message in the console window saying:

Loading .Rprofile in D:/Users/YourName/R/

That means that R has found the .Rprofile file and loaded it at start-up. The .Rprofile file primarily sets the path of the *library*, which is the collection of packages you install yourself. Whether this was successful or not can be checked by entering the console window in RStudio, typing the command below and hit Enter.

```
.libPaths()
```

If your installation went fine, you should see an output like the following. If the output lacks the first entry, your installation was not successful and you need to check all the above steps.

[1] "D:/Users/YourName/R/Rlibrary" "C:/Program Files/R/R-3.3.0/library"

2.1.1 Installing CRAN Packages

While R comes with a set of standard packages, thousands of packages are available to enhance functionality for every purpose you can think of. Most packages are available from the *Comprehensive R Network Archive (CRAN)*.

For example, the package *foreign* is delivered with R and provides functions to read data files in various formats, e.g. SPSS files. The package *haven* is a rather new package, with enhanced functionality and usability. It is not delivered with R, hence, we have to fetch it.

Generally, packages need to be *installed once* on your system and to be *loaded everytime* you need them. Installation is fairly straightforward once your R environment has been set up correctly and you have an Internet connection.

In this book, we will use a number of additional packages from CRAN. The listed packages below are all required packages, which can be loaded using the `library(package)` command. The package *tidyverse* is a metapackage that installs and loads a number of modern packages. The ones being used in this book are

- dplyr and tidyr for data manipulation;
- ggplot for graphics;
- haven for reading and writing files from other statistical packages;
- readr for reading and writing text-based data files (e.g. CSV);
- readxl for reading Excel files;
- stringr for string matching and manipulation.

```
## tidyverse
library(tidyverse)

## data manipulation
library(openxlsx)

## plotting
library(gridExtra)

## regression models
library(rstanarm)

## other
library(devtools) ## only needed for installing from Github
library(knitr)
```

```
## non-CRAN packages
library(mascutils)
library(bayr)
```

We start by *checking the packages*:

1. Create a new R file by `File --> New file --> R script`
2. Copy and paste the above code to that file and run it. By repeatedly pressing `Ctrl-Return`, you run every line one-by-one. As a first- time user with a fresh installation, you will now see error messages like

Error in library(tidyverse) : there is no package called 'tidyverse'

This means that the respective package is not yet present in your R library. Before you can use the package *tidyverse*, you have to install it from CRAN. For doing so, use the built-in package management in RStudio, which fetches the package from the Web and is to be found in the tab *Packages*. The first time, you may have to select a repository and refresh the package list, before you can find and install packages. Then click `Install`, enter the names of the missing package(s) and install. On the R console, the following command downloads and installs the package *tidyverse*.

```
install.packages(``tidyverse'')
```

CRAN is like a giant stream of software pebbles, shaped over time in a growing tide. Typically, a package gets better with every version, be it in reliability or versatility, so you want to be up-to-date. RStudio has a nice dialogue to update packages and there is the R command:

```
update.packages(``tidyverse'')
```

Finally, run the complete code block at once by selecting it and pressing `Ctrl-Enter`. You will see some output to the console, which you should check once again. Unless the output contains any error messages (like above), you have successfully installed and loaded all packages.

Note that R has a somewhat idiosyncratic jargon: many languages, such as Java or Python call "libraries" what R calls "packages". *The* library in R is strictly the set of packages installed on your computer and the `library` command loads a package from the library.

2.1.2 Installing Packages from GitHub

Two packages, *mascutils* and *bayr*, are written by the author of this book. They have not yet been committed to CRAN, but they are available on *GitHub* which is a general-purpose versioning system for software developers and a few authors.

Fortunately, with the help of the *devtools* package, it is rather easy to install these packages, too. Just enter the RStudio console and type:

```
library(devtools)
install_github(''schmettow/mascutils'')
install_github(''schmettow/bayr'')
```

Again, you have to do that only once after installing R and you can afterwards load the packages with the `library` command. Only if the package gets an update to add functionality or remove bugs, you need to run these commands again.

2.1.3   A First Statistical Program

After you have set up your R environment, you are ready to run your first R program (you will not yet understand all the code, but as you proceed with this book, all will become clear):

1. Stay in the file where you have inserted and run the above code for loading the packages.
2. Find the *environment tab* in RStudio. It should be empty.
3. Copy and paste the code below into your first file, right after library commands.
4. Run the code lines one-by-one and observe what happens (in RStudio: Ctrl-Enter).

```
set.seed(42)
## Simulation of a data set with 100 participants
## in two between-subject conditions
N <- 100
levels <- c(''control'', ''experimental'')
Group <- rep(levels, N / 2)
age <- round(runif(N, 18, 35), 0)
outcome <- rnorm(N, 200, 10) + (Group == ''experimental'') * 50
Experiment <- tibble(Group, age, outcome) %>% as_tbl_obs()
Experiment
```

With seven lines of code, you have simulated the data for an experiment with two conditions (Table 2.1). The following code produces two so-called density plots, which indicate how the simulated values are distributed along variable Outcome (Fig. 2.1).

```
## Plotting the distribution of outcome
Experiment %>%
  ggplot(aes(x = outcome)) +
  geom_density(fill = 1)

## ... outcome by group
```

Table 2.1 Data set with 4 variables, showing 8 of 100 observations

Obs	Group	Age	Outcome
22	Experimental	20	249
26	Experimental	27	256
43	Control	19	207
61	Control	29	200
80	Experimental	18	252
88	Experimental	20	262
89	Control	19	195
97	Control	24	195

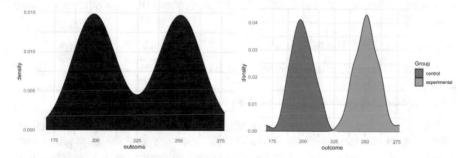

Fig. 2.1 Density of simulated data

```
Experiment %>%
  ggplot(aes(fill = Group, x = outcome)) +
  geom_density()
```

Then, we move on to estimating a statistical model and produce a summary of the estimation in Table 2.2

```
## ... statistical model comparing the groups

model <- stan_glm(
  formula = outcome ~ Group,
  data = Experiment
)

fixef(model)
```

Table 2.2 Coefficient estimates with 95% credibility limits

Fixef	Center	Lower	Upper
Intercept	198.6	196.1	201.3
Groupexperimental	52.3	48.6	55.9

Observe Console, Environment and Plots. Did you see

- how the *Environment* window is populated with new variables (Values and Data)?
- a table appears in the *Console*, when executing the `summary(Experiment)` command?
- how the "camel-against-the-light" in *Plots* tab morphed into "two-piles-of-colored-sugar"?

Congratulations! You have just

- simulated data of a virtual experiment with two groups,
- plotted the data and
- estimated a Bayesian regression model that compares the two groups.

Isn't it amazing, that in less than 20 simple statements we have just reached the level of a second-year bachelor student? Still, you may find the R output a little inconvenient, as you may want to save the output of your data analysis. Not long ago that really was an issue, but in the past few years R has become a great tool for *reproducable research*. The most simple procedure of saving your analysis for print or sharing is as follows:

1. to save the R file you have created by hitting `CTRL-S` and selecting a directory and name.
2. in RStudio, open `File --> Compile notebook` and select Word as a format.
3. Hit `Compile`.

A new Word document should appear that shows all code and the output. Now, you can copy and paste the graphics into another document or a presentation.

2.1.4   Bibliographic Notes

Getting started with Rstudio (presentation)

Getting started with Rstudio (ebook)

rstudio cheat sheets is a collection of beautifully crafted cheat sheets for ggplot, dplyr and more. I suggest you print the data mangling and ggplot cheat sheets and always keep them on your desk.

The tidyverse is a metapackage that loads all core tidyverse packages by Hadley Wickham.

2.2 Learning R: A Primer

This book is for applied researchers in design sciences, whose frequent task is to analyze data and report it to stakeholders. Consequently, the way I use R in this book capitalizes on interactive data analysis and reporting. As it turns out, a small fraction of R, mostly from the tidyverse, is sufficient to write R code that is effective and fully transparent. In most cases, a short chain of simple data transformations tidies the raw data which can then be pushed into a modeling or graphics engine that will do the hard work. We will not bother (ourselves and others) with usual programming concepts such as conditionals, loops and the somewhat eccentric approaches to functional programming. At the same time, we can almost ignore all the clever and advanced routines that underlay statistical inference and production of graphics, as others have done the hard work for us.

R mainly serves three purposes, from easy to advanced: 1. interactive data analysis, 2. creating data analysis reports and 3. developing new statistical routines.

With R, one typically *works interactively through a data analysis*. The analysis often is a rather routine series of steps, like

1. load the data;
2. make a scatterplot;
3. run a regression;
4. create a coefficient table.

A program in R is usually developed iteratively: once you've loaded and checked your data, you progress to the next step of your analysis, test it and proceed. At every step, one or more new objects are created in the environment, capturing intermediate and final results of the analysis:

1. a data frame holding the data;
2. a graphics object holding a scatterplot;
3. a model object holding the results of a regression analysis;
4. a data frame for the coefficient table.

As R is an interpreter language, meaning there are no tedious compile-and-run cycles in everyday R programming, you develop the analysis as it happens. It is even normal to jump back and forth in an R program, while building it.

R is a way to *report and archive* what precisely you have been doing with your data. In statistics, mathematical formulas are the common form of unambiguously describing a statistical model. For example, the following equation defines a linear regression model between the observed outcome y and the predictor x:

$$\mu_i = \beta_0 + \beta_1 x_i$$
$$y_i \sim N(\mu_i, \sigma)$$

As we will later see 4.3.1, in R's formula language the same model is unambiguously specified as

Table 2.3 Data set with 2 variables, showing 7 of 7 observations

Obs	Score
1	1
2	2
3	4
4	3
5	5
6	6
7	50

y ~ x

R is currently the *lingua franca* of statistical computing. As a programming language, R has the same precision as math but is more expressive. You can specify not only complex models but also graphics and the steps of data checking and preparation. As an example, consider an outlier removal rule:

> An observation is valid if it does not exceed the tenfold of the observation mean.

We just applied our own rule of outlier removal to the data. Others may consider this rule invalid or arbitrary. Disagreement is virtue in science and one can only disagree with what one actually sees. In R, the researcher *formally reports* what precisely has been done with the data. For example, the same outlier removal rule is unambiguously specified by the following code (the first line just simulates some data). The results are shown in Table 2.3.

```
D <- tibble(score = c(1, 2, 4, 3, 5, 6, 50, 800)) %>%
   as_tbl_obs()

D %>% filter(score < mean(score))
```

Finally, R is a way to *develop and share statistical programs*. Thousands of packages in the R ecosystem cover almost all statistical problems you can imagine. As a programming language, R has been designed for that particular purpose. Under the hood of R, a bunch of generic, yet powerful, principles purrs to make it a convenient language for typical problems in statistical computation. Readers with programming experience can fly over the R basics that follow. But, as a specific purpose language R has a few idiosyncrasies you should know about:

In almost all programming languages, the first element of a list has the index zero. We got used to it, but for beginners it is another hurdle that is unnecessary. Mathematicians, catholiques, software developers in bars and everyone, young or old, count

"one", "two" ,"three".

And so does R:

```
c(1:3)[1:3]
```

```
## [1] 1 2 3
```

Counting from one is perhaps the most lovable idiosyncrasy of R. But, let's also welcome people who have experience with other programming languages:

The first thing one has to know about R is that it is a *functional programming* language. A function simply is a programmed procedure that takes data as input, applies some transformation and returns data as output. That sounds trivial, but there is an important difference to most other languages: Different from procedures in Pascal or object- oriented methods (in Java or Python), functions are forbidden to modify any external object. A certain function is a black box, but one can be sure that the only thing it does is return a new object.

At the same time, functions are first-class citizens in R and can be called every-where, even as an *argument to another function*. The *purrr* package is famous for functions that call functions, also called high-level functions, such as map or rerun.

The routine application of higher level functions is to apply a transformation to a list of objects. In a majority of programming languages, you would put this in a loop and this is where programmers often have to re-learn, when they get started with R. Believe me on one thing: Once you have wrapped your head around functional programming, you will program the same procedure in a quarter of the time with half the code and your program will run significantly faster. My general advice is

Whenever you think you need a loop, you don't.

For me, it helped to imagine the following: loops carry the notion of a chain of data that moves over a fixed transformation device. In functional programming languages, data processing routines can be assembled as hierarchies of functions, where typically a high-level function (a functional) is responsible for navigating the data, calling lower-level functions to do the actual processing.

If you come from relational databases, you have something in common with the statistician: you both think in the transformation of tables. Not coincidently, the features in *dplyr*, the tidy data transformation engine, are clearly borrowed from SQL. You will also feel at home with the idea of reports powered by functional chunks embedded in a templating system.

For object orientation folks, R is a good choice, but you have to get used to it. First, it gives you the choice of several object orientation systems, which sometimes requires installing a package. The so-called *S3 system* is the original. It is rather limited and some even call it informal. The approach is as simple as it is unusual. At its heart, it is a methods dispatcher that handles inheritance and overloading of functions. S3 puts methods first, whereas objects of a class simply get a tag for the dispatcher.

Beginners are at peace with all of this. You can count as you do. Functional programming is intuitive for working on data. And because of S3, the function summary always does something useful.

2.2.1 Assigning and Calling Objects

Any statistical analysis can be thought of as a production chain. You take the raw data and process it into a neat data table, which you feed into graphics and regression engines or summarize by other means. At almost every step, there is an input and an output object.

Objects are a basic feature of R. They are temporary storage places in the computer's memory. Objects always have a name chosen by the programmer. By its name, a stored object can be found back at any time. Two basic operations apply for all objects: an object is stored by *assigning* it a name and it is retrieved by *calling* its name. If you wanted to store the number of observations in your data set under the name N_obs, you use the assignment operator <-. The name of the variable is to the left of the operator, the assigned value is to the right of it.

```
N_obs <- 100
```

Now, that the value is stored, you can call it any time by simply calling its name:

```
N_obs
```

```
## [1] 100
```

Just calling the name prints the value to the Console. In typical interactive programming sessions with R, this is already quite useful. But, you can do much more with this mechanism.

Often, what you want is to do calculations with the value. For example, you have a repeated measures study and want to calculate the average number of observations per participant. For this, you need the number of observations and the number of participants. The below code creates both objects, does the calculation (right of <-) and stores it in another object avg_N_Obs

```
N_Obs <- 100
N_Part <- 25
avg_N_Obs <- N_Obs / N_Part
avg_N_Obs
```

```
## [1] 4
```

Objects can exist without a name, but are volatile, then. They cannot be used any further. The following arithmetic operation does create an object, a single number. For a moment or so, this number exists somewhere in your computer's memory, but once it is printed to the screen, it is gone. Of course, the same expression can be called again, resulting in the same number. But, strictly, it is a different object.

```
N_Obs / N_Part ## gone after printing
```

```
## [1] 4
```

```
N_Obs / N_Part ## same value, different object
```

```
## [1] 4
```

There even is a formal way to show that the two numbers, although having the same value assigned, are located at different addresses. This is just for the purpose of demonstration and you will rarely use it in everyday programming tasks:

```
tracemem(N_Obs / N_Part)
```

```
## [1] ``<00000000B45F1AB8>''
```

```
tracemem(N_Obs / N_Part)
```

```
## [1] ``<00000000B464DF50>''
```

2.2.2 Vectors

Notice the [1] that R put in front of the single value when printing it? This is an *index*. Different from other programming languages, all basic data types are *vectors* in R. Vectors are containers for storing many values *of the same type*. The individual values are addressed by an index. If V is a vector of numbers, V[1] calls the first element, V[2] the second, asf. In R, *indices start counting with 1*, which is different from most other languages that start at zero. And if you have a single value only, this is just a vector of length one.

For statistics programming having vectors as basic data types makes perfect sense. Any statistical data is a collection of values. What holds for data is also true for functions applied to data. Practically, all frequently used mathematical functions work on vectors; take the following example:

```
X <- rnorm(100, 2, 1)
mean(X)
```

```
## [1] 1.99
```

The rnorm command *produces* a vector of length 100 from three values. More precisely, it does 100 random draws from a normal distribution with mean 2 and an SD of 1. The mean command takes the collection and *reduces* it to a single value. By the way, this is precisely what we call *a statistic: a single quantity that characterizes a collection of quantities*.

2.2.3   Basic Object Types

Objects can be of various *classes*. In R, the common basic classes are logical, factor, character, integer and numeric. Besides that, programmers can define their own complex classes, for example, to store the results of regression models.

Objects of type *logical* store the two levels TRUE, FALSE, like presence or absence of a treatment, or passed and failed test items. With Boolean operators, one can compute new logical values, for example:

```
Apple <- TRUE
Pear <- FALSE

Apple & Pear ## and
```

```
## [1] FALSE
```

```
Apple | Pear ## or
```

```
## [1] TRUE
```

More generally, logical values can be used for categorization, when there are only two categories, which is called a *dichotomous variable*. For example, gender is usually coded as a vector of characters ("m", "f", "f"), but one can always do

```
is_female <- c(FALSE, TRUE, TRUE)
is_male <- c(T, F, F)
```

Programmers are lazy folks when it comes to typing, therefore R allows you to abbreviate TRUE and FALSE as shown above. As a consequence, one should never assign objects the name reserved for logical values, so don't do one of the following:

```
## never do this
TRUE <- ''All philosophers have beards''
F <- ''All gods existed before the big bang''
42 * F
```

The class `numeric` stores real numbers and is therefore abundant in statistical programming. All the usual arithmetic operations apply

```
a <- 1.0
b <- a + 1
sqrt(b)
```

```
## [1] 1.41
```

Objects of class `integer` are more specific as they store natural numbers, only. This often occurs as counts, ranks or indices.

```
friends <- c(
  anton = 1,
  berta = 3,
  carlo = 2
)
order(friends)
```

```
## [1] 1 3 2
```

The usual arithmetic operations apply, although the result of the operation may no longer be `integer`, but `numeric`

```
N <- 3
sum_of_scores <- 32
mean_score <- 32 / 3
mean_score
```

```
## [1] 10.7
```

```
class(mean_score)
```

```
## [1] ''numeric''
```

Surprisingly, logical values can be used in arithmetic expressions, too. When R encounters value `TRUE` in an arithmetic context, it replaces it with 1, zero otherwise. Used with multiplication, this acts like an on/off switch, which we will put to use for building factorial models.

```
TRUE + TRUE
```

```
## [1] 2
```

```
sqrt(3 + TRUE)
```

```
## [1] 2
```

```
is_car <- c(TRUE, TRUE, FALSE) ## bicycle otherwise
wheels <- 2 + is_car * 2
wheels
```

```
## [1] 4 4 2
```

Data sets usually contain variables that are not numeric, but partition the data into groups. For example, we frequently group observations by the following:

- `Part`: participant;
- `Condition`: experimental condition;
- `Design`: one of several designs;
- `Education`: level of education (e.g. low, middle or high).

Two object types apply for grouping observations: *factor* and *character*. While factors specialize in grouping observations, character objects can also be used to store longer text, say the description of a usability problem. The following identifies two conditions in a study, say a comparison of designs A and B. Note how the factor identifies its *levels* when called to the screen:

```
design_char <- c(``A'', ``B'', ``B'', ``A'')
design_char
```

```
## [1] ``A'' ``B'' ``B'' ``A''
```

```
design_fact <- factor(c(``A'', ``B'', ``B'', ``A''))
design_fact
```

```
## [1] A B B A
## Levels: A B
```

Statistical analyses deal with real-world data whichever so often is messy. Frequently, a planned observation could not be recorded, because the participant decided to quit or the equipment did not work properly or the Internet collapsed. Users of certain legacy statistics packages got used to coding missing observations as -999 and then declared this a missing value. In R, *missing values are first-class citizens*. Every vector of a certain class can contain missing values, which are identified as NA.

Most basic statistics functions, like mean(), sd() or median(), act conservatively when the data contains missing values. If there is a single NA in the variable to be summarized, the result is NA. While this is good in the sense of transparency, much of the time what the researcher wants is to have the summary statistic with NA values being removed, first.

```
clicks <- c(3, NA, 2)
mean(clicks)
```

```
## [1] NA
```

```
mean(clicks, na.rm = T)
```

```
## [1] 2.5
```

This book is about programming and statistics at the same time. Unfortunately, there are a few terms that have a particular meaning in both domains. One of those is a "variable". In statistics, a variable usually is a property we have recorded, say the body length of persons, or their gender. In general programming, a variable is a space in the computer's memories, where results can be stored and recalled. Fortunately, R avoids any confusion and calls *objects* what is usually called a programming variable.

2.2.4 Operators and Functions

R comes with a full bunch of functions for creating and summarizing data. Let me first introduce you to functions that produce exactly one number to characterize a vector.

```
length(X)
sum(X)
mean(X)
var(X)
sd(X)
min(X)
max(X)
median(X)
```

These functions are a transformation of data. The input to these transformations is X and is given as an *argument* to the function. Other functions require more than one argument. The `quantile` function is routinely used to summarize a variable. Recall that X has been drawn from a Normal distribution of $\mu = 2$ and standard deviation $\sigma = 1$. All Normal distributions have the property that about 66% of the mass is within the range of $\mu - \sigma$ and $\mu + \sigma$. That means in turn 17% are below $\mu - \sigma$ and $66 + 17 = 83\%$ are *below* $\mu + \sigma$. The number of observations in a certain range of values is called a *quantile*. The `quantile` function operates on X, but takes an (optional) vector of quantiles as second argument:

```
quantile(X, c(.17, .83))
```

```
##   17%   83%
## 0.963 2.956
```

Most functions in R have *optional arguments* that let you change how the function performs. The basic mathematical functions all have the optional argument `na.rm`. This is a switch that determines how the function deals with missing values `NA`. Many optional arguments have *defaults*. The default of `na.rm` is `FALSE` ("return NA in case of NAs in the vector"). By setting it to `TRUE`, they are removed before operation.

```
B <- c(1, 2, NA, 3)
mean(B)
```

```
## [1] NA
```

```
mean(B, na.rm = TRUE)
```

```
## [1] 2
```

Most of the more complex routines in R have an abundance of parameters, most of which have reasonable defaults, fortunately. To give a more complex example, the first call of `stan_glm` performs a Bayesian estimation of the grand mean model. The second does a Poisson grand mean model with 5000 iterations per the MCMC chain. As `seed` has been fixed, every subsequent run will produce the exact same chains. My apologies for the jargon!

```
D_1 <- tibble(X = rnorm(20, 2, 1))
M_1 <- stan_glm(X ~ 1,
  data = D_1
)

D_2 <- tibble(X = rpois(20, 2))
M_2 <- stan_glm(X ~ 1,
```

Table 2.4 Definition of common Boolean operators

A	B	!A	A & B	A | B	A == B
		not	and	or	equals
T	T	F	T	T	T
T	F	F	F	T	F
F	T	T	F	T	F
F	F	T	F	F	T

```
  family = poisson,
  seed = 42,
  iter = 5000,
  data = D_1
)
```

R brings the usual set of arithmetic operators, like +, -, *, / and more. In fact, an operator is just a function. The sum of two numbers can, indeed, be written in these two ways:

```
1 + 2
```

```
## [1] 3
```

```
`+`(1, 2)
```

```
## [1] 3
```

The second term is a function that takes two numbers as input and returns a third. It is just a different syntax, and this one is called the *Polish notation*. I will never use it throughout the rest of this book.

Another set of commonly used operators are logical; they implement *Boolean algebra*. Some common Boolean operators are shown in the truth table (Table 2.4).

Be careful not to confuse Boolean "and" and "or" with their common natural language use. If you ask: "Can you buy apples *or* pears on the market?", the natural answer would be "both". The Boolean answer is TRUE. In a requirements document, you could state "This app is for children and adults". In Boolean, the answer would be FALSE, because no one can be a child and an adult at the same time, strictly. A correct Boolean statement would be "The envisioned users can be adult or child".

Further Boolean operators exist but can be derived from the three above. For example, the exclusive OR, "either A or B", can be written as (A | B) & !(A & B). This term only gets TRUE when A or B is TRUE, but not both. In the data analysis workflow, Boolean logic is frequently used for filtering data and we re-encounter them in data transformation.

Finally, it sometimes is convenient or necessary to program own functions. A full coverage of developing functions is beyond the scope of this introduction, so I show just one simple example. If one desires a more convenient function to compute the mean that ignore missing values by default, this can be constructed as follows:

```
mean_conv <- function(x) {
  mean(x = B, na.rm = TRUE)
}

mean_conv(B)
```

```
## [1] 2
```

Notice that

- the function() function creates new functions.
- the arguments given to function(x) will be the arguments expected by the function mean_conv(x).
- The function body is enclosed by braces and carries the actual routine.

More examples of creating basic functions can be found in Sect. 3.3. As R is a functional programming language, it offers very elaborate ways of programming functions, way beyond what is found in common languages, such as Python or Java. An advanced example is given in Sect. 8.2.2.

2.2.5 Storing Data in Data Frames

Most behavioral research collects *real data* to work with. As behavior researchers are obsessed with finding associations between variables, real data usually contains several. If you have a sample of observations (e.g. participants) and every case has the same variables (measures or groups), data is stored in a table structure, where columns are variables and rows are observations.

R knows the data.frame objects to store variable-by-observation tables. Data frames are tables, where columns represent statistical variables. Variables have names and can be of different data types, as they usually appear in empirical research. In many cases, data frames are imported to R, as they represent real data. Here, we first see how to create data frames by simulation. First, we usually want some initial inspection of a freshly harvested data frame.

Several commands are available to look into a data frame from different perspectives. Another command that is implemented for a variety of classes, including data frames, is summary. For all data frames, it produces an overview with descriptive statistics for all variables (i.e. columns), matching their object type. Particularly useful for data initial screening is that missing values are listed per variable.

```
print(summary(Experiment))
```

```
##          Obs               Group
##   Min.    :   1.0   Length:100
##   1st Qu.:  25.8   Class :character
##   Median :  50.5   Mode  :character
##   Mean    :  50.5
##   3rd Qu.:  75.2
##   Max.    :100.0
##          age               outcome
##   Min.    :18.0   Min.    :170
##   1st Qu.:22.0   1st Qu.:199
##   Median :27.5   Median :223
##   Mean    :27.0   Mean    :225
##   3rd Qu.:31.0   3rd Qu.:251
##   Max.    :35.0   Max.    :277
```

The str (structure) command works on any R object and displays the hierarchical structure (if there is one):

```
str(Experiment)
```

```
## tbl_obs [100$\,\times\,$4] (S3: tbl_obs/tbl_df/tbl/data.frame)
##  $ Obs    : int [1:100] 1 2 3 4 5 6 7 8 9 10 ...
##  $ Group  : chr [1:100] ``control'' ``experimental'' ``control'' ``experimental'' ...
##  $ age    : num [1:100] 34 34 23 32 29 27 31 20 29 30 ...
##  $ outcome: num [1:100] 203 242 216 256 201 ...
```

Data frames store variables, but statistical procedures operate on variables. We need ways of accessing and manipulating statistical variables and we will have plenty. First, recall that in R the basic object types are all vectors. You can store as many elements as you want in an object, as long as they are of the same class.

Internally, data frames are a collection of "vertical" vectors that are equally long. Being a collection of vectors, the variables of a data frame can be of different classes, like character, factor or numeric. In the most basic case, you want to calculate a statistic for a single variable out of a data frame. The $ operator pulls the variable out as a vector:

Table 2.5 Results of slicing

Age	Group	Obs	Group	Age	Outcome
34	Control	1	Control	34	203
	Experimental				
	Control				

```
mean(Experiment$outcome)
```

```
## [1] 225
```

As data frames are rectangular structures, you can also access individual values by their addresses. The following commands produce three sub-tables of an Experiment (Table 2.5):

- the first *outcome* measure;
- the first three rows of *Group*;
- the complete first row.

```
Experiment[1, 3]
Experiment[1:3, 2]
Experiment[1, ]
```

Addressing one or more elements in square brackets always requires two elements, first the row, second the column. As odd as it looks, one or both elements can be empty, which just means get all rows (or all columns). Even the expression `Experiment[,]` is fully valid and will just return the whole data frame.

There is an important difference, however, when using R's classic `data.frame` as compared to dplyr's `tibble`implementation: When using single square brackets on dplyr data frames, one always gets a data frame back. That is a very predictable behavior, and very much unlike the classic: with `data.frame`, when the addressed elements expand over multiple columns, like `Experiment[, 1:2]`, the result will be a `data.frame` object, too. However, when slicing a single column, the result is a vector:

```
Exp_classic <- as.data.frame(Experiment)
class(Exp_classic[1:2, 1:2]) ## data.frame
```

```
## [1] ``data.frame''
```

```
class(Exp_classic[1, ]) ## data.frame
```

```
## [1] ``data.frame''
```

```
class(Exp_classic[, 1]) ## vector
```

```
## [1] ``integer''
```

Predictability and a few other useful tweaks made me prefer `tibble` over `data.frame`. But, many third-party packages continue to produce classic `data.frame` objects. For example, there is an alternative to package 'readxl, openxlsx, which reads (and writes) Excel files. It returns classic data.frames, which can easily be converted as follows:

```
D_foo <-
  read.xlsx(``foo.xlsx'') %>%
  as_tibble()
```

If you slice a Tibble, the result is always a Tibble, even if you pick a single cell. Sometimes, one wants to truly extract a vector. With a `tibble`, a single column can be extracted as a vector, using double square brackets, or using the $ operator.

```
Experiment[[1]] ## vector
Experiment$Group ## the same
```

Sometimes, it may be necessary to change values in a data frame. For example, a few outliers have been discovered during data screening, and the researcher decides to mark them as missing values. The syntax for indexing elements in a data frame can be used in conjunction with the assignment operator `<-`. In the example below, we make the simulated experiment more realistic by injecting a few outliers (Table 2.6). Then we discard these outliers by setting them all to NA.

```
## injecting
Experiment[2, ``outcome''] <- 660
Experiment[6, ``outcome''] <- 987
Experiment[c(1, 3), ``age''] <- -99

## printing first few observations
head(Experiment)

## setting to NA (by injection)
Experiment[c(2, 6), ``outcome''] <- NA
Experiment[c(1, 3), ``age''] <- NA
```

Besides injection, note two more features of addressing data frame elements. The first is that vectors can be used to address multiple rows, e.g. 2 and 6. In fact, the range operator `1:3` we used above is just a convenient way of creating a vector `c(1,2,3)`. Although not shown in the example, this works for columns alike.

Table 2.6 Data set with 4 variables, showing 6 of 6 observations

Obs	Group	Age	Outcome
1	Control	−99	203
2	Experimental	34	660
3	Control	−99	216
4	Experimental	32	256
5	Control	29	201
6	Experimental	27	987

The careful reader may also have noted another oddity in the above example. With `Experiment[c(2, 6),"outcome"]`, we addressed two elements, but the right-hand side of `<-` is only one value. That is a basic mechanism of R, called *reuse*. When the left-hand side is longer than the right-hand side, the right-hand side is reused as many times as needed. Many basic functions in R work like this, and it can be quite useful. For example, you may want to create a vector of 20 random numbers, where one half has a different mean as the second half of observations.

```
rnorm(20, mean = c(1, 2), sd = 1)
```

The above example reuses the two mean values 50 times, creating an alternating pattern. Strictly speaking, the `sd = 1` parameter is reused, too, a 100 times. While reuse often comes in conveniently, it can also lead to difficult programming errors. So, it is good advice to be aware of this mechanism and always carefully check the input to vectorized functions.

2.2.6   Import, Export and Archiving

R lets you import data from almost every conceivable source, given that you have installed and loaded the appropriate packages (foreign, haven or openxlsx for Excel files). Besides that, R has its own file format for storing data, which is *.Rda* files. With these files you can save data frames (and any other object in R), using the `save(data, file = "some_file.Rda")` and `load(file = "some_file.Rda")` commands.

A few people create their data tables directly in R, but have legacy data sets in Excel (*.xslx*) and SPSS files (*.sav*). Moreover, the data can be produced by electronic measurement devices (e.g. electrodermal response measures) or programmed experiments can provide data in different forms, for example, as *.csv* (comma-separated-values) files. All these files can be opened by the following commands:

```
## Text files
Experiment <-
    read_csv(``Data/Experiment.csv'') %>%
```

```
  as_tbl_obs()

## Excel
Experiment <-
  read_excel(''Data/Experiment.xlsx'', sheet = 1) %>%
  as_tbl_obs()

## SPSS (haven)
Experiment <-
  read_sav(''Data/Experiment.sav'') %>%
  as_tbl_obs()

## SPSS (foreign)
Experiment <-
  read.spss(''Data/Experiment.sav'', to.data.frame = TRUE) %>%
  as_tbl_obs()
```

Note that I gave two options for reading SPSS files. The first (with an underscore) is from the newer haven package (part of tidyverse). With some SPSS files, I experienced problems with this command, as it does not convert SPSS's data type *labeled* (which is almost the same as an R factor). The alternative is the classic `read.spss` command which works almost always, but as a default it creates a list of lists, which is not what you typically want. With the extra argument, as shown, it behaves as expected.

This is also a good moment to address the notorious `as_tbl_obs()`, whenever I simulate or read data. The command is from the Bayr package. Its main purpose is to produce a useful display of what is in the data. A regular Tibble (or Data.frame) object puts the whole data table into your report. If you first call it a *table of observations* (tbl_obs), it will only print eight randomly selected observations (rows), plus, hold our breath, automatic table captions in your report. The second function of `as_tbl_obs()` is to add a variable Obs, which is just a sequential identifier.

Remember, data frames are objects in the memory of your computer, and as such volatile. Once you leave your R session, they are gone. Once you have a data frame imported and cleaned, you may want to store it to a file fopr future use. Like for reading, many commands are available for writing all kinds of data formats. If your workflow is completely based on R, you can conveniently use R's own format for storing data, Rdata files (Rda). For storing a data frame and then reading it back (in your next session), simply do

```
save(Experiment, file = ''Data/Experiment.Rda'')
load(file = ''Data/Experiment.Rda'')
```

Note that with `save` and `load`, all objects are restored by their original names, without using any assignments. Take care, as this will not overwrite any object with the same name. Another issue is that for the `save` command you have to explicitly refer to the `file` argument and provide the file path as a character object. In RStudio, begin typing `file=""`, put the cursor between the quotation marks and hit `Tab`, which opens a small dialogue for navigation to the desired directory.

Once you have loaded, prepared and started to analyze a data frame in R, there is little reason to go back to any legacy program. Still, the `haven` and `foreign` packages contain commands to write to various file formats. I'll keep that as an exercise for the reader.

2.2.7   Case Environments

This book features more than a dozen case studies. Every case will be encountered several times and multiple objects are created along the way: data sets, regressions, graphics, tables, you name it. That posed the problem of naming the objects, so that they are unique. I could have chosen object names, like `BrowsingAB_M_1`, `AUP_M_1`, etc. But, this is not what you normally would do, when working on one study at a time. Moreover, every letter you add to a line of code makes it more prone to errors and less likely that you, dear reader, are typing it in and trying it out yourself.

For these reasons, all cases are enclosed in *case environments* and provided with this book. For getting a case environment to work in your session, it has to be loaded from the respective R data file first:

```
load(``BrowsingAB.Rda'')
```

In R, *environments* are containers for collections of objects. If an object `BAB1` is placed in an environment `BrowsingAB`, it can be called `BrowsingAB$BAB1`. This way, no brevity is gained (Table 2.7). Another way to assess objects in an environment is to *attach the environment first* as

```
attach(BrowsingAB)
BAB1
```

Calling `attach` gets you into the *namespace* of the environment (formally correct: the namespace gets imported to your working environment). All objects in that namespace become immediately visible by their mere name. The `detach` command leaves the environment, when you are done. When working with the case environments, I strongly recommend detaching before attaching another environment.

All case environments provided with this book contain one or more data sets. Many of the cases are synthetic data which has been generated by a simulation function. This function, normally called `simulate`, is provided with the case environment, too. That gives you the freedom to produce your own data sets with the same structure, but different effects. Generally, calling the simulation function without any further arguments exactly reproduces the synthetic data set provided with the case environment.

```
simulate() ## exactly reproduces the data frame BAB1
```

Simulation functions have parameters by which you can tune the data-generating process. Table 2.8 shows a data set of only six ToT observations. These observations are perfect in a sense, because `sd = 0` effectively removed the random component.

Table 2.7 Data set with 15 variables, showing 8 of 200 observations

Obs	Part	Task	Design	Gender	Education	Age	Far_sighted	Small_font	ToT	Clicks	Returns	Rating	Age_shft	Age_cntr
53	53	1	A	M	High	64	FALSE	FALSE	33.3	1	0	2	44	13.83
59	59	1	A	F	Middle	63	FALSE	FALSE	152.6	4	3	4	43	12.83
69	69	1	A	M	Middle	74	TRUE	FALSE	146.4	8	0	3	54	23.83
125	125	1	B	F	Low	50	FALSE	TRUE	76.0	2	0	2	30	−0.17
166	166	1	B	M	High	62	FALSE	TRUE	44.9	0	0	1	42	11.83
170	170	1	B	F	Middle	47	FALSE	TRUE	18.0	1	1	2	27	−3.17
187	187	1	B	M	Middle	43	TRUE	TRUE	161.7	6	2	3	23	−7.17
190	190	1	B	F	Low	60	FALSE	TRUE	111.3	3	2	2	40	9.83

Table 2.8 Data set with 13 variables, showing 8 of 60 observations

Obs	Part	Task	Design	Gender	Education	age	Far_sighted	Small_font	ToT	clicks	returns	rating
25	1	5	A	F	Middle	56	TRUE	FALSE	191.7	10	3	5
43	1	3	B	F	Middle	56	TRUE	TRUE	232.6	12	5	6
2	2	1	A	F	Middle	42	TRUE	FALSE	110.5	7	2	3
14	2	3	A	F	Middle	42	TRUE	FALSE	163.8	8	1	4
56	2	5	B	F	Middle	42	TRUE	TRUE	139.1	11	0	4
28	4	5	A	F	High	22	TRUE	FALSE	107.1	3	0	3
34	4	1	B	F	High	22	TRUE	TRUE	89.6	4	1	2
24	6	4	A	M	Low	45	FALSE	FALSE	103.1	7	1	2

```
simulate(n_Part = 6, sd_epsilon = 0) ## just 6 observations
```

Furthermore, once you delve deeper into R, you can critically inspect the simulation function's code for its behavioral and psychological assumptions (working through the later chapters on data management and simulation will help).

```
simulate ## calling a function without parentheses prints code
```

Finally, the case environments contain all objects that have been throughout this book. This is especially useful for the regression models, as fitting these can take from a few seconds to hours.

Note that working with environments is a tricky business. Creating these case environments in an efficient way was more difficult than you may think. Therefore, I do *not* recommend using environments in everday data analysis, with one exception: at any moment the current working environment contains all objects that have been created, so far. That is precisely the set of objects shown in the Environment pane of RStudio (or call `ls()` for a listing). Saving all objects and retrieving them when returning from a break is as easy as

```
save(file = ''my_data_analysis.Rda'')
## have a break
load(''my_data_analysis.Rda'')
```

Next to that, RStudio can be configured to save the current workspace on exit and reload it on the next start. When working on just one data analysis for a longer period of time, this can be a good choice.

2.2.8 Structuring Data

In the whole book, data sets are structured according to the rule *one-row-per-observation* of the dependent variable (the ORPO rule). Many researchers still organize their data tables as one row per participant, as is requested by some legacy statistics programs. This is fine in research with non-repeated measures, but will not function properly with multi-level data sets. Consider a study where two designs were evaluated by three participants using a self-report item, like "how easy to use is the interface?" Then, the *wrong way* of structuring the data would be as in Table 2.9, without multiple observations per row (A and B).

```
ORPO %>%
  # filter(Task == 1, Item == 1) %>%
  # mascutils::discard_redundant() %>%
  sample_n(8) %>%
  spread(Design, response)

ORPO %>% as_tbl_obs()
```

Table 2.9 Wide format with multiple observations per row

Part	Task	Item	A	B
1	1	2	4	
2	1	2		2
2	2	1		4
2	2	2	3	
3	1	1		4
3	1	3		1
3	2	3	6	2

Table 2.10 Data set with 6 variables, showing 8 of 36 observations

Obs	Part	Task	Design	Item	Response
1	1	1	A	1	3
16	1	2	A	2	7
28	1	2	A	3	6
31	1	1	B	3	4
2	2	1	A	1	3
8	2	1	B	1	6
17	2	2	A	2	3
33	3	1	B	3	1

The correct way structure is shown in Table 2.10. But, the ORPO rule dictates another principle: every row should have a unique identifier (besides the observation ID), which often is a combination of values. In the example above, every observation is uniquely identified by the participant identifier and the design condition. If we extend the example slightly, it is immediately apparent why the ORPO rule is justified. Imagine, the study actually asked three participants to rate two different tasks on two different designs by three self-report items. By the ORPO rule, we can easily extend the data frame as below (showing a random selection of rows). I leave it up to the reader to figure out how to press such a data set in the wide legacy format.

Using identifiers is good practice for several reasons. First, it reduces problems during manual data entry. Second, it allows to efficiently record data in multi-method experiments and join them automatically. Lastly, the identifiers will become statistically interesting by themselves when we turn to linear mixed-effects models and the notion of *members of a population* 6.5. Throughout the book, I will use standard names for recurring identifier variables in design research:

- Part,
- Design,
- Item and
- Task.

Note that usually these entities get numerical identifiers, but these numbers are just labels. Throughout, variables are written in Uppercase when they are entities, but not real numbers. An exception is the trial order in experiments with massive repeated measures. These get a numerical type to allow exploring effects over time such as learning, training and fatigue.

2.2.9 Data Transformation

Do you wonder about the strange use of %>% in my code above? This is the tidy way of programming data transformations in R.

The so-called magritte operator %>% is part of the *dplyr/tidyr* framework for data manipulation. It chains steps of data manipulation by connecting transformation functions, also called piping. In the following, we will first see a few basic examples. Later, we will proceed to longer transformation chains and see how graceful dplyr piping is, compared to the classic data transformation syntax in R.

Importing data from any of the possible resources will typically give a data frame. However, often the researcher wants to *select* or *rename* variables in the data frame. Say, you want the variable *Group* to be called *Condition*, omit the variable *age* and store the new data frame as *Exp*. The select command does all this. In the following code, the data frame Experiment is piped into select. The variable *Condition* is renamed to *Group*, and the variable *outcome* is taken as is. All other variables are discarded (Table 2.11).

```
Exp <-
  Experiment %>%
  select(Condition = Group, outcome) %>%
  as_tbl_obs()
Exp
```

Table 2.11 Data set with 3 variables, showing 8 of 100 observations

Obs	Condition	Outcome
3	Control	216
12	Experimental	252
13	Control	206
30	Experimental	239
37	Control	198
51	Control	212
60	Experimental	251
65	Control	183

Table 2.12 Data set with 3 variables, showing 8 of 96 observations

Condition	Age	Outcome
Control	24	212
Experimental	27	251
Experimental	26	240
Experimental	28	257
Experimental	22	264
Control	21	200
Control	18	194
Control	26	191

Another frequent step in data analysis is cleaning the data from missing values and outliers. In the following code example, we first "inject" a few missing values for age (which were coded as -99) and outliers (>500) in the outcome variable. Note that I am using some R commands that you don't need to understand by now. Then we reuse the above code for renaming (this time keeping *age* onboard) and add some filtering steps (Table 2.12).

```
## rename, then filtering
Exp <-
  Experiment %>%
  select(Condition = Group, age, outcome) %>%
  filter(outcome < 500) %>%
  filter(age != -99)
Exp
```

During data preparation and analysis, new variables are created routinely. For example, the covariate is often shifted to the center before using linear regression (Table 2.13).

```
mean_age <- mean(Exp$age)
Exp <- Exp %>%
  mutate(age_cntrd = age - mean_age)
Exp
```

Finally, for the descriptive statistics part of your report, you probably want to summarize the outcome variable per experimental condition. The following chain of commands first groups the data frame, then computes means and standard deviations. At every step, a data frame is piped into another command, which processes the data frame and outputs a data frame (Table 2.14).

```
Exp %>%
  group_by(Condition) %>%
  summarize(
```

Table 2.13 Data set with 4 variables, showing 8 of 96 observations

Condition	Age	Outcome	Age_cntrd
Control	31	207	4.15
Experimental	28	239	1.15
Control	30	196	3.15
Experimental	32	253	5.15
Control	24	200	−2.85
Control	29	200	2.15
Experimental	20	262	−6.85
Control	22	196	−4.85

Table 2.14 Data set with 4 variables, showing 8 of 96 observations

Condition	Age	Outcome	Age_cntrd
Experimental	29	261	2.146
Experimental	18	241	−8.854
Control	32	183	5.146
Control	33	189	6.146
Experimental	27	256	0.146
Experimental	32	239	5.146
Experimental	21	249	−5.854
Experimental	34	250	7.146

```
  mean = mean(outcome),
  sd = sd(outcome)
)
```

Condition	Mean	Sd
Control	198	9.05
Experimental	251	9.43

Exp

2.2.10 Plotting Data

Good statistical figures can vastly improve your and your readers' understanding of data and results. This book introduces the modern ggplot2 graphics system of R.

Every plot starts with piping a data frame into the ggplot(aes(...)) command. The aes(...) argument of ggplot creates the *aesthetics*, which is a *mapping between variables and features of the plot* (and only remotely has something to do with beauty). Review the code once again that produces the piles of sugar: the aesthetics map the variable *Group* on the fill color, whereas *outcome* is mapped to the x-axis. For a plot to be valid, there must at least one layer with a *geometry*. The above example uses the density geometry, which calculates the density and maps it to the y-axis.

The ggplot2 plotting system knows a full set of geometries, like

- scatterplots with `geom_point()`,
- smooth line plots with `geom_smooth()`,
- histograms with `geom_histogram()`,
- boxplots with `geom_boxplot()` and
- my personal favorite: horizontal density diagrams with `geom_violin()`.

For a brief demonstration of ggplots basic functionality, we use the `BAB1` data set of the BrowsingAB case. We attach the case environment and take a glance at the data (Table 2.15)):

```
attach(BrowsingAB)
BAB1 %>% as_tbl_obs()
```

The BrowsingAB case is a virtual series of studies, where two websites were compared by how long it takes users to complete a given task, time-on-task (ToT). Besides the design factor, a number of additional variables exist that could possibly play a role for ToT, too. We explore the data set with ggplot.

We begin with a plot that shows the association between the age of the participant and ToT. Both variables are metric and suggest themselves be put on a 2D plane, with coordinates x and y, a *scatterplot* (Fig. 2.2).

```
BAB1 %>%
  ggplot(aes(x = age, y = ToT)) +
  geom_point()
```

Let's take a look at the elements of the command chain: The first two lines pipe the data frame into the ggplot engine.

```
BAB1 %>%
  ggplot()
```

At that moment, the ggplot engine "knows" which variables the data frame contains and hence are available for the plot. It does not yet know which variables are being used, and how. The next step is, usually, to consider a basic (there exist more than 30) *geometry* and put it on a *layer*. The scatterplot geometry of ggplot is `geom_point`:

```
BAB1 %>%
  ggplot() +
  geom_point()
```

Table 2.15 Data set with 15 variables, showing 8 of 200 observations

Obs	Part	Task	Design	Gender	Education	Age	Far_sighted	Small_font	ToT	Clicks	Returns	Rating	Age_shft	age_cntr
43	43	1	A	M	Low	24	FALSE	FALSE	186.9	6	0	2	4	−26.2
54	54	1	A	M	Middle	77	TRUE	FALSE	65.3	5	1	2	57	26.8
55	55	1	A	M	Low	39	FALSE	FALSE	137.7	9	0	4	19	−11.2
58	58	1	A	M	Low	27	FALSE	FALSE	7.5	4	1	2	7	−23.2
85	85	1	A	F	High	67	TRUE	FALSE	107.8	1	1	2	47	16.8
162	162	1	B	M	Middle	27	FALSE	TRUE	28.5	1	0	1	7	−23.2
165	165	1	B	M	Middle	22	FALSE	TRUE	56.4	2	1	1	2	−28.2
173	173	1	B	M	Middle	32	FALSE	TRUE	65.1	2	1	2	12	−18.2

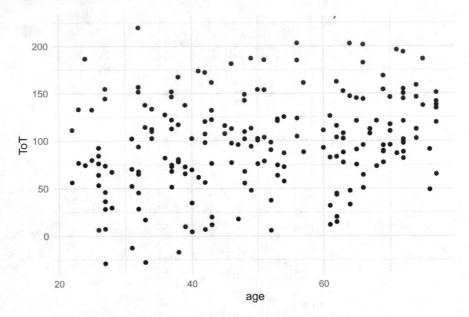

Fig. 2.2 Scatterplot showing the assiciation between age and ToT

The last step is the *aesthetic mapping*, which tells ggplot the variables to use and how to map them to *visual properties* of the geometry. The basic properties of points in a coordinate system are the x- and y-positions:

```
BAB1 %>%
  ggplot(aes(x = age, y = ToT)) +
  geom_point()
```

The function `aes` creates a mapping where the aesthetics per variable are given. When we call `aes` directly, we see that it produces a table with the mappings.

```
aes(x = age, y = ToT)
```

```
## Aesthetic mapping:
## * `x` -> `age`
## * `y` -> `ToT`
```

One tiny detail in the above chain has not yet been explained: the +. When choosing the geometry, you actually *add a layer* to the plot. This is, of course, not the literal mathematical sum. Technically, what the author of the ggplot2 package did was to *overload* the + operator. A large set of ggplot functions can be combined in a myriad of ways, just using +. The overloaded + in ggplot is a brilliant analogy: you can infinitely chain ggplot functions like you can create long sums. You can store the

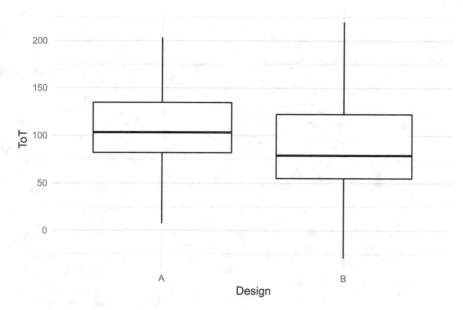

Fig. 2.3 A boxplot

ggplot object and later modify it by adding functions. The analogy has its limits, though: other than sums, order matters in ggplot combinations: the first in the chain is always ggplot and layers are drawn upon each other.

Let's move on with a slightly different situation that will result in a different geometry. Say, we are interested in the distribution of the time-on-task measures under the two designs. We need a geometry that visualizes the distribution of quantitative variables split by a grouping variable, factor. The boxplot does the job (Fig. 2.3):

```
BAB1 %>%
  ggplot(aes(x = Design, y = ToT)) +
  geom_boxplot()
```

The boxplot maps ToT to y (again). The factor Design is represented as a split on the x-axis. Interestingly, the boxplot does not represent the data as raw as in the scatterplot example. The geometry actually performs an analysis on ToT, which produces five statistics: min, first quartile, median, third quartile and max. These statistics define the vertical positions of bars and end points.

Now, we combine all three variables in one plot: how does the association between ToT and age differ by design? As we have two quantitative variables, we stay with the scatterplot for now. As we intend to separate the groups, we need a property of points to distinguish them. Points offer several additional aesthetics, such as color, size and shape. We choose color, and add it to the aesthetic mapping by aes (Fig. 2.4). Note that it does not matter whether you use the British or American way of writing (colour vs. color).

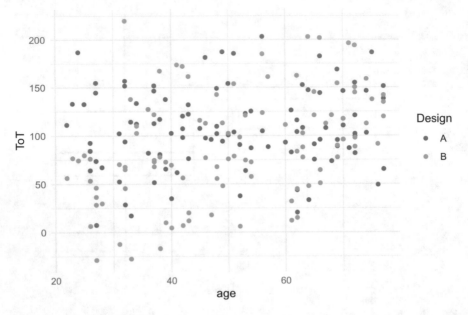

Fig. 2.4 A grouped scatterplot

```
BAB1 %>%
  ggplot(aes(x = age, y = ToT, color = Design)) +
  geom_point()
```

Now, we can distinguish the groups visually, but there is too much clutter to discover any relation. With the boxplot we saw that some geometries do not represent the raw data, but summaries (statistics) of data. For scatterplots, a geometry that does the job of summarizing the trend is geom_smooth. This geometry summarizes a cloud of points by drawing a LOESS-smooth line through it. Note how the color mapping is applied to all geometry layers (Fig. 2.5).

```
BAB1 %>%
  ggplot(aes(x = age, y = ToT, color = Design)) +
  geom_point() +
  geom_smooth()
```

We see a highly interesting pattern: the association between age and ToT follows two slightly different mirrored sigmoid curves.

Now that we have represented three variables with properties of geometries, what if we wanted to add a fourth one, say education level? Formally, we could use another aesthetic, say shape of points, to represent it. You can easily imagine that this would no longer result in a clear visual figure. For situations, where there are many factors, or factors with many levels, it is impossible to reasonably represent them in one plot.

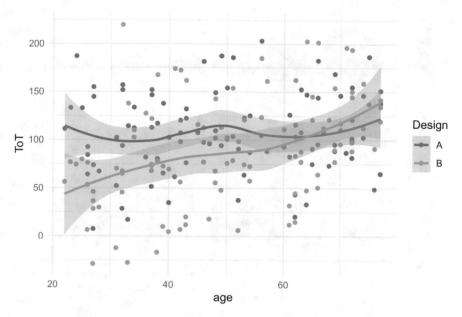

Fig. 2.5 A scatterplot with smoothed lines

The alternative is to use *facetting*. A facet splits the data by a grouping variable and creates one single plot for every group (Fig. 2.6).

```
BAB1 %>%
  ggplot(aes(x = age, y = ToT, color = Design)) +
  geom_point() +
  geom_smooth() +
  facet_grid(Education ~ .)
```

See how the `facet_grid` command takes a formula, instead of just a variable name. This makes faceting the primary choice for highly dimensional situations. For example, we may also choose to represent both factors, Design and education by facets (Fig. 2.7):

```
BAB1 %>%
  ggplot(aes(x = age, y = ToT)) +
  geom_point() +
  geom_smooth() +
  facet_grid(Education ~ Design)
```

Note how the color aesthetic, although unnecessary, is kept. It is possible to map several aesthetics (or facets) to one variable, but not vice versa.

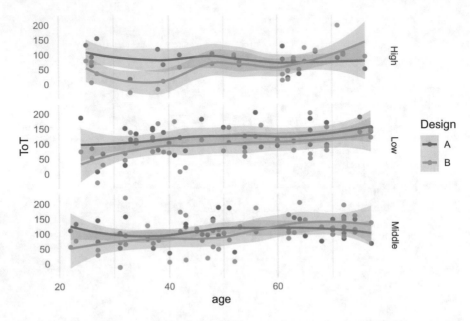

Fig. 2.6 With facets, groups can be distinguished

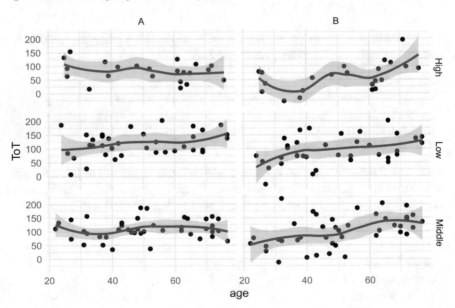

Fig. 2.7 Facetting by two factors (or more) results in a grid

2.2.11 Fitting Regression Models

Above we have seen examples of functions that boil down a vector to a single statistic, like mean. R has several functions that summarize data in a more complex way. One function with a wide range of applications is the `lm` command that applies regression models to data (provided as data frames).

In the following, we will use another simulated data frame `Exp` to demonstrate linear models. To make this more interesting, we simulate `Exp` in a slightly advanced way, with quantitative associations between variables. Note how the *expected value* μ is created by drawing on the variables `Condition` and `age`. The last step adds (somewhat) realistic noise to the measures, by drawing from the normal distribution with a mean of *mu*.

```
N_Obs <- 20
set.seed(42)
Exp <-
  tibble(
    Obs = 1:N_Obs,
    Condition = rep(
      c(``Experimental'', ``Control''),
      N_Obs / 2
    ),
    age = runif(N_Obs, 18, 35),
    mu = 200 + (Condition == ``Control'') * 50 + age * 1,
    outcome = rnorm(N_Obs, mu, 10)
  )
```

The experiment involves two groups, which in classic statistics would clearly point to what is commonly referred to as *ANOVA*. As it will turn out in 4.3.1, old-fashioned ANOVA can be replaced by a rather simple regression model that I call comparison of groups model (CGM). The estimation of regression models is done by a *regression engine*, which basically is a (very powerful) R command. The specification for any regression model is given in R's formula language. Learning this formula language is key to unleashing the power of regression models in R. We can perform a CGM on the data frame `Exp` using the regression engine `stan_glm`. The desired model estimates the effect of `Condition` on `outcome`. This produces a regression object that contains an abundance of information, much of it being of little interest for now. (A piece of information that it does *not* contain is F-statistics and p-values; and that is why it is not an ANOVA, strictly speaking!) The foremost question is how strong the difference between the groups is. The `clu` command extracts the parameter estimates from the model to answer the question (Table 2.16).

```
M_1 <-
  stan_glm(outcome ~ Condition,
    data = Exp
  )

clu(M_1)
```

Table 2.16 Parameter estimates with 95% credibility limits

Parameter	Fixef	Center	Lower	Upper
Intercept	Intercept	275.6	264.2	286.0
ConditionExperimental	ConditionExperimental	−47.8	−62.5	−31.9
sigma_resid		16.8	12.3	24.5

Table 2.17 Parameter estimates with 95% credibility limits

Parameter	Fixef	Center	Lower	Upper
Intercept	Intercept	220.29	132.1	306.69
Age	Age	1.09	−1.9	4.17
Sigma_resid		30.11	22.3	43.43

Another classic model is *linear regression*, where outcome is predicted by a metric variable, say age. Estimating such a model with stan_glm looks like this, and Table 2.17 shows the estimated parameters.

```
M_2 <-
  stan_glm(outcome ~ age,
    data = Exp
  )

clu(M_2)
```

If you are interested in both at the same time, you can combine that in one model by the following formula. As a result, Table 2.18 now has three parameters, two of which are coefficients (fixef).

```
M_3 <-
  stan_glm(outcome ~ Condition + age,
    data = Exp
  )

clu(M_3)
```

Table 2.18 Parameter estimates with 95% credibility limits

Parameter	Fixef	Center	Lower	Upper
Intercept	Intercept	220.1	178.744	261.79
ConditionExperimental	ConditionExperimental	−50.4	−63.321	−37.06
Age	Age	2.0	0.551	3.45
Sigma_resid		14.2	10.309	20.87

A statistical model has several components, for example, the coefficients and residuals. Models are complex objects, from which a variety of inferences can be made. For example, the coefficient estimates can be extracted and used for prediction. This is what `fixef()` does in the above code.

A number of functions can be used to extract certain aspects of the model. For example:

- `fixef(model)` extracts the linear coefficients.
- `residuals(model)` extracts the measurement errors.
- `predict(model)` extracts the expected values.

These will all be covered in later chapters.

2.2.12 Knitting Statistical Reports

As you have seen throughout this chapter, with R you can effectively manage data, create impressively expressive graphics and conveniently estimate statistical models. Then usually comes the painful moment where all this needs to be assembled into a neat report. With R and RStudio, it has never been easier than that. In fact, complete books have been written in R, like the one you are reading.

A *minimal statistical report* contains four elements:

1. a recap of the research question;
2. description of how the statistical model relates to the research question;
3. a few figures or tables that answer the research question;
4. an explanation of the results.

Of these four elements, three are pure text. For a minimal report, it is fairly convenient to use a word processor software for the text, craft the figure in R and copy it. One problem with this approach is that a *scrutable statistical report* contains at least the following *additional* elements:

1. procedures of data preparation (sources, transformations, variable names, outlier removal);
2. data exploration (ranges of variables, outlier discovery, visualizing associations, etc.);
3. model estimation (formula specification, convergence checks);
4. model criticism (normality of residuals, etc.).

In advanced statistical workflows, this is then multiplied by the number of models, an iterative selection process. Because it is easy to lie with statistics, these elements are needed to build a fundament of credibility. Full transparency is achieved when another researcher can exactly reproduce all steps of the original analysis. It is obvious that the easiest way to achieve this is to hand over the full R script.

The most user-friendly way to achieve both, a good-looking report and full transparency, is to write a document that contains all before mentioned: text, graphics,

```
# Results

In the study we examined

1. whether on average users can rent a car in 99 seconds
2. and if we can say that with sufficient certainty

## Data exploration


```{r}
summary(D)
```


```{r}
summary(D)
```


All variables show good variation.

Regression

```{r}
M_1 <- stan_lm(ToT ~ 1, data = D)
```

```{r}
coef(M_1) %>% knitr::kable()
```


Our main observations are:

+ the 99 seconds claim is not supported
+ time-on-task measures are not normally distributed
```

Fig. 2.8 A minimal statistical report in markdown

tables and R code. In the R environment, such mixed documents can be written in the *markdown/knitr* framework.

Markdown implements a simple markup language; with that, you can typeset simple, structured texts in a plain ASCII editor. Later in the workflow, such a markup document is transformed into one of the various output formats that are rendered by the respective programs, such as Microsoft Word or an HTML browser.

The example in Fig. 2.8 is an alternation of markup text and *chunks*, those weirdly enclosed pieces of R code. While the text is static, the chunks are processed by the knitr engine, evaluating the enclosed R code and knitting the output into a document. Very conveniently, when the output is a figure, it will be inserted into the document right away. The `kable` command from the knitr package, in turn, produces neatly rendered tables from data frame objects. By default, the R code is shown, too, but that can be customized.

The minimal workflow for statistical reporting with knitr is as follows:

1. Use markdown right away, covering all steps of your data analysis, i.e. a scrutable report. You may even start writing when only one part of your data gathering is completed, because due to the dynamic chunks, updating the report when new data arrives is just a button click away.
2. When the data analysis is complete, compile the scrutable report to Word format.
3. Extract the passages, figures and tables for a minimal statistical report. This is your results section.
4. Provide the scrutable report as appendix or supplementary material.

In the notion of this chapter, this is just to get you started and knitr is so tightly integrated with the RStudio environment that I don't even bother to explain the commands for knitting a document. Once acquainted with the basics, markdown provides a few additional markup tokens, like footnotes, hyperlinks or including images. The customization options and add-ons for knitr are almost endless, and various interesting add-ons are available, just to mention two:

1. The bookdown package provides an infrastructure for writing and publishing longer reports and books.
2. With the shiny package, one can add dynamic widgets to HTML reports. Think of a situation, where your statistical model is more complicated, than a linear regression line or a few group means say you are estimating a polynomial model or a learning curve. Then, with a simple shiny app, you can enable your readers to understand the model by playful exploration.

2.3 Further Reading

1.R for Data Science is a book co-authored by Hadley "Tidy" Wickham. 1. The Grammar of Graphics, [1] is the formal framework for the ggplot engine. 1.ggplot2 Version of Figures in "25 Recipes for Getting Started with R" for readers who are familiar with the legacy plotting commands in R. 1. Introduction to dplyr for Faster Data Manipulation in R introduces dplyr, the next generation R interface for data manipulation, which is used extensively in this book. 1. Quick-R is a comprehensive introduction to many common statistical techniques with R. 1. Code as manuscript features a small set of lessons with code examples, assignments and further resources. For if you are in a haste. 1. bookdown: Authoring Books and Technical Documents with R Markdown fully unleashes the power of knitr for writing and publishing longer reports and books. 1. Rstudio Cheatsheets a growing collection of cheatsheets for tidy R and more.

Reference

1. Wilkinson L (2005) The grammar of graphics. Statistics and computing, 2nd edn. Springer, New York. ISBN: 0-387-24544-8. https://doi.org/10.1007/0-387-28695-0

Chapter 3
Elements of Bayesian Statistics

As human beings, we make our decisions on what has happened to us in the past. For example, we trust a person or a company more, when we can look back at a series of successful transactions. And we have a remarkable capability to recall what has just happened, but also what happened yesterday or years ago. By integrating over all the evidence, we form a view of the world we forage. When evidence is abundant, we vigorously experience a feeling of certainty or lack of doubt. That is not to deny, that in a variety of situations, the boundedness of the human mind kicks in and we become terrible decision makers. This is for a variety of psychological reasons, to name just a few:

- Plain forgetting.
- The primacy effect: recent events get more weight.
- Confirmation bias: evidence that supports a belief is actively sought for, counter-evidence gets ignored.
- The hindsight bias: once a situation has taken a certain outcome, we believe that it had to happen that way.

The very aim of scientific research is to avoid the pitfalls of our minds and act as rational as possible by translating our theory into a formal model of reality, gathering evidence in an unbiased way, and weigh the evidence by formal procedures. This weighing of evidence using data essentially is *statistical modeling* and statistical models in this book all produce two sorts of numbers: *magnitude of effects* and *level of certainty*. In applied research, real-world decisions depend on the evidence, which has two aspects: first, the strength of effects and the level of certainty we have reached.

Bayesian inferential statistics grounds on the idea of accumulating evidence, where past data is not lost. *Certainty* (or *strength of belief* or *credibility* or *credence*) in Bayesian statistics is formalized as a *probability scale (0 = impossible, 1 = certain)*. The level of certainty is determined by two sources, everything that we already know about the subject and the data we just gathered. Both sources are only

© Springer Nature Switzerland AG 2021
M. Schmettow, *New Statistics for Design Researchers*,
Human–Computer Interaction Series,
https://doi.org/10.1007/978-3-030-46380-9_3

seemingly different, because when new data is analyzed, a transition occurs from what you knew before, *prior belief*, to what you know after seeing the data, *posterior belief*. In other words, by data, the current belief gets an update.

Updating our beliefs is essential for acting in rational ways. The first section of this chapter is intended to tell the Big Picture. It puts statistics into the context of decision-making in design research. For those readers with a background in statistics, this section may be a sufficient introduction all by itself.

In the remainder of this chapter, the essential concepts of statistics and Bayesian analysis will be introduced from the ground up. First, we will look at descriptive statistics and I will introduce basic statistical tools, such as summary statistics and figures. Descriptive statistics can be used effectively to explore data and prepare the statistical modeling, but they lack one important ingredient: information about the level of certainty.

Section 3.4 first derives probability from set theory and relative frequencies, before we turn to the famous Bayes theorem Sect. 3.4.5, followed by an introduction to Bayesian thinking Sect. 3.4.6.

Then we go on to basic concepts of statistical modeling, such as the likelihood, and we finish with the Bayes theorem, which does the calculation of the posterior certainty from prior knowledge and data. Despite the matter, I will make minimal use of mathematical formalism. Instead, I use R code as much as possible to illustrate the concepts. If you are not yet familiar with R, you may want to read Sect. 2.2 first, or alongside.

Section 3.5 goes into the practical details of modeling. A statistical model is introduced by its two components: the structural part, which typically carries the research question or theory, followed by a rather deep account of the second component of statistical models: the random part.

3.1   Rational Decision-Making in Design Research

- I see clouds. Should I take my umbrella?
- Should I do this bungee jump? How many people came to death by jumping? (More or less than alpine skiing?) And how much fun is it really?
- Overhauling our company website will cost us EUR 100.000. Is it worth it?

All the above cases are examples of decision-making under uncertainty. The actors aim for maximizing their outcome, be it well being, fun or money. But, they are uncertain about what will really happen. And their uncertainty occurs on two levels:

1. One cannot precisely foresee the exact outcome of one's chosen action:

- Taking the umbrella with you can have two consequences: if it rains, you have the benefit of staying dry. If it does not rain, you have the inconvenience of carrying it with you.
- You don't know if you will be the rare unlucky one, who's bungee rope breaks.

- You don't know by how much the new design will attract more visitors and how much the income will raise.

2. It can be difficult to precisely determine the benefits or losses of potential outcomes:

- How much worse is your day when carrying a useless object with you? How much do you hate moisture? In order to compare the two, they must be assessed on the same scale.
- How much fun (or other sources of reward, like social acknowledgments) is it to jump a 120 m canyon? And how much worth is your own life to you?
- What is the average revenue generated per visit? What is an increase of recurrence rate of, say, 50% worth?

Once you know the probabilities of all outcomes and the respective losses, *decision theory* provides an intuitive framework to estimate these values. *Expected utility U* is the sum product of *outcome probabilities P* and the involved *losses*.

In the case of the umbrella, the decision is between two options: taking an umbrella versus taking no umbrella, when it is cloudy.

$P(\text{rain})$		$=0.6$
$P(\text{no rain})$	$=1 - P(\text{rain})$	$=0.4$
$L(\text{carry})$		$=2$
$L(\text{wet})$		$=4$
$U(\text{umbrella})$	$=P(\text{rain})L(\text{carry}) + P(\text{no rain})L(\text{carry}) = L(\text{carry})$	$=2$
$U(\text{no umbrella})$	$=P(\text{rain})L(\text{wet})$	$=2.4$

Tables 3.1, 3.2 and 3.3 develop the calculation of expected utilities U in a step-by-step manner:

```
attach(Rainfall)

Outcomes <-
  tibble(
    outcome = c(``rain'', ``no rain''),
    prob = c(0.6, 0.4)
  )
Outcomes

Actions <-
  tibble(action = c(``umbrella'', ``no umbrella''))

Losses <-
```

Table 3.1 Probabilities of outcomes

Outcome	Prob
Rain	0.6
No rain	0.4

Table 3.2 Losses conditional on outcome and action

Action	Outcome	Prob	Loss
Umbrella	Rain	0.6	2
No umbrella	Rain	0.6	4
Umbrella	No rain	0.4	2
No umbrella	No rain	0.4	0

Table 3.3 Expected losses

Action	Expected_loss
Umbrella	2.0
No umbrella	2.4

```
expand.grid(
  action = Actions$action,
  outcome = Outcomes$outcome
) %>%
join(Outcomes) %>%
mutate(loss = c(2, 4, 2, 0))
Losses

Utility <-
  Losses %>%
  mutate(conditional_loss = prob * loss) %>%
  group_by(action) %>%
  summarise(expected_loss = sum(conditional_loss))
Utility
```

We conclude that, given the high chance for rain and the conditional losses, the expected loss is larger for not taking an umbrella with you. It is rational to take an umbrella when it is cloudy.

3.1.1 *Measuring Uncertainty*

As we have seen above, a decision requires two investigations: outcomes and their probabilities, and the assigned loss. Assigning loss to decisions is highly context-dependent and often requires domain-specific expertise. The issues of probabilistic processes and the uncertainty that arises from them are basically what the idea of *New Statistics* represents. We encounter uncertainty in two forms: first, we usually have just a limited set of observations to draw inference from, this is *uncertainty of parameter estimates*. From just 20 d of observation, we cannot be absolutely certain about the true chance of rain. It can be 60%, but also 62% or 56%. Second, even if we precisely knew the chance of rain, it does not mean we could make a certain statement of the future weather conditions, which is *predictive uncertainty*. For a perfect forecast, we had to have a complete and exact figure of the physical properties of the atmosphere and a fully valid model to predict future states from it. For all non-trivial systems (which excludes living organisms and weather), this is impossible.

Review the rainfall example: the strategy of taking an umbrella with you has proven to be superior under the very assumption of *predictive uncertainty*. As long as you are interested in long-term benefit (i.e. optimizing the average loss on a long series of days), this is the best strategy. This may sound obvious, but it is not. In many cases, where we make decisions under uncertainty, the decision is not part of a homogeneous series. If you are a member of a startup team, you only have this one chance to make a fortune. There is not much opportunity to average out a single failure on future occasions. In contrast, the investor, who lends you the money for your endeavor, probably has a series. You and the investor are playing by very different rules. For the investor, it is rational to optimize his strategy toward a minimum average loss. The entrepreneur is best advised to keep the maximum possible loss at a minimum.

As we have seen, predictive uncertainty is already embedded in the framework of rational decision-making. Some concepts in statistics can be of help here: the uncertainty regarding future events can be quantified and the process of model selection can assist in finding the model that provides the best predictive power.

Still, in our formalization of the Rainfall case, what magically appears are the estimates for the chance of rain. Having these estimates is crucial for finding an optimal decision, but they are created outside of the framework. Furthermore, we pretended to know the chance of rain exactly, which is unrealistic. Estimating parameters from observations is the reign of statistics. From naive calculations, statistical reasoning differs by also regarding the uncertainty of estimates. Generally, we aim for making statements of the following form:

"With probability p, the attribute A is of magnitude X."

In the umbrella example above, the magnitude of interest is the chance of rain. It was assumed to be 60%. This appears extremely high for an average day. A more realistic assumption would be that the probability of rainfall is 60% *given the observation of a cloudy sky*. How could we have come to the belief that with 60% chance, it will rain when the sky is cloudy? We have several options, here:

Table 3.4 Data set with 3 variables, showing 8 of 20 observations

Obs	Cloudy	Rain
1	TRUE	FALSE
2	TRUE	TRUE
9	FALSE	TRUE
10	TRUE	TRUE
12	TRUE	TRUE
14	TRUE	TRUE
19	TRUE	FALSE
20	FALSE	FALSE

1. Supposed, you know that, on average, it rains 60% of all days, it is a matter of common sense that the probability of rain must be equal or larger than that when it's cloudy.
2. You could go and ask a number of experts about the association between clouds and rain.
3. You could do some systematic observations yourself.

Imagine, you have recorded the coincidences of clouds and rainfall over a period of, let's say, 20 d (Table 3.4):

```
Rain
```

Intuitively, you would use the average to estimate the probability of rain under every condition (Table 3.5).

```
Rain %>%
  group_by(cloudy)
```

We can feed these probabilities into the decision framework as outlined above. The problem is that we obtained just a few observations to infer the magnitude of the parameter $P(rain|cloudy) = 60\%$. Imagine, you would repeat the observation series on another 20 d. Due to random fluctuations, you would get a more or less different series and different estimates for the probability of rain. More generally, the *true* parameter is only imperfectly represented by any sample, it is not unlikely that it is close to the estimate, but it could be somewhere else, for example, $P(rain|cloudy) = 55.872\%$.

The trust you put in your estimation is called *level of certainty* or *belief* or *confidence*. It is the primary aim of statistics to rationally deal with uncertainty, which involves to *measure the level of certainty* associated with any statement derived from the data. So, what would be a good way to determine certainty? Think for a moment. If you were asking an expert, how would you do that to learn about magnitude and uncertainty regarding $P(rain|cloudy)$?

Table 3.5 Chance of rain depending on cloudiness of the sky

Obs	Cloudy	Rain
1	TRUE	FALSE
2	TRUE	TRUE
3	TRUE	FALSE
4	FALSE	FALSE
5	TRUE	TRUE
6	FALSE	FALSE
7	FALSE	FALSE
8	FALSE	FALSE
9	FALSE	TRUE
10	TRUE	TRUE
11	TRUE	TRUE
12	TRUE	TRUE
13	FALSE	FALSE
14	TRUE	TRUE
15	FALSE	TRUE
16	TRUE	FALSE
17	FALSE	TRUE
18	FALSE	FALSE
19	TRUE	FALSE
20	FALSE	FALSE

Maybe, the conversation would be as follows:

YOU: What is the chance of rain, when it's cloudy?

EXPERT: Wow, difficult question. I don't have a definite answer.

YOU: Oh, c'mon. I just need a rough answer. Is it more like 50%-ish, or rather 70%-ish?

EXPERT: Hmm, maybe somewhere between 50 and 70%.

YOU: Then, I guess, taking an umbrella with me is the rational choice of action.

Note how the expert gave two end points for the parameter in question, to indicate the location and the level of uncertainty. If she had been more certain, she had said "between 55 and 65%". While this is better than nothing, it remains unclear which level of uncertainty is enclosed. Is the expert 100%, 90% or just 50% sure the true chance is in the interval? Next time, you could ask as follows:

...

EXPERT: Hmm, maybe somewhere between 70–90%

YOU: What do you bet? I'm betting 5 EUR that the true parameter is outside the range you just gave.

EXPERT: I dare you! 95 EUR it's inside!

The expert feels 95% certain that the parameter in question is in the interval. However, for many questions of interest, we have no expert at hand (or we may not even trust them altogether). Then we proceed with option 3: making our own observations.

3.1.2 Benchmarking Designs

The most basic decision in practical design research is whether a design fulfills an external criterion. External criteria for human performance in a human-machine system are most common, albeit not abundant, in safety-critical domains.

Consider Jane: she is a user experience researcher at the mega-large rent-a-car company smartr.car. Jane was responsible for an overhaul of the customer interface for mobile users. The goal of the redesign was to streamline the user interface, which had grown wild over the years. Early customer studies indicated that the app needed a serious visual de-cluttering and stronger funneling of tasks. 300 person months went into the re-development and the team did well: a recent A/B study had shown that users learned the smartr.car v2.0 fast and could use its functionality very efficiently. Jane's team is prepared for the roll-out when Marketing comes up with the following request:

> Marketing: We want to support market introduction with the following slogan: "rent a car in 99 s".

> Jane: Not all users manage a full transaction in that short time. That could be a lie.

> Marketing: Legally, the claim is fine if it holds on average.

> Jane: That I can find out for you.

Jane takes another look at the performance of users in the smartr. car v2.0 condition. As she understands it, she has to find out whether the average of all recorded time-on-tasks with smartr.car 2.0 is 99 s or better. Here is how the data looks like (Fig. 3.1):

```
attach(Sec99)

Ver20 %>%
  ggplot(aes(x = ToT)) +
  geom_histogram()
```

The performance is not completely off the 99 s, many users are even faster. Jane figures out that she has to ask a more precise question, first, as the slogan can mean different things, like

- All users can do it within 99 s.
- At least one user can do it.
- Half of the users can do it.

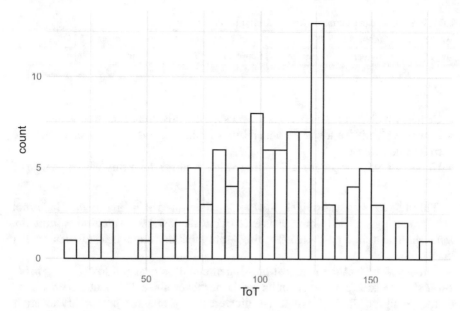

Fig. 3.1 Distribution of ToT

Jane decides to go the middle way and chooses the population average, hence the average ToT must not be more than 99 s. Unfortunately, she had only tested a small minority of users and therefore cannot be certain about the true average:

```
mean(Ver20$ToT)
```

```
## [1] 106
```

Because the sample average is uncertain, Jane is afraid that Marketing could use this as an argument to ignore the data and go with the claim. Jane sees no better way than quantifying the chance of being wrong using a statistical model, which we will learn to know as the *Grand Mean Model* (4.1). The following code estimates the model and shows the estimated coefficient (Table 3.6).

```
M_1 <-
  Ver20 %>%
  stan_glm(ToT ~ 1, data = .)

P_1 <-
  posterior(M_1)

coef(P_1)
```

Let's see what the GMM reports about the population average and its uncertainty. The table above is called a *CLU table* because it reports three estimates per coefficient:

Table 3.6 Coefficient estimates with 95% credibility limits

Model	Parameter	Type	Fixef	Center	Lower	Upper
M_1	Intercept	Fixef	Intercept	106	99.8	112

- Center, which (approximately) is the most likely position of the true value.
- Lower, which is the lower 95% credibility limit. There is a 2.5% chance that the true value is lower.
- Upper, the 95% upper limit. The true value is larger than this with a chance of 2.5%.

This tells Jane that most likely the average time-on-task is *Intercept*. That is not very promising, and it is worse: 99 is even below the lower 95% credibility limit. So, Jane can send a strong message: The probability that this claim is justified is smaller than 2.5%.

Luckily, Jane had the idea that the slogan could be changed to *"rent a card in 1-1-1s"*. The 95% credibility limits are in her favor since 111 is at the upper end of the credibility limit. It would be allowed to say that the probability to err is not much smaller than 2.5%. But Jane desires to make an accurate statement. But what precisely is the chance that the true population average is 111 or lower? In Bayesian analysis, there is a solution to that. When estimating such a model, we get the complete distribution of certainty, called the posterior distribution. In fact, a CLU table with 95% credibility limits is just a summary of the posterior distribution. This distribution is not given as a function, but has been generated by a (finite) random walk algorithm, known as Markov chain Monte Carlo. At every step (or most, to be precise), this algorithm jumps to another set of coordinates in parameter space and a frequency distribution arises that can be used to approximate levels of certainty. Figure 3.2 shows the result of the MCMC estimation as a frequency distribution (based on 4000 iterations in total), divided into the two possible outcomes.

```
P_1 %>%
  filter(parameter == "Intercept") %>%
  mutate(outcome = ifelse(value <= 111,
    ''111 s or shorter'',
    "longer than 111 s"
  )) %>%
  ggplot(aes(
    x = value,
    fill = outcome
  )) +
  geom_histogram(binwidth = 2)
```

In a similar manner to how the graph above was produced, a precise certainty level can be estimated from the MCMC frequency distribution contained in the posterior object. Table 3.7 shows that the 111 s holds with much better certainty.

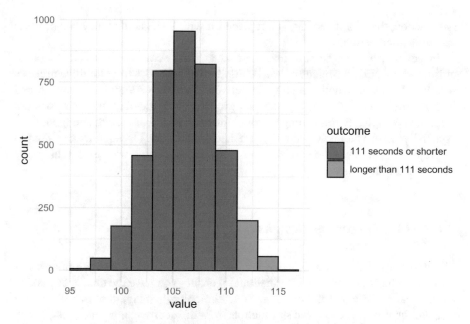

Fig. 3.2 A histogram of MCMC results split by the 111-s criterion

Table 3.7 Level of certainty that the population average is 111 s or better

Certainty
0.935

```
P_1 %>%
  filter(parameter == "Intercept") %>%
  summarise(certainty = mean(value <= 111))
```

The story of Jane is about decision-making under risk and under uncertainty. We have seen how easily precise statements on uncertainty can be derived from a statistical model. But regarding rational decision-making, this is not an ideal story: What is missing is a systematic analysis of losses (and wins). The benefit of going with the slogan has never been quantified. How many new customers it will really attract and how much they will spend cannot really be known upfront. Let alone, predicting the chance to lose in court and what this costs are almost unintelligible. The questions must be allowed, what good is the formula for utility, when it is practically impossible to determine the losses. And if we cannot estimate utilities, what are the certainties good for?

Sometimes, one possible outcome is just so bad that the only thing that practically matters is to avoid it at any costs. Losing a legal battle often falls into this category and the strategy of Marketing/Jane effectively reduced this risk: they dismissed a risky action, the 99 s statement, and replaced it with a slogan that they can prove is true with good certainty.

In general, we can be sure that there is at least some implicit calculation of utilities going on in the minds of Marketing. Perhaps that is a truly intuitive process, which is felt as an emotional struggle between the fear of telling the untruth and love for the slogan. This utility analysis probably is inaccurate, but that does not mean it is completely misleading. A rough guess always beats complete ignorance, especially when you know about the attached uncertainty. Decision makers tend to be prejudiced, but even then probabilities can help find out to what extent this is the case: Just tell the probabilities and see who listens.

3.1.3   Comparison of Designs

The design of systems can be conceived as a choice between design options. For example, when designing an informational website, you have the choice of making the navigation structure flat or deep. Your choice will change the usability of the website, hence your customer satisfaction, rate of recurrence, revenue, etc. Much practical design research aims at making good choices and from a statistical perspective that means to compare the outcomes of two (or more) design options. A typical situation is to compare a redesign with its predecessor, which will now be illustrated by a hypothetical case:

Violet is a manager of an e-commerce website and at present, a major overhaul of the website is under debate. The management team agrees that this overhaul is about time and will most likely increase the revenue per existing customer. Still, there are considerable development costs involved and the question arises whether the update will pay itself in a reasonable time frame. To answer this question, it is not enough to know that revenues increase, but an more accurate prediction of *how much precisely* is gained. In order to return the investment, the increase must be in the ballpark of 10% increase in revenue. For this purpose, Violet carries out a user study to compare the two designs. Essentially, she observes the transactions of 50 random customers using the current system with 50 transactions with a prototype of the new design. The measured variable is the money every user spends during the visit. The research question is: *By how much do revenues increase in the prototype condition?* Figure 3.3 shows the distribution of measured revenue in the experiment.

```
attach(Rational)

RD %>%
  ggplot(aes(x = Euro, fill = Design)) +
  geom_density(alpha = 0.5)
```

There seems to be a slight benefit for the prototype condition. But, is it a 10% increase? The following calculation shows Violet that it could be the case (Table 3.8).

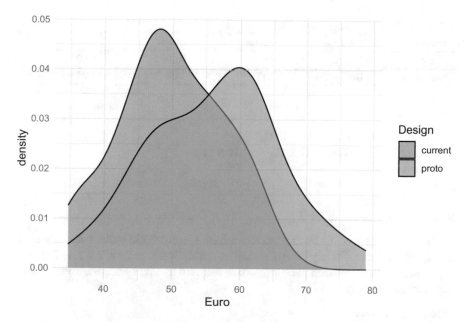

Fig. 3.3 Density plot comparing the revenue of two designs

Table 3.8 Comparing the mean revenue of two designs

Design	Mean_revenue
Current	49.9
Proto	56.3

```
RD %>%
  group_by(Design) %>%
  summarize(mean_revenue = mean(Euro))
```

Like in the previous case, testing only a sample of 100 users out of the whole
population leaves room for uncertainty. So, how certain can Violet be? A statistical
model can give a more complete answer, covering the magnitude of the improvement,
as well as a level of certainty. Violet estimates a model that compares the means
of the two conditions Sect. 4.3.1, assuming that the randomness follows a Gamma
distribution Sect. 7.3.1.

```
library(rstanarm)
library(tidyverse)
library(bayr)

M_1 <-
  RD %>%
```

Table 3.9 Coefficient estimates with 95% credibility limits

Parameter	Fixef	Center	Lower	Upper
Intercept	Intercept	49.90	46.99	53.05
Designproto	Designproto	1.13	1.04	1.23

```
stan_glm(Euro ~ Design,
   family = Gamma(link = "log"),
   data = .
)
```

```
P_1 <- posterior(M_1)
```

The coefficients of the Gamma model are on a logarithmic scale, but when exponentiated, they can directly be interpreted as multiplications Sect. 7.2.1.1. That precisely matches the research question, which is stated as a percentage increase, rather
than a difference (Table 3.9).

```
coef(P_1, mean.func = exp)
```

The results tell Violet that, most likely, the average user spends 49.904 Euro with
the current design. The prototype seems to increase the revenue per transaction by
a factor of 1.127. That would be a sufficient increase; however, this estimate comes
from a small sample of users and there remains a considerable risk that the true
improvement factor is much weaker (or stronger). The above coefficient table tells
that with a certainty of 95%, the true value lies between 1.039 and 1.225. But, what
precisely is the risk of the true value being lower than 1.1? This information can be
extracted from the model (or the posterior distribution):

```
N_risk_of_failure <-
  P_1 %>%
  filter(parameter == "Designproto") %>%
  summarize(risk_of_failure = mean(exp(value) < 1.1))
```

```
paste0("risk of failure is ", c(N_risk_of_failure))
```

```
## [1] "risk of failure is 0.28425"
```

So, the risk of failure is just below 30%. With this information in mind, Violet
now has several options:

1. Deciding that 28.425% is a risk she *dares* to take and recommend going forward
   with the development.
2. *Continue testing* more users to reach a higher level of certainty.
3. Improve the model by taking into account sources of evidence from the past,
   i.e. *prior knowledge*.

Table 3.10 Data set with 3 variables, showing 8 of 20 observations

Obs	Project	Revenue_increase
2	2	1.016
6	6	1.014
8	8	1.003
9	9	1.072
13	13	0.998
14	14	0.979
17	17	1.037
19	19	1.041

3.1.4 Prior Knowledge

It is rarely the case that we encounter a situation as a *blank slate*. Whether we are correct or not, when we look at the sky in the morning, we have some expectations on how likely there will be rain. We also take into account the season and the region and even the very planet is sometimes taken into account: the Pathfinder probe carried a bag of high-tech gadgets to planet Mars. However, the included umbrella was for safe landing only, not to cover from precipitation, as Mars is a dry planet.

In most behavioral research, it still is the standard that every experiment had to be judged on the produced data alone. For the sake of objectivity, researchers were not allowed to take into account previous results, let alone their personal opinion. In Bayesian statistics, you have the choice. You can make use of external knowledge, but you don't have to.

Violet, the rational design researcher, has been designing and testing e-commerce systems for many years and has supervised several large-scale roll-outs. So the current project is not a new situation, at all. From the top of her head, Violet produces the following table to capture her past twenty projects and the increase in revenue that had been recorded afterward (Table 3.10).

```
attach(Rational)

D_prior
```

On this data set, Violet estimates another grand mean model that essentially captures prior knowledge about revenue increases after redesign:

```
M_prior <-
  D_prior %>%
  stan_glm(revenue_increase ~ 1,
    family = Gamma(link = "log"),
    data = .,
    iter = 5000
```

Table 3.11 Coefficient estimates with 95% credibility limits

Model	Parameter	Type	Fixef	Center	Lower	Upper
M_prior	Intercept	Fixef	Intercept	1.02	0.882	1.18

```
)

P_prior <- posterior(M_prior)
```

Note that the above model is a so-called Generalized Linear Model with a Gamma shape of randomness, which will be explained more deeply in Sect. 7.3.

Table 3.11 shows the results. The mean increase was Intercept and without any further information, this is the best guess for revenue increase in any future projects (of Violet). A statistical model that is based on such a small number of observations usually produces very uncertain estimates, which is why the 95% credibility limits are wide. There even remains a considerable risk that a project results in a decrease in revenue, although that has never been recorded. (In Gamma models, coefficients are usually multiplicative, so a coefficient < 1 is a decline).

```
coef(P_prior, mean.func = exp)
```

Or graphically, we can depict the belief as in Fig. 3.4:

```
P_prior %>%
  filter(parameter == "Intercept") %>%
  mutate(value = exp(value)) %>%
  ggplot(aes(x = value)) +
  geom_density() +
  xlab("Strength of prior belief")
```

The population average (of projects) is less favorable than what Violet saw in her present experiment. If the estimated revenue on the experimental data is correct, it would be a rather extreme outcome. And that is a potential problem because extreme outcomes are rare. Possibly, the present results are overly optimistic (which can happen by chance) and do not represent the true change revenue, i.e. on the whole population of users. In Bayesian Statistics, mixing present results with prior knowledge is a standard procedure to correct this problem. In the following step, she uses the (posterior) certainty from M_prior and employs it as prior information (by means of a Gaussian distribution). Model M_2 has the same formula as M_1 before, but combines the information of both sources, data and prior certainty.

```
T_prior <-
  P_prior %>%
  filter(parameter == "Intercept") %>%
  summarize(mean = mean(value), sd = sd(value))
```

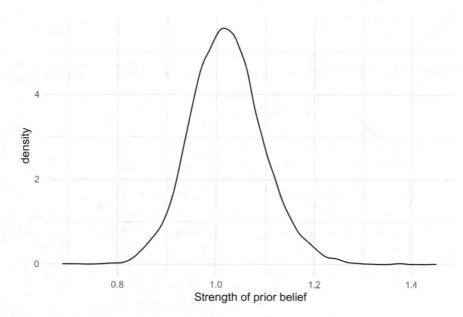

Fig. 3.4 Prior knowledge about a parameter is expressed as a distribution

Table 3.12 Coefficient estimates with 95% credibility limits

Model	Parameter	Center	Lower	Upper
M_1	Designproto	1.13	1.04	1.23
M_2	Designproto	1.10	1.02	1.19

```
M_2 <-
  stan_glm(
    formula = Euro ~ Design,
    prior_intercept = normal(0, 100),
    prior = normal(T_prior[[1, 1]], T_prior[[1, 2]]),
    family = Gamma(link = "log"),
    data = RD
  )

P_2 <- posterior(M_2)
```

Note that the standard deviation here is saying how the strength of belief is distributed for the average revenue. It is not the standard deviation in the population of projects. Table 3.12 and Fig. 3.5 show a comparison of the models with and without prior information.

```
P_comb %>%
  ggplot(aes(x = model, y = value)) +
```

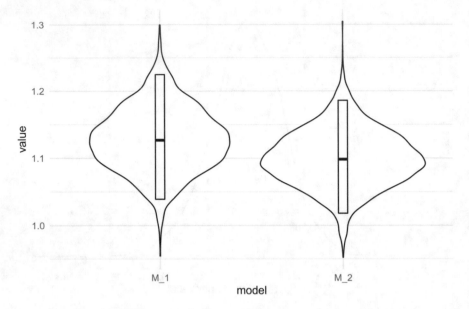

Fig. 3.5 Comparison of expected revenue increase with and without prior information

```
geom_violin() +
geom_crossbar(
   data = coef(P_comb),
   aes(y = center, ymin = lower, ymax = upper),
   width = 0.05
)
```

Model M_2 reduces the estimated expected revenue by a small amount. But, remember that Violet has to meet the criterion of 110% in revenue. In the following, she extracts the risk of failure (revenue smaller than 110%) from the posterior distribution (Table 3.13).

```
P_comb %>%
  mutate(outcome = value < 1.1) %>%
  group_by(model) %>%
  summarize(risk_to_fail = mean(outcome))
```

So what should Violet report to decision makers? Something like this: "The data from the study tells us that our chance of success is around two-thirds. *However*, in my long career, I have never actually reached such an increase in revenue, so I'd rather say the chance of success is more around 50%."

Table 3.13 Estimated risk to fail with prior (M2) and without (M1)

Model	Risk_to_fail
M_1	0.284
M_2	0.512

3.2 Observations and Measures

The statistical models presented in this book have in common that there is exactly one measure, which we call the *outcome*. In design research, outcome variables directly represent the current value of a design or an aspect of it. This section provides an overview of the types of outcome variables.

3.2.1 Interaction Sequences

A general concept in design is to think of purposes as *user tasks*. A user task can be defined as an initial state, a desired outcome and a procedure to get there. The knowledge required to follow the procedure can be found in two major locations: the users' mind (mental model) and the interface (design model). A principle of user-centered design is to create a design model that matches the users' current representation of the task or easily enters the users' mind, at least. The first is called *intuitiveness* of a design; the latter *ease-of-learning*.

A highly intuitive design matches the users' mental model and can be used out-of-the-box, without the requirement to instruct or train a user. Intuitiveness relies on the match between design and mental model. Whereas the design model is explicit, the mental model needs to be elicited from the users' mind. Eliciting procedural mental models is difficult. You may think it is sufficient to just ask users about the idea of a procedure, but that is a limited approach. If I ask you about the precise steps in preparing a cup of coffee in your kitchen, that probably is more demanding and error-prone than to ask you to prepare an actual cup of coffee. Two reasons make up for this discrepancy:

1. The human mind has separate facilities for procedural knowledge and declarative knowledge. If I ask you about a procedure, you first have to make a translation.
2. The more automated a task is, the less available it is to your conscious mind.

Our ability to verbalize our actions is limited. If there were no such verbalization limit, designing for tasks would be simple: just ask! Only mind-reading is more convenient. In user-centered design, verbal inquiries are a central method. But, results from user interviews can be incomplete or biased.

An example of incompleteness is that users sometimes fail to report what they think is obvious. For example, in modern computer desktop applications, a function to undo a step is standard and probably it is one of the most frequently used functions. In other types of systems, for example database-driven information systems, implementing an Undo function is non-trivial, because database records can be changed by multiple users. It can be implemented by so-called roll-back mechanisms, but these reduce the performance and storage capacity of the system. When collecting user requirements for such a system, the developer has little interest in Undo, whereas the user has huge interest, but does not mention it. If that is not resolved during the design process, there will be trouble.

Verbal reports of action sequences are often incomplete. But, if there is something even worse, then it is the limited ability of humans to imagine new situations or novel ways of doing something. Imagine you had a time machine and you would travel back to the year 1981, which is a year before the series Knight Rider went on the broadcast. If you would ask car drivers from that era how they would envision a navigation assistant device, you would probably end up with something that looks more like a Star Trek computer console than with anything comparable to the modern navigation device.

One central principle of user-centered design is the *direct observation* of users.By directly observing how a person prepares a cup of coffee, we can learn about the details of behavior and close the verbalization gap. By observing many action sequences, we can carve out detailed user requirements or fix an existing design. Observing user interactions does not require one-way mirrors and nights of video coding. Because of the verbalization gap, a lot can be learned just by watching over the users' shoulder. The method of *think-aloud usability testing* even goes one step further and combines behavior observation with verbalization.

Interaction sequences can sometimes be collected without a human observer. Log files of web servers provide sequences of users navigating the website. Plugin software is available that records keystrokes and mouse actions on computers. The difficult part is the following: When observing 50 users while doing a non-trivial task, no two interaction sequences are exactly the same (if I had to bet on it). By itself, there is little value without further means of interpretation and this can go two ways up: qualitative and quantitative.

The *qualitative design researcher* will collect interaction sequences, as well as verbal reports, and shuffle them around until an intelligible picture emerges. One way to describe the purpose of user testing is to *find out all possible ways how things can go wrong*. Every break-down that is observed at least once in a sample of test users tells a story of what may happen to hundreds or thousands of users in the future. That is why in the early development phases, qualitative research rules.

The *quantitative* researcher will aim at deriving measures from the interaction sequence. Formally, *to measure* means assigning numbers to observed sequences, so that these can be brought into an *order*, at least. If the original data is qualitative, we need some method of transformation that gives us measures.

Sometimes, you have to go a long way up the qualitative route, before you can derive useful measures. In [1], we coded sequences from nurses using an infusion pump. Individual sequences were compared to an optimal reference path. The closer a user stays on this path, the better. But how to measure similarity? We used the

Levensthein distance, which takes two sequences, the optimal path and the observed path, and determines the minimum number of edits to transform one sequence into the other. This results in a score for error proneness, the *deviation from optimal path*.

Another example is a study we did on the active user paradox. We recorded interaction sequences of users doing editing tasks with graphics software. The sessions were recorded and analyzed using a behavioral coding scheme. First, events were classified on a low level (e.g. "reading the handbook", "first time trying a function") and later aggregated to broader classes (e.g. "exploratory behavior"). The number of exploratory events then served as a measure for the exploratory tendencies of the participant.

3.2.2 Performance Measures

User errors are qualitative by nature and need a transformation to be used as outcome variables. Other aspects of performance can be measured directly. A useful framework for outcome measures is the classic concept of *usability*, which the ISO 9142-11 defines by the following three high-level criteria:

- Effectiveness: can users accomplish their tasks?
- Efficiency: what resources have to be spent for a task, e.g. time.
- Satisfaction: how did the user like it?

While these criteria originated in the field of Human-Computer Interaction, they can easily be adapted to compare everything that people do their work with. Even within the field, it has been adapted to hundreds of studies and a hundred ways are reported of assessing these criteria.

Effectiveness is often measured by *completion rate (CR)*. A classic waterfall approach would be to consult the user requirements documents and identify the, let's say eight, crucial tasks the system must support. User tests might then show that most users fail at the two tasks, and a completion rate of 75% is recorded for the system. Completion rate is only a valid effectiveness measure with *distinct tasks*. Strictly, the set of tasks also had to be *complete*, covering the whole system. When completion rate is taken from a series of *repetitive tasks*, it depends on whether it is effective or efficient. It is effective when a failed operation is unrepairable, such as a traffic accident, data loss on a computer or medical errors. But, who cares for a single number between 0 and 1, when the user test provides such a wealth of information on *why* users failed? Effectiveness, in the sense of task completion, is primarily a qualitative issue and we shall rarely encounter it in this book.

A more subtle notion of effectiveness is the *quality of outcome*, and despite the very term, it is a measure. (Perhaps, it should better be called *level of perfection*.) Reconsider the AUP study, where participants had to modify a given graphic, e.g. change some colors and erase parts of it. Of course, some participants worked neatly, whereas others used broader strokes (literally). There are several ways to rank all results by quality and thereby create an outcome variable.

Efficiency is where it really gets quantitative as we ask about resources: time, attention, strain, distraction and Euros. Efficiency can be measured in a variety of ways: time-on-task (ToT), clicks, mental workload or time spent watching the traffic while driving.

Counting the *number of clicks* before someone has found the desired piece of information is a coarse, but easy to acquire and intuitive measure of efficiency, and so is *time-on-task (ToT)*.

ToT and other performance measures can be very noisy. The general recipe to reduce noise and improve certainty is to collect more data. The obvious way of doing this is by increasing the sample size, but that can be costly. A more efficient way to reduce uncertainty with a given sample is to collect more data per participant, which is called *repeated measures*. Chapter 6 will introduce models that deal with repeated measures in a straightforward way.

Counting steps-to-completion or errors often requires the laborious process of interaction analysis. Measures of duration are much easier to obtain and in many situations, they are spot-on: In usability studies, *time-on-task* is a direct measure of efficiency. When controlling a car in dense city traffic, a few hundred milliseconds is what makes huge difference and therefore *reaction time* is a valid performance measure. In experimental cognitive research, reaction times have been successfully used in countless experiments to reveal the structure of the mind.

3.2.3   Satisfaction and Other Feelings

The standard definition of usability defines three levels of usability, two performance-related effectiveness and efficiency, and satisfaction. The latter has long been held the enfant terrible of the three. That's not a big surprise, as satisfaction is about the *feelings* of users.

Early research in the 1990s took enough with a few rating scales, that measure satisfaction, as the *absence of negative feelings*. Later, when the user experience era took off, a wave of constructs and measures washed over the research community; here are just a few examples:

- Beauty.
- Hedonic quality.
- Coolness.
- Credibility.
- Meaning of life.

Feelings are a tricky business when it comes to measuring them. Most frequently, rating scales are employed, and often the same author makes the remark that the study should be replicated with more objective measures for emotional states, such as physiological measures or implicit measures. However, I haven't seen many studies where such measures produced good results.

Despite all criticism, *self-report rating scales* are still the primary method of measuring feelings toward designs. Rating scale instruments exist for a variety of concepts, but they come in only a few forms: first, there exist single-item or multi-item scales. *Single-item* instruments are the hydrogen of rating scales. Because they are so short, they cause little interruption and are therefore useful for obtaining repeated measures over time. That is very valuable when the goal is to track feelings for an extended period of time. For example, the effect of learning can be seen in a decline of cognitive workload over time. From a methodological point-of-view, single-item scales are inferior, because many quality checks rest on having multiple items (see Sect. 6.8).

Multi-item rating scales are the standard. Participants or users respond to a number of statements that have an overarching theme. In contrast to single items, multi-item scales are amenable to a number of procedures for quality check, such as reliability. Whereas a psychometric assessment requires the data on item level, for the purpose of design evaluation, multi-item ratings are often aggregated as total scores, such as the *average score*. However, aggregation always causes a loss in information, and with the multi-level models presented in Sect. 6.8, this is also no longer required.

Next to the number of items, rating scale instruments differ in *cardinality of the response*, which is the number of possible responses to an item. By far, most rating scales use between four and nine *ordered bins*. In contrast, so-called *visual analog* rating scales measure on a continuum. This can be done on paper using a ruler to translate the response into numbers or using a slider bar in a computer program.

Finally, rating scales have either *unipolar or bipolar anchoring*. Many rating scales put labels (instead of just numbers) on the minimum and the maximum bins. With a unipolar item, the left anchor is neutral, whereas the right is not, like in

0: Dull … 1: Bliss

Dull is not the opposite of bliss, it is the absence of it. (Just like Zero is not the opposite of One.) one example of a bipolar scales is

−1: Ugly … + 1: Beautiful

Another consideration is with binned (rather than continuous) bipolar scales. If such a scale has an uneven number, the center bin is neutral.

−1:Ugly … 0:Neutral … +1:Beautifuly

Sometimes, it is useful that participants have the opportunity for a neutral answer, for example, when the participant may just not know:

The help pages of the program are written in a clear language.

−1: Not at all … 0: I didn't notice +1: … Totally

Especially with long questionnaires, it can happen that participants are getting bored and just always respond neutral. In such a case, an even number of bins, i.e. the absence of a neutral response, force participants to make a choice of direction, at least.

What kind of rating scale you use has consequences for your statistical model. As we will see in Sect. 6.8, multi-level models are a good match for multi-item rating scales. What also matters for the choice of model is whether you have been using a visual analog scale or a binned scale. Data from visual analog scales is more easily treated, by either a Gaussian Sect. 6.8 or a Beta linearized model Sect. 7.4.2. Both are relatively lean methods and easy to report. For binned rating scales, the complicated beast called ordinal logistic regression Sect. 7.4.1 applies. My advice would be to use visual analog scales, whenever possible, even if this means to not exactly following the original instructions for the scale.

While rating scales are prevalent for measuring feelings, that does not mean there are no other, more objective, ways. There has been some buzz about *physiological measures*, like galvanic skin response or EEG, lately. In our own lab, I have seen these measures fail more often than succeed for the evaluation of products (such as wine or floor cleaning robots).

Implicit measures are means to assess certain attitudes or feelings by means of experimental setups. For example, we once tried to measure technophile attitude (geekism) using a variant of the classic Stroop task. In [2], we showed pictures of computers to a sample of students, followed by the Stroop task, which means that participants had to name the ink color of a color-printed word (e.g. "explore" in color Red). It was conceived that reaction time increases when a participant experiences a strong association, like how good it felt to build a computer all by yourself. The initial success was soon washed away by a failure to reproduce these results. Another implicit method sometimes proposed is the Approach-Avoidance task, which has gotten some merits in research on addiction and racism. In simple terms, participants (or users) are asked to push or pull a joystick and it seems that they pull faster when they see something they like (a bottle of booze) and push faster when they dislike what they see (a photograph of war victims). However, I have seen this approach failing to produce relevant results in a design comparison experiment. Generally, such experiments produce reaction time differences below the 100 ms mark and therefore many trials are needed to carve out any differences. At the same time, I have doubts that the emotional reactions toward, say, computer interfaces play in the same league as the stimuli used in research on addiction or racism research. Emotional responses in design research may just be too mellow to disturb cognitive processes with a strength that is measurable.

3.3   Descriptive Statistics

In empirical research, we systematically gather observations. Observations of the same kind are usually subsumed as variables. A set of variables that have been gathered on the same sample are called a data set, which typically is a table with variables in columns. In the most general meaning, *a statistic* is a single number that somehow represents relevant features of a data set, such as

- Frequency: how many measures of a certain kind can be found in the data set?
- Mean: do measures tend to be located left (weak) or right (strong) on a scale?
- Variance: are measures close together or widely distributed along the scale?
- Association: does one variable X tend to change when another variable Y changes?

3.3.1 Frequencies

```
attach(Sec99)
```

The most basic statistics of all probably is the number of observations on a variable x, usually denoted by n_x. The number of observations is a rough indicator of the amount of data that has been gathered. In turn, more data usually results in better accuracy of statistics and higher levels of certainty can be reached.

```
nrow(Ver20$ToT)
```

```
## NULL
```

The number of observations is not as trivial as it may appear at first. In particular, it is usually not the same as the sample size, for two reasons: First, most studies employ repeated measures to some extent. You may have invited $N_{Part} = 20$ participants to your lab, but each participant is tested on, let's say, $N_{Task} = 5$ tasks, the number of observations is $N_{Obs} = N_{Part} N_{Task} = 100$. Second, taking a valid measure can always fail for a variety of reasons, resulting in *missing values (NA)*. For example, in the 99 s study, it has happened that a few participants missed to fill in their age on the intake form. The researcher is left with fewer measures of age n_{age} than there were participants.

```
N_obs <- function(x) sum(!is.na(x))
N_obs(Ver20$age)
```

```
## [1] 100
```

Another important issue is the distribution of observations across groups (Table 3.14). Again, the number of observations in a group is linked to the certainty we can gain on the statistics of that group. Furthermore, it is sometimes important to have the distribution match the proportions in the population, as otherwise biases may occur.

```
Ver20 %>%
  group_by(Gender) %>%
  summarize(n())
```

The table above shows the so-called *absolute frequencies*. Often, we have to compare frequencies of two groups of different size, and it often is more appropriate to report *relative frequencies* or *proportions* (Table 3.15):

```
n_Gender <- N_obs(Ver20$Gender)

Ver20 %>%
```

Table 3.14 Absolute frequencies of gender

Gender	n()
Female	59
Male	41

Table 3.15 Relative frequencies of gender

Gender	Rel_freq
Female	0.59
Male	0.41

```
group_by(Gender) %>%
summarize(rel_freq = n() / n_Gender)
```

Summarizing frequencies of metric measures, such as time-on-task (ToT) or the number of errors, is useful too. However, a complication arises from the fact that continuous measures do not naturally fall into groups. Especially in duration measures, no two measures are exactly the same.

```
length(unique(Ver20$Gender))
```

```
## [1] 2
```

```
length(unique(Ver20$ToT))
```

```
## [1] 100
```

The answer to this problem is *binning*: the scale of measurement is divided into a number of adjacent sections, called bins, and all measures that fall into one bin are counted. For example, we could use bins of 10 s and assess whether the bin with values larger than 90 and smaller or equal to 100 is representative in that it contains a large proportion of values. If we put such a binned summary of frequencies into a graph, that is called a *histogram* (Fig. 3.6).

```
bin <- function(x, bin_width = 10) floor(x / bin_width)
* bin_width
n_ToT <- N_obs(Ver20$ToT)

Ver20 %>%
  mutate(bin = bin(ToT)) %>%
  group_by(bin) %>%
  summarize(rel_freq = n() / n_ToT) %>%
  ggplot(aes(x = bin, y = rel_freq)) +
  geom_col()
```

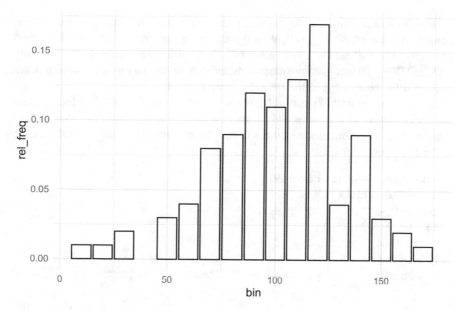

Fig. 3.6 Histogram showing relative frequencies

Strictly spoken, grouped and binned frequencies are not one statistic, but a vector of statistics. It approximates what we will later get to know more closely as a *distribution* Sect. 3.5.2.

3.3.2 Central Tendency

Reconsider the rational design researcher Jane Sect. 3.1.2. When asked about whether users can complete a transaction within 99, she looked at the population average of her measures. The population average is what we call the *(arithmetic) mean*. The mean is computed by summing over all measures and dividing by the number of observations. The mean is probably the most often used measure of central tendency, but two more are being used and have their own advantages: *median* and *mode* (Table 3.16).

```
my_mean <- function(x) sum(x) / N_obs(x) ## not length()
my_mean(Ver20$ToT)
```

```
## [1] 106
```

Note that I am using function N_obs() from Sect. 3.3.1, not length(), to not accidentally count missing values (NA).

Imagine a competitor of the car rental company goes to court to fight the 99-s claim. Not an expert in juridical matters, my suggestion is that one of the first questions to be regarded in court probably is: what does "rent a car in 99 s" actually promise? One way would be the mean ("on average users can rent a car in 99 s"), but here are some other ways to interpret the same slogan:

"50% (or more) of users can …". This is called the *median*. The median is computed by ordering all measures and identifying the element right in the center. If the number of observations is even, there is no one center value, and the mean of the center pair is used, instead.

```
my_median <- function(x) {
  n <- length(x)
  center <- (n + 1) %/% 2
  if (n %% 2 == 1) {
    sort(x, partial = center)[center]
  } else {
    mean(sort(x, partial = center + 0:1)[center + 0:1])
  }
}
```

```
my_median(Ver20$ToT)
```

Actually, the median is a special case of so-called *quantiles*. Generally, quantiles are based on the order of measures and an X% quantile is that value where X% of measures are equal to or smaller. The court could decide that 50% of users is too lenient as a criterion and could demand that 75% of users must complete the task within 99 s for the slogan to be considered valid.

```
quantile(Ver20$ToT, c(.50, 0.75))
```

```
## 50% 75%
## 108 125
```

A common pattern to be found in distributions of measures is that a majority of observations are clumped in the center region. The point of the highest density of a distribution is called the *mode*. In other words, the mode is the region (or point) that is most likely to occur. For continuous measures, this once again poses the problem that every value is unique. Sophisticated procedures exist to smooth over this inconvenience, but by the simple method of binning, we can construct an approximation of the mode: just choose the center of the bin with the highest frequency. This is just a crude approximation. Advanced algorithms for estimating modes can be found in the R package *modeest*.

```
mode <- function(x, bin_width = 10) {
  bins <- bin(x, bin_width)
```

Table 3.16 Summary of central tendency statistics

Mean_ToT	Median_ToT	Mode_ToT
106	108	145

```
  bins[which.max(tabulate(match(x, bins)))]
+ bin_width / 2
}

mode(Ver20$ToT)
```

```
  ## [1] 145
```

```
Ver20 %>%
  group_by() %>%
  summarize(
    mean_ToT = mean(ToT),
    median_ToT = median(ToT),
    mode_ToT = mode(ToT)
  )
```

The table above shows the three statistics for central tendency side-by-side. Mean and median are close together. This is frequently the case, but not always. Only if a distribution of measures is completely symmetric, mean and median perfectly coincide. In Sect. 3.5.2, we will encounter distributions that are not symmetric. The more a distribution is skewed, the stronger the difference between mean and median increases (Fig. 3.7).

To be more precise, for left-skewed distributions, the mean is strongly influenced by few, but extreme, values in the left tail of the distribution. The median only counts the number of observations to both sides and is not influenced by how extreme these values are. Therefore, it is located more to the right. The mode does not regard any values other than those in the densest region and just marks that peak. The same principles hold in reversed order for right-skewed distributions.

To summarize, the mean is the most frequently used measure of central tendency, one reason being that it is a so-called *sufficient statistic*, meaning that it exploits the full information present in the data. The median is frequently used when extreme measures are a concern. The mode is the point in the distribution that is most typical.

3.3.3 Dispersion

In a symmetric distribution with exactly one peak, mean and mode coincide and the mean represents the most typical value. But, a value being *more* typical does *not*

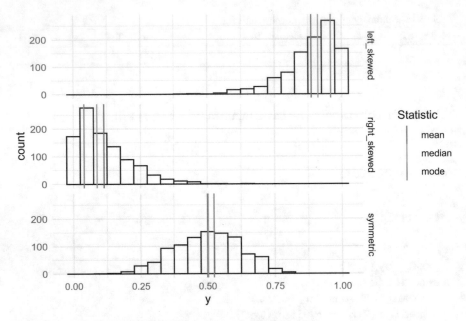

Fig. 3.7 Left-skewed, right-skewed and symmetric distributions

mean it is *very* typical. That depends on how the measures are dispersed over the whole range. In the figure below, the center value of the narrow distribution contains 60% of all measures, as compared to 40% in the wide distribution, and is therefore more representative (Fig. 3.8).

```
D_disp <-
  tribble(
    ~y, ~narrow, ~wide,
    1, 0, 1,
    2, 2, 2,
    3, 6, 4,
    4, 2, 2,
    5, 0, 1
  ) %>%
  gather(Distribution, frequency, -y)


D_disp %>%
  ggplot(aes(
    x = y,
    y = frequency
  )) +
```

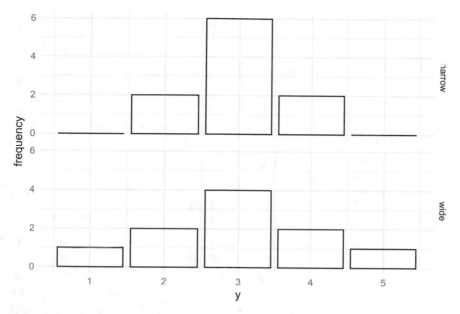

Fig. 3.8 Narrow and wide distributions

```
facet_grid(Distribution ~ .) +
geom_col()
```

A very basic way to describe the dispersion of a distribution is to report the *range* between the two extreme values, *minimum* and *maximum*. These are easily computed by sorting all values and selecting the first and the last element. Coincidentally, they are also special cases of quantiles, namely the 0% and 100% quantiles.

A *boxplot* is a commonly used geometry to examine the shape of dispersion. Similar to histograms, boxplots use a binning mechanism and are useful for continuous measures. Whereas histograms use equidistant bins on the scale of measurement, boxplots create four bins based on 25% quantile steps (Fig. 3.9). These are also called *quartiles*.

```
Ver20 %>%
  ggplot(aes(y = ToT)) +
  geom_boxplot()
```

The min/max statistics only uses just these two values and therefore does not fully represent the amount of dispersion. A statistic for dispersion that exploits the full data is the *variance*, which is the mean of squared deviations from the mean. Squaring the deviations makes variance difficult to interpret, as it no longer is on the same scale as the measures. The *standard deviation* solves this problem by taking the square root of variance. By reversing the square, the standard deviation is on the same scale as the original measures and can easily be compared to the mean (Table 3.17).

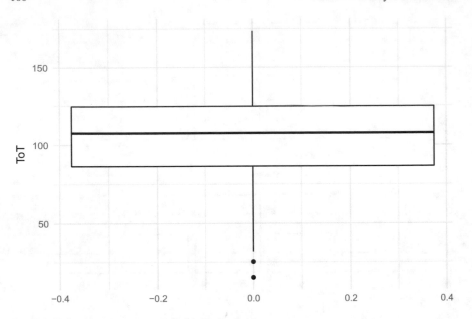

Fig. 3.9 A boxplot shows quartiles of a distribution

Table 3.17 Summary table with five dispersion statistics

Min (ToT)	Max (ToT)	Range (ToT)	Var (ToT)	sd (ToT)
15.2	174	158	966	31.1

```
min <- function(x) sort(x)[1]
max <- function(x) quantile(x, 1)
range <- function(x) max(x) - min(x)
var <- function(x) mean((mean(x) - x)^2)
sd <- function(x) sqrt(var(x))

Ver20 %>%
  summarize(
    min(ToT),
    max(ToT),
    range(ToT),
    var(ToT),
    sd(ToT)
  )
```

Table 3.18 Possible associations between any two variables

Between	Categorical	Metric
Categorical	Frequency cross tables	Differences in mean
Metric		Correlations

3.3.4 Associations

- Are elderly users slower at navigating websites?
- How does reading speed depend on font size?
- Is the result of an intelligence test independent from gender?

In the previous section, we have seen how all individual variables can be described by location and dispersion. A majority of research deals with associations between measures and the present section introduces some statistics to describe them. Variables represent properties of the objects of research and fall into two categories: *Metric variables* represent a measured property, such as speed, height, money or perceived satisfaction. *Categorical variables* put observations (or objects of research) into non-overlapping groups, such as experimental conditions, persons who can program or cannot and type of education. Consequently, associations between any two variables fall into precisely one of three cases, as shown in Table 3.18.

```
tribble(
  ~between, ~categorical, ~metric,
  "categorical", "frequency cross tables", "differences in mean",
  "metric", "", "correlations"
)
```

3.3.4.1 Categorical Associations

Categorical variables group observations, and when they are *both categorical*, the result is just another categorical case and the only way to compare them is using relative frequencies. To illustrate the categorical-categorical case, consider a study to assess the safety of two syringe infusion pump designs, called Legacy and Novel. All participants of the study are asked to perform a typical sequence of operation on both devices (categorical variable Design) and it is recorded whether the sequence was completed correctly or not (categorical variable Correctness, Table 3.19).

```
attach(IPump)

D_agg %>%
  filter(Session == 3) %>%
  group_by(Design, completion) %>%
  summarize(frequency = n()) %>%
```

Table 3.19 Summary of task completion

Design	FALSE	TRUE
Legacy	21	4
Novel	22	3

Table 3.20 A cross table with relative frequencies

Design	FALSE	TRUE
Legacy	0.84	0.16
Novel	0.88	0.12

```
ungroup() %>%
spread(completion, frequency)
```

Besides the troubling result that incorrect completion is the rule, not the exception, there is almost no difference between the two designs. Note that in this study, both professional groups were even in number. If that is not the case, absolute frequencies are difficult to compare and we better report *relative frequencies*. Note how every row sums up to 1 in Table 3.20:

```
D_agg %>%
  filter(Session == 3) %>%
  group_by(Design, completion) %>%
  summarize(frequency = n()) %>%
  group_by(Design) %>%
  mutate(frequency = frequency / sum(frequency)) %>%
  ungroup() %>%
  spread(completion, frequency)
```

In addition, absolute or relative frequencies can be shown in a stacked *bar plot* (Fig. 3.10).

```
D_agg %>%
  ggplot(aes(x = Design, fill = completion)) +
  geom_bar()
```

3.3.4.2 Categorical-Metric Associations

Associations between *categorical and metric* variables are reported by *grouped location statistics*. In the case of the two infusion pump designs, the time spent to complete the sequence is compared in comparison-of-means Table 3.21.

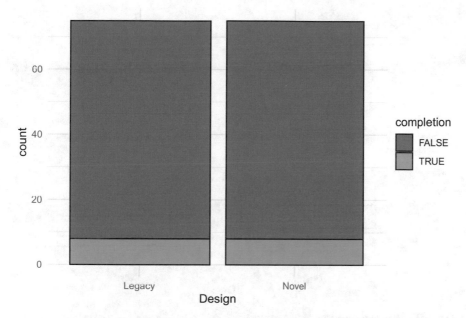

Fig. 3.10 A stacked bar plot with absolute frequencies

Table 3.21 Comparison of group means

Design	Mean_ToT	sd_ToT
Legacy	151.0	62.2
Novel	87.7	33.8

```
D_agg %>%
  filter(Session == 3) %>%
  group_by(Design) %>%
  summarize(
    mean_ToT = mean(ToT),
    sd_ToT = sd(ToT)
  )
```

For the illustration of categorical-metric associations case, *boxplots* have proven useful. Boxplots show differences in central tendency (median) and dispersion (other quartiles) simultaneously. In Fig. 3.11, we observe that Novel produces shorter ToT and also seems to be less dispersed.

```
D_agg %>%
  ggplot(aes(x = Design, y = ToT)) +
  geom_boxplot()
```

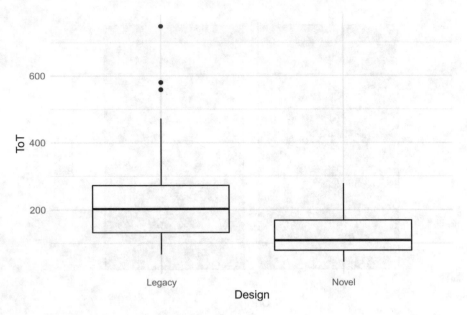

Fig. 3.11 Boxplot comparison of two groups

3.3.4.3   Covariance and Correlation

For associations between a pair of metric variables, *covariance* and *correlations* are commonly employed statistics.

A covariance is a real number that is *zero* when there really is *no association* between two variables. When two variables move into the *same direction*, covariance is *positive*. When they move in *opposite directions*, covariance is *negative*.

For an illustration, consider the following hypothetical example of a study on the relationship between mental ability and performance in a minimally invasive surgery (MIS) task. MIS tasks are known to involve a lot of visual-spatial cognition, which means that performance on other visual-spatial tasks should be associated.

The following code simulates such a set of measures from a multivariate-normal distribution. The associations are defined as a matrix of correlations and are then up-scaled by the standard error to result in covariances. Later, we will do the reverse to obtain correlations from covariances (Table 3.22).

```
cor2cov <- function(cor, sd) diag(sd) %*% cor %*% t(diag(sd))

cor_mat <- matrix(c(
  1, 0.95, -.5, 0.2,
 0.95, 1, -.5, 0.2,
  -.5, -.5, 1, 0.15,
 0.2, 0.2, 0.15, 1
), ncol = 4)
sd_vec <- c(.2, 0.2, 40, 2)
```

Table 3.22 Data set with 5 variables, showing 8 of 300 observations

Obs	MRS_1	MRS_2	ToT	Corsi
17	1.97	1.93	165	5.75
25	2.10	2.08	144	6.93
44	2.20	2.13	125	3.31
58	1.70	1.68	204	4.10
68	2.22	2.25	161	5.54
77	2.20	2.23	108	4.62
225	1.91	1.75	146	3.48
272	2.04	2.07	132	8.50

```
mean_vec <- c(2, 2, 180, 6)

D_tests <-
  mvtnorm::rmvnorm(300,
    mean = mean_vec,
    sigma = cor2cov(cor_mat, sd_vec)
  ) %>%
  as_tibble() %>%
  rename(MRS_1 = V1, MRS_2 = V2, ToT = V3, Corsi = V4) %>%
  as_tbl_obs()

D_tests
```

The following function computes the covariance of two variables. The covariance between the two MRS scores is positive, indicating that they move in the same direction.

```
my_cov <- function(x, y) {
  mean((x - mean(x)) * (y - mean(y)))
}

my_cov(D_tests$MRS_1, D_tests$MRS_2)
```

```
## [1] 0.0407
```

The problem with covariances is that, like variances, they are on a square scale (a product of two numbers), which makes them difficult to interpret. This is why later we will transform covariances into correlations, but for understanding the steps to go there, we have to understand the link between variance and covariance. The formula for covariance is (with $E(X)$ the mean of X)

$$\mathrm{cov}_{XY} = \frac{1}{n} \sum_{i=1}^{n} (x_i - E(X))(y_i - E(Y))$$

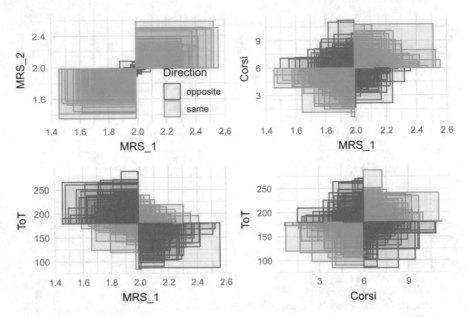

Fig. 3.12 Illustration of covariance. Every rectangle represents a product of two measures. Same-direction rectangles have a positive area; opposite-direction rectangles have a negative area. The sum of all rectangles is the covariance

Covariance essentially arises by the multiplication of differences to the mean, $(x_i - E(X))(y_i - E(Y))$. When for one observation both factors go in the same direction, be it positive or negative, this term gets positive. If the association is strong, this will happen a lot, and the whole sum gets largely positive. When the deviations systematically move in the opposite direction, such that one factor is always positive and the other negative, we get a large negative covariance. When the picture is mixed, i.e. no clear tendency, covariance will stay close to zero.

Figure 3.12 is an attempt at a geometric illustration of the multiplication as the area of rectangles. Rectangles with equal directions (blue) are in the upper-right and lower-left quadrant. They overwhelm the opposite-direction rectangles (red), which speaks for a strong positive association. The associations between MRT_1 and Corsi, as well as between Corsi and ToT, seem to have a slight overhead in the same direction, so the covariance is positive, but less strong. A clear negative association exists between MRS_1 and Corsi. It seems these two tests have some common ground.

If we compare the formulas of covariance and variance, it is apparent that variance is just covariance of a variable with itself $((x_i - E(X))^2 = (x_i - E(X))(x_i - E(X))$.

That gives rise to a compact form to show all covariances and variances between a bunch of variables at once. Table 3.23 is a *variance-covariance matrix* produced

Table 3.23 Variance-covariance matrix

	Obs	MRS_1	MRS_2	ToT	Corsi
Obs	7525.00	1.106	1.159	−33.50	11.971
MRS_1	1.11	0.043	0.041	−4.25	0.106
MRS_2	1.16	0.041	0.043	−4.13	0.104
ToT	−33.50	−4.246	−4.127	1515.49	7.615
Corsi	11.97	0.106	0.104	7.62	4.185

by the command `cov`. It shows the variance of every variable in the diagonal and the mutual covariances in the off-diagonal cells.

```
cov(D_tests)
```

As intuitive the idea of covariance is, as unintelligible is the statistic itself for reporting results. The problem is that covariance is not a pure measure of association, but is contaminated by the dispersion of X and Y. For that reason, two covariances can only be compared if the variables have the same variance. As this is usually not the case, it is impossible to compare covariances. The *Pearson correlation coefficient* r solves the problem by rescaling covariances by the product of the two standard deviations:

$$r_XY = \frac{cov_{XY}}{sd_X sd_Y}$$

```
my_cor <- function(x, y) {
  cov(x, y) / (sd(x, na.rm = T) * sd(y, na.rm = T))
}


my_cor(D_tests$MRS_1, D_tests$MRS_2)
```

```
## [1] 0.952
```

Due to the standardization of dispersion, r will always be in the interval $[-1, 1]$ and can be used to evaluate or compare the strength of association, independent of the scale of measurement.

That makes it the perfect choice when associations are being compared to each other or to an external standard. In the field of psychometrics, correlations are ubiquitously employed to represent *reliability* and *validity* of psychological tests (6.8). *Test-retest stability* is one form to measure reliability and it is just the correlation of the same test taken on different days. For example, we could ask whether mental rotation speed as measured by the mental rotation task (MRT) is stable over time, such that we can use it for long-term predictions, such as how likely someone will become a good surgeon. Validity of a test means that it represents what it was intended for,

Table 3.24 A table of correlations

	Obs	MRS_1	MRS_2	ToT	Corsi
Obs	1.000	0.062	0.065	−0.010	0.067
MRS_1	0.062	1.000	0.952	−0.526	0.250
MRS_2	0.065	0.952	1.000	−0.513	0.245
ToT	−0.010	−0.526	−0.513	1.000	0.096
Corsi	0.067	0.250	0.245	0.096	1.000

and that requires an external criterion that is known to be valid. For example, we could ask how well the ability of a person to become a minimally invasive surgeon depends on spatial cognitive abilities, like mental rotation speed. Validity could be assessed by taking performance scores from exercises in a surgery simulator and do the correlation with mental rotation speed. A correlation of $r = 0.5$ would indicate that mental rotation speed as measured by the task has rather limited validity. Another form is called *discriminant validity* and is about how specific a measure is. Imagine another test as part of the surgery assessment suite. This test aims to measure another aspect of spatial cognition, namely the capacity of the visual-spatial working memory (e.g. the Corsi block tapping task). If both tests are as specific as they claim to be, we would expect a particularly low correlation.

And similar to covariances, correlations between a set of variables can be put into a correlation table, such as Table 3.24. This time, the diagonal is the correlation of a variable with itself, which is a perfect correlation and therefore equals 1.

```
cor(D_tests)
```

Another way to illustrate a bunch of correlations is shown in Fig. 3.13. It was produced by the `ggpairs` command from the *GGally* package. For entirely continuous measures, it shows:

- The association between a pair of variables as a scatterplot and a correlation coefficient.
- The observed distribution of every measure as a density plot.

(In earlier versions of the command, correlations were given without p-values. In my opinion, forcing p-values on the user was not a good choice.)

```
D_tests %>%
  GGally::ggpairs(upper = )
```

Correlations give psychometricians a comparable standard for the quality of measures, irrespective of what scale they are on. In an exploratory analysis, one often seeks to get a broad overview of how a bunch of variables is associated. Creating a correlation table of all variables is no hassle and allows us to get a broad picture of the situation.

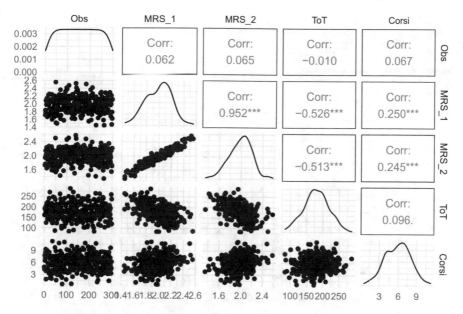

Fig. 3.13 A pairs plot showing raw data (left triangle), correlations (right) and individual distribution (diagonal)

While correlations are ubiquitous in data analysis, they do have limitations: First, a correlation only uncovers linear trends, whereas the association between two variables can take any conceivable form. The validity of correlations depends on how salient the feature of linear trend is. Figure 3.14 shows a few types of associations where correlations are not adequate. In the example, Y_2 is associated with X in a parabolic form, which results in zero correlation. Also, the curvature of an exponentially rising association (Y_1) is captured insufficiently. For that reason, I recommend that correlations are always cross-checked by a scatterplot. Another situation where covariances and correlations fail is when there is simply no variance. It is almost trivial, but for observing how a variable Y changes when X moves is that both variables actually vary. There simply is no covariance without variance.

```
tibble(
  x = (0:100) / 10,
  y_1 = rnorm(101, exp(x) / 100, x * 2),
  y_2 = rnorm(101, (x - 5)^2, 3)
) %>%
  ggpairs(lower = list(continuous = "smooth"))
```

As we have seen, for every combination of two categorical and metric variables, we can produce summary statistics for the association, as well as graphs.

While it could be tempting to primarily use summary statistics and rather omit statistical graphs, the last example makes clear that some statistics like correlation

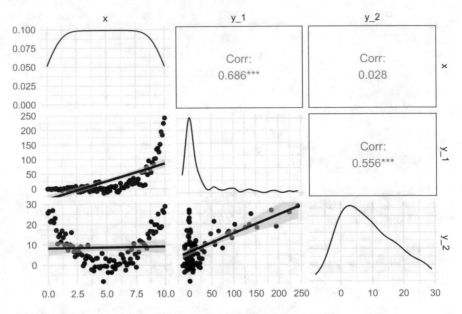

Fig. 3.14 Some shapes of associations where correlation is not adequate

are making assumptions on the shape of the association. The different graphs we have seen are much less presupposing and can therefore be used to check the assumptions of statistics and models.

3.4 Bayesian Probability Theory

Mathematics is emptiness. In its purest form, it does not require or have any link to the real world. That makes math so difficult to comprehend and beautifully strange at the same time. Sometimes a mathematical theory describes real-world phenomena, but we have no intuition about it. A classic example is Einstein's General Relativity Theory, which assumes a curved space, rather than the straight space our senses are tuned to. Our minds are Newtonian and the closest to the intuitive understanding we can get is the imagination of the universe as a four-dimensional mollusk, thanks to Einstein.

Math can also be easy, even appear trivial, if mathematical expressions directly translate into familiar ideas and sensations. I recall how my primary school teacher introduced the sum of two numbers as removing elements from one stack and place it on the second (with an obvious stop rule). Later, as a student, I was taught how the sum of two numbers is defined within the Peano axiomatic theory of natural numbers. As it turned out, I knew this already, because they just formalized the procedure I was taught as a kid. The formal proof for $1 + 1 = 2$ is using just the same elements as me shifting blocks between towers.

In this section, I will introduce *Probability theory*, which is largely based on another mathematical theory that many people find intuitive, *Set theory*. The formal theory of probability, the Kolmogorov axioms, may be somewhat disappointing from an ontological perspective, as it just defines rules for when a set of numbers can be regarded as probabilities. But calculating actual probabilities is rather easy and a few R commands will suffice to start playing with set theory and probability. The most tangible interpretation of probabilities is that the probability of an event to happen, say getting a Six when rolling a dice, coincides with the relative frequency of Six in a (very long) sequence of throws. This is called the *frequentist interpretation* of probability and this is how probability will be introduced in the following. While thinking in terms of relative frequency in long-running sequences is rather intuitive, it has limitations. Not all events we want to assign a probability can readily be imagined as a long-running sequence, for example

- The probability that your house burns down (you only have this one).
- The probability that a spaceship will safely reach Mars (there's only this one attempt).
- The probability that a theory is more true than another (there's only this pair).

The *Bayesian interpretation* of probability is essentially the same as the frequentist but is more relaxed as it does *not* require that all probabilities are measured through relative frequencies in long-running sequences. Bayesian thinking includes the idea that probabilities can also be a *degree of belief*, which can, but doesn't have to be grounded in long-running series. In the following, I will present in broad strokes how the theory of probability emerges from set theory and can be set into motion by computing relative frequencies of sets and subsets. Then, I will introduce the *likelihood*, which is a concept equally used in classic and Bayesian statistics. After clarifying the differences between frequentist and Bayesian ideas of measuring probability, *Bayes' theorem* is introduced as the formal underpinning of all Bayesian statistics. We will see how the likelihood and idea of *certainty as probability* combine to a scientific framework that emphasizes the incremental updating of our knowledge about the world we measure.

3.4.1 Some Set Theory

The mathematical concept of probability can most intuitively be approached by thinking in terms of relative frequency in long-running sequences. Actually, it is not even required to think of a sequence (where events have an order). It suffices to assume a set of events that emerge from one experiment.

A mathematical *set* is a collection of elements taken from a domain (or universe, more dramatically). These can either be defined by stating all the elements, like $S = \{red, yellow, green, off\}$ or by a characterizing statement, like

Table 3.25 Data set with 4 variables, showing 8 of 30 observations

Obs	Timely	Harmful	Success
2	TRUE	TRUE	FALSE
8	TRUE	FALSE	TRUE
9	TRUE	FALSE	TRUE
16	TRUE	FALSE	TRUE
18	TRUE	FALSE	TRUE
21	FALSE	TRUE	FALSE
25	FALSE	FALSE	TRUE
27	FALSE	FALSE	TRUE

S := possible states of a Dutch traffic light

The elements should be clearly identified, but need not have a particular order. (If they do, this is called an *ordered set*, the set of natural numbers is an example). Sets can have all possible sizes, which is called the *cardinality* of a set:

- Finite (and countable) like the states of a traffic light.
- Empty like "all opponents who can defeat Chuck Norris" {} or $\oslash$.
- Infinite, but countable, like the natural numbers N.
- Infinite, uncountable, like the real numbers R.

You may wonder now whether you would ever need such a strange concept as uncountable infinite sets in your down-to-earth design research. Well, the set of primary interest in every design study is the possible outcomes. Sometimes, these are finite, like {success, failure}, but when you measure durations or distances, you enter the realm of real numbers. We will set this issue aside for the moment and return to it later in the context of continuous distributions of randomness.

In order to introduce the mathematical concept of probability, we first have to understand some basic operations on sets. For an illustration, imagine a validation study for a medical infusion pump, where participants were given a task and the outcome was classified by the following three criteria (Table 3.25):

- Was the task goal achieved successfully?
- Was the task completed timely (e.g. one minute or below)?
- Were there any operation errors along the way with potentially harmful conse-
  quences?

D_sets

Note how the data table makes use of logical values to assign each observation a membership (or not) to each of the three sets. We can use the filter command to create all kinds of subsets and actually that would carry us pretty far into set theory. In the following, I will introduce set theory the Programming way, but use the package Sets, as it most closely resembles the mathematical formalism, it replaces. We begin with loading the package, which unfortunately uses the `%>%` operator for its own purpose.

```
library(sets)
## masks %>% operator. don't use in conjunction with
dplyr
```

```
All <- as.set(D_sets$Obs)
Success <- as.set(filter(D_sets, Success)$Obs)
Harmful <- as.set(filter(D_sets, Harmful)$Obs)
Timely <- as.set(filter(D_sets, Timely)$Obs)
```

Once there is more than one set in the game, set operators can be used to create all kinds of new sets. We begin with the *set difference*, which removes elements of one set from another (if they exist), for example the set of all successful tasks that were not completed in time. Note how the package Sets uses the minus operator to remove elements of one set (Timely) from another (Success).

```
Success - Timely
```

```
## {24L, 25L, 26L, 27L, 28L, 29L}
```

Using the set difference, we can produce *complementary set* which includes all elements that are not included in a set.

```
Failure <- All - Success
Harmless <- All - Harmful
Delayed <- All - Timely
```

In probability theory this corresponds with the probability of an event (Success) and its *counter-event* (Failure). A set and its complementary set taken together produce the *universal set*, which in probability theory is the *sure event* with a probability of One. To show that we can use *set union*, which collects the elements of two separate sets into one new set, for example re-uniting a set with its complementary,

```
Success | Failure == All
```

```
## {7L, 8L, 9L, 10L, 11L, 12L, 13L,
## 14L, 15L, 16L, 17L, 18L, 24L, 25L,
## 26L, 27L, 28L, 29L, FALSE}
```

or creating the set of all observations that were failure or delayed (or both):

```
Failure | Delayed
```

```
## {1L, 2L, 3L, 4L, 5L, 6L, 19L, 20L,
##   21L, 22L, 23L, 24L, 25L, 26L, 27L,
##   28L, 29L, 30L}
```

Another commonly used set operator is the *intersect*, which produces a set that contains only those elements present in both original sets, like the set of timely and successful task completions.

```
Success & Timely
```

```
## {7L, 8L, 9L, 10L, 11L, 12L, 13L,
##   14L, 15L, 16L, 17L, 18L}
```

All successful observations are also harmless. But not all harmless observations were successful. In set theory, Success is therefore a *subset* of Harmless. The subset operator differs from those discussed so far, in that it does not produce a new set, but a truth value (also called logical or Boolean). Per definition, two *equal* sets are also subsets of each other. The < operator is more strict and it means *proper subsets*, where being a subset has just one direction.

```
# subset
Success <= Harmless
```

```
## [1] TRUE
```

```
# proper subset
Success < Harmless
```

```
## [1] TRUE
```

```
# set equality
Success == Harmless
```

```
## [1] FALSE
```

```
Success == (All - Failure)
```

```
## [1] TRUE
```

The example above demonstrates the, figuratively, smallest concept of set theory. The *empty set* has the special property of being a subset of all other set:

```
set() < Success
```

```
## [1] TRUE
```

The empty set is important for the intersect operator to work properly. It may happen that two sets do not share any elements at all. It would be problematic if the intersect operator only worked if common elements truly existed. In such a case, the intersection of two sets is the empty set. Sets that have an empty intersection are called *disjunct sets* (with complementary sets as a special case). The package Sets, which defines all operators on sets so far, is lacking a dedicated function for disjunctness, but this is easily defined using the intersect function:

```
is_disjunct <- function(x, y) set_is_empty(x & y)
is_disjunct(Success, Harmful)
```

```
## [1] TRUE
```

So far, we have only seen sets of atomic elements, where all elements are atomic, i.e. they are not sets themselves.

With a little more abstraction, we can also conceive a set that has other sets as its elements. The set of sets that are defined by the three performance criteria and their complementary sets is an obvious example:

```
set(Success, Failure, Harmful, Harmless, Timely, Delayed)
```

```
## {<<set(9)>>, <<set(10)>>,
## <<set(12)>>, <<set(18)>>,
## <<set(20)>>, <<set(21)>>}
```

For the formal introduction of probability, we need two concepts related to sets of sets: First, a *partition of a set* is a set of non-empty subsets such that every element is assigned to exactly one subset. The subsets of successes and its complementary set, all failures, are such a partition. Second, the *power set* is the set of all possible subsets in a set. Even with a rather small set of 20 elements, this is getting incredibly large, so let's see it on a smaller example:

```
S <- set(1, 2, 3)
P <- set_power(S)
P
```

```
## {{}, {1}, {2}, {3}, {1, 2}, {1, 3},
## {2, 3}, {1, 2, 3}}
```

The power set is tantamount to the definition of probability that follows, because it has two properties: first, for every subset of S, it also contains the complementary set. That is called *closed under complementarity*. Second, for every pair of subsets of S, P, it also contains the union, and it is called *closed under union*. In the same way, power sets are also *closed under intersection*. Generally, all sets of subsets that fulfill these three requirements are called Σ algebras. The mathematical theory of Σ algebras is central for the mathematical definition of all measures.

Without going into too much depth on measurement theory, a measure is a mapping from the domain of empirical observations to the domain of numbers, such that certain operations in the domain of measurement work consistently with numerical operations. One example is the following: if you have two towers of blocks, L and R, next to each other and you look at them from one side, then the following rule applies for translating between the world of sensations and the world of sets:

L L R   <- Observer L   R L   R If you can see the top of tower L, when looking from the right side, then tower L larger than tower R is build with *more* blocks than tower R. Probabilities are measures and in the next section, we will see how numerical operations on probabilities relate to set operations in a Σ algebra. We will also see that relative frequencies are measures of probability.

3.4.2 Probability

In the following, I will outline the formal theory of probability and use the same fictional validation study to illustrate the relevant concepts introduced in the previous section. The performance of participants was classified by the three two-level criteria, success, harm and timeliness. Every recorded outcome therefore falls into one of eight possible sets and relative frequencies (π, pi) are a purposeful way to summarize the data (Table 3.26).

```
N_sets <- nrow(D_sets)

D_freq <-
  D_sets %>%
  group_by(Success, Harmful, Timely) %>%
  summarize(n = n()) %>%
  ungroup() %>%
  complete(Success,
    Harmful,
    Timely,
    fill = list(n = 0)
  ) %>% # adds empty events
  mutate(pi = n / sum(n))

D_freq
```

Table 3.26 Absolute and relative frequencies of eight distinct subsets

Success	Harmful	Timely	n	pi
FALSE	FALSE	FALSE	1	0.033
FALSE	FALSE	TRUE	2	0.067
FALSE	TRUE	FALSE	3	0.100
FALSE	TRUE	TRUE	6	0.200
TRUE	FALSE	FALSE	6	0.200
TRUE	FALSE	TRUE	12	0.400
TRUE	TRUE	FALSE	0	0.000
TRUE	TRUE	TRUE	0	0.000

Let's examine, on an abstract level, what has happened here:

1. The set of events has been partitioned into eight non-overlapping groups, which cover the three-way intersections. The first row, for example, is the intersect of the three sets Failure, Harmless and Delayed (see the previous section).
2. All subsets got a real number assigned by the operation of relative frequencies which produces numbers between (and including) Zero and One.
3. Hidden property is that, if we unite all sets, we get the universal set and, not coincidentally, if we sum over the frequencies, the result is One:

```
sum(D_freq$pi)
```

```
## [1] 1
```

Back to formal: The mathematical theory of probability departs from a set of *outcomes* Ω and a Σ algebra F defined on Ω. An element E of F therefore is a set of outcomes, which is called an *event*.

The eight three-way interaction sets above are a partition of Ω, but not a Σ-algebra. As disjunct sets, they are closed under intersection for trivial reasons, but they are not closed under union. For that we had to add a lot of possible outcomes, all counter-sets to start with. The point is that we can construct all these subsets using filter commands and produce relative frequencies, like above.

Probability as an axiomatic theory is defined by the three *Kolmogorov axioms*:

The *first Kolmogorov axiom* states that a probability is a non-negative real number assigned to every event. The computation of relative frequencies satisfies this condition hands down.

The first axiom defines a lower border of Zero for a probability measure; the *second Kolmogorov axiom* is taking care of an upper limit of One. This happens indirectly by stating that the set of all observations Ω (which is an element of F) is assigned a probability of One. In the table of relative frequencies, that is not yet covered, but we can easily do so:

Table 3.27 A cross table with frequencies

Success	n	pi
FALSE	12	0.4
TRUE	18	0.6

```
D_sets %>%
  # no group_by
  summarize(pi = n() / N_sets) %>%
  c()
```

```
## $pi
## [1] 1
```

So far, the theory only cared for assigning numbers to events (subsets), but provides no means to operate on probabilities. The *third Kolmogorov axiom* establishes a relation between the union operator on sets and the sum operator on probabilities by stating that the probability of a union of disjunct events is the sum of the individual probabilities. We can approve this to be true for the relative frequencies. For example, the question could be: Is the set of all successful observations the union of successful timely observations. Indeed, the relative frequency of all successful events is the sum of the two and satisfies the third axiom (Table 3.27).

```
D_sets %>%
  group_by(Success) %>%
  summarize(n = n()) %>%
  mutate(pi = n / sum(n))
```

The Kolmogorov axioms establish a probability measure and let us do calculations on disjunct subsets. That would be a meager toolbox to do calculations with probabilities. What about all the other set operators and their possible counterparts in the realm of numbers? It is one of the greatest wonders of the human mind that the rich field of reasoning about probabilities spawns from just these three axioms and a few set-theoretic underpinnings. To just give one very simple example, we can derive that the probability of the complement of a set A is $P(\Omega/A) = 1 - P(A)$:

1. From set theory follows that a set A and its complement Ω/A are disjunct, hence axiom 3 is applicable: $P(A \cup \Omega/A) = P(A) + P(\Omega/A)$.
2. From set theory follows that a set A and its complement Ω/A form a partition on Ω. Using axiom 2, we can infer

$$
\begin{aligned}
A \cup \Omega/A &= \quad \Omega \\
\Rightarrow \quad P(A) + P(\Omega/A) = P(\Omega) &= \quad 1 \\
\Rightarrow \quad P(\Omega/A) &= \quad 1 - P(A)
\end{aligned}
$$

Table 3.28 Joint subsets and their complements

Success	Timely	pi
FALSE	FALSE	0.133
FALSE	TRUE	0.267
TRUE	FALSE	0.200
TRUE	TRUE	0.400

Table 3.29 Conditional probabilities

Harmful	n	pi
FALSE	21	0.7
TRUE	9	0.3

The third axiom tells us how to deal with probabilities when events are disjunct. As we have seen, it applies for defining more general events. How about the opposite direction, calculating probabilities of more special events? In our example, two rather general events are Success and Timely, whereas the intersection events Success *and* Timely are more special. The probability of two events occurring together is called *joint probability* P(Timely $\cap$ Success). The four joint probabilities on the two sets and their complements are shown in Table 3.28.

```
D_sets %>%
    group_by(Success, Timely) %>%
    summarize(pi = n() / N_sets) %>%
    ungroup()
```

As joint probability asks for simultaneous occurrence, it treats both involved sets symmetrically: P(Timely $\cap$ Success) = P(Successes $\cap$ Timely). What if you are given one piece of information first, such as "this was a successful outcome", and you have to guess the other "Was it harmful?" (Table 3.29). That is called *conditional probability* and in this case, it is Zero. But what is the conditional probability that, when you know an event was a failure, it really caused harm?

P(Harmful|Success)

```
D_sets %>%
    group_by(Harmful) %>%
    summarize(n = n()) %>%
    mutate(pi = n / sum(n))
```

In the manner of a speed-accuracy trade-off, there could be a relationship between Timely and Harm. Participants who rush through the task are likely to make more harmful errors. We would then expect a different distribution of probability of harm by whether or not task completion was timely.

Table 3.30 Conditional probabilities

Timely	Harmful	n	pi
FALSE	FALSE	7	0.7
FALSE	TRUE	3	0.3
TRUE	FALSE	14	0.7
TRUE	TRUE	6	0.3

```
D_sets %>%
  group_by(Timely, Harmful) %>%
  summarize(n = n()) %>%
  mutate(pi = n / sum(n)) %>%
  ungroup()
```

In Table 3.30, see how conditional probabilities sum up to one *within* their condition. In this case, the conditional probabilities for harm are the same for successes and failures. As a consequence, it is also the same as the overall probability, hence

$$P(\text{Harm}|\text{Timely}) = P(\text{No harm}|\text{Timely}) = P(\text{Timely})$$

This situation is called *independence of events* and it means that knowing about one variable does not help in guessing the other. In Statistics, *conditional probability* and *independence of events* are tightly linked to *likelihoods* and *Bayes' theorem* Sect. 3.4.5.

3.4.3   Likelihood

In the previous section, we have seen how to create probabilities from relative frequencies in data and how to do basic calculations with those probabilities. Using these concepts, we will see in the following how data can be used for inference. Inference means to draw conclusions about theoretical models. In the following, this will be illustrated in the example of rolling dices, where the default theory is that the dice is fair, hence the probability of Six is assumed to be π_{Six}. For the matter here, we take the theory of the dice being fair into the equation, as a conditional probability, in words: "Conditional on this dice being fair, the chance of rolling Six is $1/6$".

$$P(y = \text{Six}|\pi_{\text{Six}} = 1/6)$$

When such a standard dice is rolled twice, how likely is an outcome of two times Six? We use probability theory: It is one dice but the results of the rolls are otherwise independent; for example, the probability to roll a Six does not wear off over time or anything like that.

Because of independence, the joint probability of rolling two times Six is just the product:

$$P(y_1 = \text{Six and } y_2 = \text{Six} | \pi = 1/6)$$
$$= P(y_1 = \text{Six} | \pi = 1/6) \times P(y_2 = \text{Six} | \pi = 1/6)$$
$$= 1/36$$

The joint probability of all data points is called the *Likelihood* and generalizes to situations where the probabilities of events are not the same, for example: What is the probability of the one dice being a Four, the second a Five and the third a Three or a Six?

$$P(y_1 = \text{Four and } y_2 = \text{Five and } y_3 = \text{Three or Six}) = \frac{1}{6} \times \frac{1}{6} \times \frac{1}{3} = \frac{1}{108}$$

Notice how the likelihood gets smaller in the second example. In fact, likelihoods are products of numbers between zero and one and therefore become smaller with every observation that is added. In most empirical studies, the number of observations is much larger than two or three and the likelihood becomes inexpressibly small. Consider the following results from 16 rolls.

```
set.seed(42)
Events <- c("One", "Two", "Three", "Four", "Five", "Six")
Result <- sample(Events, 16, replace = T)
pi <- 1 / 6
Likelihood <- pi^length(Result)
```

The likelihood of this result, given that it is a fair dice, is $\frac{1}{6}^{16} = 3.545 \times 10^{-13}$. Therefore, one usually reports the *logarithm of the likelihood (log-likelihood)*. This results in "reasonable" negative numbers. Why negative? Because all likelihood are fractions of One (the identity element of multiplication), which results in a negative logarithm.

```
(logLik <- log(Likelihood))
```

```
## [1] -28.7
```

The dice rolling example above has a twist, assumed that we may enter $\pi = 1/6$, because we *believe* that it is a fair dice, without further notice. In other words, we needed no data, because of overwhelming prior knowledge (or theory, if you will). And now we will come to see why I took the effort to write the probabilities above as conditional probabilities. A likelihood is the probability of the data, given a parameter value. The basic idea of likelihoods is to consider data constant and vary the parameter. In such a way, we can see how the likelihood changes when we assume different values for π_{Six}.

Table 3.31 Data set with 3 variables, showing 8 of 6000 observations

Obs	Roll	Result
1214	1214	Six
1589	1589	Five
2007	2007	One
3433	3433	Four
3524	3524	One
3744	3744	Six
4174	4174	Three
4967	4967	One

Imagine we have been called in to uncover fraud with biased dices in a casino. There is suspicion that the chance of rolling a Six is lower than $1/6$. So, what is the most likely chance of rolling a Six? In the following simulation, 6000 rolls have been recorded in Table 3.31.

```
n_Rolls <- 6000

Biased_dice <-
  tibble(
    Side = as_factor(Events),
    pi = c(1 / 6 +0.02, rep(1 / 6, 4), 1 / 6 -0.02)
  )



set.seed(41)
Rolls <- tibble(
  Roll = 1:n_Rolls,
  Result = sample(Biased_dice$Side,
    prob = Biased_dice$pi,
    size = n_Rolls,
    replace = T
  )
) %>%
  as_tbl_obs()

Rolls


Rolls %>%
  ggplot(aes(x = Result)) +
  geom_bar()
```

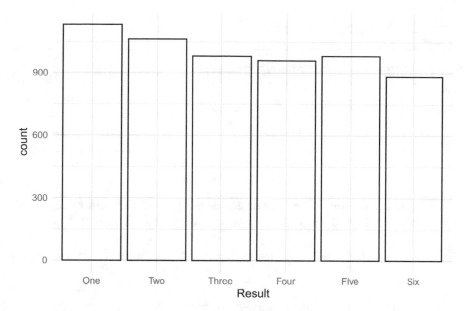

Fig. 3.15 A bar chart showing the frequencies of dice roll outcomes

Figure 3.15 shows the frequencies for the six possible outcomes. For the reason of simplicity, we focus on the events of rolling a Six, only. If we have no prior suspicion about the dice, the estimated probability is simply the relative frequency of Six (Table 3.32).

```
Rolls %>%
  group_by(Result) %>%
  summarize(pi = n() / n_Rolls)
```

In this case, we can simply note down that the *most likely value* is $\pi_{Six} = 0.147$, which is lower than the fair 0.167. But, note the slight ruggedness of the bar chart. Not a single bar is read as exactly 1/6, so the deviation of Six could have happened by chance. One way to approach this question is comparing the likelihoods $P(\text{Result} = \text{Six}|\pi = 1/6)$ and $P(\text{Result} = \text{Six}|\pi = 0.147)$. For that purpose, we create a new event variable Six, that indicates whether a roll is a Six (TRUE) or not (FALSE). Further, a *distribution function* is required that assigns these events their probabilities. Distribution functions can take very complicated forms Sect. 3.5.2, but in the case here, it is the rather simple *Bernoulli distribution*.

The log-likelihood function of the Bernoulli distribution is just the sum of log-probabilities of any roll y_i.

$$LL_{\text{Bern}}(Y|\pi) = \sum_i \log(d_{\text{Bern}}(y_i, \pi))$$

Table 3.32 Frequencies of outcome in dice rolls

Result	pi
One	0.189
Two	0.177
Three	0.163
Four	0.160
Five	0.164
Six	0.147

Now, we can determine the *ratio of likelihoods LR* with different values for π. Note that on the logarithmic scale, what was a ratio becomes a difference.

$$LR = \exp(LL_{\text{Bern}}(\text{Rolls}, 0.147) - LL_{\text{Bern}}(\text{Rolls}, \frac{1}{6}))$$

```
Rolls <- Rolls %>%
  mutate(Six = (Result == "Six"))

dbern <- function(y, pi) if_else(y, pi, 1 - pi)
LL_bern <- function(pi) sum(log(dbern(Rolls$Six, pi)))

pi_fair <- 1 / 6
pi_est <-0.147

exp(LL_bern(pi_est) - LL_bern(pi_fair))
```

```
## [1] 4846
```

Now, recall what a likelihood is: the probability of the observed data, under a certain model. Here, the data is almost 5000 times more likely with $p = 0.147$. In classic statistics, such likelihood ratios are routinely been used for the comparison of models.

Previously, I have indicated that the relative frequency gives us the most likely value for parameter π (the case of a Bernoulli distributed variable), the *maximum likelihood estimate (MLE)*. The MLE is that point in the parameter range (here [0; 1]), which maximizes the likelihood. It is the point where the data is most likely. In a similar way, the mean of Gaussian distributed measures is the maximum likelihood estimate for the distribution parameter μ. But, more advanced models do not have such a closed form, i.e. a formula that you can solve. Parameter estimation in classic statistics heavily grounds on numerical procedures to find *maximum likelihood estimates*, which I will outline now:

The probability function $d_{\text{Bern}}(y_i, \pi)$ has two parameters that vary, the result of a roll y_i and the assumed chance pi. The likelihood function, as we use it here, in contrast, takes the data as fixed and only varies on parameter π. By varying the parameter and reading the resulting likelihood of data, we can numerically interpolate the MLE. The most basic numerical interpolation method is a grid search, which starts at the left boundary of parameter range, zero in this case, and walks in small steps along a grid to the right boundary (one). By convention, maximum likelihood estimation is performed by *minimizing the negative log-likelihood*. For convenience, the following likelihood function has been vectorized to make it work smoothly in a tidy processing chain.

```
LL_bern <- function(pi) map_dbl(pi, function(x)
sum(log(dbern(Rolls$Six, x))))

LL_bern(c(0.1, 0.2))
```

```
## [1] -2572 -2563
```

```
LL_grid <-
  tibble(pi = seq(.01, 0.99, by = 0.01)) %>%
  mutate(
    nlogLik = -LL_bern(pi),
    rank = min_rank(nlogLik),
    MLE = (rank == 1)
  )
```

```
LL_grid %>%
  ggplot(aes(x = pi, y = nlogLik)) +
  geom_line() +
  geom_point(data = filter(LL_grid, MLE), color = "Red") +
  geom_text(data = filter(LL_grid, MLE), label = "MLE", color =
"Red", nudge_y = -500)
```

Figure 3.16 shows the maximum likelihood or rather its negative logarithm. Because we use the *negative* log-likelihood, the value for π with maximum likelihood is the minimum of the likelihood curve (Table 3.33). Here, $\pi_{\text{MLE}} = 0.15$, which is very close to the relative frequency we obtained above. The slight deviation is due to the limited resolution of the grid, but it is always possible to be more accurate by using a finer grid.

```
LL_grid %>%
  filter(rank == 1)
```

In classic statistics, MLE is one of the most common methods for estimating parameters from models. However, most of the time, data is more abundant and there is more than one parameter. It is possible to extend the grid method to as many parameters as the model contains by just creating multidimensional grids and walk

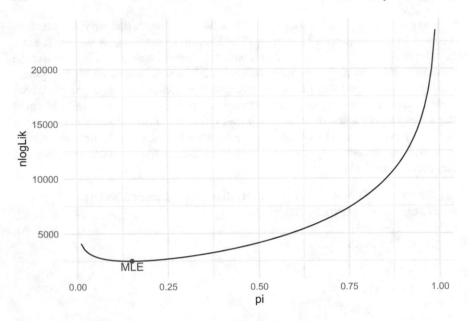

Fig. 3.16 Estimating parameter pi by maximum likelihood estimation

Table 3.33 The maximum likelihood is the lowest rank of negative log-likelihood values

pi	nlogLik	Rank	MLE
0.15	2507	1	TRUE

through them by the likelihood function. However, already a two-dimensional grid of rather coarse 100×100 would require the computation of 10.000 likelihoods. Classic statisticians have therefore developed optimization methods to identify the MLE more efficiently. Soon, we will turn our attention to Bayesian estimation, where the likelihood plays a central role in estimation, too Sect. 3.6.

3.4.4 Bayesian and Frequentist Probability

All statisticians believe that relative frequencies satisfy Kolmogorov's axioms, but not everyone thinks that this is the only way to measure probability. This is where frequentist and Bayesian statistics diverge: Frequentists believe that *only relative frequencies* are valid measures for probability, whereas Bayesians believe that *certainty* is a measure of probability, too. As subtle as this may sound, it has remarkable consequences in context with Bayes' theorem.

QUESTION: What is the chance that this dice will fall on Six?

Table 3.34 Frequentist 95% confidence intervals

	2.5 %	97.5 %
(Intercept)	99.8	112

FREQUENTIST: I can only answer this question after a long-running series of dice rolls.

BAYESIAN: I am 50% certain that this is a trick question, so I'd say 50% it never falls on Six.

If this is not a trick question, this seems to be a dice from a well-known manufacturer, so I'd say 1/6.

FREQUENTIST (rolles eyes): And how does the manufacturer know?

BAYESIAN (sighs): ... by a long-running series of experiments.

The frequentist in the caricature is someone sticking to the principles: every probability must be produced by relative frequencies, which must be produced in repetitions of the same experiment. The Bayesian has no problem with long-running sequences, but feels confident to use other sources of information. In a strictly frequentist view, this is like pulling numbers, just in the unit interval, out of the thin air. But, as we will see, the Bayes theorem is amazingly useful when we allow for probabilities that don't derive from long-running sequences. These are called *prior probabilities* and they can be used to factor in prior knowledge about the world.

Consequently, a Bayesian also accepts that levels of certainty after the experiment can be reported as probabilities. In contrast, a frequentist must insist that certainty can be interpreted as long-running series. In frequentist statistics, a common way to express one's level of certainty is the infamous p-value. And this is its definition: *A result is called statistically significant on level* $\alpha = 0.05$ *if drawing from the null distribution (an infinite number of times) will produce the observed result or a larger result in no more than 5% of cases.*

Another, and more preferable, way of expressing one's certainty about a parameter (say, the population mean) is the *95% confidence interval*, which is expressed as two end points (Table 3.34).

```
attach(Sec99)

Ver20 %>%
  lm(ToT ~ 1, data = .) %>%
  confint()
```

It is common to say "we can be 95% certain that the true values are between these bounds", but the 95% confidence interval really is defined by assuming an (infinite) set of replications of the very same experiment and using relative frequencies: *The 95% confidence interval is constructed in such a way that, if the same experiment were repeated an infinite number of times, in 95% of these repetitions, the true value is contained in the interval.*

You are not alone when you lack intuition of what the definition says and when you feel unease about where all these experiments are supposed to come from. It seems as if a true frequentist cannot imagine the future other than by a series of long-running experiments. In Bayesian statistics, the level of certainty is expressed as a *proposition about one's state of knowledge*, like: *Based on my data I am 95% sure that there is a difference.* Equating the level of certainty with probability directly, without taking the detour via relative frequencies, may be a little lax, but it leads to remarkably intuitive statements on uncertainty. In Bayesian statistics, the *credibility interval* is defined as: *With a probability of 95%, the true value is contained.* Since there seems to be no external criterion (such as a series of experiments, imagined or not), Bayesian statistics often faced the criticism of being subjective. In fact, if we imagine a certainty of 95% as some number, in the researcher's mind, that might be true. But, it is quite easy to grasp certainty as an objective quantity when we assume that there is something at stake for the researcher and that she aims for a rational decision. In the previous chapter, I have illustrated this idea by the example of carrying an umbrella with you (or not) and the 99s claim. Generally, it helps to imagine any such situation as a gamble: if you bet 1 EUR that the true population mean is outside the 95% credibility interval, as a rational person I would put 19 EUR against.

In effect, the Bayesian certainty is a probability in mathematical terms, without the necessity to implement it as a relative frequency. That liberates our reasoning from the requirement to think of long-running series. In particular, it allows us to enter non-frequentist probabilities into the Bayes theorem, resulting in a statistical framework that captures the dynamics of belief in science Sect. 3.4.6. Before we come to that, I will explain the Bayes theorem in another context of updating knowledge, medical diagnostics.

3.4.5 Bayes' Theorem

Bayes' theorem emerges from formal probability theory and therefore is neither Bayesian nor frequentist. Essentially, the theorem shows how to calculate a conditional probability of interest $P(A|B)$ from a known conditional probability $P(B|A)$ and two marginal probabilities $P(A)$ and $P(B)$:

$$P(A|B) = \frac{P(A)P(B|A)}{P(B)}$$

The proof of the theorem is rather simple and does not require repetition here. But, Bayes' theorem can lead to rather surprising conclusions, which can be illustrated by an example of a medical screening test, as follows:

In 1980, the human immunodeficiency virus (HIV) was discovered and since then has become a scourge for humanity. Given that the first outbursts of the disease raged among homosexual men, it is not really surprising that some conservative politicians quickly called for action and proposed a mandatory test for everyone, with the results to be registered in a central database. Without much of a stretch, it may seem justifiable to store (and use) the information that someone is carrying such a dangerous disease. The problem is with those people who do not carry it, but could be misdiagnosed. These are called *false-positives*. Let's assume the power of a screening test has been assessed by examining samples of participants where it is fully known whether someone is a carrier of the virus $C+$ or not $C-$. The result is a *specificity* of 95%, meaning that 95% of $C-$ are diagnosed correctly $(P(T-|C-))$, and a *sensitivity* of 99%, meaning that 99% with $C+$ are diagnosed correctly $(P(T+|C+))$. The question that Bayes' theorem can answer in such a situation is *How many citizens would be registered as HIV carrying, although they are not?* For this to work, we must also know the probability that someone randomly chosen from the population is a carrier $(P(C+))$ and the proportion of positive test results $P(T+)$.

$$
\begin{aligned}
P(C+) & & &=0.0001 \\
P(C-) &=1 - P(C+) & &=0.9999 \\
P(T+|C+) & & &=0.99 \\
P(T-|C+) &=1 - P(T-|C+) & &=0.01 \\
P(T-|C-) & & &=0.95 \\
P(T+|C-) &=1 - P(T-|C-) & &=0.05 \\
P(T+) &=P(C+)P(T+|C+) + P(C-)P(T+|C-) &&\approx0.05 \\
P(T-) &=1 - P(T+) & &\approx0.95
\end{aligned}
$$

How do these numbers arise? $P(C+)$ is the proportion of HIV carriers in the whole population. If you have no test at all, that is your best guess for whether a random person has the virus, your *prior knowledge*. Then, the validation study of the test provides us with more *data*. The study examined the outcome of the test $(T+$ or $T-)$ in two groups of participants, those that were knowingly carriers $C+$ and those that were not $C-$. This is where the four conditional probabilities come from. Finally, we need the expected proportion of positive test results $P(T+)$, which we compute as a marginal probability over the two conditions. Because non-carriers $C-$ dominate the population by so much, the marginal probability for a positive test is almost the same as the probability for a positive test among non-carriers $P(T+|C-)$.

All conditional probabilities here emerge from a validation study where it is known upfront whether someone is a carrier or not. What matters for the application of the screening test is the reverse: what is learned by test about carrier status? In the following, the test is being characterized by two types of errors that can occur: false alarms and misses.

- False alarms: What is the probability that someone will be registered as a carrier, although being a non-carrier? That is: $P(C - |T+)$. When the false alarm rate is low, the test is called to have good *specificity*.
- Misses: Which proportion of the tested population are carriers, but have a negative test result (and act accordingly)? That is: $P(C + |T-)$. When the probability of misses is low, the test is called to have good *sensitivity*.

Using Bayes' theorem, we obtain the following probability for false alarms:

$$P(C - |T+) = \frac{P(C-)P(T + |C-)}{P(T+)}$$
$$\approx \frac{0.9999 \times 0.05}{05}$$
$$\approx 0.9999$$

Obviously, testing the whole population with the screening test would result in disaster. Practically everyone who is registered as a carrier in the database is really a non-carrier. In turn, the probability that a person has the virus despite a negative test result is

$$P(C + |T-) = \frac{P(C+)P(T - |C+)}{P(T-)}$$
$$\approx \frac{0.0001 \times 0.01}{0.95}$$
$$\approx 0.000001$$

We see a strong asymmetry in how useful the test is in the two situations. The specificity of the test is rather low and stands no chance against the overwhelming prevalence of non-carriers. In the second use case, prevalence and high test sensitivity work in the same direction, which results in a fantastically low risk to err. That is what Bayes' theorem essentially does: it combines prior knowledge (prevalence, $P(C+)$) against obtained evidence and produces *posterior* knowledge. In the following section, we will see how this makes Bayes' theorem a very useful tool in a context that is all about updating knowledge, like in science. In the case of medical diagnostics, the probability $P(C + |T+)$ can be called a posterior probability, but it becomes prior knowledge in the very moment that new data arrives and we can update our knowledge once again. A reasonable strategy arises from the asymmetry of certainties: a negative test almost certainly coincides with being a non-carrier, whereas identifying true carriers remains problematic. Follow-up research should therefore capitalize on reducing false alarms and use a test with extreme specificity (= absence of false alarms) at the expense of sensitivity.

3.4.6 Bayesian Dynamics of Belief

Bayes' formula is just a law that follows directly from probability theory. It can easily be illustrated in terms of frequencies: If the number of false alarms is very small in a small group, it gets large in a very large group. What makes such an innocent formula the patron of Bayesian Statistics?

Bayes' formula can be seen as a sort of knowledge processing device. In the example of the HIV test, what we want to know is how likely it is that someone is infected. That is something we can already do without any test if we have an idea about the prevalence of infections. It already helps to know that only 1 in 10.000 has it. It is a rare disease, so usually no reason to get paranoid! In contrast, if you are running a blood bank, knowledge of prevalence is just not good enough and a test is required. This test is used not to make up our minds, but to update our minds. Bayes' formula is just a rational way of updating knowledge by combing what one knew before and what one learns from the present data. A Bayesian estimation takes *prior knowledge* $P(\theta)$ and the *likelihood* $P(\text{Data}|\theta)$, representing the data as input and the output is *posterior knowledge* $P(\theta|\text{Data})$:

$$P(\theta|\text{Data}) = \frac{P(\theta)P(\text{Data}|\theta)}{P(\text{Data})}$$

As it turns out, the marginal likelihood $P(Data)$ cannot be known or easily estimated. The reason why we can still use the Bayes rule for estimation is that this term does not depend on the parameter vector θ, which is our search space, meaning that it is practically a constant. For parameter estimation, the Bayes rule can be reduced to saying that the posterior certainty is *proportional to* the product of prior certainty and evidence:

$$\text{posterior} \propto \text{prior} \times \text{likelihood}$$

Recall that the likelihood is the probability of the data at hand, given parameter θ. This is typical for frequentist statistics, which assumes that there is one true value and all randomness is caused by fluctuations in the set of possible samples. Your data is just one fish from the pond. Bayesians typically feel that data is the real thing and that parameter θ is never really true, but represents the current state of knowledge.

Brains process data, too, and some argue that the behavior of brains can be described as Bayesian engines. It is true that prior knowledge is something we use everyday, and many things we do know because of our genes. For example, parents sometimes report that their toddlers abruptly start to reject food that is green. This is often perceived as stubborn behavior, because of vitamins, fiber, lack of sugar and the greenhouse effect. If it is true, that our ancestors headed their ways through a savannah, the child may actually be right. Savannah flora's worst enemy is vegetarian savannah animals, and in an arms race, plants have developed an abundance of weapons, such as a tough structure, scarcity of nutrients, thorns, blades and poisons. The child knows that green stuff usually is not edible or even dangerous. This prior knowledge is so overwhelming that it costs modern parents a lot of patience to update their children's knowledge of food, and reportedly many fail. A Bayesian statistician would call this a *strong prior*.

Science is what only some central nervous systems do, but the principle is the same: we have a theory which we are unsure about; data is collected and after that, we may find this theory more likely or reject it. Testing theories is not a one-shot. Some theories have been tested many times. For example, in the famous Stroop effect, participants have to name the ink color of a word. When the word is itself a color word and refers to a different color, response times typically increase. This effect has been replicated in many dozens of published studies and, probably, thousands of student experiments.The accumulated evidence is so strong that, would someone repeat the experiment another time and find the reverse effect, no one would seriously take this as a full debunk of decades of research. In Bayes' formula, prior and posterior are both probabilities, which means we can use the posterior from experiment n as prior for experiment $n + 1$, or:

Today's posterior is tomorrow's prior.

There is no principled difference between prior and posterior knowledge. They are just degrees of belief at different points in time, expressed as probabilities. Both can differ in strength: prior knowledge can be firm when it rests on an abundance of past evidence. But, prior knowledge can also be over-ruled when a lot of data disproves it. Evidence in data varies in strength: for example, the more observations, the larger the (negative) likelihood becomes, which means stronger evidence. If measures are more accurate (and less disturbed by randomness), smaller sample sizes suffice to reach conclusions of similar strength. This is why larger sample sizes are preferred and why researchers try to improve their methods.

The problem with frequentist statistics is that it has not developed general methods to incorporate prior knowledge in the analysis. It is even worse: When practicing null hypothesis significance testing, you strictly *must not update* your degree of belief during the study and act accordingly. Neither is there a way to express one's prior belief when doing a t-test nor may you adjust sample size ad hoc until satisfactory certainty is reached. Classic data analysis pretends as if no one has ever done any such an experiment before. Also, it is strictly forbidden to invite further participants to the lab, when the evidence is still too weak. If you planned the study with, say, $N = 20$, this is what you must do, no less no more. If you reach your goal with less participants, you must continue testing. If you are unsatisfied with the level of certainty, the only permissible action is to dump your data and start over from zero. The frequentist denial of incremental knowledge is not just counter-intuitive in all science, it is a millstone around the neck of every researcher.

3.5   Statistical Models

It is a scientific, maybe even naturalistic, principle that every event to happen has its causes (from the same universe). The better these causes are understood, the better will be all predictions of what is going to happen the next moment, given that one knows the complete state of the universe and the laws of physics. *Laplace demon* is a classic experiment of thought on the issue: the demon is said to have perfect knowledge of laws of physics and about the universe's current state. Within naturalistic thinking, the demon should be able to perfectly predict what is going to happen in the next moment. Of course, such an entity could never exist, because it would actually be a computer that matches the universe in size (and energy consumption). In addition, there are limits to how precisely we can measure the current state, although physicists and engineers have pushed the limits very far. Behavioral science frequently lacks this precision, which results in rather imperfect knowledge about the state. We are often left with a good amount of uncertainty.

When Violet did her experiment to prove the superiority of design B, the only two things she knew about the state of affairs were that the participant sitting in front of her is member of a very loose group of people called the "typical user" and the design he was exposed to. That is painstakingly little information on what's currently going on in the participant's central nervous system. Her lack of knowledge is profound but still not a problem as the research question was on a gross scale itself, too. Not what happens to individual users needed to be described, but just the difference in *average* duration.

Imagine Violet and a colleague had invented a small game where they both guess the time-on-task of individual participants as they enter the lab. Who comes closest wins. As both players are smart people, they do not just randomly announce numbers, but let themselves guide by data of previous sessions. A very simple but reasonable approach would be to always guess what the average ToT in all previous sessions has been. In Sect. 4.1, we will call this a grand mean model.

Of course, Violet would never expect her grand mean model to predict the accurate outcome of a session. Still, imagine a device that has perfect knowledge of the website, the complete current neural state of the participant and the physical environment both are in. As an all-knowing device, it would also have complete knowledge of how neural states change. With this device, Jane could always make a perfect prediction of the outcome. Unfortunately, real design researchers are far from Laplace demonism. Routinely borrowing instruments from social sciences, the precision of measurement is humble and the understanding of neural processes during web navigation is highly incomplete. Participants vary in many complex ways in their neural state and this makes a myriad of *small unmeasured forces (SMURF)* that can steer individual users toward or away from the average. Laplace demon would have perfect knowledge of all forces and would produce a perfect prediction. Violet, in contrast, is completely ignorant of any SMURFs and her predictions will be way off many times.

A common way to conceive this situation is that all measures are composed of a *structural part*, that captures the relation between known and measured forces and a *random part*, that serves as a bucket for unmeasured forces.

$$\text{Measure}_i = \text{structural part} + \text{random part}_i$$

Note that Measure and Random part both have an observation-level index i, which means they are *unique* per observation i. The structural part does not have such an index, because it is usually designed as a *universal* statement, a proposition that holds for all the observations. If this was different, there would be no way to make predictions from the model. After a minimally sufficient introduction to the matter, the remainder of this section will focus on the random part and we will discover that randomness is *not* completely arbitrary, but falls into certain *shapes of randomness*. And for the scope of this book, a *statistical model* is defined as a *mechanism that separates the structural from the random part* to some extent.

3.5.1   The Structural Part

Generally, statistical models consist of these two parts: a structural part that describes the association between measures and the random part, which is the sum of all small unmeasured forces (SMURFs). The structural part of statistical models is called so because it describes what all observations supposedly have in common. The structural part is what encodes the structure of a study and the dependencies between measures.

The most simple structure is just that an observation was taken on a member of a population. If we speak of a population (rather than a set), we typically imply that members of the population have something in common. The most simple structural part is therefore taking the mean of the population, which is also called a Grand Mean Model (4.1). From here on, μ_i is the result of the structural part for one observation, which for a GMM is just a constant β_0.

$$\mu_i = \beta_0$$

We will see throughout Chaps. 4 and 6 how the structural part encodes complex dependencies between measures.

The structural part makes a universal statement about the relationship between measures. This can basically be anything. However, in many (if not most) statistical models, it is common to separate the set of measures into exactly one *response* (or outcome, or dependent variable) and a set of predictor variables. In the GMM above, there are no predictors, just a constant value.

In the guessing game, Violet could try to improve her guesses, by also taking the age of participants into account. Older people tend to be slower. Violet could create a plot from past records (Fig. 3.17)). The ellipsoid form of the point cloud indicates that ToT is somehow depending on age. Violet draws a straight line with

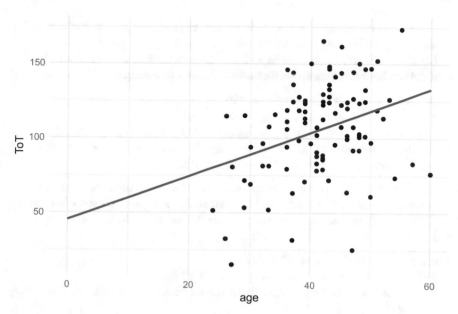

Fig. 3.17 A linear association between Age and ToT

an upward slope to approximate the relationship. It seems that zero-year-old persons have an average ToT of around 45 s, which increases to around 120 s for 50-year old. Arithmetically, this is an increase of around 1.5 s per year of age.

```
##
## Call:
## lm(formula = ToT ~ age, data = Sec99$Ver20)
##
## Coefficients:
## (Intercept)          age
##       45.31         1.46
```

```
Sec99$Ver20 %>%
  ggplot(aes(x = age, y = ToT)) +
  geom_point() +
  geom_smooth(method = "lm", se = F, fullrange = T) +
  xlim(0, 60)
```

Violet can use this information to improve her chance of winning. Instead of stoically calling the population mean, she uses a linear function as predictor: 45 + (age)1.5. This is called a *linear association* and the general notation is

$$\mu_i = \beta_0 + \beta_1 x_{1i}$$

where β_0 is the intercept value, X_1 is a measure (age) and β_1 is a *coefficient*. The primary purpose of using a model on data is to estimate the coefficients.

Linear models are very common in statistical modeling, but the structural part of a model can basically take all mathematical forms. For example:

- Two predictors with a linear relationship: $\mu_i = \beta_0 + \beta_1 x_{1i} + \beta_1 x_{2i}$.
- A parabolic relationship: $\mu_i = \beta_0 + \beta_1 x_{1i} + \beta_2 x_{2i}^2$.
- A non-linear learning curve: $\mu_i = \beta_{\text{asym}}(1 + \exp(-\beta_{\text{rate}}(x_{\text{training}} + \beta_{\text{pexp}})))$.
- The difference between groups A and B, where x_1 is a membership (dummy) variable coded as $A \rightarrow x_1 := 0, B \rightarrow x_1 := 1$: $\mu_i = \beta_0 + \beta_1 x_{1i}$.

In the vast majority of cases, the structural part is the one of interest, as this is where researchers transform their theoretical considerations or practical questions into a mathematical form. The parameters of the likelihood function are being estimated and answer the urging questions, such as

- Is the design efficient enough? (β_0)
- By how much does performance depend on age? (β_1)
- Under which level of arousal does performance peak? (determining the stationary point of the parabola)
- How fast people learn by training? (β_{rate})
- By how much design B is better than A? (β_1)

A subtle, but noteworthy, feature of the structural part is that μ_i and x_i have indicators i. Every observation i has its own measures and therefore the realization of the structural part gets a unique expected value. In contrast, the coefficients β_0, β_1 asf. are universal values that apply for all observations.

When all measures y, x are known and all coefficients β have been estimated, we can solve the structural part and obtain a unique value μ_i for all observations. Considering that $y_i = \mu_i +$ random part, that means we can also view model estimation of a model as a separation of structural part and random part. Unfortunately, it is not sufficient to just have measures and a structural part. We also need to know the shape of randomness and put this into the model.

3.5.2 Distributions: Shapes of Randomness

Review the formula Measure$_i$ = structural part + random part$_i$. What do we actually have? It turns out that the only parts we know for sure are measures y_i and $x_{.i}$. The structural part contains the answer to our research question, so this is what we want to estimate. Unfortunately, there is another unknown, the *random part*, which we literally need to subtract to get to our answers. Obviously, this would never work if the random part was random in the sense of being completely arbitrary. Fortunately, randomness is not arbitrary, but has a shape, which is described as a probability (or density) distribution. These distributions typically belong to a certain family of distribution functions, e.g. Poisson distributions or Gaussian distributions. By assuming a certain shape of randomness, we know a lot more about the random component, which will make it possible to flesh out the structure. Choosing the most appropriate distribution therefore is a crucial step in creating a valid statistical model. In this section, I will introduce in more depth how probability and density distributions describe the shape of randomness.

3.5.2.1 Probability Mass and Density

The random part of a statistical model contains all (small) unmeasured forces on the response y_i. When using the grand mean model, the only information we are using is that the person is from the target population. Everything else is left to the unobserved SMURFs and that goes into the random part of the model. Fortunately, SMURFs don't work completely arbitrary and in practice, there is just a small number of recognizable shapes randomness can take. These patterns can be formulated mathematically as either *probability mass functions (PMFs)* or *probability density functions (PDFs)*. The difference between PMF and CDF is that PMFs only work for discrete measures, such as anything that is countable, whereas CDFs also apply for continuous measures, such as ToT. In general, any PMF can also be called a CDF, but it is instructive to start with a case of discrete measures.

In the case of discrete measures, a PMF assigns *probabilities to possible outcomes*. Let's see an example: A participant is asked to complete three tasks of constant difficulty, that is a chance of .3 to be solved. The outcome variable of interest is the number of correct results, which can take the values 0, 1, 2 or 3. Under idealized conditions (but not removing randomness), a Binomial distribution assigns every possible outcome a probability to occur, it is given as

$$P(y|p, k) = \binom{k}{y} p^y (1 - p)^{k-y}$$

Binomial distributions with probabilities of success $p = 0.3$ and $k = 3$ tasks are shown in Fig. 3.18:

```
D_three_tasks <-
  tibble(
    y = -1:4,
    outcome = as.character(y),
    probability = dbinom(y, size = 3, prob = 0.3),
    cumul_prob = pbinom(y, size = 3, prob = 0.3)
  )


D_three_tasks %>%
  ggplot(aes(x = outcome, y = probability)) +
  geom_col(fill = 1) +
```

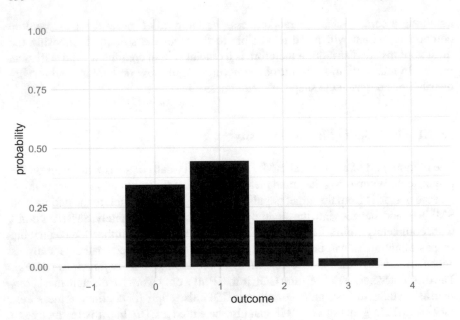

Fig. 3.18 Binomial distributions

```
ylim(0, 1) +
theme(legend.position = "none")
```

As we can see, there exist four possible outcomes for a sequence of three tasks: zero, one, two and three tasks correct. We also see that the most likely outcome is one correct task, which occurs with a probability of $P(y = 1) = 0.441$. At the same time, it is surprisingly likely to fail at all tasks, $P(y = 0) = 0.343$. We may also look at *combined events*, say the probability for less than two correct. That is precisely the sum $P(y \leq 1) = P(y = 0) + P(y = 1) = 0.784$. We can bundle basic events by adding up the probabilities. An extreme case of that is the universal event that includes all possible outcomes. You can say with absolute certainty that the outcome is, indeed, within zero and three, and certainty means the probability is 1, or $P(0 \leq y \leq 3) = 1$. Simply in order to comply with the third Kolmogorov axiom, all PMFs have *probability mass of One*. More precisely, the area covered by the function must be exactly One. Another extreme outcome is that four out of three tasks are correct, which is impossible, or $P(y > 3) = 0$.

The number of successes is a countable measure and is therefore called *discrete*. If we want to obtain the probability of combined events, we just have to sum probabilities over all the included events, which is like stacking the blocks in the figure above. This approach fails if the outcome is not discrete, but *continuous*. On a continuous scale, every outcome is a one-dimensional line, in the strictly geometrical sense. Because it has an area of zero, the probability mass of any such point is zero.

For example, the probability that the outcome of a continuous measure is *exactly* 42.18 is zero.

When the measure is continuous, rather than discrete, we cannot assign non-zero probabilities to exact outcomes. But, we can give non-zero probabilities to *ranges of outcome*. Consider the distribution of intelligence quotients (IQ) scores. Strictly spoken, the IQ is not continuous, but for instructional reasons, let us assume it was and we can give the IQ with arbitrary precision, for example 115.0, 100.00010... or $\pi * 20$..

IQ scores are often *designed to follow the Gaussian* distribution with a mean of 100 and a standard error of 15, as shown in (Fig. 3.19).

```
D_IQ <- tibble(
  IQ = 0:2000 / 10,
  density = dnorm(IQ, 100, 15),
  cdf = pnorm(IQ, 100, 15),
  SE = (IQ > 85) * (IQ <= 115) * density,
  around_100 = (IQ >= 99) * (IQ <= 101) * density,
  PDF_85 = (IQ < 85) * density,
  PDF_115 = (TQ < 115) * density,
  label = str_c("P(IQ < ", IQ, ")")
)


D_IQ %>%
  ggplot(aes(x = IQ, y = density)) +
  geom_area(fill = NA, color = 1) +
  geom_vline(aes(xintercept = 100, color = "Prob(IQ = 100.00) = 0")) +
  labs(color = NULL) +
  geom_area(fill = NA)
```

We observe that the most likely IQ is 100 and that almost nobody reaches scores higher than 150 or lower than 50. But, how likely is it to have an IQ of exactly 100? The answer is Zero. With continuous measures, we can no longer think in blocks that have a certain area. In fact, the probability of having an IQ of *exactly* 100.00...0 is exactly zero. That is why continuous outcome variables cannot be stated to have a PMF, but a *probability density distribution (PDF)*. In the example of the above Gaussian distribution, we can still identify the point of highest density (IQ = 100), but the density scale is *not probabilities*. What CDFs share with PDFs is that the area under the curve is always exactly One. In addition, probabilities still arise from density when taking intervals of values, which is nothing but combined events. Before we return to that, another way of specifying statistical distributions must be introduced.

A cumulative distribution function is the *integral* of a PDF or CDF. *Cumulative distribution functions (CDFs)* render how probability mass increases when moving steadily from left to right over the outcome scale. Because probability and density are non-negative, a CDF always is *monotonously increasing*. In Fig. 3.20, we see the CDF of the three-tasks situation. The function starts at Zero, then moves upward in increments and reaches One at the right end of the scale.

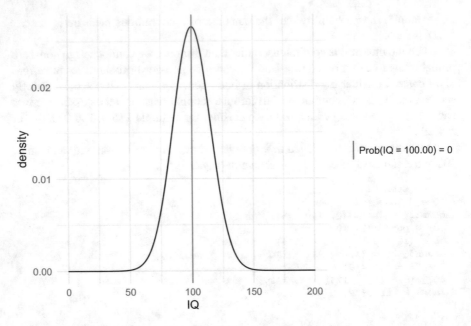

Fig. 3.19 Gaussian distribution of hypothetical IQ scores

```
D_three_tasks %>%
  ggplot(aes(x = y, y = cumul_prob)) +
  geom_step() +
  ylim(0, 1) +
  xlim(0, 4)
```

Using the CDF, the probability for any outcome to be in a certain range can be written as the difference between the upper and the lower limit of cumulative probability. For example, the probability of having zero or one task correct is

$P(\text{correct} \leq 1) = \text{CDF}_{Binom}(x = 2, k = 3, p = 0.3)$

or

```
pbinom(1, 3, 0.3)
```

```
## [1] 0.784
```

On the PDF, we calculated the probability of combined events by summing. With the PDF, we can calculate the probability for any range by subtracting the lower limit from the upper limit. The probability of more than one tasks correct is

$P(\text{correct} \geq 2) = \text{CDF}_{Binom}(x = 3, k = 3, p = 0.3) - \text{CDF}_{Binom}(x = 1, k = 3, p = 0.3)$

```
pbinom(3, 3, 0.3) - pbinom(1, 3, 0.3)
```

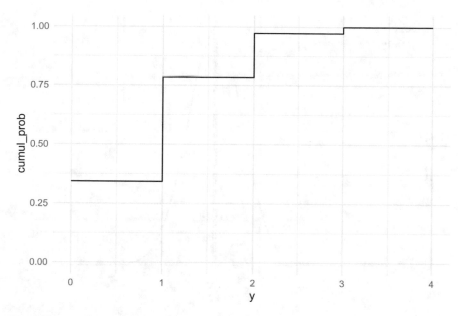

Fig. 3.20 The CDF of a discrete outcome is a step function

```
## [1] 0.216
```

With this method, we can also treat PDFs and obtain probabilities for intervals of values. Practically, nobody is really interested in infinite precision, anyhow. When asking *"what is the probability of IQ = 100?"*, the answer is *"zero"*, but what was really meant was: *"what is the probability of an IQ in a close interval around 100?"*. Once we speak of intervals, we clearly have areas larger than zero. Figure 3.21 shows the area in the range from 99 to 101.

```
D_IQ %>%
  ggplot(aes(x = IQ, y = density)) +
  geom_line() +
  geom_area(aes(y = around_100))
```

The size of the area is precisely the probability of such an event (IQ between 85 and 115). But, how large is this area exactly? As the distribution is curved, we can no longer simply stack virtual blocks. It is the CDF giving us the probability mass up to a certain value, i.e. the area under the curve up to a point. Continuous distributions have CDFs, too, and Fig. 3.22 shows the CDF for the IQs. We observe how the curve starts to rise from zero at around 50, has its steepest point at 100, just to slow down and run against 1.

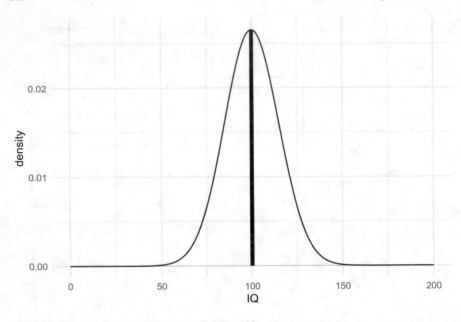

Fig. 3.21 The area around 100 has a small, but positive mass

```
D_IQ %>%
  ggplot(aes(x = IQ, y = cdf)) +
  geom_line(size = 2) +
  geom_step(
    data = filter(
      D_IQ,
      IQ %in% c(0, 85, 115, 200)
    ),
    color = "red"
  ) +
  geom_label(
    data = filter(
      D_IQ,
      IQ %in% c(0, 85, 115, 200)
    ),
    aes(label = label),
    color = "red",
    hjust = "left"
  ) +
  xlim(0, 250)
```

Underneath the smooth CDF, a discrete probability function reduces the continuum into three horizontal intervals, that have a certain total height associated, as well

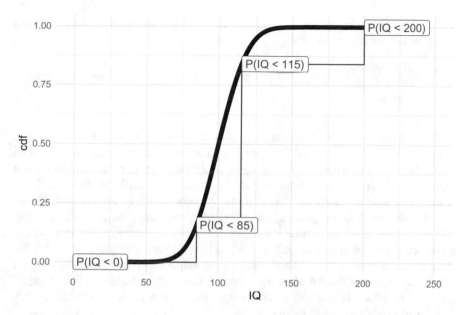

Fig. 3.22 Continuous distributions have smooth cumulative functions, which can be reduced to a step function

as a stepsize. The height is the total probability up to this point, whereas stepsize is the probability for an IQ measure to fall within an interval. By dividing the full range into steps, we can assign probabilities to intervals of values, by simple subtractions on the CDF:

$$
\begin{aligned}
CDF(IQ \geq 99) &= 0.473 \\
CDF(IQ \leq 101) &= 0.527 \\
CDF(99 \leq IQ \leq 101) &= P(IQ \leq 101) - P(IQ \leq 99) \\
&= 0.683
\end{aligned}
$$

To summarize, a probability density function (PDF) is a function that covers an area of exactly One. A probability mass function (PDF) is a discrete density function, where the area is composed of discrete blocks. A PDF has the special property to return plain probabilities at any given point. With continuous measures, this does not work. By using the CDF, we can extract probabilities of intervals of values.

3.5.2.2   Features of Shape

Density distributions can take a variety of shapes. Most distributions are shaped as one hill, like the two distributions covered in the previous section. This means that there is just one maximum point of density and is called a *unimodal* function. Besides discreteness or continuity, as covered in the previous section, unimodal distributions can have several other features:

1. Range of support.
2. Location on the x-axis.
3. Dispersion.
4. Skew.

In this book, I advocate the thoughtful choice of density distributions rather than doing batteries of goodness-of-fit to confirm that one of them, often the Gaussian, is an adequate approximation. It usually is straightforward to determine whether a measure is discrete (like everything that is counted) or (quasi)continuous and that is the most salient feature of distributions. A second, nearly as obvious, feature of any measure is its range. Practically, all physical measures, such as duration, size or temperature have natural lower bounds, which typically results in scales of measurement which are non-negative. Counts have a lower boundary, too (zero), but there can be a known upper bound, such as the number of trials. *Range of support* will be an important feature when we approach Generalized Linear Models Chap. 7 and is covered there in more detail. For now, it suffices to say that all standard density distributions fall into one of three classes:

1. *Unbound* distributions range from minus to plus infinity and are suitable for measures that are practically unbound. One example is using the Gaussian distributions for IQ scores.
2. Distributions *bound at zero* cover the range from zero up to plus infinity. It is suitable for measures that have a natural lower boundary (of zero) and no upper boundary for practical reasons. An example is the number of errors during the execution of a complex task.
3. *Double-bound* distributions have a lower and an upper limit. Typically the lower limit is zero. An example is the distribution of task success that we saw in the previous section.

Location of a distribution is the most important feature for almost all statistical models covered later in this book. When we say: "Time-on-task increases by 1.5 s per year of age", this translates into a shift on the x-axis. The mean of the ToT distribution is 90 for a 30-year old, 91.5 for a 31-year old and 120 for a 50-year-old person. When an experimenter asks for the difference between two designs in ToT, this is purely about location. In the class of models covered in this book, location is always indicated by the arithmetic mean. Still, it can theoretically also be represented by the median or the mode (in the case of unimodality). Figure 3.23 shows three Gaussian distributions shifted in location.

```
tibble(location = c(90, 91.5, 120), sd = 10) %>%
  ggplot(aes(x = location)) +
  stat_function(
    fun = dnorm,
    args = list(mean = 90, sd = 10),
```

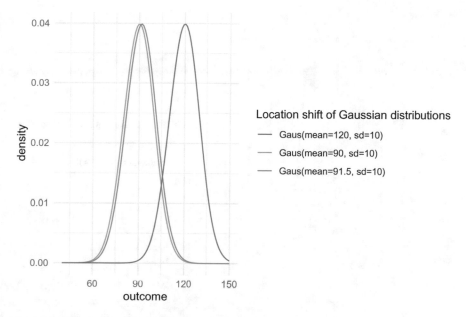

Fig. 3.23 Three location-shifted Gaussian distributions

```
  mapping = aes(colour = "Gaus(mean=90, sd=10)")
) +
stat_function(
  fun = dnorm,
  args = list(mean = 91.5, sd = 10),
  mapping = aes(colour = "Gaus(mean=91.5, sd=10)")
) +
stat_function(
  fun = dnorm,
  args = list(mean = 120, sd = 10),
  mapping = aes(colour = "Gaus(mean=120, sd=10)")
) +
xlim(40, 150) +
labs(
  colour = "Location shift of Gaussian distributions",
  x = "outcome", y = "density"
)
```

Dispersion represents the level of *variation* around the center of the distribution. In Gaussian distributions, this is given by the standard deviation (or variance). The most significant impact of dispersion is that spreading out a distribution reduces its overall density at any point. In unimodal distributions, we can think of the mode as the most typical value, the one you should place your bet on. With more variance,

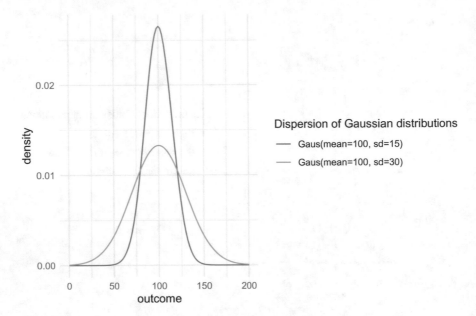

Fig. 3.24 Two Gaussian distributions with different variance

the density at this point is reduced, and you should not bet too hard on it anymore. IQ measures usually have a mode at a value of 100, with a standard deviation of 15. The density of a usual IQ distribution at an IQ of 100 is 0.027. If IQs had a standard deviation of 30, the density at 100 would be reduced to 0.013. If you were in the game to guess an unfamiliar person's IQ, in both cases, 100 would be the best guess, but you had a considerable higher chance of being right, when variance is low (Fig. 3.24).

```
tibble(location = 100) %>%
  ggplot(aes(x = location)) +
  stat_function(
    fun = dnorm,
    args = list(mean = 100, sd = 15),
    mapping = aes(colour = "Gaus(mean=100, sd=15)")
  ) +
  stat_function(
    fun = dnorm,
    args = list(mean = 100, sd = 30),
    mapping = aes(colour = "Gaus(mean=100, sd=30)")
  ) +
  xlim(0, 200) +
  labs(
    colour = "Dispersion of Gaussian distributions",
```

```
  x = "outcome", y = "density"
)
```

Large location shifts (between experimental conditions) are usually a delight for researchers, as most often research questions are about location changes. In contrast, large dispersion is often associated with uncertainty (or imperfect measures). In Gaussian models, this uncertainty or error is directly represented as the standard deviation of residuals, also called the *standard error*. We will re-encounter this idea when turning to model criticism 8.1.

Dispersion also plays a role as a measure for *variation within a population*, such as the differences in IQ. This is most prominent in psychometric situations, where we want to discern between individuals. A psychometric tool, such as the IQ test, must produce dispersion, otherwise, it would not discern between individuals. We will re-encounter this idea when turning to multi-level models 6.

Most distributions routinely used in statistics have one or two parameters. Generally, if there is one parameter, this determines both, location and dispersion, with Poisson distributions being one example. Two-parameter distributions can vary location and dispersion, to some extent. However, for most distributions, both parameters are tied to location and dispersion, simultaneously, and in sometimes convoluted ways. The Gaussian distribution is a special case as parameter μ purely does location, whereas σ is just dispersion.

As was said above, most statistical models use the mean of distribution to render differences between situations. The mean is but one measure of central tendency, with the median and the model being alternatives. If a distribution is symmetric, such as Gaussian distributions, these three parameters are the same. The mean divides the distribution into two areas of the same size, and it is the point of highest density. The Gaussian distribution owes its symmetry to the fact that it has the same range of support in both directions, looking from the mean of the distribution. That is different for zero-bound distributions, which run to plus infinity to the right, but hit a hard limit to the left. These distributions are asymmetric, which typically means that the left side runs steeper than the right side. Such distributions are called to be left-skewed. An example is the Poisson distribution, which will be covered in more detail below. Double-bound distributions, such as Binomial distributions or *Beta distributions* (see Fig. 3.25), can also be right-skewed, when the mean of the distribution is approaching the right boundary. When moving the mean from left to right, the distribution starts left-skewed, takes a symmetric form in the center of the range and then continues with increasing right skew. The following illustration shows that for the Beta distribution, which has a range of support between (not including) Zero and One. At the same time, this illustration conveys another important relationship between features of shape: a distribution that approaches a boundary also is less dispersed.

```
tibble(location = c(0.25, 0.5, 0.75)) %>%
  ggplot(aes(x = location)) +
  stat_function(
    fun = dbeta,
    args = list(shape1 = 2, shape2 = 8),
    mapping = aes(colour = ''Beta(mean = 0.25)''))
```

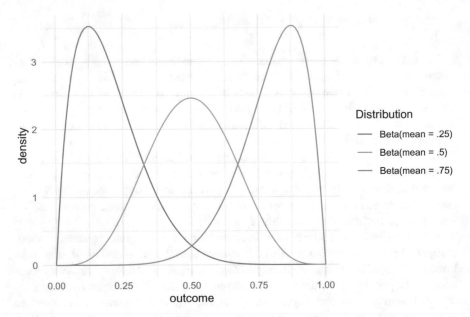

Fig. 3.25 Beta distributions have smaller variance when approaching either boundary

```
) +
stat_function(
   fun = dbeta,
   args = list(shape1 = 5, shape2 = 5),
   mapping = aes(colour = ``Beta(mean = 0.5)'')
) +
stat_function(
   fun = dbeta,
   args = list(shape1 = 8, shape2 = 2),
   mapping = aes(colour = ``Beta(mean = 0.75)'')
) +
xlim(0, 1) +
labs(colour = "Distribution", x = "outcome", y = "density")
```

A common problem in statistical modeling is using a symmetric distribution, in particular the Gaussian, when the distribution really is highly skewed. This will be treated in more depth in Chap. 7.

Many dozens of distribution functions are known in statistical science and are candidates to choose from. In the first orientation, our choice can ground on obvious characteristics of measures, such as discrete/continuous or range, but that is sometimes not sufficient. For example, the pattern of randomness in three tasks falls into a binomial distribution only, when all trials have the same chance of success. If the tasks are very similar in content and structure, learning is likely to happen and the chance of success differs between trials. Using the binomial distribution when chances are not constant leads to mistaken statistical models.

For most distributions, strict mathematical descriptions exist for under which circumstances randomness takes this particular shape. Frequently, there are one or more natural phenomena that accurately fall into this pattern, such as the number of radioactive isotope cores decaying in a certain interval (Poisson distributed) or the travel of a particle under Brownian motion (Gaussian). This is particularly the case for the canonical four random distributions that follow: Poisson, Binomial, Exponential and Gaussian. My goal here is not to bother anyone with formalism, but to introduce my readers to think about distributions as arising from data-generating processes.

3.5.2.3 Binomial Distributions

A very basic performance variable in design research is task success. Think of devices in high-risk situations such as medical infusion pumps in surgery. These devices are remarkably simple, giving medication at a certain rate into the bloodstream for a given time. Yet, they are operated by humans under high pressure and must therefore be extremely error-proof in handling. Imagine, the European government would set up a law that manufacturers of medical infusion pump must prove a 90% error-free operation in routine tasks. A possible validation study could be as follows: a sample of $N = 30$ experienced nurses are invited to a testing lab and asked to complete ten standard tasks with the device. The number of error-free task completions per nurse is the recorded performance variable to validate the 90% claim. Under somewhat idealized conditions, namely that all nurses have the same proficiency with the device and all tasks have the success chance of 90%, the outcome follows a *Binomial distribution* and the results could look like Fig. 3.26.

```
set.seed(1)
```

```
tibble(succs = rbinom(30, 10, 0.9)) %>%
  ggplot(aes(x = succs)) +
  geom_histogram(binwidth = 1) +
  scale_x_continuous(breaks = 0:10, limits = c(0, 11))
```

Speaking about the Binomial distribution in terms of *successes in a number of attempts* is common. As a matter of fact, *any* binary classification of outcomes is amenable for Binomial modeling, like on/off, red/blue and male/female.

An example in web design research is the rate of visitor return, resulting in a variable, that has two possible outcomes:: 0 for one-timers and 1 for returners. This is in fact a special case of the Binomial distribution with $k = 1$ attempts (the first visit is not counted) and is also called *Bernoulli distribution* (Fig. 3.27, top row).

```
mascutils::expand_grid(
  k = c(1, 10, 20),
  p = c(0.2, 0.5, 0.9),
  succs = 0:20
) %>%
```

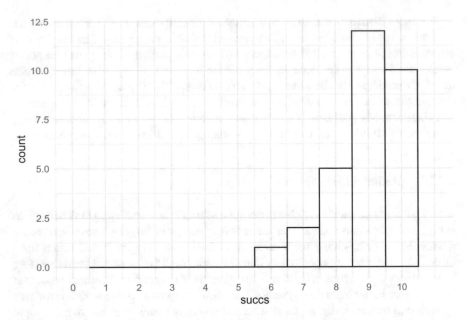

Fig. 3.26 Successes in a set of equal tasks follow a Binomial distribution

```
mutate(probability = dbinom(succs, k, p)) %>%
ggplot(aes(x = succs, y = probability)) +
geom_step() +
facet_grid(k ~ p) +
labs(x = "number of successes")
```

Binomial distributions have two parameters: p is the chance of success and k is the number of attempts. p is a probability and therefore can take values in the range from zero to one. The probability of success determines the location of distribution in that. With larger p, the distribution moves to the right. The mean of Binomial distributions is the probability scaled by the number of attempts, Mean $= kp$. Logically, there cannot be more successes than k, but with larger k, the distribution gets wider, where the variance is the odds scaled by the number of attempts, Var $= kp(1 - p)$. As mean and variance depend on the exact same parameters, they cannot be set independently. In fact, the relation is parabolic, so that variance is largest at $p = 0.5$, but decreases toward both boundaries. A Binomial distribution with say $k = 10$ and $p = 0.4$ always has mean 4 and variance 2.4. This means, in turn, that an outcome with a mean of 4 and a variance of 3 is not Binomially distributed. This occurs frequently when the success rate is not identical across trials. A common solution is to use plugin distributions, where the parameter p itself is distributed, rather than fixed. A common distribution for p is the *beta* distribution and the *logit-normal* distribution is an alternative.

The Binomial distribution has two boundaries, zero below and the number of attempts k above. Hence, Binomial distributions also require that there is a clearly

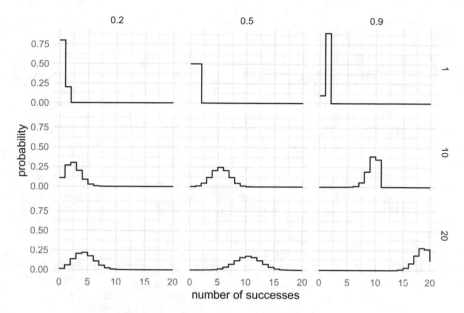

Fig. 3.27 Binomial distributions

defined number of attempts. For example, the number of times a customer returns to a website does not have a natural interpretation of the number of attempts, because attempts can happen at any moment. Literally, every single moment is an opportunity to go online and hire a car, even many times a day, if you are a holiday planner. At the same time, for a typical customer, the per-day chance to hire a car is minuscule. Under these conditions, we get an infinite number of attempts, or a really large at least, say $k = 365$ days. At the same time, the rate is very small, e.g. $p = 1.5/365$ (Fig. 3.28).

```
set.seed(42)
tibble(rentals_per_year = rbinom(1000,
  size = 365,
  prob = 1.5 / 365
)) %>%
  ggplot(aes(x = rentals_per_year)) +
  geom_histogram()
```

This is a workable solution to display the number of events per period, but it remains a little odd because the question really is about events per timespan, not success per attempt. When events per timespan are the question, the process is better covered by the *Poisson distributions*.

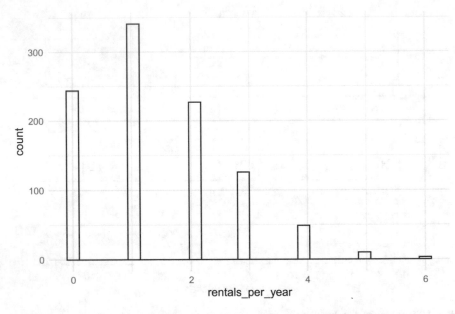

Fig. 3.28 Binomial distribution with a very small p and a very large number of attempts

3.5.2.4   Poisson Distributions

Poisson distributions can mathematically be derived from Binomial distributions with a very small probability of success with infinite attempts. This implies that Poisson distributions have no upper limit. In design research, a number of measures have no clearly defined upper limit:

- Number of erroneous actions.
- Frequency of returns.
- Behavioral events, e.g. showing exploratory behavior.
- Physiological events, such as the number of peaks in galvanic skin response.

These measures can often be modeled as *Poisson distributed*. A useful way to think of unbound counts is that they can happen at every moment, but with a very small chance. Think of a longer interaction sequence of a user with a system, where errors are recorded. It can be conceived as an almost infinite number of opportunities to err, with a very small chance of something to happen.

Poisson distributions possess only one parameter λ (lambda), that is strictly positive and determines mean and variance of the distribution alike: $\lambda = \text{Mean} = \text{Var}$ (Fig. 3.29). As a result, distributions farther from Zero are always more dispersed. Because Poisson distributions have a lower boundary, they are *asymmetric*, with the left tail always being steeper. Higher λs push the distribution away from the boundary and the skew diminishes. Poisson distributions with a large mean can therefore be approximated by Gaussian distributions:

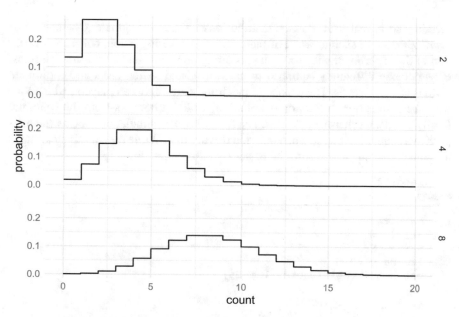

Fig. 3.29 Poisson distributions

$$Y \sim \text{Pois}(\lambda) \Rightarrow Y \overset{.}{\sim} \text{Gaus}(\mu = \lambda, \sigma = \sqrt{\lambda})$$

```
mascutils::expand_grid(
  lambda = c(2, 4, 8),
  count = 0:20
) %>%
  mutate(probability = dpois(count, lambda)) %>%
  ggplot(aes(x = count, y = probability)) +
  geom_step() +
  facet_grid(lambda ~ .)
```

For an illustration, consider a video game, *subway surfers*, where the player jumps and runs a little blue avatar on the roof of a train and catches items passing by. Many items have been placed into the game, but catching a single one is very difficult. The developers are aware that a too low success rate would demotivate players as much as when the game is made too easy. In this experiment, only one player is recorded, and in wonderful ways, this player never suffers from fatigue or is getting better with training. The player plays 100 times and records the catches after every run. In this idealized situation, the distribution of catches would, approximately, follow a Poisson distribution.

Because mean and variance are tightly linked, only a certain amount of random-ness can be contained at a location. If there is more randomness, and that is almost certainly so in real data, Poisson distributions are not appropriate. One speaks of *overdispersion* in such a case. For understanding overdispersion, consider a variation of the experiment with 1000 players doing one game and less restrictive rules. Players come differently equipped to perform visual search tasks and coordinate actions at high speeds. The chance of catching varies between players, which violates the assumption of Poisson distribution, which it borrows from the Binomial family, a constant chance of success. The following data simulation shows what happens to a count distribution when individuals vary in λ. While the overall mean stays the same, variation in measures increases (Fig. 3.30).

```
set.seed(42)
N_obs <- 200

D_single <-
  tibble(
    Part = 1,
    lambda = 20,
    catches = rpois(N_obs, lambda)
  )


D_multi <-
  tibble(
    Part = c(1:N_obs) + 1,
    part_variation = log(rnorm(N_obs, 0, 5)),
    lambda = 20,
    catches = rpois(N_obs, lambda * part_variation)
  )

grid.arrange(
  qplot(D_single$catches,
    xlab = "Catches of single participant, constant lambda",
    xlim = c(0, 100)
  ),
  qplot(D_multi$catches,
    xlab = "Catches of multiple participants, varying lambda",
    xlim = c(0, 100)
  )
)
```

Another area for trouble can be Poisson distributions' lower boundary of exactly Zero. Often this works well, a person can perform a sequence with no errors, catch zero items or have no friends on social media. But, you cannot complete an interaction sequence in zero steps, have a conversation with less than two statements or be a customer with zero customer contacts. If the lower bound is obvious, such as the minimum necessary steps to complete a task. In such a case, a count that starts at zero can be created easily:

$$\text{additional steps} = \text{steps} - \text{neccessary steps}$$

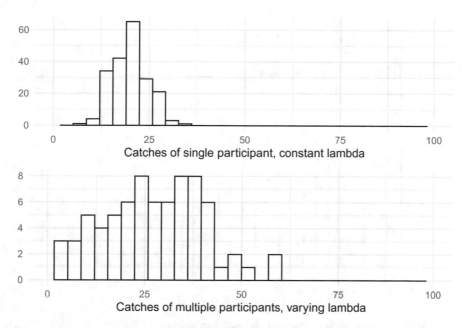

Fig. 3.30 When lambda varies, the distribution becomes overdispersed

Another frequent problem at the lower bound is zero-inflation. In traffic research, the frequency of going by bus can be an interesting variable to measure acceptance of public transport. If we would make such a survey, e.g. "How many times have you taken the bus the last seven days?", it is not unlikely, that we get a distribution like in Fig. 3.31.

```
tibble(
  uses_public_transport = rbernoulli(1000, 0.8),
  bus_rides = rpois(1000, uses_public_transport * 4)
) %>%
  ggplot(aes(x = bus_rides)) +
  geom_histogram()
```

In this scenario, the population is not homogenous but falls into two classes, those who use public transport and those who just never do. The result is a *zero-inflated* distribution. A way to deal with this is using hurdle models, which are called as such, because you first have to jump over the hurdle to use public transport, before you are in the game.

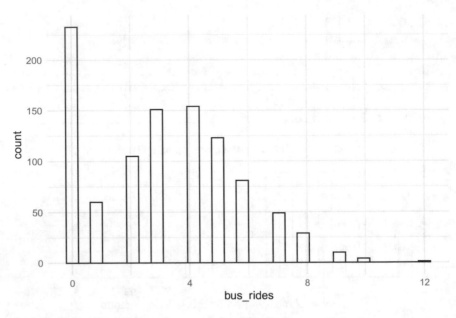

Fig. 3.31 Hidden classes can produce zero-inflated distribution

3.5.2.5 Exponential Distribution

Exponential distributions apply for measures of duration. Exponential distributions have the same generating process as Poisson distributions, except, that the *duration between events to happen* is the variable of interest, rather than the number of events in a given time. Under the idealized conditions of a Subway Surfers player with constant ability to catch items, the duration between any two catches is exponentially distributed.

Just like Poisson distributions, Exponential distributions have one parameter, called rate and frequently written as λ. Figure 3.32 illustrates Exponential distributions with varying rates.

```
ggplot(tibble(x = c(0, 20)), aes(x = x)) +
  stat_function(
    fun = dexp,
    args = list(rate = 1 / 2),
    mapping = aes(colour = "Exp(1/2)")
  ) +
  stat_function(
    fun = dexp,
    args = list(rate = 1 / 4),
    mapping = aes(colour = "Exp(1/4)")
  ) +
```

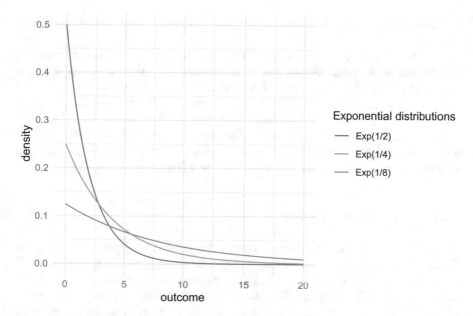

Fig. 3.32 Exponential distributions

```
stat_function(
  fun = dexp,
  args = list(rate = 1 / 8),
  mapping = aes(colour = "Exp(1/8)")
) +
labs(
  colour = "Exponential distributions",
  x = "outcome", y = "density"
)
```

Durations are common measures in design research, most importantly, time-on-task and reaction time. Unfortunately, the exponential distribution is a poor approximation of the random pattern found in duration measures. That is for three reasons: first, Exponential distributions have just one parameter, which means that mean and variance are tightly linked as Mean $= 1/\lambda$ and Var $= 1/\lambda^2$. Like with Poisson distributions, this does not allow extra variance, e.g. between participants. Second, the distribution always starts at zero, whereas human reactions always require some basic processing, and be this just the velocity of signals traveling in nerve cells, which is far below the speed of sound (in air). And third, the exponential process has one special property, which is called *memoryless-ness*. That basically means that the probability for an event to happen is completely independent of how long one has been waiting for it. In basic physical systems, like nucleus decay, this is truly the case. But, if a person works on a task, the chance of task completion usually increases when time progresses.

The one thing that Exponential distributions are getting right about durations (in contrast to the frequently employed Gaussian distribution) is the asymmetry. Durations have a lower boundary and that will always produce some skew. For the stated reasons, pure exponential distributions themselves are rarely used in statistical modeling, but two- and three-parameter distributions, like Gamma or Exponential-Gaussian, are extensions of Exponential distributions. Gamma distributions provide a scale parameter for incorporating extra variance, whereas Exponential-Gaussian distributions can be used when the lower boundary is not zero, but positive 7.3.

3.5.2.6   Gaussian Distributions

The best known distributions are *Gaussian distributions* or *Normal distributions*. These distributions arise mathematically under the assumption of a myriad of small unmeasured forces (SMURF) pushing performance (or any other outcome) up or down. As SMURFs work in all directions independently, their effects often average out and the majority of observations stay clumped together in the center, more or less. The physical process associated with Gaussian distribution is Brownian motion, the movement of small particles caused by bumping into molecules of warm fluid. Imagine, you are standing blind-folded in the middle of a tunnel, which is frequented by blind-folded passengers moving uncoordinated in both directions of the tunnel. Passengers will randomly bump into you from both directions, and this pushes you sometimes forward, sometimes backward. The total travel caused by many of these small pushes is approximately Gaussian distributed. By tendency, the small pushes cancel each other out, such that the most likely position after say 100 bumps will be close to where you started (Zero). When this experiment is repeated very often, a Gaussian distribution arises, as in Fig. 3.33

```
set.seed(2)

rtravel <- function(n, bumps = 100) {
  map_int(1:n, function(x) as.integer(sum(sample(c(-1, 1), x, replace = T))))
}

D_Tunnel <-
  tibble(
    Part = 1:1000,
    travel = rtravel(n = 1000)
  )
D_Tunnel %>%
  ggplot(aes(x = travel)) +
  geom_histogram(stat = "density")
```

Gaussian distributions take two parameters: μ marks the location of the mean of the distribution (Fig. 3.34). Because distributions are symmetric, the mean coincides with the median and mode of the distribution. The second parameter σ represents the dispersion of the random pattern. When randomness is pronounced, the center of the distribution gets less mass assigned, as the tails get thicker (Fig. 3.34). Different

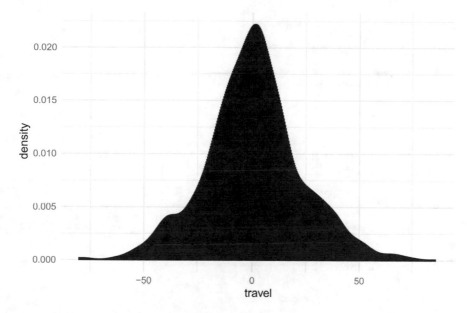

Fig. 3.33 Gaussian distribution emerging from travel by bumps

from Poisson and Binomial distributions, the mean and variance of the distribution can be set independently and therefore overdispersion is never an issue.

```
ggplot(tibble(x = c(-4, 4)), aes(x = x)) +
  stat_function(
    fun = dnorm,
    args = list(mean = 0, sd = 1),
    mapping = aes(colour = "Gaus(0, 1)")
  ) +
  stat_function(
    fun = dnorm,
    args = list(mean = -1.5, sd = 0.5),
    mapping = aes(colour = "Gaus(-1.5, 0.5)")
  ) +
  stat_function(
    fun = dnorm,
    args = list(mean = 0.5, sd = 2),
    mapping = aes(colour = "Gaus(0.5,1.5)")
  ) +
  labs(
    colour = "Gaussian distributions",
    x = "outcome", y = "density"
  )
```

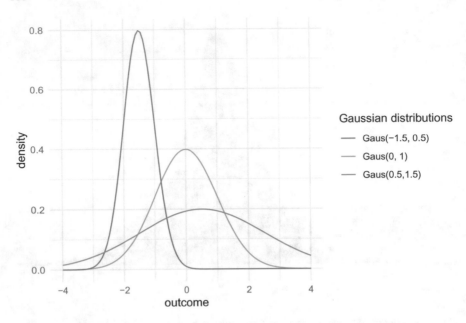

Fig. 3.34 Gaussian distributions

As illustrated by the Tunnel example, Gaussian distributions have the most compelling interpretation of summarizing the effect of SMURFs. Therefore, they are useful to capture randomness in a broad class of regression models and other statistical approaches.

The Gaussian distribution is called "normal" because people normally use it. For many decades, it was the standard distribution to tackle almost every statistical problem. That is so because statistical models with Gaussian shape of randomness can be computed very efficiently. Indeed, Gaussian distributions are often good approximations, which goes back to the *central limit theorem*. Basically, this theorem proves what we have passingly observed at binomial and Poisson distributions: the more they move to the right, the more symmetric they get. The central limit theorem proves that, in the long run, a wide range of distributions are indistinguishable from the Gaussian distribution. But, the keyword is *in the long run*. As a general rule, Gaussian distributions approximate other distributions well when the majority of measures stay far from the natural boundaries. That is the case in experiments with very many attempts and moderate chances (e.g. signal detection experiments) when counts are in the high numbers (number of clicks in a complex task) or with long durations and little variance in duration. However, in the remainder of this book, especially in Chap. 7, we will encounter numerous real data sets where the Gaussian distribution is not a good approximation. Gaussian models may be convenient to set up and interpret, but strictly speaking, a Gaussian model is always wrong. And that is for one particular reason: Gaussian distributions are unbound, but there is not a single measure in any scientific discipline that really has no limits.

These rules are no guarantee and careful model criticism is essential. We will return to this issue in Sect. 8.1.

Nowadays, computing power has evolved to a point where efficient approximations are less needed. Especially with the advent of Bayesian modeling, statistical users have a plethora of distributions to choose from, and we will see more of them when Generalized Linear Models are introduced Chap. 7. Most of the time, choosing an appropriate shape for randomness is straightforward, and doing so makes a model less prone to criticism Sect. 8.1.

3.6 Toward Bayesian Estimation

Frequentist statistics falls short of recognizing that research is incremental. Bayesian statistics embraces the idea of a gradual increase in certainty when new data arrives. Why has Bayesian statistics not been broadly adopted earlier? The reason is that Bayesian estimation was computationally infeasible for many decades. In practice, the innocent multiplication of prior probability and the likelihood of Bayes becomes a multiplication of two density distributions, which results in complex integrals, which in most cases have no analytic solution. If you have enjoyed a classic statistics education, you may recall how the computation of an ANOVA could be carried out on paper and pencil in a reasonable time (e.g. during an exam). And that is precisely how statistical computations have been performed before the advent of electronic computing machinery. In the frequentist statistical framework, ingenious mathematicians have developed procedures that were rather efficient to compute. That made statistical data analysis possible in those times.

Expensive computation is in the past. Modern computers can simulate realistic worlds in real time and the complex integrals in Bayesian statistics they solve hands down. When analytic solutions do not exist, the integrals can still be solved using numerical procedures. Numerical procedures have been used in frequentist statistics, too, for example the iterative least-squares algorithm applies for Generalized Linear Models, Newton-Rapson optimizer can be used to find the maximum likelihood estimate and bootstrapping produces accurate confidence limits. However, these procedures are too limited as they fail for highly multidimensional problems as they are common in advanced regression models.

Today, more and more researchers leave frequentist statistics alone and enter the world of Bayesian Statistics. Partly, this may be due to the replicability crisis of 2015, which has shown that, in general, behavioral researchers are not capable of carrying out frequentist statistics, correctly. As a result, the incorrect use of null hypothesis testing and p-values has fully undermined the discipline of Psychology and that may just be the tip of the iceberg.

I assume that the majority of researchers, who started using Bayesian statistics, are just thrilled by the versatility of Bayesian estimation and its natural interpretation. To name just one example for the latter, Frequentist statisticians emphasize the randomness of sampling. It all goes by asking: how would an estimate change when we draw another sample? This is best seen by the definition of the frequentist *confidence interval*: "the confidence level represents the frequency (i.e. the proportion) of possible confidence intervals that contain the true value of the unknown population parameter." Interestingly, when asked about the definition, most researchers answer: "the range, in which the true value falls with a certainty of 95%." Ironically, this is precisely the definition of the Bayesian *credibility interval*. It seems that thinking of certainty by itself, not through frequencies, is more natural than a long series of imagined replications of the same experiment.

The other reason for Bayesian Statistics gaining ground is that today's implementations offer endless possibilities. In frequentist statistics, you would find an implementation for, say, linear models with a Beta shape of randomness Sect. 7.4.2. But, if your research design is multi-level, say for psychometric evaluation, you would be less lucky. You would find plenty of implementations for psychometrics, but none supports Beta distribution. With Bayesian implementations, that is the past. In Sect. 6.8, I will show how multi-level models can replace classic tools for psychometric data, and in Sect. 7.4.2, we use Beta distribution on that model and I will explain why this is the better choice. The greatest advantage is that all these possibilities are governed by just one implementation, the Brms engine, which even allows us to add custom distributions, like Beta-binomial distribution Sect. 7.2.3.2. The most astonishing fact is accomplished by a relatively simple algorithm, called Markov chain Monte Carlo sampling.

Most Bayesian estimation engines these days ground on a numerical procedure called *Markov chain Monte Carlo (MCMC)* sampling, which we will closely examine in Sect. 4.1.1. This method differs from the earlier mentioned in that it grounds on a random walk. The closest frequentist counterpart to MCMC is the bootstrapping algorithm, which draws many samples from data (how could it be different) and computes the estimates many times. Bayesian estimation with MCMC turns this upside down, by randomly drawing possible parameter values and computing the posterior probability many times. Similar to bootstrapping, the basic MCMC algorithm is so simple, it can be explained on half a page and implemented with 25 lines of code. Despite its simplicity, the MCMC algorithm is applicable to practically all statistical problems one can imagine. Being so simple and generic at the same time must come at some costs. The downside of MCMC sampling still is computing time. Models with little data and few variables, like the examples in Sect. 3.1, are estimated within a few seconds. Multi-level models, which we will encounter later in this book, can take hours and large psychometric models can take up to a few days of processing time.

The particular merit of the MCMC algorithm is that it not only delivers accurate point estimates in almost any situation, but it also produces the full *posterior probability distribution*. This lets us characterize a parameter's magnitude and degree of (un-)certainty. Let's run an analysis on the 20 rainfall observations to see how this happens.

```
attach(Rainfall)

M_1 <-
  Rain %>%
```

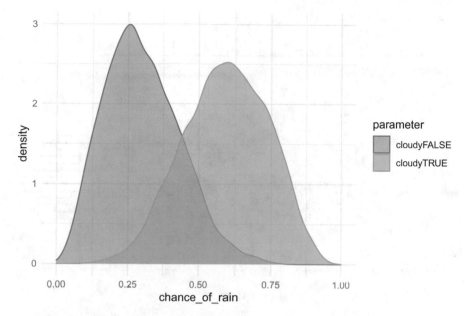

Fig. 3.35 Posterior distribution of two parameters

```
stan_glm(rain ~ cloudy - 1,
   family = binomial,
   data = .
)
```

What the estimation does is to calculate the *posterior distribution* from the observations. The *posterior distribution* contains the probability (more precisely, the *density*) for all possible values of the parameter in question. The following density plot
represents our belief about the parameter $P(rain|cloudy)$ after we have observed
twenty days (Fig. 3.35).

```
posterior(M_1) %>%
  filter(type == "fixef") %>%
  mutate(chance_of_rain = plogis(value)) %>%
  ggplot(aes(
    x = chance_of_rain,
    fill = parameter,
    col = parameter
  )) +
  geom_density(alpha = 0.5) +
  xlim(0, 1)
```

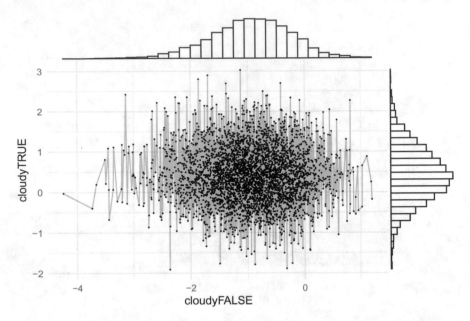

Fig. 3.36 Marginal posterior distributions emerging from a two-dimensional parameter space

From the posterior distribution, we can deduct all kinds of summary statistics, such as

1. The most likely value for a parameter in question is called the *posterior mode* and, when prior knowledge is absent, is the same as the frequentist *maximum likelihood estimate*.
2. The average of parameter values, weighted by their probability is called the *posterior mean*.
3. A defined range to express 95% (or any other level of) certainty is the *95% credibility interval*.

We can also pull non-standard summary statistics from the posterior distribution. For example, in Sect. 5.5.1, we will ask how valid a third-degree polynomial is for rendering the Uncanny Valley effect.

Coming back to MCMC random walk, how is the posterior distribution actually produced. The MCMC makes a particular type of random walk through parameter space, where more likely regions are visited more often. Basically, the posterior distribution is approximated by a frequency distribution of the visited values. See the random walk in action in the following figure! Note how the gray connecting lines show the jumps in the MCMC random walk and how the marginal frequency distributions emerge (Fig. 3.36).

```
G_mcmc <-
  posterior(M_1) %>%
  select(iter, chain, fixef, value) %>%
  spread(fixef, value) %>%
```

```
ggplot(aes(x = cloudyFALSE, y = cloudyTRUE)) +
geom_point(size = 0.1) +
geom_line(alpha = 0.3)
```

```
ggExtra::ggMarginal(G_mcmc, type = "histogram")
```

3.7 On Priors and Defaults

Bayesian priors are a wonderful idea. Who would not like to make the best of their knowledge? In the remainder of this book, I will *not* further introduce Bayesian priors and I owe you an explanation of how they can be used and why I don't use them. Let's first take a look at the continuum of certainty.

Like any knowledge, prior knowledge is certain to a degree. An example of *over-whelming prior* knowledge is an IQ score, which is designed to follow a Gaussian distribution with a mean of 100 and a standard deviation of 15. IQ scores are also designed to be non-discriminating. Rumors are that a certain professor unknowingly used such an IQ test to identify gender differences in intelligence. A Bayesian model with overwhelming priors will always return the prior itself.

Strong prior knowledge can exist in the form of earlier experiments. For example, the famous Stroop task is an experiment on human cognition that has been replicated hundreds of times. In the Stroop task, two conditions are mainly compared: the congruent and the incongruent conditions, and the experiment has been repeated so many times that we have a pretty good idea of typical reaction times. For example, someone could ask whether a certain deficit in cognitive functioning could be detected by the Stroop task. This seems like a clinical trial experiment with a diagnosed group versus the healthy control group. Because we have strong knowledge about the RT distribution in the population of young and healthy Psychology students, the experiment can effectively be reduced to only assess diagnosed participants.

Strong priors are the most useful because we need to collect less data. Strong priors are only available, when similar experiments have been conducted in the past and the results have been recorded, properly. In the domain of design research, repetition of rare experiments and any variation of circumstances can have significant effects. Design research simply is a *domain of weak prior knowledge*.

Weak prior knowledge is unspecific knowledge about effects. A certain experimentalist may not know the precise population average in the Stroop task, but would expect the majority RTs to be in the range 300–2000 ms. For the research question, this is rather useless information, but for the process of estimation, it is not. The MCMC algorithm is a random walk in a highly dimensional space and every little guidance is useful.

The use of priors is a complex task on its own. For one thing, priors are specified as distribution functions. When the MCMC algorithm dances its random walk on Experiment 1, the result is a frequency distribution, which can take any shape. In contrast, the result is *not* a distribution function. Before we can use the results of

Experiment 1 as priors for Experiment 2, we first have to identify the distribution. The knowledge required to do that in a correct way for the models presented in this book would fill a book on its own.

Still, there can be repetitions of the same experiment, leading to valuable prior knowledge. For example, the experiment on the Uncanny Valley effects, which I will present in Sect. 5.5, was our third replication of [3]. All four experiments, including the original, share most of the stimuli (robot faces), the experimental design (a three-way design-o-metric encounter Sect. 6.8.4) and the instrument of measurement (Eeriness ratings). The purpose of the fourth experiment was to estimate most precisely, at which point emotional reactions toward human-like faces take a plunge, the trough of the Uncanny Valley. From the first three experiments, we had a good approximation of where the trough is. That means we can and should use this information. The thing is I do not have to specify priors as I own the data of the previous two replications and I have a copy of the original data. With the methods described in this book, I can just merge the four data sets and run my model with full prior knowledge, circumventing the formal specification of priors.

Bayes' formula requires that there is a prior distribution. It can be totally flat, but it still is a distribution. Both regression engines used throughout this book allow user-specified priors for all parameters in a model. Unfortunately, the interface for doing that is anything but user-friendly. Fortunately, it seems that weak priors can effectively be automated. Rstanarm [4] and Brms [5] both run on the whole class of Generalized Linear Multi-level Models without user-specified priors. In personal communication, Paul Bürkner, author of the brms package, was confident that the weakly informative priors generated by his implementation are safe to use for the models presented in this book. Just a little less confident, the rstanarm package warns the user that priors have been automatically generated and that there is the possibility that running the model in a future version of the package may result in different results.

For the data and models at hand, I don't expect that future updates on the algorithm for prior specification will require me to update the conclusions I have drawn. It rather reflects that specification of priors is still an art. Even in more recent books, the recommendations for prior specification differ. When the warning message is gone, the time has come to write an artisan chapter on prior specification.

3.8   Further Readings

1. Giving priors an inferior role in this book was a pragmatic choice and this does not make me proud. For readers who want to pursue into this direction, I recommend

   a. Reference [6] for a start, who builds this topic from ground up and provides a user-friendly interface for the simultaneous specification of likelihood and prior.
   b. Reference [7] for the most explicit treatment of prior specification.

2. Readers who now feel that they thoroughly need to re-think Statistics [6], a book that truly deserves its title.
3. Reference [6] also provides a more in-depth, yet accessible, introduction to the theory of statistical distributions. He explains why the Normal distribution is called "Normal" and draws fascinating connections with Information Theory.
4. An extensive set of statistical distributions is cataloged in [7]. Another good source on this topic is Wikipedia List of Probability Distributions.
5. Reference [8] uses a phantastic metaphor to explain the MCMC algorithm.

References

1. Schnittker R et al (2016) Combining situated cognitive engineering with a novel testing method in a case study comparing two infusion pump interfaces. Appl Ergon 55:16–26. https://doi.org/10.1016/j.apergo.2016.01.004 July
2. Schmettow M, Noordzij ML, Mundt M (2013) CHI '13 extended abstracts on human factors in computing systems. ACM Press, New York. https://doi.org/10.1145/2468356.2468722
3. Mathur MB, Reichling DB (2016) Navigating a social world with robot partners: a quantitative cartography of the Uncanny Valley. Cognition 146:22–32. https://doi.org/10.1016/j.cognition.2015.09.008 Jan.
4. Goodrich B, et al (2020) rstanarm: bayesian applied regression modeling via Stan. R package version 2.21.1. https://mc-stan.org/rstanarm
5. Bürkner P-C (2017) brms: an r package for bayesian multilevel models using stan. J Stat Softw 80(1):1–28. https://doi.org/10.18637/jss.v080.i01
6. McElreath R (2018) Statistical rethinking. Chapman and Hall/CRC, Boca Raton. https://doi.org/10.1201/9781315372495
7. Gelman A, et al (2013) Bayesian data analysis. Chapman and Hall/CRC, Boca Raton. https://doi.org/10.1201/b16018
8. McElreath R (2020) Markov chain monte carlo, pp. 263–298. Chapman and Hall/CRC, Boca Raton. https://doi.org/10.1201/9780429029608-9

Part II
Models

Chapter 4
Basic Linear Models

Linear models answer the question of how one quantitative outcome, say ToT, decreases or increases, when a condition changes.

First, I will introduce the most basic LM. The grand mean model (GMM) produces just a single coefficient, the grand mean in the population. That can be useful when there exists an external standard to which the design must adhere to. In R, the GMM has a formula, like this: `ToT ~ 1`. At the example of the GMM, I describe some basic concepts of Bayesian linear models. On the practical side of things, CLU tables are introduced, which is one major workhorse to report our results.

The most obvious application of LM comes next: in linear regression models (LRM), a metric predictor (e.g. age) is linked to the outcome by a linear function, such as $f(x) = \beta_0 + \beta_1 x$. In R, this is: `ToT ~ 1 + age`. Below is a very practical section that explains how simple transformations can make the results of an estimation more clear. Correlations work in similar situations as LRMs, and it is good to know what the differences and how correlations are linked to linear slope parameters. I end this section with a warning: the assumption of linearity is limited to a straight line and this is violated not by some, but all possible data.

A very common type of research question is how an outcome changes under different conditions. In design research this is always the case, when designs are compared. Expressed as a formula, a *factorial model* looks just like an LRM: `ToT ~ 1 + Design`. The rest of the section is dedicated to the techniques that make it possible to put a qualitative variable into a linear equation. Understanding these techniques opens the door to making your own variants that exactly fit your purpose, such as when a factor is ordered and you think of it as a stairway, rather than treatments. Finally, we will see how ordered factor models can resolve non-linear relationships, as they appear with learning curves.

© Springer Nature Switzerland AG 2021
M. Schmettow, *New Statistics for Design Researchers*,
Human–Computer Interaction Series,
https://doi.org/10.1007/978-3-030-46380-9_4

4.1 Quantification at Work: Grand Mean Models

Reconsider Jane from Sect. 3.1. She was faced with the problem that potential competitors could challenge the claim "rent a car in 99 s" and in consequence drag them to court. More precisely, the question was "will users on average be able ...", which is nothing but the *population mean*. A statistical model estimating just that, we call a *grand mean model* (GMM). The GMM is the most simple of all models, so in a way, we can also think of it as the "grandmother of all models". Although it is the simplest of all, it is of useful application in design research. For many high-risk situations, there often exist minimum standards for performance to which one can compare the population mean; here are a few examples:

- with a medical infusion pump, the frequency of decimal input error (giving the tenfold or the tenth of the prescribed dose) must be below a bearable level;
- the checkout process of an e-commerce website must have a cancel rate not higher than ...
- the timing of a traffic light must be designed to give drivers enough time to hit the brakes.

A GMM predicts the *average* expected level of performance in the population (β_0). Let's start with a toy example: When you want to predict the IQ score of a totally random and anonymous individual (from this population), the population average (which is standardized to be 100) is your best guess. However, this best guess is imperfect due to the individual differences and chances are rather low that 100 is the perfect guess.

```
# random IQ sample, rounded to whole numbers
set.seed(42)
N <- 1000
D_IQ <- tibble(
  score = rnorm(N, mean = 100, sd = 15),
  IQ = round(score, 0)
)

# proportion of correct guesses
pi_100 <- sum(D_IQ$IQ == 100) / N
str_c(``Proportion of correct guesses (IQ = 100): '', pi_100)
```

```
## [1] "Proportion of correct guesses (IQ = 100): 0.031"
```

This best guess is imperfect, for a variety reasons:

1. People differ a lot in intelligence.
2. The IQ measure itself is uncertain. A person could have had a bad day, when doing the test, whereas another person just had more experience with being tested.
3. If test items are sampled from a larger set, tests may still differ a tiny bit.

4. The person is like the Slum Dog Millionaire, who by pure coincidence encountered precisely those questions, he could answer.

In a later chapter, we will investigate on the sources of randomness Chap. 6. But, like all other models in this chapter, the GMM is a *single-level linear model*. This single level is the *population level* and all unexplained effects that make variation are collected in ϵ_i, the *residuals* or *errors*, which are assumed to follow a Gaussian distribution with center zero and *standard error* σ_ϵ.

Formally, a GMM is written as follows, where μ_i is the *predicted value* of person i and β_0 is the population mean β_0, which is referred to as *Intercept*; see Sect. 4.3.1.

$$\mu_i = \beta_0$$
$$y_i = \mu_i, +\epsilon_i$$
$$\epsilon_i \sim \text{Gaus}(0, \sigma_\epsilon)$$

This way of writing a linear model only works for Gaussian linear models, as only here, the residuals are symmetric and are adding up to Zero. In Chap. 7, we will introduce linear models with different error distributions. For that reason, I will use a slightly different notation throughout:

$$\mu_i = \beta_0$$
$$y_i \sim \text{Gaus}(\mu_i, \sigma_\epsilon)$$

The notable difference between the two notations is that in the first we have just one error distribution. In the second model, every observation actually is taken from its own distribution, located at μ_i, albeit with a *constant variance*.

Enough about mathematic formulas for now. In R, regression models are specified by a dedicated formula language, which I will develop step-by-step in this chapter. This formula language is not very complex, and at the same time provides a surprisingly high flexibility for specification of models. The only really odd feature of this formula language is that it represents the intercept β_0 with 1. To add to the confusion, the intercept means something different, depending on what type of model is estimated. In GMMs, it is the grand mean, whereas in group-mean comparisons, it is the mean of one reference group Sect. 4.3.1 and in linear regression, it has the usual meaning as in linear equations.

Only estimating the population mean may appear futile to many, because interesting research questions seem to involve associations between variable. However, sometimes it is as simply as comparing against an external criterion to see whether there may be a problem. Such a case was construed in Sect. 3.1: Is it legally safe to claim a task can be completed in 99 s? In R, the analysis unfolds as follows: completion times (ToT) are stored in a data frame, with one observation per row.

This data frame is send to the R command `stan_glm` for estimation, using `data = D_1`. The formula of the grand mean model is `ToT ~ 1`. To the left of the ~ (*tilde*) operator is the outcome variable. In design research, this often is a performance measure, such as time-on-task, number of errors or self-reported cognitive workload.

The right-hand side specifies the *deterministic part*, containing all variables that are used to predict performance.

```
attach(Sec99)

M_1 <- stan_glm(ToT ~ 1, data = D_1)
```

The result is a complex model object; the summary command produces a detailed overview of how the model was specified, the estimated parameters, as well as some diagnostics.

```
summary(M_1)
```

```
##
## Model Info:
##  function:     stan_glm
##  family:       gaussian [identity]
##  formula:      ToT ~ 1
##  algorithm:    sampling
##  sample:       4000 (posterior sample size)
##  priors:       see help('prior_summary')
##  observations: 100
##  predictors:   1
##
## Estimates:
##                mean    sd    10%    50%
## (Intercept)   106.0   3.2  101.9  106.0
## sigma          31.5   2.2   28.7   31.4
##                90%
## (Intercept)   110.0
## sigma          34.4
##
## Fit Diagnostics:
##                mean    sd    10%   50%   90%
## mean_PPD     105.9    4.5  100.2 105.9 111.8
##
## The mean_ppd is the sample average posterior predictive distribution of
## the outcome variable (for details see help('summary.stanreg')).
##
## MCMC diagnostics
##                 mcse Rhat n_eff
## (Intercept)     0.1  1.0  2191
## sigma           0.0  1.0  2591
## mean_PPD        0.1  1.0  2902
## log-posterior   0.0  1.0  1666
##
## For each parameter, mcse is Monte Carlo standard error, n_eff is a crude
## measure of effective sample size, and Rhat is the potential scale reduction
## factor on split chains (at convergence Rhat=1).
```

For the researcher, the essential part is the parameter estimates. Such a table must contain information about the location of the effect (left or right, large or small) and the uncertainty. A more common form than the summary above is to present a central tendency and lower and upper credibility limits for the degree of uncertainty. The

Table 4.1 Parameter estimates with 95% credibility limits

Parameter	Fixef	Center	Lower	Upper
Intercept	Intercept	106.0	99.7	112.2
Sigma_resid		31.4	27.5	36.1

Table 4.2 Coefficient estimates with 95% credibility limits

Parameter	Type	Fixef	Center	Lower	Upper
Intercept	Fixef	Intercept	106	99.7	112

CLU tables used in this book report the median for the center and the 2.5% and 97.5% lower and upper quantiles, which is called a 95% credibility interval. The less certain an estimate is, the wider is the interval. Due to the Bayesian interpretation, it is legit to say that the true value of the parameter is within these limits with a certainty of 95%. The `clu` command from the Bayr package produces such a parameter table from the model object (Table 4.1).

```
clu(M_1)
```

The `clu` command being used in this book is from the accompanying R package `bayr`. The tables it produces contain all parameter estimates, including linear coefficients and distributional parameters. In all linear models, the distributional parameter is the standard error. Often, the distributional parameters are of lesser interest and `clu` comes with sibling commands to only show the coefficients (Table 4.2):

```
coef(M_1)
```

Note that the Rstanarm regression engine brings its own `coef` command to extract estimates, but this often report the center estimates only.

```
rstanarm:::coef.stanreg(M_1)
```

```
## (Intercept)
##         106
```

In order to always use the convenient commands from package Bayr, it is necessary to load Bayr after package Rstanarm.

```
library(rstanarm)
library(bayr)
```

Then, Bayr overwrites the commands for reporting to produce consistent coefficient tables (and others), which can go into a report, as they are.

A GMM is the simplest linear model and as such makes absolute minimal use of knowledge when doing its predictions. The only thing one knows is that test persons come from one and the same population (humans, users and psychology students). Accordingly, individual predictions are very inaccurate. From the GMM, we will depart in two directions. First, in the remainder of this chapter, we will add predictors to the model, for example, age of participants or experimental conditions. These models will improve our predictive accuracy by using additional knowledge about participants and conditions of testing.

Reporting a model estimate together with its level of certainty is what makes a statistic *inferential* (rather than merely descriptive). In Bayesian statistics, the posterior distribution is estimated (usually by means of MCMC sampling) and this distribution carries the full information on certainty. If the posterior is widely spread, an estimate is rather uncertain. You may still bet on values close to the center estimate, but you should keep your bid low. Some authors (or regression engines) express the level of certainty by means of the standard error. However, the standard deviation is a single value and has the disadvantage that a single value does not represent non-symmetric distributions well. A better way is to express certainty as limits, a lower and an upper. The most simple method resembles that of the median by using quantiles.

It is common practice to explain and interpret coefficient tables for the audience. My suggestion of how to *report regression results* is to simply walk through the table row-by-row and for every parameter make *three statements*:

1. What the parameter says;
2. a quantitative statement based on the central tendency;
3. an uncertainty statement based on the CIs.

In the present model that is:

The *intercept* (or β_0) is the population average and is in the region of 106 s, which is pretty far from the target of 99 s. The certainty is pretty good. At least we can say that the chance of the true mean being 99 s or smaller is pretty marginal, as it is not even contained in the 95% CI.

And for σ:

The population mean is rather not representative for the observations as the standard error is almost one-third of it. There is much deviation from the population mean in the measures.

From here on, we will build up a whole family of models that go beyond the population mean, but have effects. A *linear regression model* can tell us what effect *metric predictors*, like age or experience, have on user performance. Section 4.2 *Factorial models* can be used for experimental conditions, or when comparing designs.

Table 4.3 MCMC posterior with 4000 samples of 2 parameters in 1 model(s)

Model	Parameter	Type	Fixef	Count
M_1	Intercept	fixef	Intercept	1
M_1	sigma_resid	disp		

4.1.1 Do the Random Walk: Markov Chain Monte Carlo Sampling

So far, we have seen how linear models are specified and how parameters are interpreted from standard coefficient tables. While it is convenient to have a standard procedure, it may be useful to understand how these estimates came into being. In Bayesian estimation, an approximation of the *posterior distribution (PD)* is the result of running the engine and is the central point of departure for creating output, such as coefficient tables. PD assigns a degree of certainty for every possible combination of parameter values. In the current case, you can ask the PD, where and how certain the population mean and the residual standard error are, but you can also ask how certain are we that the population mean is smaller than 99 s and σ is smaller than 10?

In a perfect world, we would know the analytic formula of the posterior and derive statements from it. In most non-trivial models, though, there is no such formula one can work with. Instead, what the regression engine does is to approximate the PD by a random-walk algorithm called Markov chain Monte Carlo sampling (MCMC).

The stan_glm command returns a large object that stores, among others, the full random walk. This random walk represents the posterior distribution almost directly. The following code extracts the posterior distribution from the regression object and prints it. When calling the new object (class: tbl_post) directly, it provides a compact summary of all parameters in the model, in this case the intercept and the residual standard error (Table 4.3).

```
attach(Sec99)

P_1 <- posterior(M_1)
P_1
```

The 99 s GMM has two parameters and therefore the posterior distribution has three dimensions: the parameter dimensions β_0, σ and the probability density. Three dimensional plots are difficult to put on a surface, but for somewhat regular patterns, a density plot with dots does a sufficient job (Fig. 4.1, left).

```
P_1 %>%
  select(chain, iter, parameter, value) %>%
  spread(parameter, value) %>%
  ggplot(aes(x = Intercept, y = sigma_resid)) +
  stat_density_2d(geom = ''point'', aes(size = after_stat(density)), n = 20, contour = F) +
  xlim(95, 115) +
  ylim(25, 40)

P_1 %>%
```

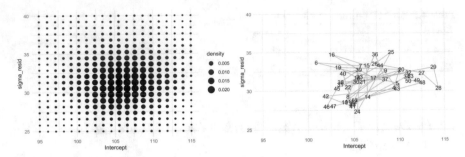

Fig. 4.1 Left: The sampled posterior distribution of a GMM. Right: 50 iterations of the MCMC random walk

```
filter(iter <= 50) %>%
select(iter, parameter, value) %>%
spread(parameter, value) %>%
ggplot(aes(x = Intercept, y = sigma_resid, label = iter)) +
geom_text() +
geom_path(alpha = .3) +
xlim(95, 115) +
ylim(25, 40)
```

Let's see how this landscape actually emerged from the random walk. In the current case, the *parameter space* is two-dimensional, as we have μ and σ. The MCMC procedure starts at a deliberate point in parameter space. At every iteration, the MCMC algorithm attempts a probabilistic jump to another location in parameter space and stores the coordinates. This jump is called probabilistic for two reasons: first, the new coordinates are selected by a random number generator and second, it is either carried out or not, and that is probabilistic, too. If the new target is in a highly likely region, it is carried out with a higher chance. This sounds circular, but it provenly works. More specifically, the MCMC sampling approach rests on a general proof that the emerging frequency distribution converges toward the true posterior distribution. This property is called *ergodicity*, and it means we can take the *relative frequencies* of jumps into a certain area of parameter space as an approximation for our degree of belief that the true parameter value is within this region.

The regression object stores the MCMC results as a long series of positions in parameter space. For any range of interest, it is the relative frequency of visits that represents its certainty. The first 50 jumps of the MCMC random walk are shown in Fig. 4.1(right). Apparently, the random walk is not fully random, as the point cloud is more dense in the center area. This is where the more probable parameter values lie. One can clearly see how the MCMC algorithm jumps to more likely areas more frequently. These areas become more dense and, finally, the cloud of visits will approach the contour density plot above.

The more complex regression models grow, the more dimensions the PD gets. The linear regression model in the next chapter has three parameter dimensions, which is difficult to visualize. Multi-level models Chap. 6 have hundreds of parameters, which is impossible to intellectually grasp at once. Therefore, it is common to use the

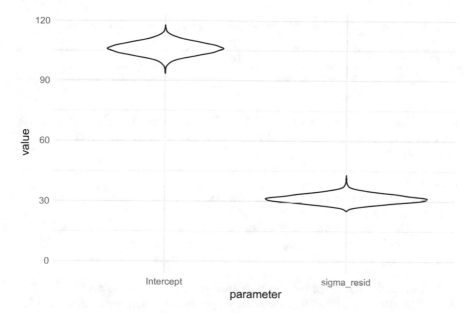

Fig. 4.2 Violin plots for (marginal) posterior density

marginal posterior distributions (MPD), which gives the density of one coefficient at a time. My preferred geometry for plotting multiple MPDs side-by-side is the violin plot.

```
P_1 %>%
  ggplot(aes(x = parameter, y = value)) +
  geom_violin() +
  ylim(0, NA)
```

In Fig. 4.2, we can spot that the most likely value for average time-on-task is 106.14. Both distributions have a certain spread. With a wider PD, far-off values have been visited by the MCMC chain more frequently. The probability mass is more evenly distributed, and there is less certainty for the parameter to fall in the central region. In the current case, a risk-averse decision maker would maybe take the credibility interval as "reasonably certain".

Andrew and Jane expect some skepticism from the marketing people, and some lack in statistical skills, too. What would be the most comprehensible single number to report? As critical decisions are involved, it seems plausible to report the risk to err: how certain are they that the true value is more than 99 s? We inspect the histograms. The MPD of the intercept indicates that the average time-on-task is rather unlikely in the range of 99 s or better. But what is the precise probability to err for the 99 s statement? The above summary with `coef()` does not accurately answer the question. The CI gives lower and upper limits for a range of 95% certainty in total. What is needed is the certainty of $\mu \geq 99$. Specific questions deserve precise

Table 4.4 Estimating the certainty for average ToT being larger than 99 (111) seconds

p_99	p_111
0.985	0.059

answers. And once we have understood the MCMC chain as a frequency distribution, the answer is easy: we simply count how many visited values are larger than 99 or 111 (Table 4.4).

```
P_1 %>%
  filter(parameter == ''Intercept'') %>%
  summarize(
    p_99 = mean(value >= 99),
    p_111 = mean(value >= 111)
  )
```

It turns out that the certainty for average time-on-task above 99 is an overwhelming 0.985. The alternative claim that the average completion time is better than 111 s has a rather moderate risk to err (0.059).

4.1.2 Likelihood and Random Term

In formal language, regression models are usually specified by *likelihood functions* and one or more *random terms* (exactly one in linear models). The likelihood represents the common, predictable pattern in the data. Formally, the likelihood establishes a link between *predicted values* μ_i and predictors. It is common to call predictors with the Greek letter β (beta). If there is more than one predictor, these are marked with subscripts, starting at zero. The "best guess" is called the *expected value* and is denoted with μ_i ("mju i"). If you just know that the average ToT is 106 s and you are asked to guess the performance of the next user arriving in the lab, the reasonable guess is just 106 s.

$$\mu_i = \beta_0$$

Of course, we would never expect this person to use 106 s, exactly. All observed and imagined observations are more or less clumped around the expected value. The *random term* specifies our assumptions on the pattern of randomness. It is given as distributions (note the plural), denoted by the $\sim$ (tilde) operator, which reads as "is distributed". In the case of linear models, the assumed distribution is always the Normal or *Gaussian distribution*. Gaussian distributions have a characteristic bell curve and depend on two parameters: the mean μ as the central measure and the standard deviation σ giving the spread.

$$y_i \sim \text{Gaus}(\mu_i, \sigma_\epsilon)$$

The random term specifies how all unknown sources of variation take effect on the measures, and these are manifold. Randomness can arise due to all kinds of individual differences, situational conditions and, last but not least, measurement errors. The Gaussian distribution sometimes is a good approximation for randomness and linear models are routinely used in research. In several classic statistics books, the following formula is used to describe the GMM (and likewise more complex linear models):

$$y_i = \mu_i + \epsilon_i$$
$$\mu_i = \beta_0$$
$$\epsilon_i \sim \text{Gaus}(0, \sigma_\epsilon)$$

First, it is to say that these two formulas are mathematically equivalent. The primary difference to our formula is that the *residuals* ϵ_i are given separately. The pattern of residuals is then specified as a single Gaussian distribution. Residual distributions are a highly useful concept in modeling, as they can be used to check a given model. Then the classic formula is more intuitive. The reason for separating the model into likelihood and random term is that it works in more cases. When turning to Generalized Linear Models (GLM) in Chap. 7, we will use other patterns of randomness that are no longer additive, like in $\mu_i \mid \epsilon_i$. As I consider the use of GLMs an element of professional statistical practice, I use the general formula throughout.

4.1.3 Working with the Posterior Distribution

Coefficient tables are the standard way to report regression models. They contain all effects (or a selection of interest) in rows. For every parameter, the central tendency (center, magnitude and location) is given, and a statement of uncertainty, by convention 95% credibility intervals (CI).

```
attach(Sec99)
```

The object M_1 is the model object created by stan_glm. When you call summary, you get complex listings that represent different aspects of the estimated model. These aspects and more are saved inside the object in a hierarchy of lists. The central result of the estimation is the *posterior distribution (PD)*. With package Rstanarm, the posterior distribution is extracted as follows (Table 4.5):

```
P_1_wide <-
  as_tibble(M_1) %>%
```

Table 4.5 Rstanarm reports posterior samples in a wide format, with one row per iteration (eight shown)

Iter	Intercept	Sigma
3439	109.3	32.3
66	105.9	28.8
813	106.8	30.4
923	108.0	32.9
1420	107.8	31.7
3076	99.2	32.7
1436	107.5	30.2
1991	104.8	31.7

Table 4.6 A wide CLU table extracted from a wide posterior object

c_Intercept	l_Intercept	u_Intercept	c_sigma	l_sigma	u_sigma
106	99.7	112	31.4	27.5	36.1

```
rename(Intercept = `(Intercept)`) %>%
mutate(Iter = row_number()) %>%
mascutils::go_first(Iter)

P_1_wide %>%
  sample_n(8)
```

The resulting data frame is actually a matrix, where each of the 4000 rows is one coordinate the MCMC walk has visited in a two-dimensional parameter space Sect. 4.1.1. For the purpose of reporting parameter estimates, we could create a CLU table as follows (Table 4.6):

```
P_1_wide %>%
  summarize(
    c_Intercept = median(Intercept),
    l_Intercept = quantile(Intercept, 0.025),
    u_Intercept = quantile(Intercept, 0.975),
    c_sigma = median(sigma),
    l_sigma = quantile(sigma, 0.025),
    u_sigma = quantile(sigma, 0.975)
  )
```

As can be seen, creating coefficient tables from wide posterior objects is awful and repetitive, even when there are just two parameters (some models contain hundreds of parameters). The additional effort would be needed to get a well-structured table. The package Bayr extracts posterior distributions into a *long for-*

Table 4.7 A long table for posterior samples stores one value per row (rather than one iteration)

Iter	Parameter	Value
1136	Intercept	103.5
3726	Sigma	29.3
823	Intercept	104.2
2151	Intercept	110.2
1581	Sigma	28.2
56	Sigma	29.8
1669	Sigma	32.8
2401	Intercept	103.9

Table 4.8 A long CLU table extracted from a long posterior table

Parameter	Center	Lower	Upper
Intercept	106.0	99.7	112.2
Sigma	31.4	27.5	36.1

mat. This works approximately as can be seen in the following code, which employs `tidyr::pivot_longer` to make the wide Rstanarm posterior long (Table 4.7).

```
P_1_long <-
  P_1_wide %>%
  pivot_longer(!Iter, names_to = ''parameter'')

P_1_long %>%
  sample_n(8)
```

With long posterior objects, summarizing over the parameters is more straight-forward and produces a long CLU table, such as Sect. 4.8. In other words: Starting from a long posterior makes for a tidy workflow.

```
P_1_long %>%
  group_by(parameter) %>%
  summarize(
    center = median(value),
    lower = quantile(value, 0.025),
    upper = quantile(value, 0.975)
  )
```

With the Bayr package, the `posterior` command produces such a long posterior object. When called, a Bayr posterior object (class *Tbl_post*) identifies itself by telling the number of MCMC samples, and the estimates contained in the model, grouped by *type of parameter* (Table 4.9).

Table 4.9 MCMC posterior with 4000 samples of 2 parameters in 1 model(s)

Model	Parameter	Type	Fixef	Count
M_1	Intercept	Fixef	Intercept	1
M_1	Sigma_resid	disp		

Table 4.10 Parameter estimates with 95% credibility limits

Parameter	Fixef	Center	Lower	Upper
Intercept	Intercept	106	99.7	112

Table 4.11 Coefficient estimates with 95% credibility limits

Parameter	Type	Fixef	Center	Lower	Upper
Intercept	Fixef	Intercept	106	99.7	112

```
P_1 <- bayr::posterior(M_1)
P_1
```

The most important benefit of posterior extraction with Bayr is that parameters are classified. Note how the two parameters `Intercept` and `sigma` are assigned different parameter types: fixed effect (which is a population-level coefficient) and dispersion. This classification allows us to filter by type of parameter and produce CLU tables, such as Table 4.10.

```
P_1 %>%
  filter(type == ''fixef'') %>%
  clu()
```

Bayr also provides shortcut commands for extracting parameters of a certain type. The above code is very similar to how the `bayr::fixef` command is implemented. Note that `coef` and `fixef` can be called on the Rstanarm model object, directly, making it unnecessary to first create a posterior table object (Table 4.11).

```
coef(M_1)
```

4.1.4 Center and Interval Estimates

The authors of Bayesian books and the various regression engines have different opinions on what to use as a center statistic in a coefficient table. The best known options are the mean, the median and the mode. The following code produces these statistics and the results are shown in Table 4.12.

Table 4.12 Various center statistics and 95% quantiles

Parameter	Mean	Median	Mode	q_025	q_975
Intercept	106.0	106.0	106	99.7	112.2
Sigma_resid	31.5	31.4	31	27.5	36.1

```
attach(Sec99)

T_1 <-
  P_1 %>%
  group_by(parameter) %>%
  summarize(
    mean = mean(value),
    median = median(value),
    mode = mascutils::mode(value),
    q_025 = quantile(value, 0.025),
    q_975 = quantile(value, 0.975)
  )
kable(T_1, caption = ''Various center statistics and 95% quantiles'')
```

We observe that for the Intercept it barely matters which center statistic we use, but there are minor differences for the standard error. We investigate this further by producing a plot with the marginal posterior distributions of μ and σ with mean, median and mode (Fig. 4.3).

```
T_1_long <-
  T_1 %>%
  gather(key = center, value = value, -parameter)

P_1 %>%
  ggplot(aes(x = value)) +
  facet_wrap(~parameter, scales = ''free_x'') +
  geom_density() +
  geom_vline(aes(
    xintercept = value,
    col = center
  ),
  data = T_1_long
  )
```

This example demonstrates how the long format posterior works together with the GGplot graphics engine. A density plot very accurately renders how certainty is distributed over the range of a parameter. In order to produce vertical lines for point estimate and limits, we first make the summary table long, with one value per row. This is not how we would usually like to read it, but it is very efficient for adding to the plot.

When inspecting the two distributions, it appears that the distribution of Intercept is completely symmetric. For the standard error, in contrast, we note a slight left

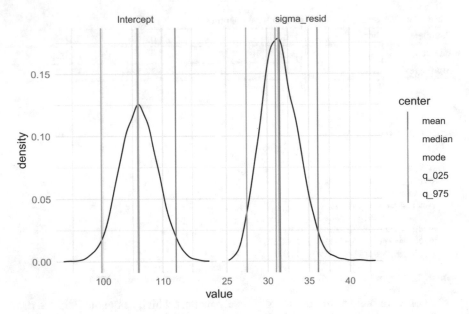

Fig. 4.3 Comparing mean, median and mode of marginal posterior distributions

skewness. This is rather typical for dispersion parameters, as these have a lower boundary. The closer the distribution sits to the boundary, the steeper becomes the left tail.

A disadvantage of the *mean* is that it may change under monotonic transformations. A monotonic transformations is a recoding of a variable x_1 into a new variable x_2 by a transformation function ϕ (*phi*) such that the order of values stays untouched. Examples of monotonic functions are the logarithm ($x_2 = \log(x_1)$), the exponential function ($x_2 = \exp(x_1)$), or simply $x_2 = x_1 + 1$. A counter-example is the quadratic function $x_2 = x_1^2$. In data analysis, monotonous transformations are used a lot. Especially Generalized Linear Models make use of monotonous link functions to establish linearity Sect. 7.1.1. Furthermore, the mean can also be highly influenced by outliers.

The *mode* of a distribution is its point of highest density. It is invariant under monotonic transformations. It also has a rather intuitive meaning as the most likely value for the true parameter. Next to that, the mode is compatible with classic maximum likelihood estimation. When a Bayesian takes a pass on any prior information, the posterior mode should precisely match the results of a classic regression engine (e.g. glm). The main disadvantage of the mode is that it has to be estimated by one of several heuristic algorithms. These add some computing time and may fail when the posterior distribution is bimodal. However, when that happens, you probably have a more deeply rooted problem than just deciding on a suitable summary statistic.

The *median* of a distribution marks the point where half the values are below and the other half are equal or above. Technically, the median is just the 50% quantile of the distribution. The median is extremely easy and reliable to compute, and it

Table 4.13 Posterior medians and 95% credibility limits

Parameter	Center	Lower	Upper
Intercept	106.0	99.7	112.2
Sigma_resid	31.4	27.5	36.1

shares the invariance of monotonous transformations. This is easy to conceive: The median is computed by ordering all values in a row and then picking the value that is exactly in the middle. Obviously, this value only changes if the order changes, i.e. a non-monotonous function was applied. For these advantages, I prefer using the median as center estimates. Researchers who desire a different center estimate can easily write their own `clu`.

In this book, *2.5% and 97.5% certainty quantiles* are routinely used to form *95% credibility intervals (CI)*. There is nothing special about these intervals; they are just conventions, Again, another method exists to obtain CIs. Some authors prefer to report the *highest posterior density interval (HPD)*, which is the narrowest interval that contains 95% of the probability mass. While this is intriguing to some extent, HPDs are not invariant to monotonic transformations either.

So, the parameter extraction commands used here give the median and the 2.5% and 97.5% limits. The three parameters have in common that they are quantiles, which are handled by R's `quantile` command. To demystify the `clu`, here is how you can make a basic coefficient table yourself, Table 4.13:

```
P_1 %>%
  group_by(parameter) %>%
  summarize(
    center = quantile(value, 0.5),
    lower = quantile(value, 0.025),
    upper = quantile(value, 0.975)
  ) %>%
  ungroup()
```

Note that the posterior contains samples of the dispersion parameter σ, too, which means we can get CIs for it. Classic regression engines don't yield any measures of certainty on dispersion parameters. In classic analyses, σ is often denounced as a nuisance parameter and would not be used for inference. I believe that measuring and understanding sources of variation are crucial for design research and several of the examples that follow try to build this case, especially Sects. 6.5 and 7.5. Therefore, the capability of reporting uncertainty on all parameters, not just coefficients, is a surplus of Bayesian estimation.

4.2 Walk the Line: Linear Regression

In the previous section, we have introduced the most basic of all regression models:
the grand mean model. It assigns rather coarse predictions, without any real predictors. Routinely, design researchers desire to predict performance based on *metric
variables*, such as

- previous experience,
- age,
- font size,
- intelligence level and other innate abilities,
- level of self-efficacy, neuroticism or other traits and
- number of social media contacts.

To carry out such a research question, the variable of interest needs to be measured
next to the outcome variable. And, the variable must vary. You cannot examine the
effects of age or font size on reading performance, when all participants are of the
same age and you test only one size. Then, for specifying the model, the researcher
has to come up with an expectation of how the two are related. Theoretically, that can
be any mathematical function, but practically, a *linear function* is often presumed.
Figure 4.4 shows a variety of linear relations between two variables x and y.

```
expand_grid(
  intercept = c(0, 1, 2),
  slope = c(-.5, 0, 1.5),
  x = -3:3
) %>%
  arrange(x) %>%
  mutate(
    y = intercept + x * slope,
    slope = as.factor(slope),
    intercept = as.factor(intercept)
  ) %>%
  ggplot(aes(x = x, y = y, color = slope)) +
  geom_line() +
  facet_grid(~intercept)
```

A linear function is a straight line, which is specified by two parameters: *intercept*
β_0 and *slope* β_1:

$$f(x_1) = \beta_0 + \beta_1 x_{1i}$$

The intercept is *"the point where a function graph crosses the x-axis"*, or more
formally

$$f(x_1 = 0) = \beta_0$$

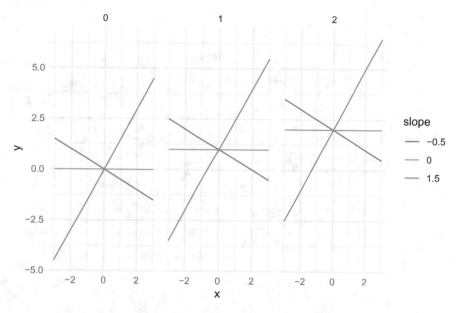

Fig. 4.4 Linear terms differing by intercepts and slopes

The second parameter β_1 is called the *slope*. The slope determines the steepness of the line. When the slope is 0.5, the line will rise up by 0.5 on Y, when moving one step to the right on X.

$$f(x_1 + 1) = \beta_0 + \beta_1 x_{1i} + \beta_1$$

There is also the possibility that the slope is zero. In such a case, the predictor has no effect and can be left out. Setting $\beta_1 = 0$ produces a horizontal line, with y_i being constant over the whole range. This shows that the GMM is a special case of LRMs, where the slope is fixed to zero, hence $\mu_i = \beta_0$.

Linear regression gives us the opportunity to discover how ToT can be predicted by age (x_1) in the BrowsingAB case. In this hypothetical experiment, two designs A and B are compared, but we ignore this for now. Instead, we ask: are older people slower when using the Internet? Or: is there a linear relationship between age and ToT? The structural term is

$$\mu_i = \beta_0 + \beta_1 \text{age}_i$$

This literally means with every year of age, ToT increases by β_1 seconds. Before we run a linear regression with stan_glm, we visually explore the association between age and ToT using a scatterplot. The blue line in the graph is a so-called a *smoother*, more specifically a LOESS. A smoother is an estimated line, just as a linear function. But it is way more flexible. Where the linear function is a straight

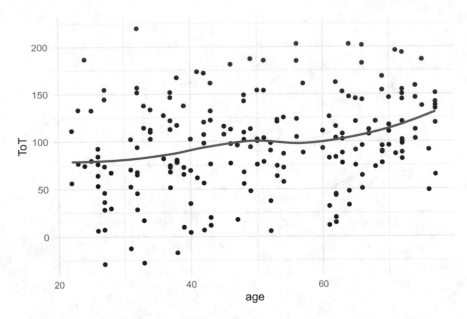

Fig. 4.5 Using a scatterplot and smoother to check for linear trends

stick fixed at a pivotal point, LOESS is more like a pipe cleaner. Here, LOESS shows a more detailed picture of the relation between age and ToT. There is a rise between 20 and 40, followed by a stable plateau, and another rise starting at 60. Actually, that does not look like a straight line, but at least there is a steady upwards trend (Fig. 4.5).

```
attach(BrowsingAB)

BAB1 %>%
   ggplot(aes(x = age, y = ToT)) +
   geom_point() +
   geom_smooth(se = F, fullrange = F)
```

In fact, the BrowsingAB simulation contains what one could call a psychological model. The effect of age is partly due to the farsightedness of participants (making them slower at reading), which more or less suddenly kicks in at a certain range of age. At this point in time it must suffice to approximate the course through a linear function. To estimate the model, we use the stan_glm command in much the same way as before, but add the predictor age. The command will internally check the data type of your variable, which is a metric in this case. Therefore, it is treated as a *metric predictor* (sometimes also called covariate).

```
M_age <-
   BAB1 %>%
   stan_glm(ToT ~ 1 + age,
```

Table 4.14 Coefficient estimates with 95% credibility limits

Parameter	Fixef	Center	Lower	Upper
Intercept	Intercept	57.17	34.053	79.53
Age	Age	0.82	0.401	1.24

```
    data = .
  )

coef(M_age)
```

Is age associated with ToT? Table 4.14 tells us that with every year of age, users get 0.82 seconds slower, which is considerable. It also tells us that the predicted performance at age = 0 is 57.17.

4.2.1   Transforming Measures

In the above model, the intercept represents the predicted ToT at `age == 0`, of a newborn. We would never seriously put that forward in a stakeholder presentation, trying to prove that babies benefit from the redesign of a public website, would we? The prediction is bizarre because we intuitively understand that there is a discontinuity up the road, which is the moment where a teenager starts using public websites. We also realize that over the whole life span of a typical web user, say 12 years to 90 years, age actually is a proxy variable for two distinct processes: the rapid build-up of intellectual skills from childhood to young adulthood and the slow decline of cognitive performance, which starts approximately, when the first of us get age-related farsightedness. Generally, with linear models, one should avoid making statements about a range that has not been observed. Linearity, as we will see in 7.1.1, it always is just an approximation for a process that truly is non-linear.

Placing the intercept where there is no data has another consequence: the estimate is rather uncertain, with a wide 95% CI, $57.17[34.05, 79.54]_{CI95}$. As a metaphor, think of the data as a hand that holds a stick, the regression line and tries to push a light switch. The longer the stick, the more difficult it becomes to hit the target.

4.2.1.1   Shifting and Centering

Shifting the predictor is a pragmatic solution to the problem: "Shifting" means that the age predictor is moved to the right or the left, such that point zero is in a region populated with observations. In this case, two options seem to make sense: either the intercept is in the region of youngest participants, or it is the sample average, which is then called *centering*. To shift a variable, just subtract the amount of units (years)

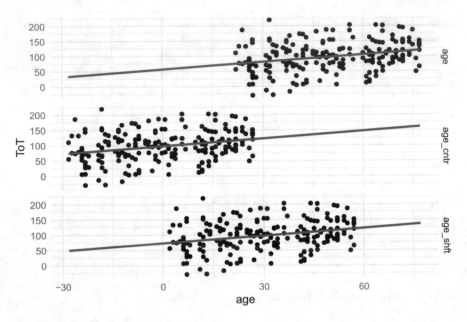

Fig. 4.6 Shifting and centering of variable Age

where you want the intercept to be. The following code produces a shift of −20 and a centering on the original variable age:

```
BAB1 <-
  BAB1 %>%
  mutate(
    age_shft = age - 20,
    age_cntr = age - mean(age)
  )

BAB1 %>%
  tidyr::gather(''predictor'', ''age'', starts_with(''age'')) %>%
  ggplot(aes(x = age, y = ToT)) +
  facet_grid(predictor ~ .) +
  geom_point() +
  geom_smooth(se = F, method = ''lm'', fullrange = T)
```

By shifting the age variable, the whole data cloud is moved to the left (Fig. 4.6). To see what happens on the inferential level, we repeat the LRM estimation with the two shifted variables:

```
M_age_shft <-
  stan_glm(ToT ~ 1 + age_shft, data = BAB1)

M_age_cntr <-
  stan_glm(ToT ~ 1 + age_cntr, data = BAB1)
```

Table 4.15 Coefficient estimates with 95% credibility limits

Model	Parameter	Fixef	Center	Lower	Upper
M_age	Intercept	Intercept	57.17	34.053	79.53
M_age	age	age	0.82	0.401	1.24
M_age_cntr	Intercept	Intercept	98.04	91.521	104.21
M_age_cntr	age_cntr	age_cntr	0.82	0.395	1.24
M_age_shft	Intercept	Intercept	73.20	59.117	87.75
M_age_shft	age_shft	age_shft	0.82	0.395	1.23

We combine the posterior distributions into one multi-model posterior and read the *multi-model coefficient table* (Table 4.15):

```
P_age <-
  bind_rows(
    posterior(M_age),
    posterior(M_age_shft),
    posterior(M_age_cntr)
  )

coef(P_age)
```

```
## [1] "BAB1"
```

When comparing the regression results, the shifted intercepts have moved to higher values, as expected. Surprisingly, the simple shift is not exactly 20 years. This is due to the high uncertainty of the first model, as well as the relation not being exactly linear (see Figure XY). The shifted age predictor has a slightly better uncertainty, but not by much. This is because the region around the lowest age is only scarcely populated with data. Centering, on the other hand, results in a highly certain estimate, due to the dense data. The slope parameter, however, practically does not change, neither in magnitude nor in certainty.

Shift (and centering) move the scale of measurement and make sure that the intercept falls close (or within) the cluster of observations. Shifting does not change the unit size, which is still in years. For truly metric predictors, changing the unit is not desirable, as the unit of measurement is natural and intuitive.

4.2.1.2   Rescaling

Most rating scales are not natural units of measure. Most of the time it is not meaningful to say: "the user experience rating improved by one". The problem has two
roots, as I will illustrate by the following four rating scale items:

This product is …

1. easy to use |1 ... X ... 3 ... 4 ... 5 ... 6 ... 7|
   difficult to use
2. heavenly |-----X----------------------------|
   hellish
3. neutral |1   ...   2   ...   3   ...   4|
   uncanny

If we would use these three scales to assess a single design, how would the raw
data look like? In the following, I use a random number generator from package
Mascutils for simulation of rating scale responses (Table 4.16).

```
library(mascutils)

set.seed(42)
Raw_ratings <-
  tibble(
    Part = 1:100,
    easy_difficult = rrating_scale(100, 0, 0.5,
      ends = c(1, 7)
    ),
    heavenly_hellish = rrating_scale(100, 0, 0.2,
      ends = c(0, 10),
      bin = F
    ),
    neutral_uncanny = rrating_scale(100, -0.5, 0.5,
      ends = c(1, 5)
```

Table 4.16 Data set with 5 variables, showing 8 of 100 observations

Obs	Part	Easy_difficult	Heavenly_hellish	Neutral_uncanny
8	8	4	4.94	2
24	24	5	4.50	2
25	25	6	5.00	3
70	70	5	5.45	2
74	74	3	5.84	3
80	80	3	5.00	3
84	84	4	5.15	3
91	91	5	5.10	2

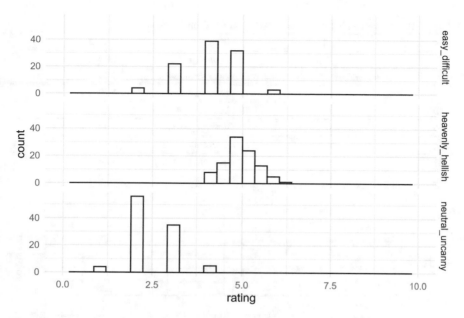

Fig. 4.7 Distribution of three rating scale items

```
    )
  ) %>%
  as_tbl_obs()
```

Raw_ratings

In the following, we are comparing the results of these three items. However, data came in a wide format, as you would use to create a correlation table. For a tidy analysis, we first make the data set long. Ratings are now classified by the item they came from (Table 4.17). From this, we can produce a grid histogram (Fig. 4.7).

```
D_ratings <-
  Raw_ratings %>%
  select(-Obs) %>%
  pivot_longer(!Part, 1:3, names_to = ``Item'', values_to = ``rating'') %>%
  as_tbl_obs()

D_ratings
```

```
D_ratings %>%
  ggplot(aes(x = rating)) +
  facet_grid(Item ~ .) +
  geom_histogram() +
  xlim(0, 10)
```

Table 4.17 Data set with 4 variables, showing 8 of 300 observations

Obs	Part	Item	Rating
3	1	neutral_uncanny	1.00
10	4	easy_difficult	5.00
16	6	easy_difficult	4.00
149	50	heavenly_hellish	4.47
195	65	neutral_uncanny	2.00
224	75	heavenly_hellish	5.43
231	77	neutral_uncanny	3.00
243	81	neutral_uncanny	3.00

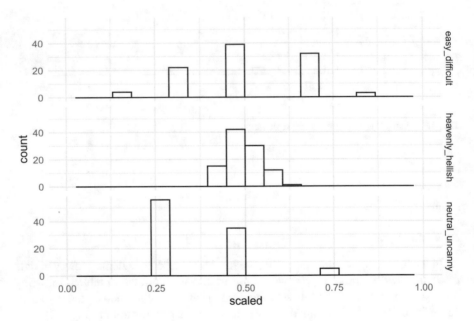

Fig. 4.8 Distribution of three rating scale items with standardized boundaries

The first problem is that rating scales have been designed with different end points. The first step when using different rating scales is shifting the left end point to zero and dividing by the range of the measure (`upper - lower` boundary). That brings all items down to the range from zero to one. Note how the following tidy code joins `D_ratings` with a table `D_Items`. That adds the lower and upper boundaries for every observation, from which we can standardize the range (Fig. 4.8).

```
D_Items <- tribble(
  ~Item, ~lower, ~upper,
  ``easy_difficult'', 1, 7,
  ``heavenly_hellish'', 0, 10,
```

```
  ''neutral_uncanny'', 1, 5
)


D_standard <-
  D_ratings %>%
  left_join(D_Items, by = ''Item'') %>%
  mutate(scaled = (rating - lower) / (upper - lower))

D_standard %>%
  ggplot(aes(x = scaled)) +
  facet_grid(Item ~ .) +
  geom_histogram(bins = 20) +
  xlim(0, 1)
```

This partly corrects the horizontal shift between scales. However, the ratings on the third item still are shifted relative to the other two. The reason is that the first two items have the neutral zone right in the center, whereas the third item is neutral at its left end point. Those are called bipolar and monopolar items. The second inconsistency is that the second item uses rather extreme anchors (end point labels, which produce a tight accumulation in the center of the range). You could say that on a cosmic scale people agree. The three scales have been rescaled by their *nominal range*, but they differ in their observed variance.

By *z-transformation* a measure is shifted, not by its nominal boundaries but by *observed standard deviation*. A set of measures is z-transformed by centering it and scaling it by its own standard deviation.

```
D_ratings %>%
  group_by(Item) %>%
  mutate(zrating = (rating - mean(rating)) / sd(rating)) %>%
  ungroup() %>%
  ggplot(aes(x = zrating)) +
  facet_grid(Item ~ .) +
  geom_histogram(bins = 10)
```

By z-transformation, the three scales now exhibit the same mean location and the same dispersion, Table 4.9. This could be used to combine them into one general score. Note, however, that information is lost by this process, namely the differences in location or dispersion. If the research question is highly detailed, such as "Is the design consistently rated low on uncanniness?" this can no longer be answered from the z-transformed variable.

Finally, sometimes researchers use *logarithmic transformation* of outcome measures to reduce what they perceive as pathologies of the data. In particular, many outcome variables do not follow a Normal distribution, as the random term of linear models assumes, but are left-skewed. Log transformation often mitigates such problems. However, as we will see in Chap. 7, linear models can be estimated gracefully with a random component that precisely matches the data as it comes. The

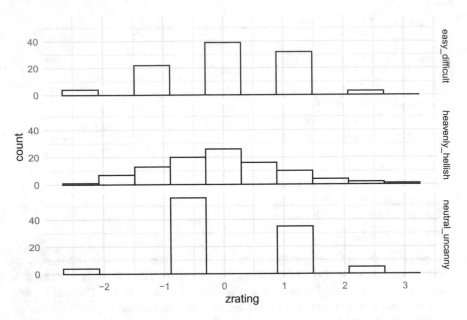

Fig. 4.9 Z-transformation removes differences in location and dispersion

following time-on-task data is from the IPump study, where nurses have tested two infusion pump interfaces. The original ToT data is strongly left-skewed, which can be mitigated by log transformation (Fig. 4.10).

```
attach(IPump)

D_pumps %>%
  mutate(log_ToT = log(ToT)) %>%
  select(Design, ToT, log_ToT) %>%
  gather(key = Measure, value = value, -Design) %>%
  ggplot(aes(x = value, color = Design)) +
  facet_wrap(Measure ~ ., scale = ``free'') +
  geom_density()
```

Count measures and durations are notorious for non-symmetric error distribution. By log transformation one often arrives at a reasonably Gaussian distributed error. However, the natural unit of the measure (seconds) gets lost by the transformation, making it very difficult to report the results in a quantitative manner.

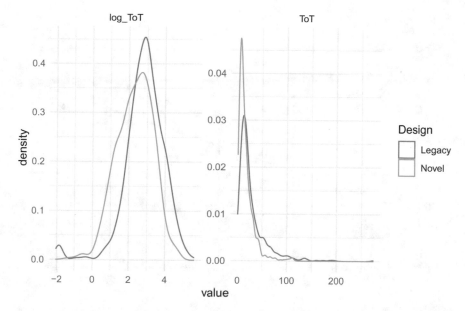

Fig. 4.10 Log transformation can be used to bend highly left-skewed distributions into a more symmetric shape

4.2.2   Correlations

LRM renders the quantitative relationship between two metric variables. Another commonly known statistic that seems to do something similar is Pearson's correlation statistic r (3.3.4). In the following, we will see that a tight connection between correlation and linear coefficients exists, albeit both having their own advantages. For a demonstration, we reproduce the steps on a simulated data set where X and Y are linearly linked (Fig. 4.11):

```
set.seed(42)
D_cor <-
  tibble(
    x = runif(50, 0, 50),
    y = rnorm(50, x * 0.2, 3)
  )

D_cor %>%
  ggplot(aes(x = x, y = y)) +
  geom_point() +
  geom_smooth(method = ``lm'', se = F)
```

Recall that r is covariance standardized for dispersion, not unsimilar to z-transformation Sect. 4.2.1 and that a covariance is the mean squared deviance

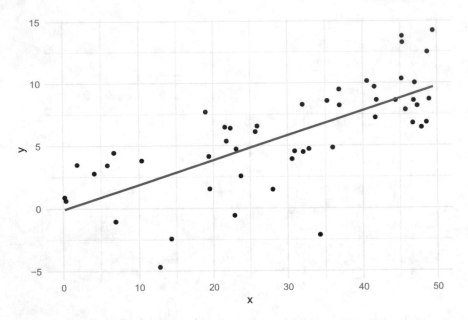

Fig. 4.11 A linear association between X and Y

from the population mean. This is how the correlation is decontaminated from the idiosyncrasies of the involved measures, their location and dispersion. Similarly, the slope parameter in an LRM is a measure of association, too. It is agnostic of the overall location of measures since this is captured by the intercept. However, dispersion remains intact. This ensures that the slope and the intercept together retain information about location, dispersion and association of data, and we can ultimately make predictions. Still, there is a tight relationship between Pearson's r and a slope coefficient β_1, namely

$$r = \beta_1 \frac{\sigma_X}{\sigma_Y}$$

For the sole purpose of demonstration, we here resort to the built-in non-Bayesian command lm for doing the regression.

```
M_cor <- stan_glm(y ~ x, data = D_cor)

beta_1 <- coef(M_cor)$center[2]

r <- beta_1 * sd(D_cor$x) / sd(D_cor$y)
cat(``the correlation is: '', r)


## the correlation is:   0.715
```

The clue with Pearson's r is that it normalized the slope coefficient by the variation found in the sample. This resembles z-transformation as was introduced in Sect. 4.2.1. In fact, when both, predictor and outcome, are z-transformed before estimation, the coefficient equals Pearson's r almost precisely. The minor deviation stems from the relatively short MCMC chains.

```
M_z <-
  D_cor %>%
  mutate(
    x_z = (x - mean(x)) / sd(x),
    y_z = (y - mean(y)) / sd(y)
  ) %>%
  stan_glm(y_z ~ x_z,
    data = .
  )

beta_1 <- coef(M_z)$center[2]

cat(''On z standardized outcomes the coefficient is'', beta_1)
```

```
## On z standardized outcomes the coefficient is 0.717
```

Pearson's r spawns from a different school of thinking than Bayesian parameter estimation: analysis of variance (ANOVA). Roughly, this family of methods draws on the idea of dividing the *total variance* of the outcome variable into two components: *explained variance* and *residual variance*. The very formula of the variance parameter reveals its connection to covariance (it is even allowed to say that variance is the covariance of a variable with itself):

$$\text{Var}_X = \frac{1}{n} \sum_{i=1}^{n} (x_i - E(X))^2$$

In ANOVA models, when explained variance is large, as compared to residual variance, the F-statistic goes up and stars twinkle behind the p-value. While I am far from promoting any legacy approaches, here, a scaleless measure of association strength bears some intuition in situations, where at least one of the involved variables has no well-defined scale. That is in particular the case with rating scales. Measurement theory tells that we may actually transform rating scales fully to our liking, if just the order is preserved (ordinal scales). That is a pretty weak criterion and, strictly speaking, forbids the application of linear models (and ANOVA) altogether, where at least sums must be well defined (interval scales).

From Pearson's r, another interesting parameter can be derived. The coefficient of determination r^2 is obtained. Because it is squared, it ranges from zero to one, eliminating the direction of an effect. The coefficient of determination allows it to compare predictors by the amount of variance they explain.

To sum it up, Pearson r and r^2 are useful statistics to express the strength of an association, when the scale of measurement does not matter or when one desires to compare across scales. Furthermore, correlations play a central role in psychometric and design-o-metric models (Sect. 6.8).

In regression modeling, the use of coefficients allows for predictions made in the original units of measurement. Correlations, in contrast, are unitless. Still, correlation coefficients play an important role in exploratory data analysis for the following reasons:

1. Correlations between predictors and responses are a quick and dirty assessment of the expected associations.
2. Correlations between multiple response modalities (e.g. ToT and number of errors) indicate to what extent these responses can be considered exchangeable.
3. Correlations between predictors should be checked upfront to avoid problems arising from so-called collinearity.

Linear coefficients and correlations both represent associations between measures. Coefficients preserve units of measurement, allowing us to make meaningful quantitative statements. Correlations are rescaled by the observed dispersion of measures in the sample, making them unitless. The advantage is that larger sets of associations can be screened at once and compared easily.

4.2.3   Endlessly Linear

On a deeper level, the bizarre age = 0 prediction is an example of a principle that will reoccur several times throughout this book.

In our endless universe everything is finite.

A well-understood fact about LRM is that they allow us to fit a straight line to data. A lesser regarded consequence from the mathematical underpinnings of such models is that this line extends infinitely in both directions. To fulfill this assumption, the outcome variable needs to have an infinite range, too, $y_i \in [-\infty; \infty]$ (unless the slope is zero). Every scientifically trained person and many laypeople know that even elementary magnitudes in physics are finite: all speeds are limited to $\approx$ 300.000 km/s, the speed of light, and temperature has a lower limit of $-276\,°C$ (or $0\,°K$). If there can neither be endless acceleration nor cold, it would be daring to assume any psychological effect to be infinite in both directions.

The endlessly linear assumption (ELA) is a central piece of all LRMs that is always violated in a universe like ours. So, should we never ever use a linear model and move on to non-linear models right away? Pragmatically, the LRM often is a reasonably effective approximation. At the beginning of Sect. 4.2, we have seen that the increase of time-on-task by age is not strictly linear, but follows a more complex curved pattern. This pattern might be of interest to someone studying the psychological causes of the decline in performance. For the applied design researcher, it probably suffices to see that the increase is monotonous and model it approximately by one slope coefficient. In Sect. 5.1, we will estimate the age effects for designs A and B separately, which lets us compare fairness toward older people.

Table 4.18 Data set with 7 variables, showing 8 of 300 observations

Obs	Part	Task	Design	Gender	Education	Far_sighted
191	11	2	B	F	Middle	FALSE
251	11	4	B	F	Middle	FALSE
42	12	2	A	M	Middle	FALSE
32	2	2	A	F	High	TRUE
25	25	1	A	F	Middle	FALSE
238	28	3	B	F	Low	TRUE
157	7	1	B	M	High	FALSE
248	8	4	B	M	High	FALSE

As has been said, theorists may desire a more detailed picture and see a disruption of linearity as indicators for interesting psychological processes. A literally uncanny example of such theoretical work will be given when introducing polynomial regression Sect. 5.5. For now, linear regression is a pragmatic choice, as long as

1. the pattern is monotonically increasing;
2. any predictions stay in the observed range and avoid the boundary regions, or beyond.

4.3 Factorial Models

In the previous section, we have seen how linear models are fitting the association between a metric predictor X and an outcome variable Y to a straight line with a slope and a point of intercept. Such a model creates a prediction of Y, given you know the value of measure X.

However, in many research situations, the predictor variable carries not a measure, but a *group label*. *Factor variables* assign observations to one of a set of predefined groups, such as the following variables do in the BrowsingAB case (Table 4.18):

```
attach(BrowsingAB)

BAB5 %>%
  select(Obs, Part, Task, Design, Gender, Education, Far_sighted)
```

Two of the variables, Gender and Education, clearly carry a group membership of the participants. That is a natural way to think of people groups, such as male of female, or which school type they went to. But, models are inert to anthropocentrism and can divide everything into groups. Most generally, it is always the observations, i.e. the rows in a (tidy) data table, which are divided into groups. Half of the observations have been made with design A, the rest with B.

The data also identifies the participant and the task for every observation. Although do we see numbers on participants, these are factors, not metric variables. If one had used the initials of participants, that would not make the slightest difference of what this variable tells. It also does not matter whether the researcher has actually created the levels, for example, by assigning participants to one of two design conditions, or has just observed it, such as demographic variables.

Factorial models are frequently used in experiments, where the effect of a certain condition on performance is measured. In design research, we frequently seek to compare performance of two (or more) designs. The basic factorial model, will be introduced, first Sect. 4.3.1. Sects. 4.3.2 and 4.3.3. explain what dummy variables are and how they can be used for custom factorial models. Sect. 4.3.4 introduces the absolute means model and some of its applications. Factors are not metric, but sometimes they have a natural order, for example, levels of education, or position in a sequence. In Sect. 4.3.5, we will use dummy variables one more time to build an ordered factorial model for short learning sequences.

4.3.1   A Versus B: Comparison of Groups

The most common linear model on factors is the *comparison of groups* (CGM), which replaces the commonly known analysis of variance (ANOVA). In design research, group comparisons are all over the place, for example:

- comparing designs: as we have seen in the A/B testing scenario;
- comparing groups of people, based on e.g. gender or whether they have a high school degree;
- comparing situations, like whether an app was used on the go or standing still.

In order to perform a CGM, a variable is needed that establishes the groups. This is commonly called a *factor*. A factor is a variable that identifies members of groups, like "A" and "B" or "male" and "female". The groups are called *factor levels*. In the BrowsingAB case, the most interesting factor is Design with its levels A and B.

Asking for differences between two (or more) designs is routine in design research. For example, it could occur during an overhaul of a municipal website. With the emerge of e-government, many municipal websites have grown wildly over a decade. What once was a lean (but not pretty) 1990 website has grown into a jungle over time, to the disadvantage of users. The BrowsingAB case could represent the prototype of a novel web design, which is developed and tested via A/B testing at 200 users. Every user is given the same task, but sees only one of the two designs. The design team is interested in *Do the two web designs A and B differ in user performance?* Again, we first take a look at the raw data (Fig. 4.12),

```
attach(BrowsingAB)

BAB1 %>%
  ggplot(aes(x = ToT)) +
  geom_histogram() +
  facet_grid(Design ~ .)
```

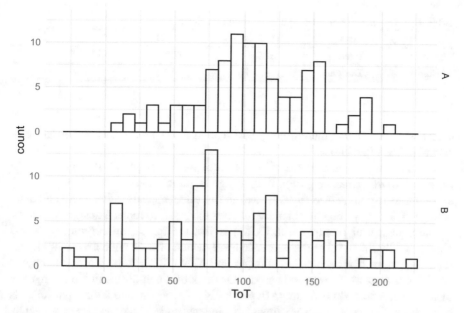

Fig. 4.12 Histogram showing ToT distributions in two groups

The difference, if it exists, is not striking. We might consider a slight advantage for design B, but the overlap is immense. We perform the CGM. Again, this is a two-step procedure:

1. The stan_glm command lets you specify a simple formula to express the dependency between one or more predictors (education) and an outcome variable (ToT). It performs the parameter estimation using the method of *Markov Chain Monte Carlo Sampling*. The results are stored in a new object M_CGM.
2. With the coef command, the estimates are extracted and can be interpreted, (Table 4.19).

```
M_CGM <-
  BAB1 %>%
  stan_glm(ToT ~ 1 + Design,
    data = .
  )
```

```
coef(M_CGM)
```

The model contains two parameters, one Intercept and one slope. Wait a second? How can you have a slope and a "crossing point zero", when there is no line, but just two groups? This will be explained further in Sects. 4.3.2 and 4.3.3. The fact is, in the model at hand, the Intercept is the *mean of a reference group*. By default, stan_glm chooses the alphabetically first group label as the reference group, in this

Table 4.19 Coefficient estimates with 95% credibility limits

Parameter	Fixef	Center	Lower	Upper
Intercept	Intercept	106.6	97.2	116.4
DesignB	DesignB	−17.5	−30.6	−4.2

case design A. We can therefore say that design A has an average performance of $106.65[97.2, 116.41]_{CI95}$.

The second parameter is the effect of "moving to design B". It is given as the *difference to the reference group*. With design B, it took users $17.49[30.62, 4.2]_{CI95}$ seconds less to complete the task. However, this effect appears rather small and there is huge uncertainty about it. It barely justifies the effort to replace design A with B.

A frequent user problem with CGMs is that the regression engine selects the alphabetically first level as the reference level, which often is not correct. Supposed, the two designs had been called Old (A) and New (B), then the regression engine would pick New as the reference group. Or think of a non-discriminating language in statistical reports. In BrowsingAB, gender is coded as f/m and female participants conquer the Intercept. But, sometimes my students code gender as v/m or w/m. Oh, my dear! The best solution is, indeed, to think upfront and try to find level names that make sense. If that is not possible, then the factor variable, which is often of type `character`, must be made a factor, which is a data type in its own right in R. When the regression engine sees a factor variable, it takes the first factor level as a reference group. That would be nice, but when a factor is created using the `as.factor`, it again takes an alphabetical order of levels. This is over-run by giving a vector of levels in the desired order. The tidy Forcats package provides further commands to set the order of factor levels.

```
Gender <- sample(c(``v'', ``m''), 4, replace = T)

factor(Gender)
```

```
## [1] m v m m
## Levels: m v
```

```
factor(Gender, c(``v'', ``m''))
```

```
## [1] m v m m
## Levels: v m
```

Table 4.20 Data set with 5 variables, showing 8 of 200 observations

Obs	Design	Design_A	Design_B	ToT
31	A	1	0	182.7
43	A	1	0	186.9
113	B	0	1	57.7
162	B	0	1	28.5
165	B	0	1	56.4
175	B	0	1	64.4
190	B	0	1	111.3
196	B	0	1	121.2

4.3.2 Not Stupid: Dummy Variables

Are we missing anything so far? Indeed, I avoided showing any mathematics on factorial models. The CGM really is a linear model, although it may not appear so, at first. So, how can a variable enter a linear model equation that is not a number? Linear model terms are a sum of products $\beta_i x_i$, but factors cannot just enter such a term. What would be the result of DesignB $\times \beta_1$?

Factors basically answer the question: *What group does the observation belong to?* This is a label, not a number, and cannot enter the regression formula. *Dummy variables* solve the dilemma by converting factor levels to numbers. This is done by giving *every level l* of factor *K* its own dummy variable *K_l*. Now every dummy represents the simple question: *Does this observation belong to group DesignB?* The answer is coded as 1 for "Yes" and 0 for "No" (Table 4.20).

```
attach(BrowsingAB)

BAB1_dum <-
  BAB1 %>%
  mutate(
    Design_A = if_else(Design == ''A'', 1, 0),
    Design_B = if_else(Design == ''B'', 1, 0)
  ) %>%
  select(Obs, Design, Design_A, Design_B, ToT)

BAB1_dum
```

The new dummy variables are numerical and can very well enter a linear formula, everyone getting its own coefficient. For a factor K with levels A, B and C, the linear formula can include the dummy variables K_{Ai} and K_{Bi}:

$$\mu_i = K_{Ai}\beta_A + K_{Bi}\beta_B$$

Table 4.21 Coefficient estimates with 95% credibility limits

Parameter	Fixef	Center	Lower	Upper
Design_A	Design_A	106.6	96.8	116.0
Design_B	Design_B	89.4	79.9	98.9

The zero/one coding acts like a switch. When $K_{Ai} = 1$, the parameter β_A is switched on and enters the sum, and β_B is switched off. An observation of group A gets the predicted value: $\mu_i = \beta_A$, vice versa for members of group B.

```
M_dummy_1 <-
  stan_glm(ToT ~ 0 + Design_A + Design_B,
    data = BAB1_dum
  )
```

```
coef(M_dummy_1)
```

In its predictions, the model M_dummy is equivalent to the CGM model M_CGM, but the coefficients mean something different. In the CGM, we got an intercept and a group difference, here we get both group means (Table 4.21). This model we call an *absolute means model (AMM)* and will discuss it in Sect. 4.3.4. First, we have to come back to the question of how the regression engine produces its dummy variables. When encountering a factorial predictor, our regression engine uses not group means, but what is called *treatment contrast coding* Sect. 4.3.3.

4.3.3 Treatment Contrast Coding

The default behavior of regression engines, when encountering a factor, is to select the first level as a reference group and estimate all other levels relative to that. Coefficients express differences. This fully makes sense if the effect of a treatment is what you are after, and is therefore called *treatment contrasts*. Treatment contrasts do not have anything special or natural to them, but are a very particular way of thinking about levels of a factor, namely that *one level is special*. In controlled experiments, this special level often is the *control condition*, whereas the coefficients are the effects of well-defined manipulations. This most prominently is the case for clinical trials, where the *placebo group* is untreated. This works well in all situations where a default situation exists and the other factor levels can be thought of as manipulations of the default:

- A redesign as an improvement over the *current design*.
- A quiet, comfortable environment is the *optimal situation* for cognitive performance.
- There is a *minimum level* of education required for most jobs.

We have seen how to create dummy variables ourselves by means of mutually exclusive on-off switches, which results in absolute means coefficients. Regression engines quietly assume that treatment effects are what the user wants and expand dummy variables in a different way: For a factor with levels A and B, the dummy for B is an on-off switch, whereas the reference level A is set *always on* (Table 4.22). This way of creating dummy variables is called *treatment contrast coding*:

```
BAB1_treat <-
  BAB1_dum %>%
  mutate(
    Intercept = 1,
    Design_B = if_else(Design == ''B'', 1, 0)
  ) %>%
  select(Obs, Design, Intercept, Design_B, ToT)
BAB1_treat
```

A frequent user problem with treatment coding is that the regression engine selects the alphabetically first level as the reference level. Supposed, the two designs had been called Old (A) and New (B), then the regression engine would pick New as the reference group. But recall the more convenient ways that were outlined earlier, Sect. 4.3.1.

The following chapters deal with more variations of factorial models. Next, we will take a closer look at the absolute means model Sect. 4.3.4, which is useful, when a reference group does not come natural. In Sect. 4.3.5, we deal with factorial models, where levels are ordered and introduce a third way of dummy coding: *stairways coding* for factors with ordered levels.

Table 4.22 Data set with 5 variables, showing 8 of 200 observations

Obs	Design	Intercept	Design_B	ToT
6	A	1	0	20.4
15	A	1	0	185.7
34	A	1	0	168.8
38	A	1	0	107.6
84	A	1	0	147.2
94	A	1	0	120.4
95	A	1	0	117.1
199	B	1	1	112.9

4.3.4 Absolute Means Model

Not all factor variables are experimental, and identifying a default can be difficult or unnatural. This often happens when the levels are just a set of conditions that you have *found as given*, such as the individuals in the human population, or all words in a language. Such is the case in the IPump study, where every session was composed of a set of tasks, such as starting the device or entering a dose. These tasks were taken from existing training material and including them as a factor could help identify areas for improvement. Although the tasks form a sequence, they are equally important for the operation. Not one can be singled out as default. Treatment coding would force us to name one default task for the Intercept.

The *absolute means model* represents all levels by their absolute means. If you put in a factorial predictor with eight levels, you will get eight coefficients, which are the mean outcomes of every level. Of course, what you can no longer do is find differences between levels.

We have seen in Sect. 4.3.2 how to create AMM dummy variables. In fact, the linear models formula language already knows two expressions (but no more) that specify an AMM.

- `0 + Task`
- `Task - 1`

In the following, we estimate an AMM using the formula method. In the IPump study, we had a sample of nurses do a sequence of eight tasks on a medical infusion pump with a novel interface design. For the further development of such a design, it may be interesting to see which tasks would most benefit from design improvements. A possible way to look at it is by saying that a longer task has more potential to be optimized. Under such a perspective, tasks are an equal set and there is no natural reference task for a CGM. Instead, we estimate the absolute group means, and visualize the CLU table as center dots and 95% credibility bars.

```
attach(IPump)

M_AMM_1 <- stan_glm(ToT ~ 0 + Task,
  data = D_Novel
)

coef(M_AMM_1) %>%
  rename(Task = fixef) %>%
  ggplot(aes(
    x = Task,
    y = center, ymin = lower, ymax = upper
  )) +
  geom_crossbar()
```

In Fig. 4.13, we can easily discover that Task 2 is by far the longest and that tasks differ a lot, overall. None of these relations can easily be seen in the CGM plot. Note

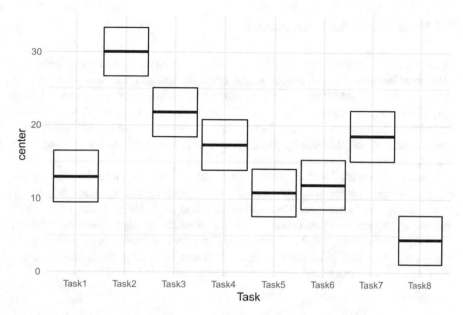

Fig. 4.13 ToT on five tasks, center estimates and 95% credibility interval

that the AMM is not a different model than the treatment effects model. It is just a *different parametrization*, which makes interpretation easier. Both models produce the exact same predictions (except for minimal variations from the MCMC random walk).

The choice between CGM and AMM depends on whether a factor represents designed manipulations or whether it is more of something that has been collected, in other words: a sample. For experimental conditions, with one default condition, a CGM is the best choice. When the factor levels are a sample of equals, an AMM is more useful. It is for now because in Sect. 6.5, we will see how random effects apply for non-human populations. .

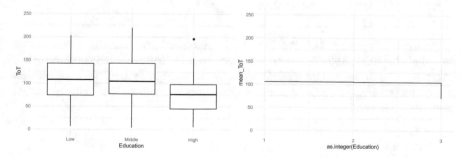

Fig. 4.14 A boxplot and a step chart showing differences in ToT by level of education

4.3.5   Ordered Factorial Models

Factors usually are not metric, which would require them to have *an order* and a unit (like years or number of errors). Age, for example, has an order and a unit, which is years. With an LRM, this makes it possible to say: "*per year of age*, participants slow down by …". The same cannot be said for levels of education. We could assign these levels the numbers 0, 1 and 2 to express the order, but we cannot assume that going from Low to Middle is the same amount of effective education as going from Middle to High.

One should not use LRM on a non-metric variable, AMM and CGM can be used, but actually they are too weak, because the coefficients do not represent the order.

For the level of education, we could use a CGM or AMM, but the graphics and regression models will just order factors alphabetically: High, Low and Middle. Note how I first change the order of levels to over-ride alphabetical ordering. In Fig. 4.14, Low and Middle are almost on the same level of performance, whereas High education has an advantage of around 30 s.

```
attach(BrowsingAB)

BAB1$Education <- factor(as.character(BAB1$Education),
   levels = c(''Low'', ''Middle'', ''High'')
)

BAB1 %>%
   ggplot(aes(x = Education, y = ToT)) +
   geom_boxplot() +
   ylim(0, 250)

BAB1 %>%
   group_by(Education) %>%
   summarize(mean_ToT = mean(ToT)) %>%
   ggplot(aes(x = as.integer(Education), y = mean_ToT)) +
   geom_step() +
   scale_x_continuous(breaks = 1:3) +
   ylim(0, 250)
```

Note that R also knows a separate variable type called ordered factors, which only seemingly is useful. At least, if we run a linear model with an officially ordered factor as a predictor, the estimated model will be so unintelligible that I will not attempt to explain it here. Instead, we start by estimating a regular CGM with treatment contrasts (Table 4.23).

```
M_OFM_1 <-
   BAB1 %>%
   stan_glm(ToT ~ 1 + Education, data = .)

coef(M_OFM_1)
```

Table 4.23 Coefficient estimates with 95% credibility limits

Parameter	Fixef	Center	Lower	Upper
Intercept	Intercept	105.989	95.2	117.0
EducationMiddle	EducationMiddle	−0.654	−15.8	14.6
EducationHigh	EducationHigh	−34.953	−52.5	−16.8

A basic ordered factor model is just a CGM where the coefficients are shown in the desired order. The second and third coefficients carry the respective difference toward level Low. EducationHigh is *not* the difference toward EducationMiddle. In this case, it makes sense to understand Middle and High as a smaller step or a larger step up from Low. It is not always like that. Sometimes, the only way of moving from the reference group to some other level implies going through all the intermediates, just like walking up a stairway. Then it makes more sense to use a model where coefficients are individual steps. In the IPump study, we looked at the speed of learning of a novel interface design by letting the participants repeat a set of tasks in three successive sessions. Here the three sessions make a stairway: going from the first to the third session always involves the second session. Before we come to that, we first have to see why Session must be an ordered factor and not a metric predictor.

The first idea that could come to mind is to take the session as a metric predictor and estimate an LRM—there is an ordering and it is the same amount of training per step, which you could call a unit. The thing with learning processes is that they are curved, more precisely, they gradually move toward an asymptote. The following curve shows the effect of a hypothetical training over 12 sessions. What we see is that the steps are getting smaller when training continues. While the amount of training is the same, the effect on performance declines, which is also called a curve of diminishing returns. The asymptote of this curve is the *maximum performance* the participant can reach, which theoretically is only reached in infinity. The following code defines an exponential learning curve function and renders the example in Fig. 4.15.

```
learning_curve <-
  function(session, amplitude, rate, asymptote) {
    amplitude * exp(-rate * session) + asymptote
  }

tibble(session = as.integer(1:12)) %>%
  mutate(ToT = learning_curve(session, 10, 0.3, 2)) %>%
  ggplot(aes(x = session, y = ToT)) +
  geom_step() +
  scale_x_continuous(breaks = 1:12)
```

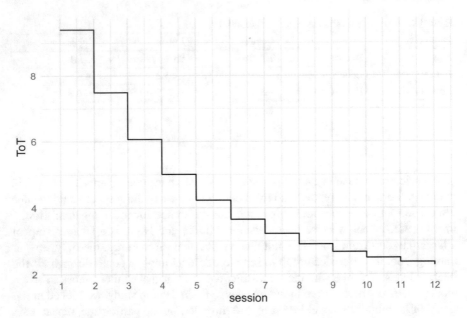

Fig. 4.15 A learning curve

LRMs can only do straight lines, which means constant effects, whereas learning curves have diminishing effects. For short learning sequences, we can use ordered factorial models, where every session becomes a level. As these levels get their own coefficients, the steps no longer have to be constant. When levels are ordered, the two end point levels (first session, last session) can serve as a natural reference group for the intercept. However, how useful would it be to express the performance in session 3 as differences to the reference level (session 1). It is more natural to think of learning to take place incrementally, like *walking up stairways* (or down), where the previous step always is your reference (Fig. 4.16).

```
attach(IPump)

D_Novel %>%
  group_by(Session, session) %>%
  summarize(mean_ToT = mean(ToT)) %>%
  ggplot(aes(x = as.integer(Session), y = mean_ToT)) +
  geom_step() +
  scale_x_continuous(breaks = 1:3)
```

This is what a factorial model with *stairways dummy coding* does. The first coefficient β_0 is the starting point, for example, the first session, and all other coefficients (β_1, β_2) are a sequence of step sizes. The expected value μ_i for session K, using stairways dummies K_0, K_1, K_2, is

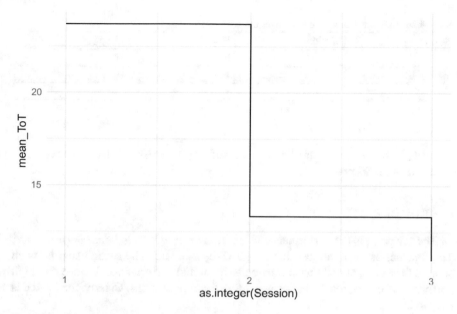

Fig. 4.16 Learning to execute a task faster over three sessions

$$\mu_i = K_{1i}\beta_0 \qquad\qquad +$$
$$K_{2i}(\beta_0 + \beta_1) \qquad +$$
$$K_{?i}(\beta_0 + \beta_1 + \beta_2)$$

Thinking of these dummy variables as switches once again: Recall that treatment dummies have an always-on reference level and exclusive switches for the other levels Sect. 4.3.2. Stairway dummies are like a *incremental switches*: when switch K is on, this implies all previous switches are on, too (Table 4.24). *Stairways-down* dummies are made as follows:

```
D_Novel <-
  D_Novel %>%
  mutate(
    Session_1 = 1,
    Step_1 = as.integer(session >= 1),
    Step_2 = as.integer(session >= 2)
  )

D_Novel %>%
  distinct(session, Session_1, Step_1, Step_2) %>%
  arrange(session)
```

Now we can run a factorial model using these stairway-down dummies, where the intercept is the upper floor and we are losing height at every step (Table 4.25).

Table 4.24 Stairways dummy coding over three sessions

Session	Session_1	Step_1	Step_2
0	1	0	0
1	1	1	0
2	1	1	1

```
M_OFM_2 <- stan_glm(ToT ~ Session_1 + Step_1 + Step_2,
   data = D_Novel
)
```

```
coef(M_OFM_2)
```

The Intercept is the performance in the first level, which is *initial performance*. The first step is huge, almost reducing ToT by one half. The second step is much smaller than the first and tiny compared to the initial performance. We see that high performance can be reached after just a few training sessions. Clearly, the device is easy to learn.

Another question that arises is what level of performance is reached in the end. Is *maximum performance* good enough, actually? Strictly, this would require a non-linear learning curve model, which would contain an estimate for maximum performance. With an OFM, the best guess we have is *final performance*. Because the second step was already small, we may believe that the asymptote is not so far anymore. And we know that final performance is a conservative estimate for maximum performance. With a *stairway-up model*, the Intercept is the basement an we walk up step-by-step (Table 4.26).

```
D_Novel <-
   D_Novel %>%
   mutate(
     Session_3 = 1,
     Step_1 = as.integer(session <= 1),
     Step_2 = as.integer(session <= 0)
   )
```

```
D_Novel %>%
```

Table 4.25 Coefficient estimates with 95% credibility limits

Parameter	Fixef	Center	Lower	Upper
Intercept	Intercept	23.71	21.55	25.896
Step_1	Step_1	−10.36	−13.31	−7.227
Step_2	Step_2	−2.38	−5.39	0.529

Table 4.26 Coefficient estimates with 95% credibility limits

Parameter	Fixef	Center	Lower	Upper
Intercept	Intercept	10.93	8.879	13.01
Step_1	Step_1	2.42	−0.717	5.44
Step_2	Step_2	10.33	7.254	13.41

```
distinct(session, Session_3, Step_1, Step_2) %>%
arrange(desc(session)) %>%
as_tibble()
```

Session	Step_1	Step_2	Session_3
2	0	0	1
1	1	0	1
0	1	1	1

```
M_OFM_3 <- stan_glm(ToT ~ Session_3 + Step_1 + Step_2,
    data = D_Novel
)
```

```
coef(M_OFM_3)
```

The Intercept is an estimate of final performance and we can ask whether this
level of efficiency is actually good enough. From a methodological perspective, the
results of this study indicate that it might often be worthwhile to let participants do
multiple sessions and observe the learning process. In particular, when users do their
tasks routinely with a device, like the nurses, initial performance can be a very poor
estimate for long-term performance.

To wrap it up: Factorial models use dummy variables to put factor levels into
the linear term of a model. These dummy variables can be understood as arrays of
switches, and we saw how they can be arranged in different patterns:

1. Exclusive on-off switches produce an AMM. An AMM is the least specified
   among factorial models; all levels are equal. Often this is the best choice when
   the levels were drawn from a population.
2. One always-on Intercept and exclusive on-off switches produce a CGM with
   treatment effects. When a default level can be identified, such as the placebo
   condition in clinical trials, treatment contrasts are a good choice.
3. Stairway dummies produce an OFM, taking one end point as the first coefficient
   and stepping up (or down). This is particularly useful for short learning curves.

The disadvantage of an OFM is that it cannot predict how performance will improve in *future* sessions. In Sect. 7.2.1.2, we will see how a Poisson regression model can linearize a learning curve and can make forecasts.

The AMM deals with a situation where a factor is under-specified to be used with treatment contrasts. It lacks the default level. Ordered factors at the opposite side, being *more specific* than treatment factors. Treatment factors identify one default level, but the rest are just a set. Quite often, factors also carry a natural order, such as level of education or position in a sequence of tasks.

Chapter 5
Multi-predictor Models

Design researchers are often collecting data under rather wild conditions. Users of municipal websites, consumer products, enterprise information systems and cars can be extremely diverse. At the same time, Designs vary in many attributes, affecting the user in many different ways. There are many variables in the game, and even more possible relations. With *multi-predictor models*, we can examine the simultaneous influence of everything we have recorded.

The first part of the chapter deals with predictors that act independent of each other: Sect. 5.1 demonstrates how two continuous linear predictors form a surface in a three-dimensional space. Subsequently, we address the case of multifactorial models in Sect. 5.2, which are very common in experimental research. In Sect. 4.3.2, we have seen how linear models unite factorial with continuous predictors. This lays the ground for combining them into grouped regression models, Sect. 5.3.

That being said, in reality it frequently happens that predictors are not acting independent on each other. Rather, the influence of one predictor changes dependent on the value of another predictor. In Sect. 5.4, conditional effects models will be introduced. As will turn out, by adding conditional effects a linear model is capable of rendering non-linear associations. The final section introduces polynomial regression as a general way to estimate even wildly non-linear relationship between a continuous predictor and the outcome variable.

5.1 On Surface: Multiple Regression Models

Productivity software, like word processors, presentation and calculation software or graphics programs have evolved over decades. For every new release, dozens of developers have worked hard to make the handling more efficient and the user experience more pleasant. Consider a program for drawing illustrations: basic functionalities, such as drawing lines, selecting objects, moving or colourizing them, have

© Springer Nature Switzerland AG 2021
M. Schmettow, *New Statistics for Design Researchers*,
Human–Computer Interaction Series,
https://doi.org/10.1007/978-3-030-46380-9_5

practically always been there. A user wanting to draw six rectangles, painting them red and arranging them in a grid pattern can readily do that using basic functionality. At a certain point of system evolution, it may have been recognized that this is what users repeatedly do: creating a grid of alike objects. With the basic functions, this is rather repetitive and a new function was created, called "copy-and-arrange". Users may now create a single object, specify rows and columns of the grid and give it a run.

The new function saves time and leads to better results. Users should be very excited about the new feature, should they not? Not quite, as [1] made a very troubling observation: adding functionality for the good of efficiency may turn out ineffective in practice, as users have a strong tendency to stick with their old routines, ignoring new functionality right away. This is called the *active user paradox (AUP)*.

Do all users behave that way? Or can we find users of certain traits that are different? What type of person would be less likely to fall for the AUP? And how can we measure resistance toward the AUP? We did a study, where we explored the impact of two user traits *need-for-cognition (ncs)* and *geekism (gex)* on AUP resistance. To measure AUP resistance, we observed users while they were doing drawing tasks with a graphics software. User actions were noted down and classified by a behavioral coding scheme. From the frequencies of exploration and elaboration actions, an individual AUP resistance score was derived. So, are users with high need-for-cognition and geekism more resistant to the AUP?

In Fig. 5.1, we first look at the two predictors, separately:

```
attach(AUP)

AUP_1 %>%
   ggplot(aes(x = ncs, y = resistance)) +
   geom_point() +
   geom_smooth(method = "lm", se = F)

AUP_1 %>%
   ggplot(aes(x = gex, y = resistance)) +
   geom_point() +
   geom_smooth(method = "lm", se = F)
```

As we will see, it is preferable to build one model with two simultaneous predictors, and this is what the present section is all about. Still, we begin with two separate LRMs, one for each predictor, and z-transformed scores, then we create one model with two predictors.

$$M1 : \mu_i = \beta_0 + \beta_{ncs} x_{ncs}$$
$$M2 : \mu_i = \beta_0 + \beta_{gex} x_{gex}$$

```
M_1 <-
   AUP_1 %>%
   stan_glm(zresistance ~ zncs, data = .)
```

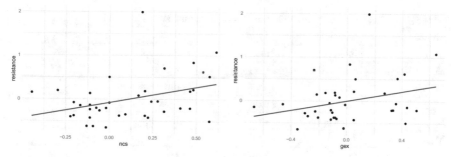

Fig. 5.1 Linear associations of NCS and Gex with Resistance

```
M_2 <-
  AUP_1 %>%
  stan_glm(zresistance ~ zgex, data = .)
```

Next, we estimate a model that includes both predictors *simultaneously*. The most practical property of the linear term is that we can include multiple predictor terms (and the intercept), just by forming the sum. In this case, this is a `multiple regression model` (MRM):

$$\mu_i = \beta_0 + \beta_{ncs} x_{ncs} + \beta_{gex} x_{gex}$$

In R's regression formula language, this is similarly straightforward. The + operator directly corresponds with the + in the likelihood formula.

```
M_3 <-
  AUP_1 %>%
  stan_glm(zresistance ~ zncs + zgex, data = .) # <--
```

For the comparison of the three models, we make use of a feature of package Bayr: the posterior distributions of arbitrary models can be combined into one multi-model posterior object, by just stacking them upon each other with `bind_rows` (Table 5.1). In effect, the coefficient table shows all models simultaneously (Table 5.2):

```
P_multi <- bind_rows(
  posterior(M_1),
  posterior(M_2),
  posterior(M_3)
)

P_multi

coef(P_multi)
```

Table 5.1 MCMC posterior with 4000 samples of 10 parameters in 3 model(s)

Model	Parameter	Type	fixef	Count
M_1	Intercept	fixef	Intercept	1
M_1	zncs	fixef	zncs	1
M_2	Intercept	fixef	Intercept	1
M_2	zgex	fixef	zgex	1
M_3	Intercept	fixef	Intercept	1
M_3	zgex	fixef	zgex	1
M_3	zncs	fixef	zncs	1
M_1	sigma_resid	disp		
M_2	sigma_resid	disp		
M_3	sigma_resid	disp		

Table 5.2 Coefficient estimates with 95% credibility limits

Model	Parameter	fixef	Center	Lower	Upper
M_1	Intercept	Intercept	−0.001	−0.325	0.314
M_1	zncs	zncs	0.372	0.065	0.687
M_2	Intercept	Intercept	0.001	−0.312	0.305
M_2	zgex	zgex	0.291	−0.034	0.618
M_3	Intercept	Intercept	−0.001	−0.302	0.306
M_3	zncs	zncs	0.295	−0.079	0.687
M_3	zgex	zgex	0.122	−0.259	0.505

Now, we can easily compare the coefficients. The intercepts of all three models are practically zero, which is a consequence of the z-transformation. Recall, that the intercept in an LRM is the point, where the predictor variable is zero. In MRM this is just the same: here, the intercept is the predicted AUP resistance score, when NCS and GEX are both zero.

When using the two predictors simultaneously, the overall positive tendency remains. However, we observe major and minor shifts: in the MRM, the coefficient of the geekism score is reduced to less than half: $0.12[-0.26, 0.5]_{CI95}$. In contrast, the impact of NCS is reduced just by a little, compared to M_1 : $0.29[-0.08, 0.69]_{CI95}$.

For any researcher who has carefully conceived a research question, this appears to be a disappointing outcome. Indeed, putting multiple predictors into a model sometimes reduces the size of the effect, compared to single-predictor models. More precisely, this happens, when *predictors are correlated*. In this study, participants who are high on NCS also tend to have more pronounced geekism (Fig. 5.2)

```
AUP_1 %>%
  ggplot(aes(x = zncs, y = zgex)) +
  geom_point() +
```

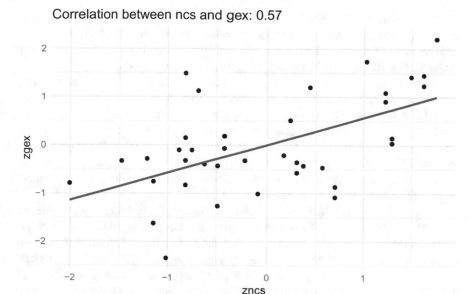

Fig. 5.2 Correlated predictors Gex and NCS

```
geom_smooth(method = "lm", se = F) +
labs(title = str_c(
    "Correlation between ncs and gex: ",
    round(cor(AUP_1$zncs, AUP_1$zgex), 2)
))
```

Participants with a higher NCS also tend to score higher on geekism. Is that surprising? Actually, it is not. People high on NCS love to think. Computers are a good choice for them, because these are complicated devices that make you think. (Many users may even agree that computers help you think, for example, when analyzing your data with R.) In turn, geekism is a positive attitude toward working with computers in sophisticated ways, which means such people are more resistant toward the AUP.

[NCS: love to think] --> [GEX: love computers] --> [resist AUP]
When such a causal chain can be established without doubt, some researchers speak of a *mediating variable* GEX. Although a bit outdated [2], *mediator analysis is correct when the causal direction of the three variables is known.* The classic method to deal with mediation is a so-called step-wise regression. However, structural equation modeling [3] can be regarded as a better option to deal with three or more variables that have complex causal connections (in theory).

We can exclude that the resistance test has influenced the personality scores, because of the order of appearance in the study. Unfortunately, in the situation here, the causal direction remains ambiguous for NCS and Gex. We can make up a story, like above, where NCS precedes GEX, but we can tell another story with a reversed causal connection, for example, Computers reward you for thinking hard and, hence, you get used to it and make it your lifestyle. If you like thinking hard, then you probably also like the challenge that was given in the experiment.

`[GEX: love computers] --> [NCS: love to think] --> [resist AUP]`
In the current case, we cannot distinguish between these two competing theories with this data alone. This is a central problem in empirical research. An example, routinely re-iterated in social science methods courses is the observation that people who are more intelligent tend to consume more fresh vegetables. Do carrots make us smart? Perhaps, but it is equally plausible that eating carrots is what smart people do. The basic issue is that a particular direction of causality can only be established, when all reverse directions can be excluded by logic.

To come back to the AUP study: There is no way to establish a causal order of predictors NCS and Gex. If nothing is known but covariation, they just enter the model simultaneously, as in model M_3. This results in a redistribution of the overall covariance and the predictors are *mutually controlled*. In M_2, the effect of GEX was promising at first, but now seems spurious in the simultaneous model. Most of the strength was just borrowed from NCS by covariation. The model suggests that loving-to-think has a considerably stronger association with AUP resistance than loving-computers.

That *may* suggest, but not prove, that NCS precedes GEX, as in a chain of causal effects, elements that are closer to the final outcome (AUP resistance) tend to exert more salient influence. But without further theorizing and experimenting, this is weak evidence of causal order.

If I would want to write a paper on geekism, NCS and the AUP, I might be tempted to report the two separate LRMs, that showed at least moderate effects. The reason why one should not do that is that separate analyses suggest that the predictors are independent. To illustrate this at an extreme example, think of a study where users were asked to rate their agreement with an interface by the following two questions, before ToT is recorded:

1. Is the interface beautiful?
2. Does the interface have an aesthetic appearance?

Initial separate analyses show strong effects for both predictors. Still, it would not make sense to give the report the title: "Beauty and aesthetics predict usability". Beauty and aesthetics are practically synonyms. For Gex and NCS this may be not so clear, but we cannot exclude the possibility that they are linked to a common factor, perhaps a third trait that makes people more explorative, no matter whether it be thoughts or computers.

So, what to do if two predictors correlate strongly? First, we always report just a single model. Per default, this is the model with both predictors simultaneously. The second possibility is to use a disciplined method of *model selection* and remove the predictor (or predictors) that does not actually contribute to prediction. The third possibility is that the results with both predictors become more interesting when including conditional effects, Sect. 5.4.

Table 5.3 Coefficient estimates with 95% credibility limits

Parameter	fixef	Center	Lower	Upper
Intercept	Intercept	105.98	93.6	117.94
DesignB	DesignB	−17.47	−31.2	−2.99
GenderM	GenderM	1.35	−12.3	15.00

Table 5.4 A two-factorial model has one reference level and two differences

Condition	F	M
A	Reference	Difference
B	Difference	

5.2 Crossover: Multifactorial Models

The very common situation in research is that multiple factors are of interest. In Sect. 4.3.5, we have seen how we can use an OGM to model a short learning sequence. That was only using half of the data, because in the IPump study, we compared two designs against each other, and both were tested in three sessions. That makes 2 × 3 conditions. Here, I introduce a multifactorial model that has *main effects only*. Such a model actually is of very limited use for the IPump case, where we need *conditional effects* to get to a valid model (Sect. 5.4).

We take as an example the BrowsingAB study: the primary research question regarded the design difference, but the careful researcher also recorded gender of participants. One can always just explore variables that one has. The following model estimates the gender effect alongside the design effect (Table 5.3).

```
attach(BrowsingAB)

M_mfm_1 <-
  BAB1 %>%
  stan_glm(ToT ~ 1 + Design + Gender, data = .)

coef(M_mfm_1)
```

By adding gender to the model, both effects are estimated simultaneously. In the following *multifactorial model (MFM)* the intercept is a reference group, once again. Consider that both factors have two levels, forming a 2 × 2 matrix, like Table 5.4.

```
tribble(
  ~Condition, ~F, ~M,
  "A", "reference", "difference",
  "B", "difference", ""
)
```

Table 5.5 Coefficient estimates with 95% credibility limits

Parameter	fixef	Center	Lower	Upper
DesignA:GenderF	DesignA:GenderF	104.3	89.5	119
DesignB:GenderF	DesignB:GenderF	89.9	75.5	104
DesignA:GenderM	DesignA:GenderM	108.4	95.1	122
DesignB:GenderM	DesignB:GenderM	88.8	75.8	102

The first one, A-F, has been set as reference group. In Table 5.4, the intercept coefficient tells that women in condition A have an average ToT of $105.98[93.65, 117.94]_{CI95}$ seconds. The second coefficient says that design B is slightly faster and that there seemingly is no gender effect.

How comes that the model only has three parameters, when there are four groups? In a CGM, the number of parameters always equals the number of levels, why not here? We can think of the 2×2 conditions as flat four groups, A-F, A-M, B-F and B-M and we would expect four coefficients, say absolute group means. This model regards the two effects as independent that means they are not influencing each other: Design is assumed to have the *same effect* for men and women.

In many multifactorial situations, one is better advised to use a model with conditional effects. Broadly, with conditional effect we can assess, how much effects influence each other. We will come back to that, but here I am introducing an extension of the AMM (Sect. 4.3.4), the *multifactorial AMM* (MAMM):

```
M_amfm_1 <- stan_glm(ToT ~ 0 + Design:Gender, data = BAB1)
```

The R formula for an AMM suppresses the intercept and uses an interaction term without main effects (as will be explained in Sect. 5.4.2). Table 5.5 carries the four group means and can be further processed as a *conditional plot*, as in Fig. 5.3.

```
coef(M_amfm_1)
```

```
coef(M_amfm_1) %>%
    separate(parameter, into = c("Design", "Gender")) %>%
    ggplot(aes(x = Design, col = Gender, y = center)) +
    geom_point(size = 2) +
    geom_line(aes(group = Gender))
```

If the two effects were truly independent, these two lines had to be parallel, because the effect of Gender had to be constant. What this graph now suggests is that there is an interaction between the two effects. There is a tiny advantage for female users with design A, whereas men are faster with B with about the same difference. Because these two effects cancel each other out, the combined effect of Gender in model M_mfm_1 was so close to zero.

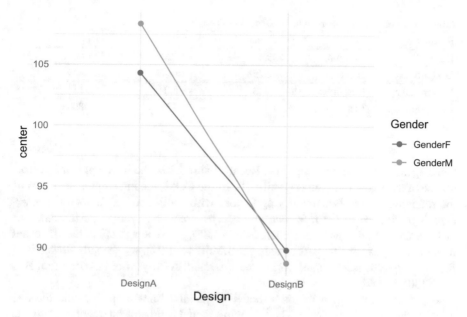

Fig. 5.3 Line graph showing conditional effects in a tow-factorial model

5.3 Line-by-Line: Grouped Regression Models

Recall that dummy variables make factors compatible with linear regression. We have seen how two metric predictors make a surface and how factors can be visualized by straight lines in a conditional plot. When a factor is combined with a metric predictor, we get a group of lines, one per factor level. For example, we can estimate the effects of age and design simultaneously, as shown in Table 5.6.

```
attach(BrowsingAB)

M_grm_1 <-
  BAB1 %>%
  stan_glm(ToT ~ 1 + Design + age_shft, data = .)

coef(M_grm_1)
```

Table 5.6 Coefficient estimates with 95% credibility limits

Parameter	fixef	Center	Lower	Upper
Intercept	Intercept	82.035	66.435	96.85
DesignB	DesignB	−17.381	−30.354	−3.67
age_shft	age_shft	0.817	0.413	1.22

Table 5.7 Coefficient estimates with 95% credibility limits

Parameter	fixef	Center	Lower	Upper
DesignA	DesignA	99.435	79.884	119.042
DesignB	DesignB	46.298	26.843	65.444
DesignA:age_shft	DesignA:age_shft	0.233	−0.346	0.813
DesignB:age_shft	DesignB:age_shft	1.420	0.854	1.980

Once again, we get an intercept first. Recall that in LRM the intercept is the performance of a 20-year old (age was shifted!). In the CGM, the intercept is the mean of the reference group. When marrying factors with continuous predictors, the *intercept is point zero in the reference group*. The predicted average performance of 20-year old with design A is $82.03[66.44, 96.85]_{CI95}$. The age effect has the usual meaning: by year of life, participants get $0.82[0.41, 1.22]_{CI95}$ seconds slower. The *factorial effect* B is a *vertical shift of the intercept*. A 20-year old in condition B is $17.38[30.35, 3.67]_{CI95}$ seconds faster.

It is important to that this is a model of parallel lines, implying that the age effect is the same everywhere. The following model estimates intercepts and slopes separately for every level, making it an *absolute mixed-predictor model (AMPM)*. The following formula produces such a model and results are shown in Table 5.7.

```
M_ampm_1 <- stan_glm(ToT ~ (0 + Design + Design:age_shft),
  data = BAB1
)

coef(M_ampm_1)
```

It turns out that the intercepts and slopes are very different for the two designs. For a 20-year old, design B works much better, but at the same time design B puts a much stronger penalty on every year of age. With these coefficients, we can also produce a conditional plot, with one line per Design condition (Fig. 5.4).

```
coef(M_ampm_1) %>%
  select(fixef, center) %>%
  mutate(
    Design = str_extract(fixef, "[AB]"),
    Coef = if_else(str_detect(fixef, "age"),
      "Slope",
      "Intercept"
    )
  ) %>%
  select(Design, Coef, center) %>%
  spread(key = Coef, value = center) %>%
  ggplot() +
  geom_abline(aes(
```

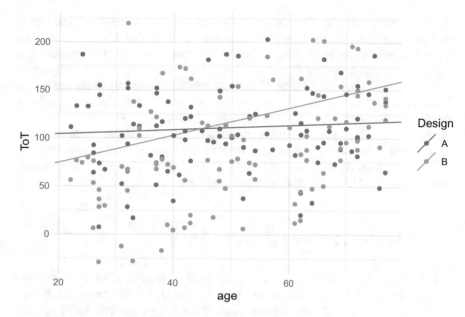

Fig. 5.4 Creating a conditional plot from intercept and slope effects

```
    color = Design,
    intercept = Intercept,
    slope - Slope
)) +
geom_point(data = BAB1, aes(
    x = age,
    col = Design,
    y = ToT
))
```

Note

- how the coefficient table is first made flat with `spread`, where Intercept and Slope become variables.
- that the Abline geometry is specialized in plotting linear graphs, but it requires its own aesthetic mapping (the global will not work).

So, if we can already fit a model with separate group means (an AMFM) or a bunch of straight lines (AMPM), why do we need a more elaborate account of conditional effects, as in Sect. 5.4.2? The answer is that conditional effects often carry important information, but are notoriously difficult to interpret. As it will turn out, conditional effects sometimes are due to rather trivial effects, such as saturation. But, like in this case, they can give the final clue. It is hard to deny that design features can work differently to different people. The hypothetical situation in BrowsingAB is that design B uses a smaller font size, which makes it harder to read with elderly users, whereas younger users have a benefit from more compactly written text.

And, sometimes, experimental hypotheses are even formulated as conditional effects, like the following: some control tasks involve long episodes of vigilance, where mind wandering can interrupt attention on the task. If this is so, we could expect people who meditate to perform better at a long-duration task, but showing no difference at short tasks. In a very simple experiment, participant's reaction time could be measured in a long and short task condition.

5.4   Conditional Effects Models

With the framework of MPM, we can use an arbitrary number of predictors. These can represent properties on different levels, for example, two design proposals for a website can differ in font size, or participants differ in age. So, with MPM we gain much greater flexibility in handling data from applied design research, which allows us to examine user-design interactions more closely.

The catch is that if you would ask an arbitrary design researcher:

Do you think that all users are equal? Or, could it be that one design is better for some users, but inferior for others?

you would in most cases get the answer:

Of course users differ in many ways and it is crucial to know your target group.

Some will also refer to the concept of usability by the ISO 9241-11, which contains the famous phrase:

"… for a specified user …"

The definition explicitly requires you to state for *for whom* you intended to design. It thereby implicitly acknowledges that usability of a design could be very different for another user group. Statements on usability are by the ISO 9241-11 definition *conditional* on the target user group.

In statistical terms, conditional statements have this form:

the effect of design *depends on* the user group.

In regression models, conditional statements like these are represented by *conditional effects*. Interactions between user properties and designs are central in design research, and deserve a neologism: *differential design effects models (DDM)*.

However, conditional effects are often needed for a less interesting reason: *saturation* occurs when physical (or other) boundaries are reached and the steps are getting smaller, for example, the more you train, the less net effect it usually has. Saturations counterpart is *amplification*, a rare one, which acts like compound glue: it will harden only if the two components are present.

5.4.1 Conditional Multiple Regression

In Sect. 4.2, we have seen how the relationship between predictor and outcome variable can be modeled as a linear term. We analyzed the relationship between age and ToT in the (fictional) BrowsingAB case and over both designs combined and observed just a faint decline in performance, which also seemed to take a wavey form.

It is commonly held that older people tend to have lower performance than younger users. A number of factors are called responsible, such as slower processing speed, lower working memory capacity, lower motor speed and visual problems. All these capabilities interact with properties of designs, such as legibility, visual simplicity and how well the interaction design is mapped to a user's task. It is not a stretch to assume that designs can differ in how much performance degrades with age.

In turn, a design can also contain compromises that limit the performance of younger users. For example, the main difference between design A and B in the BrowsingAB example is that A uses larger letters than B. Would that create the same benefit for everybody? It is not unlikely that larger letters really only matter for users that have issues with vision. Unfortunately, large letters have an adverse side effect for younger users, as larger font size takes up more space on screen and more scrolling is required. In Fig. 5.5, we take a first look at the situation.

```
attach(BrowsingAB)

BAB1 %>%
  ggplot(aes(
    x = age,
    col = Design,
    y = ToT
  )) +
  geom_point() +
  geom_smooth(se = F) +
  geom_smooth(aes(col = "combined"), se = F)
```

The graph suggests that designs A and B differ in the effect of age. Design B appears to perform much better with younger users. At the same time, it seems as if A could be more favorable for users at a high age. By adding the conditional effect `Design:age_shft`, the following model estimates the linear relationship for the designs separately. This is essentially the same model as the absolute mixed-predictor model M_ampm_1 in this chapter, which also had four coefficients, the intercepts and slopes of two straight lines. We have already seen how the GRM and the AMPM

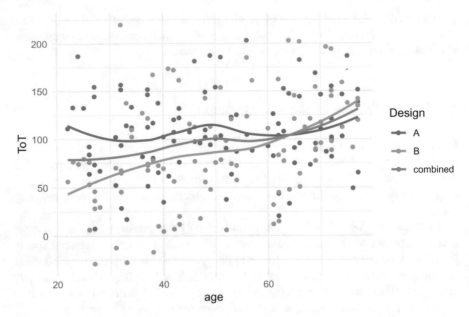

Fig. 5.5 The effect of age, combined and conditional on Design

produce different fitted responses. Predictions are independent of contrast coding, but coefficients are not. The following conditional model uses treatment contrasts, like the GRM, and we can compare the coefficients side-by-side (Table 5.8).

```
M_cmrm <-
  BAB1 %>%
  stan_glm(ToT ~ Design + age_shft + Design:age_shft,
    data = .
  )

P_comb <-
  bind_rows(
    posterior(M_grm_1),
    posterior(M_cmrm)
  )
```

```
coef(P_comb)
```

The conditional model shares the first three coefficients with the unconditional model, but only the first two, Intercept and DesignB have the same meaning.

The intercept is the performance of an average twenty-year old using design A, but the two models diverge in where to place this and the conditional model is less in favor of design A (99.99[80.39, 119.86]$_{CI95}$ seconds). Conversely, the effect

Table 5.8 Coefficient estimates with 95% credibility limits

Model	Parameter	fixef	Center	Lower	Upper
M_cmrm	Intercept	Intercept	99.992	80.392	119.858
M_cmrm	DesignB	DesignB	−53.112	−80.641	−25.913
M_cmrm	age_shft	age_shft	0.219	−0.346	0.805
M_cmrm	DesignB:age_shft	DesignB:age_shft	1.191	0.405	2.007
M_grm_1	Intercept	Intercept	82.035	66.435	96.848
M_grm_1	DesignB	DesignB	−17.381	−30.354	−3.670
M_grm_1	age_shft	age_shft	0.817	0.413	1.222

of design B at age of 20 improved dramatically: accordingly, a twenty-year old is $53.11[80.64, 25.91]_{CI95}$ faster with B.

The third coefficient Age_shift appears in both models, but really means something different. The GRM assumes that both designs have the same slope of 0.82 seconds per year. The conditional model produces one slope per design and here the coefficient refers to design A only, as this is the reference group. Due to the treatment effects, `DesignB:age_shft` is the *difference in slopes*: users loose 0.82 seconds per year with A, and on top of that $0.22[−0.35, 0.81]_{CI95}$ with design B.

5.4.2 Conditional Multifactorial Models

In a conditional multifactorial model (CMFM), the effect of one factor level depends on the level on another factor. A full CMFM has as many coefficients as there are multi-level groups and is flexible enough that all group means can be completely independent, just like an AMM does it. Let us see this on an almost trivial example, first. In the fictional BrowsingAB case, a variable `rating` has been gathered. Let us imagine this be a vague emotional rating in the spirit of user satisfaction. Some claim that emotional experience is what makes the sexes different, so one could ask whether this makes a difference for the comparison of two designs A and B (Fig. 5.6).

```
attach(BrowsingAB)

BAB1 %>%
  ggplot(aes(y = rating, x = Gender, color = Design)) +
  geom_boxplot()
```

In a first exploratory plot, it looks like the ratings are pretty consistent across gender, but with a sensitive topic like that, we better run a model, or rather two, a plain MFM and a conditional MFM:

```
M_mfm_2 <-
  BAB1 %>%
```

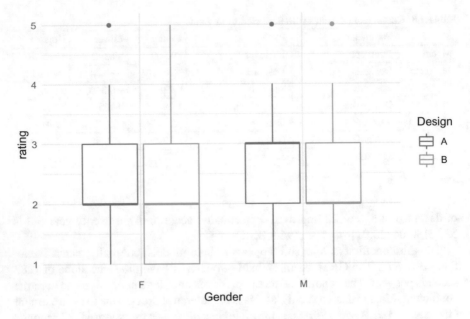

Fig. 5.6 Comparing satisfaction ratings by design and gender

```
stan_glm(rating ~ Design + Gender,
  data = .
)

M_cmfm_1 <-
  BAB1 %>%
  stan_glm(rating ~ Design + Gender + Design:Gender,
    data = .
  )

# T_resid <- mutate(T_resid, M_ia2 = residuals(M_ia2))

bind_rows(
  posterior(M_mfm_2),
  posterior(M_cmfm_1)
) %>%
  coef() %>%
  ggplot(aes(
    y = parameter, col = model,
    xmin = lower, xmax = upper, x = center
  )) +
  geom_crossbar(position = "dodge") +
  labs(x = "effect")
```

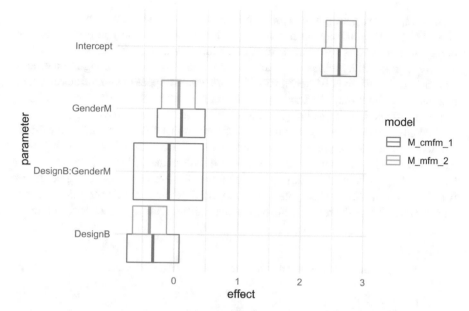

Fig. 5.7 Comparison of non-conditional and conditional two-factorial models, center estimates and 95 percent credibility intervals

The CLU plots above show both models in comparison. Both models use treatment effects and put the intercept on female users with design A. We observe that there is barely a difference in the estimated intercepts. The coefficient DesignB means something different in the models: in the MFM, it represents *the* difference between Designs. In the CMFM, it is the difference design B makes *for female users*. The same is true for GenderM: In the MFM it is *the* gender effect, whereas in the CMFM it is the gender difference *for design A*.

A note on terminology: many researchers divide the effect of conditional models into main effects (DesignB, GenderM) and interaction effects. That it is *incorrect*, because DesignB and GenderM are not main, in the sense of global. That is precisely what a conditional model does: it makes two (or more) local effects out of one global effect (Fig. 5.7).

None of the three coefficients of the MFM noticeably changed by introducing the conditional effect DesignB:GenderM. Recall that in the MFM, the group mean of design B among men is calculated by adding the two main effects to the intercept. This group mean is fixed. The conditional effect DesignB:GenderM is the difference to the fixed group in the MFM. It can be imagined as an adjustment parameter that gives the fourth group its own degree of freedom. In the current CMFM, the conditional coefficient is very close to zero, with a difference of just $-0.1[-0.65, 0.44]_{CI95}$.

It seems we are getting into a lot of null results here. If you have a background in classic statistics, you may get nervous at such a point, because you remember that in case of null results someone said: "one cannot say anything". This is true when you are testing null hypotheses and divide the world into the classes significant/non-significant. But, when you interpret coefficients, you are speaking quantities and zero is a quantity. What the MFM tells us is that male users really don't give any higher or lower ratings, *in total*, although there remains some uncertainty.

Actually, the purpose of estimating a CMFM can just be to show that some effect is unconditional. As we have seen earlier Chap. 5.2, conditional effects can cancel each other out, when combined into global effects. Take a look at the following hypothetical results of the study. Here, male and female users do not agree. If we would run an MFM in such a situation, we would get very similar coefficients, but would overlook that the relationship between design and rating is just poorly rendered (Fig. 5.8).

```
tribble(
  ~Design, ~Gender, ~mean_rating,
  "A", "F", 5.6,
  "A", "M", 5.6 + .4,
  "A", "Total", mean(c(5.6, 6.0)),
  "B", "F", 5.6 - .3,
  "B", "M", 5.6 + .4 - .3 - .6,
  "B", "Total", mean(c(5.3, 5.1))
) %>%
```

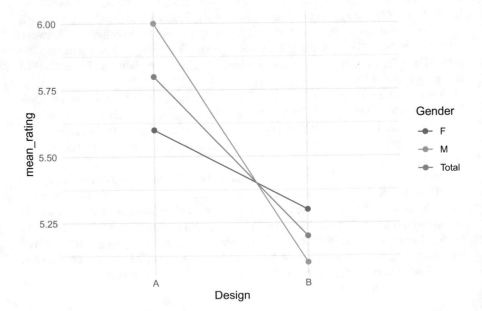

Fig. 5.8 Total versus conditional effects in a factorial model

```
ggplot(aes(x = Design, col = Gender, y = mean_rating)) +
geom_point(size = 2) +
geom_line(aes(group = Gender))
```

If something like this happens in a real design study, it may be a good idea to find out, why this difference appears and whether there is a way to make everyone equally happy. These are questions a model cannot answer. But a CMFM can show, when effects are conditional and when they are not. Much of the time, gender effects are what you rather don't want to have, as it can become a political problem. If conditional adjustment effects are close to zero that is proof (under uncertainty) that an effect is unconditional. That actually justifies the use of an MFM with global effects, only.

Let's see a more complex example of conditional MFMs, where conditional effects are really needed. In the IPump study, two infusion pump designs were compared in three successive sessions. In Sect. 4.3.5, we saw how a factorial model can render a learning curve using stairway dummies. With two designs, we can estimate separate learning curves and make comparisons. Let's take a look at the raw data in Fig. 5.9.

```
attach(IPump)

D_agg %>%
  group_by(Design, Session) %>%
  summarize(mean_ToT = mean(ToT)) %>%
  ggplot(aes(x = Session, y = mean_ToT, color = Design)) +
  geom_point() +
```

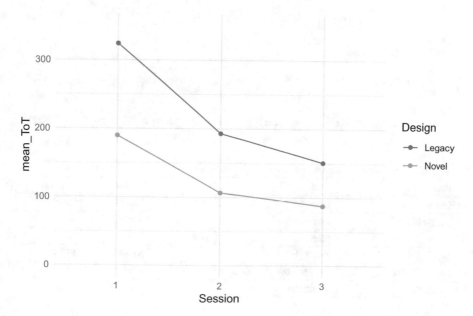

Fig. 5.9 ToT by design and session

```
geom_line(aes(group = Design)) +
ylim(0, 350)
```

We note that the learning curves do not cross, but are not parallel either, which means the stairway coefficients will be different. We need a conditional model.

The first choice to make is between treatment dummies and stairway dummies (Sects. 4.3.2, 4.3.5) both have their applications. With treatment effects, we would get an estimate for the total learning between sessions 1 and 3. That does not make much sense here, but could be interesting to compare trainings by the total effect of a training sequence.

We'll keep the stairway effects on the sessions, but have to now make a choice on where to fix the intercept, and that depends on what aspect of learning is more important. If this were any walk-up-and-use device or a website for making your annual tax report, higher initial performance would indicate that the system is intuitive to use. Medical infusion pumps are used routinely by trained staff. Nurses are using infusion pumps every day, which makes long-term performance more important. The final session is the best estimate we have for that. We create stairway dummies for session and make this conditional on Design. The results are shown in Table 5.9.

```
T_dummy <-
  tribble(
    ~Session, ~Session_3, ~Step3_2, ~Step2_1,
    "1", 1, 1, 1,
    "2", 1, 1, 0,
    "3", 1, 0, 0
  )

D_agg <-
  left_join(D_agg,
    T_dummy,
    by = "Session",
    copy = T
  ) %>%
  select(Obs, Design, Session, Session_3, Step3_2, Step2_1, ToT)
```

Table 5.9 Coefficient estimates with 95% credibility limits

Parameter	fixef	Center	Lower	Upper
Intercept	Intercept	151.1	119.406	180.4
DesignNovel	DesignNovel	−63.6	−105.107	−19.4
Step3_2	Step3_2	41.8	0.363	84.9
Step2_1	Step2_1	131.4	87.140	172.4
DesignNovel:Step3_2	DesignNovel:Step3_2	−22.4	−84.576	35.1
DesignNovel:Step2_1	DesignNovel:Step2_1	−48.2	−106.155	12.6

```
M_cmfm_2 <-
  stan_glm(ToT ~ 1 + Design + Step3_2 + Step2_1 +
    Design:(Step3_2 + Step2_1), data = D_agg)
```

```
coef(M_cmfm_2)
```

Note that ...

- Here I demonstrate a different technique to attach dummies to the data. First a coding table T_dummy is created, which is then combined with the data, using a (tidy) *join* operation.
- We have expanded the factor Session into three dummy variables, and we have to make every single one conditional. Design:(Step3_2 + Step2_1) is short for Design:Step3_2 + Design:Step2_1. But, you should *never* use the fully factorial expansion (Factor1 * Factor2), a this would make dummy variables conditional.

In conditional learning curve model, the intercept coefficient tells us that the average ToT with the Legacy in the final session is $151.11[119.41, 180.38]_{CI95}$ seconds. Using the Novel design, the nurses were $63.61[105.11, 19.37]_{CI95}$ seconds faster and that is our best estimate for the long-term improvement in efficiency.

Again, the learning step coefficients are not "main" effects, but are local to Legacy. The first step Step2_1 is much larger than the second, as is typical for learning curves. The adjustment coefficients for Novel have the opposite direction, meaning that the learning steps in Novel are smaller. That is not as bad as it sounds, for two reasons: first, in this study, the final performance counts, not the training progress. Second, and more generally, we have misused a linear model to smooth a non-linear model. Learning processes are exponential (Sect. 7.2.1.2).

Learning curves are saturation processes, which can look linear when viewed in segments, but unlike linear models, they never cross the lower boundary. This is simply, because there is a maximum performance limit, which can only be reached asymptotically. In the following section, I will argue that basically all measures we take have natural boundaries. Under common circumstances, this can lead to conditional effects which are due to saturation.

5.4.3 Saturation: Hitting the Boundaries

Recall that the three main assumptions of linear regression are Normal distributed residuals, variance homogeneity and linearity. The last arises from the basic regression formula:

$$y_i = \beta_0 + \beta_1 x_{1i}$$

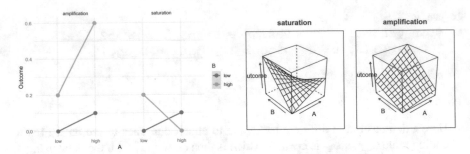

Fig. 5.10 Two forms of conditional effects: amplification and saturation

The formula basically says, that if we increase x_1 (or any other influencing variable) by one unit, y will increase by β_1. It also says that y is composed as a mere sum. In this section, we will discover that these innocent assumptions often do not hold.

In this and the next section, we will use conditional effects to account for non-linearity. We can distinguish between *saturation effects*, which are more common, and *amplification effects*. Figure 5.10 shows two attempts at visualizing saturation (and amplification).

A major flaw with the linear model is that it presumes the regression line to rise or fall infinitely. However, *in an endless universe everything has boundaries*. Just think about your performance in reading this text. Several things could be done to improve reading performance, such as larger font size, simpler sentence structure or translation into your native language. Still, there is a hard lower limit for time to read, just by the fact, that reading involves saccades (eye movements) and these cannot be accelerated any further. The time someone needs to read a text is limited by fundamental cognitive processing speed. We may be able to reduce the inconvenience of deciphering small text, but once an optimum is reached, there is no further improvement. Such boundaries of performance inevitably lead to non-linear relationships between predictors and outcome.

Modern statistics knows several means to deal with non-linearity, some of them are introduced in Sect. 7. Still, most researchers use linear models, and it often can be regarded as a reasonable approximation under particular circumstances. Mostly, this is that measures keep a distance to the hard boundaries, to avoid saturation.

When there is just one treatment repeatedly pushing toward a boundary, we get the diminishing returns effect seen in learning curves, Sect. 4.3.5. If two or more variables are pushing simultaneously, saturation can appear, too. Letter size and contrast both influence the readability of a text, but once the letters are huge, contrast no longer matters.

Before we turn to a genuine design research case, let me explain saturation effects by an example that I hope is intuitive. The hypothetical question is do two headache pills have twice the effect of one? Consider a pharmaceutical study on the effectiveness of two pain killer pills A and B. The day after a huge campus party, random strolling students have been asked to participate. First, they rate their experienced

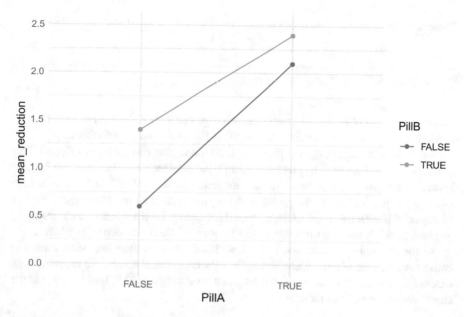

Fig. 5.11 Group means of a two-factorial model

headache on a Likert scale ranging from "fresh like the kiss of morning dew" to "dead possum on the highway". Participants are randomly assigned to four groups, each group getting a different combination of pills: no pill, only A, only B, A and B. After 30 minutes, headache is measured again and the difference between both measures is taken as the outcome measure: headache reduction. Figure 5.11

```
attach(Headache)

T_means <-
  Pills %>%
  group_by(PillA, PillB) %>%
  summarise(mean_reduction = round(mean(reduction), 1))

T_means %>%
  ggplot(aes(x = PillA, col = PillB, mean_reduction)) +
  geom_point() +
  geom_line(aes(group = PillB)) +
  ylim(0, 2.5)
```

When neither pill is given a slight spontaneous recovery seems to occur. Both pills alone are much stronger than the placebo and when giving them both, participants recover the best. However, looking more closely, the effect of two pills is just a tad stronger than the effect of A and stays far from being the sum. One could also say

Table 5.10 Comparing the coefficients of conditional and unconditional multifactorial models

fixef	M_1
Intercept	106

that the net effect of B is weaker when given together with A. When the effect of one predictor depends on the level of another, this is just a conditional effect.

So, why is the effect of two pills not the sum of the two one-pill effects? This question can be answered by contemplating what may happen when not two but five headache pills are given. If we would assume linear addition of effects, we also have to assume that participants in the group with all pills make the breathtaking experience of *negative* headache. So, certainly, the effect cannot be truly linear. All headache pills are pushing into the direction of the boundary called absence of headache.

At the example of headache pills, I will now demonstrate that saturation can cause a severe bias when not accounted for by a conditional effect. We estimate both models: a factorial unconditional MFM and a conditional MFM. Table 5.10 puts the center estimates of both models side-by-side.

```
M_mfm <- stan_glm(reduction ~ 1 + PillA + PillB,
   data = Pills
)
M_cmfm <- stan_glm(reduction ~ 1 + PillA + PillB + PillA:PillB,
   data = Pills
)

P_1 <- bind_rows(
   posterior(M_mfm),
   posterior(M_cmfm)
)

coef(P_1) %>%
   select(model, fixef, center) %>%
   spread(key = model, value = center) %>%
   # mutate(diff = M_cmfm - M_mfm)
```

Both intercepts indicate that headache diminishes due to the placebo alone, but M_mfm overestimates spontaneous recovery. At the same time, the treatment effects PillA and PillB are underestimated by M_mfm. That happens, because the unconditional model averages over two conditions, under which pill A or B are given: with the other pill or without. As M_cmfm tells, when taken with the another pill, effectiveness is reduced by −0.4. This example shows that multi-predictor models can severely underestimate effect strength of individual impact variables, when effects are conditional.

In general, if two predictors work into the same direction (here the positive direction) and the conditional adjustment effect has the opposite direction, this is most likely a *saturation effect*: the more of similar is given, the closer it gets to the natural boundaries and the less it adds.

Remember that this is really not about side effects in conjunction with other medicines. Quite the opposite: if two types of pills effectively reduce headache, but in conjunction produce a rash, this would actually be an amplification effect, Sect. 5.4.4. Whereas amplification effects are theoretically interesting, not only for pharmacists, saturation effects are a boring nuisance stemming from the basic fact that there always are boundaries of performance. Saturation effects only tell us that we have been applying *more of the similar* and that we are running against a set limit of how much we can improve things.

Maybe, saturation affects are not so boring for design research. A saturation effect indicates that two impact factors work in a similar way. That can be used to trade one impact factor for another. There is more than one way to fight pain. Distraction or, quite the opposite, meditation can also reduce the suffering. Combining meditation practice with medication attacks the problem from different angles and that may add up much better than taking more pills. For people who are allergic to pill A, though, it is good that B is a similar replacement.

If two design impact factors work in similar ways, we may also be able to trade in one for the other. Imagine a study aiming at ergonomics of reading for informational websites. In a first experiment, the researcher found that 12pt font effectively reduces reading time as compared to 10pt by about 5 seconds. But, is it reasonable to believe that increasing to 18pt would truly reduce reading time to 15 seconds?

```
D_reading_time <-
  tibble(
    font_size = c(4, 10, 12, 14, 16, 18),
    observed_time = c(NA, 40, 30, NA, NA, NA),
    predicted_time = 60 - font_size / 4 * 10
  )
```

D_reading_time

font_size	observed_time	predicted_time
4		50
10	40	35
12	30	30
14		25
16		20
18		15

Probably not. For normally sighted persons, a font size of 12 is easy enough to decipher and another increase will not have the same effect.

Researching the effect of font sizes between 8pt and 12pt font size probably keeps the right distance, with approximate linearity within that range. But what happens if you bring a second manipulation into the game with a functionally similar effect? For example, readability also improves with contrast.

Table 5.11 Data set with 6 variables, showing 8 of 40 observations

Obs	Part	font_size	font_color	mu	ToT
1	1	10pt	gray	60	66.9
2	2	12pt	gray	48	45.2
12	12	12pt	gray	48	59.4
23	23	10pt	black	50	49.1
24	24	12pt	black	46	52.1
25	25	10pt	black	50	59.5
26	26	12pt	black	46	43.8
34	34	12pt	black	46	43.0

A common conflict of interests is between the aesthetic appearance and the ergonomic properties. From an ergonomic point of view, one would probably favor a typesetting design with crisp fonts and maximum contrast. However, if a design researcher would suggest using 12pt black Arial on white background as body font, this is asking for trouble with anyone claiming a sense of beauty. Someone will insist on a fancy serif font in an understating blueish-grey tone. For creating a relaxed reading experience, the only option left is to increase the font size.

The general question arises: can one sufficiently compensate lack of contrast by setting the text in the maximum reasonable font size 12pt, as compared to the more typical 10pt? In the fictional study Reading, a 2×2 experimental study has been simulated: the same page of text is presented in four versions, with either 10pt or 12pt, and grey versus black font color (Table 5.11).

```
attach(Reading)

D_1

D_1 %>%
  ggplot(aes(
    col = font_color,
    x = font_size,
    y = ToT
  )) +
  geom_boxplot()
```

In Fig. 5.12, we see that both design choices have an impact: black letters, as well as larger letters are faster to read. But, do they add up? Or do both factors behave like headache pills, where more is more, but less than the sum. Clearly, the 12pt-black group could read fastest on average. Neither with large font, nor with optimal contrast alone has the design reached a boundary, i.e. saturation. We run two regression models, a plain MFM and a conditional MFM, that adds an interaction term. We extract the coefficients from both models and view them side-by-side:

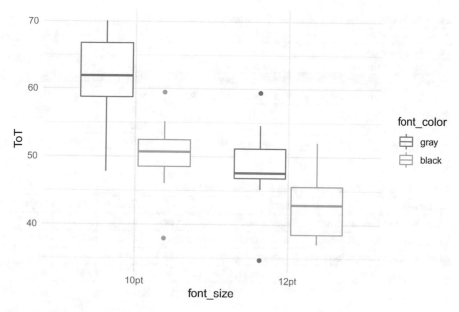

Fig. 5.12 A boxplot showing groups in a 2 × 2 experiment

```
M_mfm <- stan_glm(ToT ~ 1 + font_size + font_color,
  data = D_1
)

M_cmfm <- stan_glm(ToT ~ 1 + font_size + font_color +
  font_size:font_color,
data = D_1
)

bind_rows(
  posterior(M_mfm),
  posterior(M_cmfm)
) %>%
  coef()
```

The estimates confirm that both manipulations have a considerable effect in reducing reading time. But, as the conditional effect works in the opposite direction, this reeks of saturation: in this hypothetical case, font size acts as contrast is more-of-the-similar and the combined effects are less than the sum. This is just like taking two headache pills (Table 5.12).

If this was real data, we could assign the saturation effect a deeper meaning. It is not always obvious that two factors work in a similar way. From a psychological perspective, this would indicate that both manipulations work on similar cognitive processes, for example, visual letter recognition. Knowing more than one way to

Table 5.12 Coefficient estimates with 95% credibility limits

Model	Parameter	fixef	Center	Lower	Upper
M_cmfm	Intercept	Intercept	61.33	57.41	65.18
M_cmfm	font_size12pt	font_size12pt	−12.73	−18.00	−7.10
M_cmfm	font_colorblack	font_colorblack	−11.05	−16.50	−5.75
M_cmfm	font_size12pt:font_colorblack	font_size12pt:font_colorblack	5.55	−2.23	13.38
M_mfm	Intercept	Intercept	59.89	56.52	63.44
M_mfm	font_size12pt	font_size12pt	−9.90	−14.16	−5.86
M_mfm	font_colorblack	font_colorblack	−8.28	−12.38	−4.31

Table 5.13 Coefficient estimates with 95% credibility limits

Parameter	fixef	Center	Lower	Upper
font_size10pt:font_colorgray	font_size10pt:font_colorgray	61.2	57.5	65.2
font_size12pt:font_colorgray	font_size12pt:font_colorgray	48.5	44.5	52.1
font_size10pt:font_colorblack	font_size10pt:font_colorblack	50.1	46.1	54.2
font_size12pt:font_colorblack	font_size12pt:font_colorblack	43.0	38.9	46.9

improve on a certain mode of processing can be very helpful in design, where conflicting demands arise often and in the current case, a reasonable compromise between ergonomics and aesthetics would be to either use large fonts or black letters. Both have the strongest ergonomic net effect when they come alone.

Conditional effects are notoriously neglected in research and they are often hard to grasp for audience, even when people have a classic statistics education. Clear communication is often crucial, and conditional models are best understood by using conditional plots. A conditional plot for the 2×2 design contains the four estimated group means. These can be computed from the linear model coefficients, but often it easier to just estimate an absolute means model alongside (Table 5.13)

```
M_amm <-
  D_1 %>%
  stan_glm(ToT ~ 0 + font_size:font_color,
    data = .
  )

coef(M_amm)


T_amm <-
  coef(M_amm) %>%
  separate(fixef, c("font_size", "font_color"), sep = ":") %>%
  mutate(
    font_size = str_remove(font_size, "font_size"),
    font_color = str_remove(font_color, "font_color")
  )
```

```
G_amm <- T_amm %>%
  ggplot(aes(
    x = font_color,
    color = font_size, shape = font_size,
    y = center
  )) +
  geom_point() +
  geom_line(aes(group = font_size))
```

Note that in a CLU table the column `fixef` stores two identifiers, the level of font size and the level of font_color. For putting them on different GGplot aesthetics, we first have to rip them apart using `separate` before using `mutate` and `str_replace` to strip the group labels off the factor names. Since the coefficient table also contains the 95% certainty limits, we can produce a conditional plot with credibility intervals in another layer (`geom_errorbar`). These limits belong to the group means, and generally cannot be used to tell about the treatment effects.

```
G_amm +
  geom_crossbar(aes(ymin = lower, ymax = upper),
    width = .1
  ) +
  labs(y = "ToT")
```

Still, it gives the reader of a report some sense of the overall level of certainty. Usually, when two 95% CIs do not overlap that means that the difference is almost certainly not zero. Another useful Ggplot geometry is the violin plot, as these make the overlap between posterior distributions visible and reduce visual clutter caused by vertical error bars.

However, a violin plot requires more that just three CLU estimates. Recall from Sect. 4.1.1 that the posterior object obtained with `posterior` stores the full certainty information gained by the MCMC estimation walk. The CLU estimates, we so commonly use, are just condensing this information into three numbers (CLU). By pulling the estimated posterior distribution into the plot, we can produce a conditional plot that conveys more information and is easier on the eye.

```
P_amm <-
  posterior(M_amm) %>%
  filter(type == "fixef") %>%
  select(fixef, value) %>%
  separate(fixef, c("font_size", "font_color"), sep = ":") %>%
  mutate(
    font_size = str_replace(font_size, "font_size", ""),
    font_color = str_replace(font_color, "font_color", "")
  )


G_amm +
```

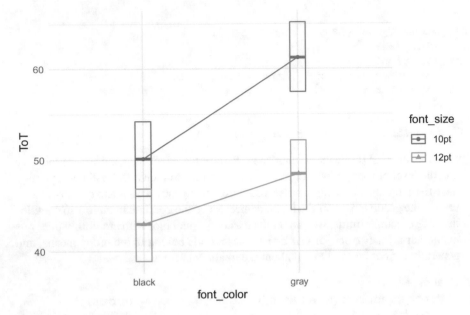

Fig. 5.13 Conditional effects of font size and font color

```
geom_violin(
  data = P_amm,
  aes(
    y = value,
    fill = font_size
  ),
  alpha = 0.5,
  position = position_identity(),
  width = .2
) +
labs(y = "ToT")
```

Note how we just add one alternative layer to the original line plot object G_amm to get the violin plot. The violin layer here gets its own data set, which is another feature of the GGplot engine.

As Figs. 5.13 and 5.14 show, ergonomics is maximized by using large fonts and high contrast. Still, there is saturation and therefore it does little harm to go with the gray font, as long as it is 12pt.

Saturation is likely to occur when multiple factors influence the same cognitive or physical system or functioning. In quantitative comparative design studies, we gain a more detailed picture on the co-impact of design interventions and can come to more sophisticated decisions.

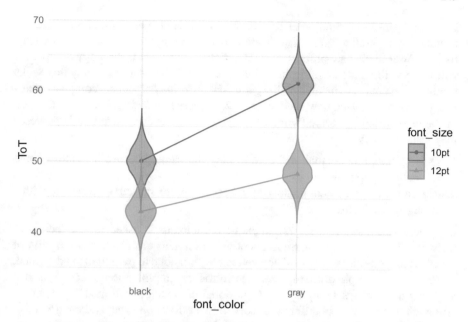

Fig. 5.14 Another way to plot conditional effects from an AMM includes posterior distributions

If we don't account for saturation by introducing conditional terms, we are prone to underestimate the net effect of any of these measures and may falsely conclude that a certain treatment is rather ineffective. Consider a large scale study that assesses the simultaneous impact of many demographic and psychological variables on how willing customers are to take certain energy saving actions in their homes. It is very likely that impact factors are associated, like higher income and size of houses. Certain action require little effort (such as switching off lights in unoccupied rooms), whereas others are time-consuming (drying the laundry outside). At the same time, customers may vary in the overall eagerness (motivation). For high effort actions, the impact of motivation level probably makes more of a difference than when effort is low. Not including the conditional effect would result in the false conclusion that suggesting high effort actions is rather ineffective.

5.4.4 Amplification: More than the Sum

Saturation effects occur when multiple impact factors act on the same system and work in the same direction. When reaching the boundaries, the change per unit diminishes. We can also think of such factors as exchangeable. *Amplification* conditional effects are the opposite: Something only really works, if all conditions are fulfilled. Conceiving good examples for amplification effects is far more challenging as compared to saturation effects. Probably this is because saturation is a rather trivial phenomenon, whereas amplification involves complex orchestration of cognitive or physiological subprocesses. Here, a fictional case on technology acceptance will serve to illustrate amplification effects. Imagine a start-up company that seeks funding for a novel augmented reality game, where groups of gamers compete for territory. For a fund raiser, they need to know their market potential, i.e. which fraction of the population is potentially interested. The entrepreneurs have two hypotheses they want to verify:

1. Only technophile persons will dare to play the game, because it requires some top-notch equipment.
2. The game is strongly cooperative and therefore more attractive for people with a strong social motif.

Imagine a study, where a larger sample of participants is asked to rate their own technophilia and sociophilia. Subsequently, participants are given a description of the planned game and were asked how much they intended to participate in the game.

While the example primarily serves to introduce amplification effects, it is also an opportunity to get familiar with conditional effects between metric predictors. Although this is not very different to conditional effects on groups, there are a few peculiarities, one being that we cannot straightforwardly make an exploratory plot. For factors, we have used box plots, but these do not apply to metric predictors. In fact, it is very difficult to come up with a good graphical representation. One might think of 3D wire-frame plots, but these transfer poorly to the 2D medium of these pages.

Another option is to create a scatterplot with the predictors on the axes and encode the outcome variable by shades or size of dots . These options may suffice to see any present main effects, but are too coarse to discover subtle non-linearity. The closest we can get to a good illustration is to artificially create groups and continue as if we had factor variables. Note, that turning metric predictors into factors is just a hack to create exploratory graphs, it is not recommended practice for linear models.

```
attach(AR_game)

library(forcats) # fct_rev

D_1 %>%
  mutate(
    Sociophile =
      fct_rev(if_else(sociophile > median(sociophile),
        "high", "low"
      )),
    Technophile =
      fct_rev(if_else(technophile > median(technophile),
        "high", "low"
      ))
  ) %>%
  ggplot(aes(y = intention, x = Technophile, col = Sociophile)) +
  geom_boxplot() +
  ylim(0, 0.5)
```

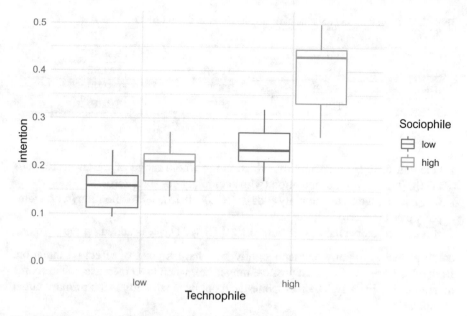

Fig. 5.15 Visualizing continuous conditional effects as factors

Table 5.14 Coefficient estimates with 95% credibility limits

Parameter	fixef	Center	Lower	Upper
Intercept	Intercept	0.273	0.258	0.288
Sociophile	Sociophile	0.114	0.076	0.153
Technophile	Technophile	0.183	0.153	0.214
Sociophile:Technophile	Sociophile:Technophile	0.164	0.081	0.244

From Fig. 5.15, it seems that both predictors have a positive effect on intention to play. However, it remains unclear whether there is a conditional effect. In absence of a better visualization, we have to rely fully on the numerical estimates of a conditional linear regression model (CMRM)

```
M_cmrm <-
  stan_glm(intention ~ 1 + sociophile + technophile +
    sociophile:technophile,
  data = D_1
  )
```

```
coef(M_cmrm)
```

Table 5.14 tells the following:

- Intention to buy is $0.27[0.26, 0.29]_{CI95}$ for people with minimum (i.e. zero) technophily and sociophily.

Table 5.15 Saturation and amplification are like Boolean Or and AND

A	B	A OR B	A AND B
FALSE	FALSE	FALSE	FALSE
FALSE	TRUE	TRUE	FALSE
TRUE	FALSE	TRUE	FALSE
TRUE	TRUE	TRUE	TRUE

- One unit change on sociophily, which is the whole range of the measure, adds $0.11[0.08, 0.15]_{CI95}$ to intention (with sociophily constant zero).
- One unit change on technophily adds $0.11[0.08, 0.15]_{CI95}$ to intention (with sociophily constant zero).
- If both predictors change one unit, $0.18[0.15, 0.21]_{CI95}$ is added *on top*

confirms that sociophily and technophily both have a positive effect on intention. Both effects are clearly in the positive range. Yet, when both increase, the outcome increases over-linearly. The sociophile-technophile personality is the primary target group.

    -> -> ->
    ->

Saturation effects are about declining net effects, the more similar treatments pile up. Amplification effects are more like two-component glue. When using only one of the components, all one gets is a smear. You have to put them together for a strong hold.

Saturation and amplification also have parallels in formal logic (Table 5.15). The logical AND requires both operands to be TRUE for the result to become TRUE. Instead, a saturation process can be imagined as logical OR. If A is already TRUE, B no longer matters.

```
tibble(
  A = c(F, F, T, T),
  B = c(F, T, F, T)
) %>%
  as_tibble() %>%
  mutate("A OR B" = A | B) %>%
  mutate("A AND B" = A & B)
```

For decision-making in design research, the notion of saturation and amplification are equally important. Saturation effects can happen with seemingly different design choices that act on the same cognitive (or other) processes. That is good to know, because it allows the designer to compensate one design feature with the other, should there be a conflict between different requirements, such as aesthetics and readability of text. Amplification effects are interesting, because they break barriers. Only if the right ingredients are present, a system is adopted by users. Many technology breakthroughs can perhaps be attributed to adding the final necessary ingredient.

Sometimes we can see that on technology that first is a failure, just to take off years later. For example, the first commercial smartphone (with touchscreen, data connectivity and apps) has been the IBM Simon Personal Communicator, introduced in 1993. Only a few thousands were made, and it was discontinued after only six months on the market. It lasted more than ten years before smartphones actually took off. What were the magic ingredients added? My best guess is it was the combination of good battery time and still fitting in your pockets.

A feature that must be present for the users to be satisfied (in the mere sense of absence-of-annoyance) is commonly called a *necessary user requirements*. That paints a more moderate picture of amplification in everyday design work: The peak, where all features work together usually, is not the magic break-through; it is the strenuous path of user experience design, where user requirements whirl around you and not a single one must be left behind.

5.4.5 *Conditional Effects and Design Theory*

Explaining or predicting complex behavior with psychological theory is a typical approach in design research. Unfortunately, it is not an easy one. While design is definitely multifactorial, with a variety of cognitive processes, individual differences and behavioral strategies, few psychological theories cover more than three associations between external or individual conditions and behavior. The design researcher is often forced to enter a rather narrow perspective or knit a patchwork model from multiple theories. Such a model can either be loose, making few assumptions on how the impact factors interact which others. A more tightened model frames multiple impact factors into a conditional network, where the impact of one factor can depend on the overall configuration. A classic study will now serve to show how conditional effects can clarify theoretical considerations.

Vigilance is the ability to remain attentive for rarely occurring events. Think of truck drivers on lonely night rides, where most of the time they spend keeping the truck on a straight 80km/h course. Only every now and then is the driver required to react to an event, like when braking lights flare up ahead. Vigilance tasks are among the hardest thing to ask from a human operator. Yet, they are safety relevant in a number of domains.

Keeping up vigilance most people perceive as tiring, and vigilance deteriorates with tiredness. Several studies have shown that reaction time at simple tasks increases when people are deprived of sleep. The disturbing effect of loud noise has been documented as well. A study by [4] examined the simultaneous influence of sleep deprivation and noise on a rather simple reaction task. They asked:

> will the effects of noise summate with those of loss of sleep to induce an even greater performance decrement or will noise subtract from the performance decrement caused by loss of sleep?

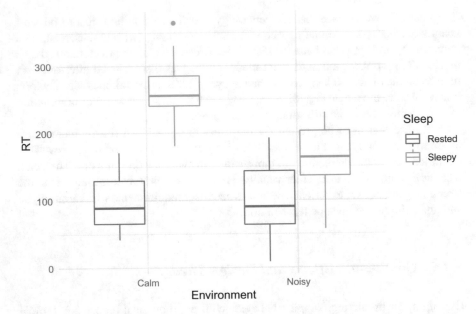

Fig. 5.16 Conditional effects of environmental noise and sleep deprivation

The theoretical argument is that sleep deprivation deteriorates the central nervous arousal system. In consequence, sleep-deprived persons cannot maintain the necessary level of energy that goes with the task. Noise is a source of irritation and therefore usually reduces performance. At the same time, loud noise has an agitating effect, which may compensate for the loss of arousal due to sleep deprivation.

The Sleep case study is a simplified simulation of Corcoran's results. Participants were divided into 2×2 groups (quiet/noisy, rested/deprived) and had to react to five signal lamps in a succession of trials. In the original study, performance measure gaps were counted, which is the number of delayed reactions (>1500 ms). Here, we just go with (simulated) reaction times, assuming that declining vigilance manifests itself in overall slower reactions (Fig. 5.16).

```
attach(Sleep)

D_1 %>%
  ggplot(aes(
    x = Environment,
    color = Sleep,
    y = RT
  )) +
  geom_boxplot()
```

Using a 2×2 model including a conditional effect, we examine the conditional association between noise and sleepiness. Note that the * operator in the model formula

Table 5.16 Coefficient estimates with 95% credibility limits

Parameter	fixef	Center	Lower	Upper
Intercept	Intercept	97.68	63.1	130.7
EnvironmentNoisy	EnvironmentNoisy	2.32	−47.7	53.9
SleepSleepy	SleepSleepy	163.58	114.2	212.4
EnvironmentNoisy:SleepSleepy	EnvironmentNoisy:SleepSleepy	−103.50	−173.4	−32.9

is an abbreviation for a fully factorial model `1 + Environment + Sleep + Environment:Sleep`. The results are shown in Table 5.16

```
M_1 <-
  D_1 %>%
  stan_glm(RT ~ Environment * Sleep, data = .)

coef(M_1)
```

Recall, that treatment contrasts were used, where all effects are given relative to the reference group quiet-rested (intercept). The results confirm the deteriorating effect of sleepiness, although its exact impact is blurred by pronounced uncertainty $163.58[114.21, 212.36]_{CI95}$. Somewhat surprisingly, noise did not affect well-rested persons by much $2.32[−47.67, 53.91]_{CI95}$. Note, however, that we cannot conclude a null effect, as the credibility limits are wide. Maybe the lack of a clear effect is because steady white noise was used, not a disturbing tumult. The effect of sleepiness on RT is partly reduced in a noisy environment $−103.5[−173.38, 32.88]_{CI95}$. This suggests that the arousal system is involved in the deteriorating effect of sleep deprivation, which has interesting consequences for the design of vigilance tasks in the real world.

These findings reverb with a well-known law in Psychology of Human Factors, the Yerkes-Dodson law, which states that human performance at cognitive tasks is influenced by arousal. The influence is not linear, but better approximated with a curve as shown in Fig. 5.17. Performance is highest at a moderate level of arousal. If we assume that sleepy participants in Corcona's study showed low performance due to under-arousal, the noise perhaps has increased the arousal level, resulting in better performance. If we accept that noise has an arousing effect, the null effect of noise on rested participants stands in opposition to the Yerkes-Dodson law: if rested participants were on an optimal arousal level, additional arousal would usually have a negative effect on performance. There is the slight possibility that Corcona has hit a sweet spot: if we assume that calm/rested participants were still below an optimal arousal level, noise could have pushed them right to the opposite point.

To sum it up, saturation and amplification effects have in common that performance is related to design features in a monotonous increasing manner, albeit not linearly. Such effects can be interpreted in a straightforward manner: when saturation occurs with

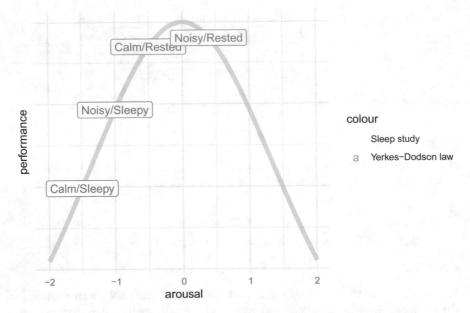

Fig. 5.17 Conditional effects explained by the Yerkes-Dodson law

multiple factors, it can be inferred that they all impact the same underlying cognitive
mechanism and are therefore interchangeable to some extent, like compensating
letter size with stronger contrast.

In contrast, amplification effects indicate that multiple cognitive mechanisms (or
attitudes) are necessarily involved. Whereas saturation effects point us at options
for compensation, amplification narrows it down to a particular configuration that
works.

The Sleep study demonstrated that conditional effects can also occur in situations
with *non monotonously increasing* relationships between design features and performance. When such a relationship takes the form of a parabole, like the Yerkes-Dodson
law, the designer (or researcher) is faced with the complex problem of finding the
sweet spot.

In the next section we will see how paraboles, but also more wildly curved relationships can be modeled using linear models with polynomial. And we will see how
sweet spots or, to be more accurate, a catastrophic spot can be identified.

5.5   Doing the Rollercoaster: Polynomial Regression Models

In the preceding sections, we used linear models with conditional effects to render
processes that are not linear, but somehow curved. These non-linear processes fell
into two classes: learning curves, saturation effects and amplification. But, what can

we do when a process follows more complex curves, with more ups and downs? In the following I will introduce polynomial regression models, which still use a linear combination, but can describe a wild variety of shapes for the association between two variables.

Robots build our cars and sometimes drive them. They mow the lawn and may soon also deliver parcels to far-off regions. In prophecies robots will also enter social domains, such as care for children and the elderly. One can imagine that in social settings emotional acceptance plays a significant role in technology adoption. Next to our voices, our faces and mimic expressions are the main source of interpersonal messaging. Since the dawn of the very idea of robots, anthropomorphic designs have been dominant. Researchers and designers all around the globe are currently pushing the limits of human-likeness of robots. (Whereas I avoid Science Fiction movies with humanoid extraterrestrians.) One could assume that emotional response improves with every small step towards perfection. Unfortunately, this is not the case. Reference [5] discovered a bizarre non-linearity in human response: people's emotional response is proportional to human-likeness, but only at the lower end. A robot design with cartoon-style facial features will always beat a robot vacuum cleaner. But, an almost anatomically correct robot face may provoke a very negative emotional response, an intense feeling of eery, which is called the *Uncanny Valley* (Fig. 5.18).

```
tibble(
  hl = seq(-1, 1, length.out = 100),
  emotional_valence = -.5 * hl + .6 * hl^3 + .2 * hl^4
```

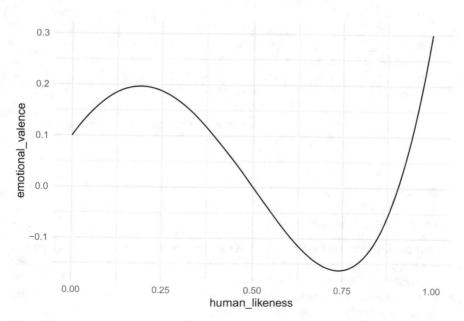

Fig. 5.18 The Uncanny Valley phenomenon is a non-linear emotional response to robot faces

```
) %>%
  mutate(human_likeness = (hl + 1) / 2) %>%
  ggplot(aes(x = human_likeness, y = emotional_valence)) +
  geom_line()
```

In [6], the observation of Mori is put to a test: Is the relationship between human-likeness and emotional response really shaped like a valley? They collected 60 pictures of robots and attached a score for human likeness to them. Then, they frankly asked their participants how much they liked the faces. For the data analysis, they calculated an average score of likeability per robot picture. Owing to the curved shape of the uncanny valley, linear regression is not applicable to the problem. Instead, Mathur et al. applied a third-degree polynomial term.

A polynomial function of degree k has the form:

$$y_i = \beta_0 x_i^0 + \beta_1 x_i^1 + \cdots + \beta_k x_i^k$$

The degree of a polynomial is its largest exponent. In fact, you are already familiar with two polynomial models. The zero-degree polynomial is the grand mean model, with $x_i^0 = 1$, which makes β_0 a constant. A first-degree polynomial is simply the linear model: $\beta_0 + \beta_1 x_{1i}$ By adding higher degrees, we can introduce more complex curvature to the association (Fig. 5.19).

```
D_poly <-
  tibble(
    x = seq(-2, 3, by = .1),
    degree_0 = 2,
    degree_1 = 1 * degree_0 + 3 * x,
    degree_2 = 0.5 * (degree_1 + 2 * x^2),
    degree_3 = 0.5 * (degree_2 + -1 * x^3),
    degree_4 = 0.4 * (degree_3 + 0.5 * x^4),
    degree_5 = 0.3 * (degree_4 + -0.3 * x^5)
  ) %>%
  gather(polynomial, y, degree_0:degree_5) %>%
  arrange(polynomial, y, x)

D_poly %>%
  ggplot(aes(x, y)) +
  geom_line() +
  facet_wrap(~polynomial)
```

Mathur et al. argue that the Uncanny Valley curve possesses two stationary points, with a slope of zero: the valley is a local minimum and represents the deepest point in the valley, the other is a local maximum and marks the shoulder left of the valley. Such a curvature can be approximated with a polynomial of (at least) third degree, which has a constant term β_0, a linear slope $x\beta_1$, quadratic component $x^2\beta_2$ and a cubic component $x^3\beta_3$.

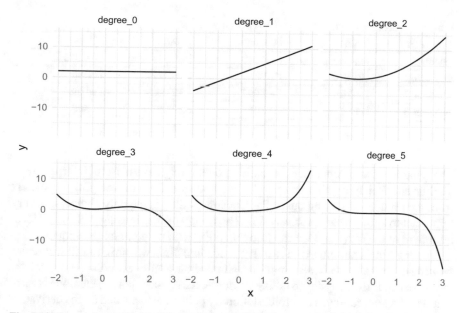

Fig. 5.19 The higher the degree of a polynomial, the more complex the association

While R provides high-level methods to deal with polynomial regression, it is instructive to build the regression manually. The first step is to add variables to the data frame, which are the predictors taken to powers ($x_k = x^k$). These variables are then added to the model term, as if they were independent predictors. For better clarity, we rename the intercept to be x_0, before summarizing the fixed effects. We extract the coefficients as usual. The four coefficients in Table 5.17 specify the polynomial to approximate the average likability responses.

```
attach(Uncanny)

M_poly_3 <-
  RK_2 %>%
  mutate(
    huMech_0 = 1,
    huMech_1 = huMech,
    huMech_2 = huMech^2,
    huMech_3 = huMech^3
  ) %>%
  stan_glm(avg_like ~ 1 + huMech_1 + huMech_2 + huMech_3,
    data = ., iter = 2500
  )
P_poly_3 <- posterior(M_poly_3)

T_coef <- coef(P_poly_3)
T_coef
```

Table 5.17 Coefficient estimates with 95% credibility limits

Parameter	fixef	Center	Lower	Upper
Intercept	Intercept	−0.449	−0.516	−0.378
huMech_1	huMech_1	0.149	−0.322	0.588
huMech_2	huMech_2	−1.092	−2.006	−0.086
huMech_3	huMech_3	0.919	0.282	1.499

The thing is, coefficients of a polynomial model rarely have a useful interpretation. Mathur and Reichling also presented a method to extract meaningful parameters from their model. If staying out of the Uncanny Valley is the only choice, it is very important to know, where precisely it is. The trough of the Uncanny Valley is a local minimum of the curve and we can find this point with polynomial techniques.

Finding a local minimum is a two step procedure: first, we must find all *stationary points*, which includes all *local* minima and maxima. Stationary points occur, where the curve bends from a rising to falling or vice versa. At these points, the slope is zero, neither rising nor falling. Therefore, stationary points are identified by the derivative of the polynomial, which is a second-degree (cubic) polynomial:

$$f'(x) = \beta_1 + 2\beta_2 x + 3\beta_2 x^2$$

The derivative $f'(x)$ of a function $f(x)$ gives the slope of $f(x)$ at any given point x. When $f'(x) > 0$, $f(x)$ is rising at x, with $f'(x) < 0$ it is falling. Stationary points are precisely those points, where $f'(x) = 0$ and can be found by solving the equation. The derivative of a third-degree polynomial is of the second degree, which has a quadratic part. This can produce a parabolic form, which hits point zero twice, once rising and once falling. A rising encounter of point zero indicates that $f(x)$ has a local minimum at x, a falling one indicates a local maximum. In consequence, solving $f'(x) = 0$ can result in two solutions, one minimum and one maximum, which need to be distinguished further.

If the stationary point is a local minimum, as the trough, slope switches from negative to positive; $f'(x)$ crosses $x = 0$ in a rising manner, which is a positive slope of $f'(x)$. Therefore, a stationary point is a local minimum, if $f''(x) > 0$.

Mathur et al. followed these analytic steps to arrive at an estimate for the position of the trough. However, they used frequentist estimation methods, which is why they could not attach a level of uncertainty to their estimate. We will apply the polynomial operations on the posterior distribution which results in a new posterior for the position of the trough.

```
library(polynom)
poly <- polynomial(T_coef$center) # UC function on center
dpoly <- deriv(poly) # 1st derivative
ddpoly <- deriv(dpoly) # 2nd derivative
stat_pts <- solve(dpoly) # finding stat points
slopes <- as.function(ddpoly)(stat_pts) # slope at stat points
```

```
trough <- stat_pts[slopes > 0] # local minimum
cat("The trough is most likely at a huMech score of ", round(trough, 2))
```

```
## The trough is most likely at a huMech score of  0.72
```

Note how the code uses high-level functions from package polynom to estimate
the location of the trough, in particular the first and second derivative d[d]poly.

Every step of the MCMC walk produces a simultaneous draw of the four parameters huMech_[0:3], and therefore fully specifies a third-degree polynomial. If
the position of the trough is computed for every step of the MCMC walk, the result
is a posterior distribution of the trough position. For the convenience, the R package
Uncanny contains a function trough(coef) that includes all the above steps.
The following code creates a data frame with one row per MCMC draw and the
four huMech variables, the function trough acts on this data frame as a matrix of
coefficients and returns one trough point per row. We have obtained the PD of the
trough.

```
devtools::install_github("schmettow/uncanny")
```

```
P_trough <-
  P_poly_3 %>%
  filter(type == "fixef") %>%
  select(chain, iter, fixef, value) %>%
  spread(fixef, value) %>%
  select(Intercept, starts_with("huMech")) %>%
  mutate(trough = uncanny::trough(.)) %>%
  gather(key = parameter)
```

This derived posterior distribution can put it into a CLU form (Table 5.18) or plot it
together with the estimated polynomial curve (Fig. 5.20)

```
P_trough %>%
  group_by(parameter) %>%
  summarize(
    center = median(value, na.rm = T),
    lower = quantile(value, .025, na.rm = T),
    upper = quantile(value, .975, na.rm = T)
  )
```

The 95% CI is a conventional measure of uncertainty and may be more or less
irrelevant. The most generous display on uncertainty is a density plot on the full
posterior. The density function just smooths over the frequency distribution of trough
draws, but makes no arbitrary choices on where to cut it.

Table 5.18 Polynomial coefficient table with 95% credibility limits

Parameter	Center	Lower	Upper
huMech_1	0.149	−0.322	0.588
huMech_2	−1.092	−2.006	−0.086
huMech_3	0.919	0.282	1.499
Intercept	−0.449	−0.516	−0.378
trough	0.715	0.650	0.801

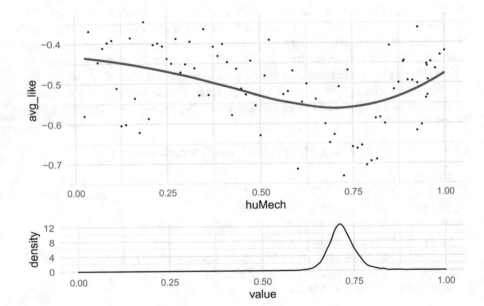

Fig. 5.20 Estimated Uncanny Valley curve and position of trough

```
RK_2$M_poly_3 <- predict(M_poly_3)$center

gridExtra::grid.arrange(
  RK_2 %>%
    ggplot(aes(x = huMech, y = avg_like)) +
    geom_point(size = .3) +
    geom_smooth(aes(y = M_poly_3), se = F),

  P_trough %>%
    filter(parameter == "trough") %>%
    ggplot(aes(x = value)) +
    geom_density() +
    xlim(0, 1),
```

```
  heights = c(.7, .3)
)
```

With reasonable certainty, we can say that the trough is at approximately two-thirds of the huMech score range. In contrast, the illustration of the uncanny valley as it used to be perpetuated from the original source places the trough at about four quarters of the scale. The Uncanny Valley effect sets in "earlier" than I thought, at least.

A closer look at the scatterplot above reveals a problem with the data set: It seems that data is sparsest right where the valley is deepest. Since there also is a lot of noise, the concern is that there actually is no trough. This can be tested on the same posterior. The `uncanny::trough` function returns a missing value, when no minimum stationary point could be found. Hence, the proportion of non-NAs is the certainty we have that a trough exists:

```
cert_trough <- 1 - mean(is.na(P_trough))
cat("Certainty that trough exists:", cert_trough)
```

```
## Certainty that trough exists: 1
```

5.5.1   Make Yourself a Test Statistic

Generally, in design research we are interested in real-world impact and this book takes a strictly quantitative stance. Rather than testing the hypothesis whether any effect exists or not, we interpret coefficients by making statements on their magnitude and uncertainty.

We evaluated the position of the local minimum, the trough. The theory goes that the Uncanny Valley effect is a disruption of a slow upwards trend, the disruption creates the shoulder and culminates in the trough. But, there is no single coefficient telling us directly that there actually are a shoulder and a trough.

Polynomial theory tells us that a cubic function *can* have two stationary points, but it can also just have one or zero. After all, straight line is a cubic, too, if we set the quadratic and cubic coefficients to zero. But that would mean that teh UNcanny Valley effect does not exist. If we run our MCMC chains long enough, they will visit spots in parameter space, where β_2 and β_3 are close to zero, or: areas where the cubic coefficient dominates, and there is just is a saddle.

When a cubic model is estimated, the MCMC walk makes random visits in a four-dimensional coefficient space, Sect. 4.1.1 (five-dimensional, if we count the error variance). These coordinates are stored *per iteration* in a posterior distribution object. Every iteration represents one possible polynomial, as is illustrated in Fig. 5.21.

```
attach(Uncanny)

post_pred(M_poly_3, thin = 100) %>%
   left_join(RK_2, by = "Obs") %>%
```

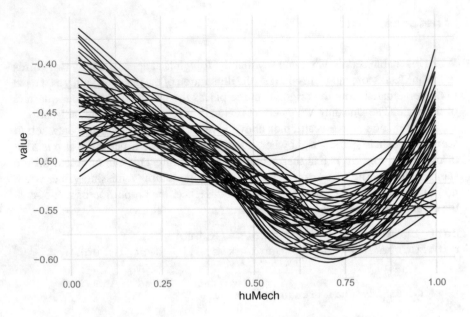

Fig. 5.21 MCMC estimation produces one polynomial per sample (40 shown)

```
ggplot(aes(x = huMech, y = value, group = iter)) +
stat_smooth(geom = "line", se = FALSE)
```

All we have to do is count the number of MCMC visits that have a trough and a
shoulder. The function `trough` in the Uncanny package (on Github) is designed to
return the position, when it exists and returns `NA` otherwise. The same goes for the
function `shoulder`, which finds the local maximum.

With these two functions, we can create a test statistics, by counting how many
of the MCMC draws represent a cubic polynomial *with* shoulder and trough.

```
# devtools::install_github("schmettow/uncanny")
library(uncanny)

P_wide <-
  P_poly_3 %>%
  filter(type == "fixef") %>%
  # as_tibble() %>%
  select(iter, parameter, value) %>%
  spread(key = parameter, value = value) %>%
  select(Intercept, starts_with("huMech")) %>%
  mutate(
    trough = uncanny::trough(.),
    shoulder = uncanny::shoulder(.),
    is_Uncanny = !is.na(trough) & !is.na(shoulder)
  )

cert_Uncanny <- mean(P_wide$is_Uncanny)
```

```
cat("The Uncanny Valley exists with a certainty of: ", cert_Uncanny)
```

```
## The Uncanny Valley exists with a certainty of:  0.999
```

So, with our data we can be pretty sure that the Uncanny Valley effect is present. Probably, there is a very tiny chance that it does not exist, which we would only catch by increasing the resolution of the posterior, i.e. running more MCMC iterations. This conclusion is remarkable also from a philosophy-of-science perspective. It was in 1970, when Masahiro Mori published his theory on the relation between human likeness and emotional response. Fifty years later this article is all but outdated in how lucidly it anticipates the emerge of human-like robots and virtual characters [5] . What can surprise the modern reader in Social Sciences is how the article abruptly stops, right where we would expect the experimental part confirming the theory.

It almost seems that Mori's theory sprang just from his own feelings, and he just left it at that. Introspection as a scientific method is likely to give seasoned researcher another uncanny feeling. But that would be unjust! In the first place, Mori made on observation his own inner world and assumed that others would feel the same. Once the world was ready for it, Mori's theory turned out to provable and immensely useful for design.

Still, I argue that we have not yet fully confirmed Mori's theory. Strictly spoken, the data of Mathur & Reichling only prove that *on average* the effect exists, because we aggregated scores over participants It would be much stronger to state: *everyone* experiences the Uncanny Valley. In essence, we could estimate the same cubic models, but *one per participant*. That requires non-aggregated data, because the analysis of very participant requires the data from every participant. The next chapter will introduce *multi-level models*, which can simultaneously estimate a model on population level and participant level. At the end of the following chapter, we will return to the Uncanny Valley with more data to feed our chains. Spoiler alert: the Uncanny Valley effect could be *universal*.

5.6 Further Readings

1. The original paper on the IPump case illustrates how Bayesian analysis can be reported in scientific journals [7].
2. Our Uncanny Valley experiment is described in detail in [8].

References

1. Carroll JM, Beth Rosson M (1987) Paradox of the active user. In: Carroll JM (ed) Interfacing thought. MIT Press, Chap 5, pp 80–111
2. Iacobucci D, Saldanha N, Deng X (2007) A meditation on mediation: evidence that structural equations models perform better than regressions. J Consum Psychol 17(2):139–153. ISSN: 1057-7408. https://doi.org/10.1016/S1057-7408(07)70020-7. http://linkinghub.elsevier.com/retrieve/pii/S1057740807700207
3. Merkle EC, Rosseel Y (2018) blavaan: Bayesian structural equation models via parameter expansion. J Stat Softw 85(4). https://doi.org/10.18637/jss.v085.i04
4. Corcoran DWJ (1962) Noise and loss of sleep. Q J Exp Psychol 14(3):78–182. ISSN: 0033-555X. https://doi.org/10.1080/17470216208416533
5. Mori M (1970) The uncanny valley. Energy 7(4):98–100. ISSN: 1070-9932. https://doi.org/10.1109/MRA.2012.2192811
6. Mathur Maya B, Reichling David B (2016) Navigating a social world with robot partners: a quantitative cartography of the Uncanny Valley. Cognition 146:22–32. https://doi.org/10.1016/j.cognition.2015.09.008
7. Schmettow M, Schnittker R, Schraagen JM (2017) An extended protocol for usability validation of medical devices: research design and reference model. J Biomed Inform 69:99–114. ISSN: 1532-0464. https://doi.org/10.1016/j.jbi.2017.03.010. http://linkinghub.elsevier.com/retrieve/pii/S153204641730059X
8. Koopman R (2019) The Uncanny Valley as a universal experience: a replication study using multilevel modelling. http://essay.utwente.nl/77172/

Chapter 6
Multilevel Models

In the previous chapters we have seen several examples of conditional effects: groups of users responding differently to design conditions, such as font size, noise and emerging technology. Dealing with differential design effects seems straight forward: identify the relevant property, record it and add an conditional effect to the model.

Identifying user properties that matter requires careful review of past research or deep theorizing, and even then it remains guesswork. Presumably, hundreds of studies attempted to explain differences in usage patterns or performance by all sorts of psychological predictors, with often limited results. That is a big problem in design research, as variation in performance can be huge and good predictors are urgently needed. Identifying the mental origins of being fast versus slow, or motivated versus bored, is extremely useful to improve the design of systems to be more inclusive or engaging.

As we will see in this chapter, individual differences can be accounted for and measured accurately without any theory of individual differences. For researchers trained in experimental social sciences it may require a bit of getting used to theory-free reasoning about effects, as it is always tempting to ask for the *why*. But in applied evaluation studies, what we often really need to know is by *how much* users vary. The key to measuring variation in a population is to create models that operate on the level of participants, in addition to the population level, for example.

- on population level, users prefer design B over A on average ($\beta_1 = 20$)
- on the participant-level, participant i preferred B over A ($\beta_{1i} = 20$), j preferred A over B ($\beta_{1j} = -5$), +

When adding a participant-level effects, we still operate with coefficients, but in contrast to single-level linear models, every participant gets their own coefficient ($\beta_1.$). The key to estimating individual parameters is simply to regard participant (Part) a grouping variable on its own, and introduce it as a factor.

The subsequent two sections introduce the basics of estimating multi-level linear models, first introducing intercept-only participant-level effects Sect. 6.1 and then

© Springer Nature Switzerland AG 2021
M. Schmettow, *New Statistics for Design Researchers*,
Human–Computer Interaction Series,
https://doi.org/10.1007/978-3-030-46380-9_6

slope (or group difference) effects Sect. 6.2. Typically, fixed and random effects
appear together in a linear multi-level model. It depends on the research question
whether the researcher capitalizes on the average outcome, the variation in the population or participant-level effects.

The participant-level is really just the factor and once it is regarded alongside the
population level, a model is multi-level. However, in multi-level linear modelling
we usually use a different type of factor, for the particpant level. The additional
idea is that the levels of the factor, hence the individuals, are part of a *population*.
The consequences of this perspective, will be discussed in Sect. 6.7: a population
is a set of entities that vary to some extent but also clump around a typical value.
And that is precisely what *random effects* do: levels are drawn from an overarching
distribution, usually the Gaussian. This distribution is estimated simultaneously to
the individual parameters (β_1.), which has advantages. We will return to a more
fundamental research case, the Uncanny Valley, and examine the *universality* of this
strange effect Sect. 6.4.

Once it is clear what the concept of random effects means for studying participant
behaviour, we will see that it transfers with grace to *non-human populations*, such
as designs, teams or questionnaire items. Three sections introduce multi-population
multi-level models: In Sect. 6.5 we will use a random effects model with four populations and compare their relative contribution to overall variance in performance.
Section 6.6 will show how multiple levels can form a hierarchy and in Sect. 6.8 we
will see that multi-level models can be employed the development of *psychometrics
tests*, that apply for people. Finally, we will see how to treat tests to compare designs,
for which I will coin the term *design-o-metrics* Sect. 6.8.4.

6.1   The Human Factor: Intercept Random Effects

Design science fundamentally deals with interaction between systems and humans.
Every measure we take in a design study is an encounter of an individual with
a system. As people differ in many aspects, it is likely that people differ in how
they use and perform with a system. In the previous chapter we have already dealt
with differences between users: in the BrowsingAB case, we compared two designs
in how inclusive they are with respect to elderly users. Such a research question
seeks for a definitive answer on what truly causes variation in performance. Years
of age is a standard demographic variable and in experimental studies it can be
collected without hassle. If we start from deeper theoretical considerations than that,
for example, we suspect a certain personality trait to play a significant role, this can
become more effort. Perhaps, you need a 24-item scale to measure the construct,
perhaps you first have to translate this particular questionnaire into three different
languages, and perhaps you have to first invent and evaluate a scale. In my experience,
personality scales rarely explain much of the variation we see in performance. It may
be interesting to catch some small signals for the purpose of testing theories, but for

Table 6.1 Population mean of ToT

mean_Pop
16

applied design research it is more important to quantify the performance variation within a population, rather than explaining it.

At first, one might incorrectly think that a grand mean model would do, take β_0 as the population mean and σ_ϵ as a measure for individual variation. The mistake is that the residuals collect all random variations sources, not just variance between individuals, in particular residuals are themselves composed of:

- inter-individual variation
- intra-individual variation, e.g. by different levels of energy over the day
- variations in situations, e.g. responsiveness of the website
- inaccuracy of measures, e.g. misunderstanding a questionnaire item

What is needed, is a way to separate the variation of participants from the rest? Reconsider the principles of model formulations: the structural part captures what is repeatable, what does not repeat goes to the random term. This principle can be turned around: If you want to pull a factor from the random part to the structural part, you need repetition. For estimating users' individual performance level, all that is needed is repeated measures.

In the IPump study we have collected performance data of 25 nurses, operating a novel interface for a syringe infusion pump. Altogether, every nurse completed a set of eight tasks three times. Medical devices are high-risk systems where a single fault can cost a life, which makes it a requirement that user performance is on a *uniformly* high level. We start the investigation with the global question (Table 6.1):

What is the average ToT in the population?

```
attach(IPump)
```

```
D_Novel %>%
  summarize(mean_Pop = mean(ToT))
```

The answer is just one number and does not refer to any individuals in the population. This is called the population-level estimate or fixed effect estimate. The following question is similar, but here one average is taken for every participant. We call such a summary *participant-level* (Table 6.2).

What is the average ToT of individual participants?

```
D_Novel %>%
  group_by(Part) %>%
  summarize(mean_Part = mean(ToT)) %>%
  sample_n(5)
```

Table 6.2 Participant-level mean ToT

Part	mean_Part
13	18.46
18	13.30
7	9.24
25	15.75
14	15.47

Table 6.3 Variation of participant-level mean ToT

sd_Part
13.8

Such a grouped summary can be useful for situations where we want to directly compare individuals, like in performance tests. In experimental research, individual participants are of lesser interest, as they are exchangeable entities. What matters is the total variation within the sample, representing the population of users. Once we have participant-level effects, the amount of variation can be summarized by the standard deviation (Table 6.3):

```
D_Novel %>%
  group_by(Part) %>%
  summarize(mean_Part = mean(ToT)) %>%
  ungroup() %>%
  summarize(sd_Part = var(mean_Part))
```

Generally, these are the three types of parameters in multi-level models: the population-level estimate (commonly called *fixed effects*), the participant-level estimates (*random effects*) and the *participant-level variation*.

Obviously, the variable Part is key to build such a model. This variable groups observations by participant identity and, formally, is a plain factor. A naive approach to multi-level modeling would be to estimate an AGM, like ToT ~ 0 + Part, grab the center estimates and compute the standard deviation. What sets a truly multi-level apart is that population-level effects, participant-level effects and variation are contained in one model and are estimated *simultaneously*. Random effects are really just factors with one level per participant. The only difference to a fixed effects factor is that the levels are assumed to follow a Gaussian distribution. This will further be explained in Sect. 6.7.

For the IPump study we can formulate a GMM model with participant-level random effect β_{p0} as follows:

$$\mu_i = \beta_0 + x_p \beta_{0p}$$
$$\beta_{p0} \sim \text{Gaus}(0, \sigma_{p0})$$
$$y_i \sim \text{Gaus}(\mu_i, \sigma_\epsilon)$$

There will be as many parameters β_{0p}, as there were participants in the sample, and they have all become part of the structural part. The second term describes the distribution of the participant-level group means. And finally, there is the usual random term. Before we examine further features of the model, let's run it. In the package `rstanarm`, the command `stan_glmer` is dedicated to estimating multi-level models with the extended formula syntax.

However, I will now introduce another Bayesian engine and use it from here on. The Brms package provides the Brm engine, which is invoked by the command `brm()`. This engine covers all models that can be estimated with `stan_glm` or `stan_glmer` and it uses the precise same syntax. All models estimated in this chapter, should also work with `stan_glmer`. However, Brms supports an even broader set of models, some of which we will encounter in Chap. 7.

The only downside of Brms is that it has to compile the model, preceding the estimation. For simple models, as in the previous chapter, the chains are running very quickly, and the extra step of compilation creates much overhead. For the models in this chapter, the chains run much slower, such that compilation time becomes almost negligible.

Both engines Brms and Rstanarm differ a lot in how they present the results. The Bayr package provides a consistent interface to extract information from model objects of both engines.

```
attach(IPump)
```

```
M_hf <- brm(ToT ~ 1 + (1 | Part), data = D_Novel)
P_hf <- posterior(M_hf)
```

The posterior of a multi-level model contains three types of variables (and the standard error)

1. the *fixed effect* captures the population average (Intercept)
2. *random effects* capture how individual participants deviate from the population mean
3. *random factor variation* (or group effects) captures the overall variation in the population.

With the `bayr` package these parameters can be extracted using the respective commands (Tables 6.4, 6.5 and 6.6):

```
fixef(P_hf)
```

```
ranef(P_hf) %>% sample_n(5)
```

```
grpef(P_hf)
```

Table 6.4 Coefficient estimates with 95% credibility limits

Model	Type	fixef	Center	Lower	Upper
M_hf	fixef	Intercept	16	14.4	17.5

Table 6.5 Coefficient estimates with 95% credibility limits

re_entity	Center	Lower	Upper
10	−0.160	−3.86	2.77
16	−0.019	−3.26	3.22
24	−0.497	−5.07	1.87
4	0.782	−1.38	5.89
1	1.091	−1.10	6.38

Table 6.6 Coefficient estimates with 95% credibility limits

Model	Type	fixef	re_factor	Center	Lower	Upper
M_hf	grpef	Intercept	Part	1.53	0.079	3.73

Random effects are factors and enter the model formula just as linear terms. To indicate that to the regression engine, a dedicated syntax is used in the model formula (recall that 1 represents the intercept parameter):

(1|Part)

In probability theory expressions, such as the famous Bayes theorem, the | symbol means that something to the left is conditional on something to the right. Random effects can be read as such conditional effects. Left of the | is the fixed effect that is conditional on (i.e. varies by) the factor to the right. In the simplest form the varying effect is the intercept and in the case here could be spoken of as:

Average ToT, conditional on the participant

Speaking of factors: So far, we have used *treatment contrasts* as lot for population-level factors, which represent the difference towards a reference level. If random effects were coded as treatment effects, we would have one absolute score for the first participants (reference group). All other average scores, we would express as differences to the reference participant. This seems odd and, indeed, has two disadvantages: first, whom are we to select as the reference participant? The choice would be arbitrary, unless we wanted to compare brain sizes against the grey matter of Albert Einstein, perhaps. Second, most of the time the researcher is after the factor variation rather than differences between any two individuals, which is inconvenient to compute from treatment contrasts.

The solution is to use a different contrast coding for random factors: *deviation contrasts* represent the individual effects as *difference* (δ) *towards the population mean*. As the population mean is represented by the respective fixed effect, we can

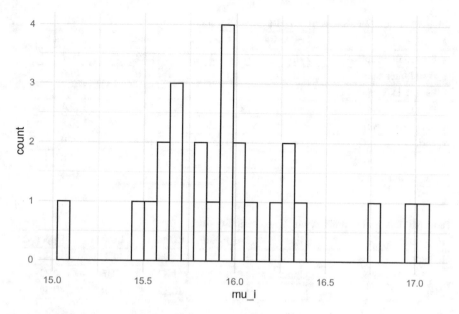

Fig. 6.1 Absolute random effect scores

compute the absolute individual predictions by adding the fixed effect to the random effect. The results are shown in Fig. 6.1.

```
tibble(mu_i = ranef(P_hf)$center +
    fixef(P_hf)$center) %>%
    ggplot(aes(x = mu_i)) +
    geom_histogram()
```

Note that first two lines in the above code only work correctly if there is just one population-level effect (i.e. a GMM). Package Bayr contains the general `re_score` to produce absolute random effects scores. This happens on the level of MCMC samples, from which CLUs can extracted, such as (Table 6.7).

```
re_scores(P_hf) %>%
    clu() %>%
    sample_n(8)
```

Finally, we can assess the initial question: are individual differences a significant component of all variation in the experiment? Assessing the impact of variation is not as straight-forward as with fixed effects. Two useful heuristics are to compare group-level variation to the fixed effects estimate (Intercept) and against the standard error:

```
P_hf %>%
    filter(type %in% c("grpef", "disp", "fixef")) %>%
    clu()
```

Table 6.7 Parameter estimates with 95% credibility limits

Parameter	re_entity	Center	Lower	Upper
r_Part[15,Intercept]	15	16.2	12.9	19.7
r_Part[2,Intercept]	2	16.1	13.0	19.6
r_Part[12,Intercept]	12	16.4	13.4	20.4
r_Part[1,Intercept]	1	17.1	14.5	22.4
r_Part[9,Intercept]	9	16.5	13.7	20.6
r_Part[4,Intercept]	4	16.9	14.2	22.0
r_Part[3,Intercept]	3	15.7	11.9	18.8
r_Part[21,Intercept]	21	15.5	11.6	18.4

Table 6.8 Parameter estimates with 95% credibility limits

Parameter	fixef	re_factor	Center	Lower	Upper
b_Intercept	Intercept		15.96	14.423	17.46
sd_Part__Intercept	Intercept	Part	1.53	0.079	3.73
Sigma			16.39	15.488	17.39

The variation due to individual differences is an order of magnitude smaller than the Intercept, as well as the standard error (Table 6.8). This lets us conclude that the novel interface works pretty much the same for every participant. If we are looking for relevant sources of variation, we have to look elsewhere. (As we have seen in Sect. 4.3.5, the main source of variation is learning.)

6.2   Multi-level Linear Regression: Variance in Change

So far, we have dealt with Intercept random effects that capture the gross differences between participants of a sample. We introduced these random effects as conditional effects like: "average performance depends on what person you are looking at". However, most research questions rather regard differences between conditions.

With *slope random effects* we can represent individual *changes* in performance. For an illustration of slope random effects, we take a look at a data set that ships with package Lme4 (which provides a non-Bayesian engine for multi-level models). 18 participants underwent sleep deprivation on ten successive days and the average reaction time on a set of tests has been recorded per day and participant. The research question is: what is the effect of sleep deprivation on reaction time and, again, this question can be asked on population level and participant level.

The participant-level plots in Fig. 6.2 shows the individual relationships between days of deprivation and reaction time. For most participants a positive linear association seems to be a good approximation, so we can go with a straight linear regression model, rather than an ordered factor model. One noticeable exception is the curve of participant 352, which is fairly linear, but reaction times get shorter with sleep deprivation. What would be the most likely explanation? Perhaps, 352 is a cheater, who slept secretly and improved by gaining experience with the task. That would explain the outstanding performance the participant reaches.

```
attach(Sleepstudy)
```

```
D_slpstd %>%
  ggplot(aes(x = days, y = RT)) +
  facet_wrap(~Part) +
  geom_point() +
  geom_smooth(se = F, aes(color = "LOESS")) +
  geom_smooth(se = F, method = "lm", aes(color = "Linear model")) +
  labs(color = "Smoothing function") +
  theme(legend.position = c(0.8, 0.1)) # !del+
```

A more compact way of plotting multi-level slopes is the spaghetti plot below. By superimposing the population level effect, we can clearly see that participants vary in how sleep deprivation delays the reactions.

```
D_slpstd %>%
  ggplot(aes(
    x = days,
    y = RT,
    group = Part
  )) +
  geom_smooth(aes(color = "participant"),
    size = .5, se = F, method = "lm"
  ) +
  geom_smooth(aes(group = 1, color = "population"),
    size = 2, se = F, method = "lm"
  ) +
  labs(color = "Level of Effect")
```

For a single level model, the formula would be RT ~ 1 + days, with the intercept being RT at day Zero and the coefficient days representing the change per day of sleep deprivation. The multi-level formula retains the population level and adds the participant-level term as a conditional statement: again, the effect depends on whom you are looking at (Fig. 6.3).

```
RT ~ 1 + days + (1 + days|Part)
```

Remember to always put complex random effects into brackets, because the + operator has higher precedence than |. We estimate the multi-level model using the Rstanarm engine.

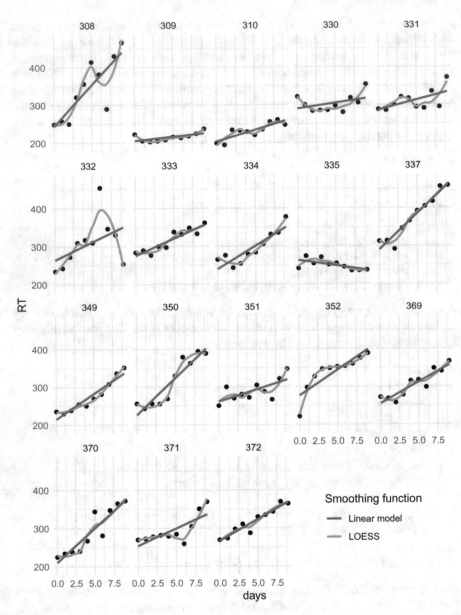

Fig. 6.2 Participant-level association between sleep deprivation and RT

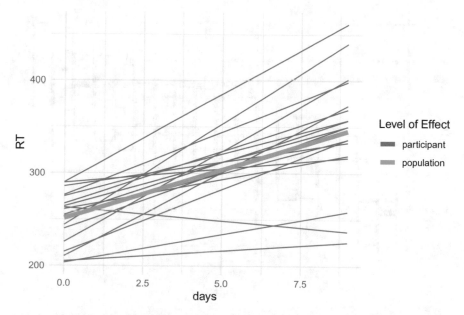

Fig. 6.3 (Uncooked) Spaghetti plot showing population and participant-level effects

Table 6.9 Population-level coefficients with random effects standard deviations

fixef	Center	Lower	Upper	SD_Part
Intercept	251.2	237.17	265.8	26.1
Days	10.5	7.01	13.8	6.4

```
M_slpsty_1 <- brm(RT ~ 1 + days + (1 + days | Part),
  data = D_slpstd,
  iter = 2000
)
```

Again, we could use the commands fixef, ranef and grpef to extract the parameters, but Bayr also provides a specialized command for multi-level tables, as Table 6.9: fixef_ml extracts the population-level estimates in CLU form and adds the participant-level standard deviation. The overall penalty for sleep deprivation is around ten milliseconds per day, with a 95% CI ranging from 7 to 14 ms. At the same time, the participant-level standard deviation is around 6.5 ms, which is considerable. One can conclude that people vary a lot in how sleep deprivation effects their alertness. Figure 6.4 shows a caterpillar plot of the slope random effects, ordered by the center estimate.

```
fixef_ml(M_slpsty_1)
```

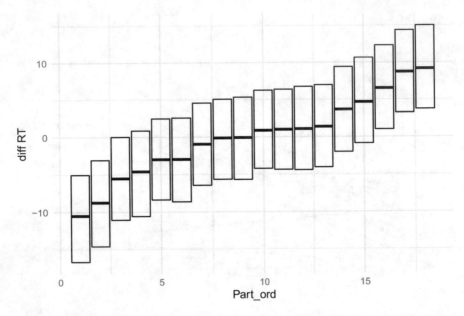

Fig. 6.4 Caterpillar plot showing individual absolute scores for effect of one day of sleep deprivation

```
ranef(M_slpsty_1) %>%
  filter(fixef == "days") %>%
  mutate(Part_ord = rank(center)) %>%
  ggplot(aes(x = Part_ord, ymin = lower, y = center, ymax = upper)) +
  geom_crossbar() +
  labs(y = "diff RT")
```

The multi-level regression model is mathematically specified as follows. Note how random coefficients $\beta_{.(Part)}$ are drawn from a Gaussian distribution with their own standard deviation, very similar to the errors ϵ_i.

$$y_i = \mu_i + \epsilon_i$$
$$\mu_i = \beta_0 + \beta_{0(Part)} + x_1\beta_1 + x_1\beta_{1(Part)}$$
$$\beta_{0(Part))} \sim \text{Gaus}(0, \sigma_{0(Part)})$$
$$\beta_{1(Part))} \sim \text{Gaus}(0, \sigma_{1(Part)})$$
$$\epsilon_i = \text{Gaus}(0, \sigma_\epsilon)$$

The second line can also be written as:

$$\mu_i = \beta_0 + \beta_{0(Part)} + x_1(\beta_1 + \beta_{1(Part)})$$

This underlines that random coefficients are additive correction terms to the population-level effect, which is what `ranef` reports. Sometimes, it is useful to

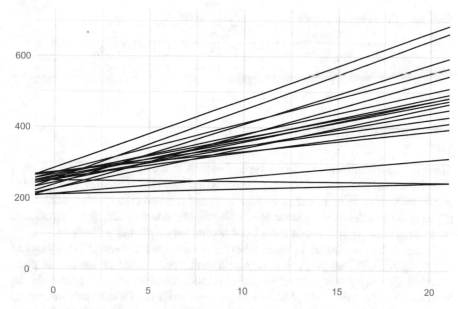

Fig. 6.5 Sleep deprivation projected

look at the total scores per participant. In package Bayr, the command `re_scores` computes absolute scores on the level of the posterior distribution. The following plot uses this command and plots two distributions: The participant-level variation in RT at Day 1 (Intercept) and after *twenty nights* of sleep interruption, (assuming that the association is linear beyond the observed range). Figure 6.5 shows the participant-level trajectories. We learn from it, that long-term sleep interruption creates a huge variance. If you design for a population where long-term sleep deprivation occurs, such as parents or doctors, and reaction time is critical, the worst case can be much, much worse than the average.

```
posterior(M_slpsty_1) %>%
  re_scores() %>%
  clu() %>%
  select(re_entity, fixef, center) %>%
  pivot_wider(names_from = fixef, values_from = center) %>%
  ggplot() +
  geom_abline(aes(
    intercept = Intercept,
    slope = days
  )) +
  xlim(0, 20) +
  ylim(0, 700)
```

Table 6.10 Coefficient estimates with 95% credibility limits

fixef	Center	Lower	Upper
Intercept	27.9	25.9	29.76
DesignNovel	−11.8	−14.5	−9.17

6.3   Thinking Multi-level

There is a lot of confusion about the type of models that we deal with in this chapter. They have also been called hierarchical models or mixed effects models. The "mixed" stands for a mixture of so called fixed effects and random effects. The problem is: if you start by understanding what fixed effects and random effects are, confusion is programmed, not only because there exist several very different definitions.

In fact, it does not matter so much whether an estimate is a fixed effect or random effect. As we will see, you can construct a multi-level model by using just plain descriptive summaries. What matters is that a model contains estimates on population level and on participant level. The benefit is, that a multi-level model can answer the same question for the population as a whole and for every single participant.

For entering the world of multi-level modeling, we do not need fancy tools. More important is to start thinking multi-level. In the following, I will introduce the basic ideas of multi-level modeling at the example of the IPump case. The idea is simple: A statistical model is developed on the population level and then we "pull it down" to the participant level.

In the IPump case, a novel syringe infusion pump design has been tested against a legacy design by letting trained nurses complete a series of eight tasks. Every nurse repeated the series three times on both designs. Time-on-task was measured and the primary research question is:

Does the novel design lead to faster execution of tasks?

```
attach(IPump)
```

To answer this question, we can compare the two group means using a basic CGM (Table 6.10)

```
M_cgm <- stan_glm(ToT ~ 1 + Design,
  data = D_pumps
)
```

```
fixef(M_cgm)
```

This model is a single-level model. It takes all observations as "from the population" and estimates the means in both groups. It further predicts that with this population of users, the novel design is faster *on average*, that means taking the whole population into account, (and forgetting about individuals).

An average benefit sounds promising, but we should be clear what it precisely means, or better what it does not mean: That there is a benefit for the population does not imply, that every individual user has precisely that benefit. It does not even imply that every user has a benefit at all. In extreme case, a small subgroup could be negatively affected by the novel design, but this could still result in a positive result on average. In the evaluation of high-risk devices like infusion pumps concerns about individual performance are real and this is why we designed the study with within-subject conditions, which allows to estimate the same model on population level and participant level. The following code produces a *multi-level descriptive model*. First, a summary on participant level is calculated, then it is summarized to obtain the population level. By putting both summaries into one figure, we are doing a multi-level analysis.

```
T_Part <-
  D_pumps %>%
  group_by(Part, Design) %>%
  summarize(mean_Part = mean(ToT))


T_Pop <-
  T_Part %>%
  group_by(Design) %>%
  summarize(mean_Pop = mean(mean_Part))
gridExtra::grid.arrange(
  nrow = 2,
  T_Pop %>%
    ggplot(aes(
      x = Design, group = NA,
      y = mean_Pop
    )) +
    geom_point() +
    geom_line() +
    ggtitle("Population-level model (average benefits)") +
    ylim(0, 60),
  T_Part %>%
    ggplot(aes(
      x = Design,
      y = mean_Part,
      group = Part, label = Part
    )) +
    geom_line() +
    ggrepel::geom_label_repel(size = 3, alpha = .5) +
    ggtitle("Participant-level model (individual benefits)") +
    ylim(0, 60)
)
```

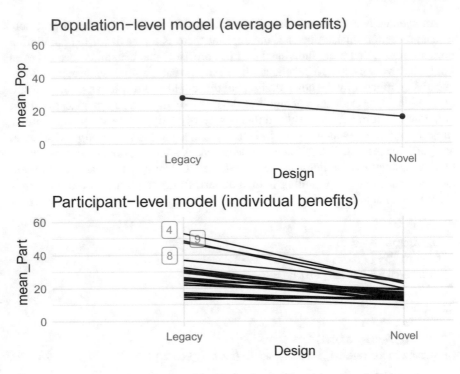

Fig. 6.6 Exploratory multi-level plot of population-level and participant-level change

Note

• how with `gridExtra::grid.arrange()` we can multiple plots into a grid, which is more flexible than using facetting
• that `ggrepel::geom_label_repel` produces non-overlapping labels in plots

Figure 6.6 is a multi-level plot, as it shows the same effect on two different levels *alongside*. In this case, the participant-level plot confirms that the trend of the population-level effects is representative. Most worries about the novel design are removed, with the one exception of participant 3, all users had net benefit from using the novel design and we can call the novel design universally better. In addition, some users (4, 8 and 9) seem to have experienced catastrophes with the legacy design, but their difficulties disappear when they switch to the novel design.

If you look again at the participant-level *spaghetti plot* (They are uncooked!) and find it similar to what you have seen before, you are right: This is an design-by-participant *conditional plot*. Recall, that conditional effects represent the change of outcome, depending on another factor. In this multi-level model, this second factor simply Part(icipant). That suggests that it is well within reach of plain linear models to estimate design-by-participant conditional effects. Just for the purpose of demonstration, we can estimate a population level model, conditioning the design effect on participants. Ideally, we would use a parametrization giving us separate Intercept and DesignNovel effects per participant, but the formula interface is not flexible enough and we would have to work with dummy variable expansion. Since this is just a demonstration before we move on to the multi-level formula extensions, I use an AMM instead. A plain linear model can only hold one level at a time, which is why we have to estimate the two separate models for population and participant levels. Then we combine the posterior objects, extract the CLU table and plot the center estimates in Fig. 6.7.

```
M_amm_pop <-
  D_pumps %>%
  stan_glm(ToT ~ 0 + Design, data = .)

M_amm_part <-
  D_pumps %>%
  stan_glm(ToT ~ (0 + Design):Part, data = .)

T_amm <-
  bind_rows(
    posterior(M_amm_pop),
    posterior(M_amm_part)
  ) %>%
  fixef() %>%
  separate(fixef, into = c("Design", "Part"))

T_amm %>%
  ggplot(aes(x = Design, y = center, group = Part, color = model)) +
  geom_line()
```

The convenience of (true) multi-level models is that both (or more) levels are specified and estimated as one model. For the multi-level models that follow, we will use a specialized engine, brm() (generalized multi-level regression) that estimates both levels simultaneously and produce multi-level coefficients. The multi-level CGM we desire is written like this:

```
M_mlcgm <-
  D_pumps %>%
  brm(ToT ~ 1 + Design + (1 + Design | Part), data = .)
```

In the formula of this multi-level CGM the predictor term (1 + Design) is just copied. The first instance is the usual population-level averages, but the second is on participant-level. The | operator in probability theory means "conditional upon" and here this can be read as *effect of Design conditional on participant*.

For linear models we have been using the coef() command to extract all coefficients. Here it would extract all coefficients on both levels. With multi-level models, two specialized command exist to separate the levels: we can extract population-level effects using the fixef() command for *fixed effects* (Table 6.11). All lower level

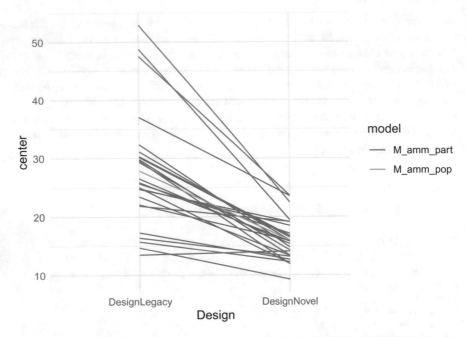

Fig. 6.7 Spaghetti plot combining the results of a population-level with a participant-level model

Table 6.11 Coefficient estimates with 95% credibility limits

fixef	Center	Lower	Upper
Intercept	27.6	23.7	31.54
DesignNovel	−11.7	−15.3	−8.05

effects can be accessed with the `ranef` command, which stands for *random effects*.
Random effects are *differences towards the population-level*. This is why random
effects are always *centered at zero*. In the following histogram, the distribution of
the DesignNovel random effects are shown. This is how much users deviate from the
average effect in the population (Fig. 6.8)

```
fixef(M_mlcgm)
```

```
ranef(M_mlcgm) %>%
  rename(Part = re_entity, `deviation` = center) %>%
  ggplot(aes(x = deviation)) +
  facet_grid(~fixef) +
  geom_histogram()
```

The distribution of random effects should resemble a *Gaussian distribution*. It is
usually hard to tell with such small sample sizes, but it seems that the Intercept effects

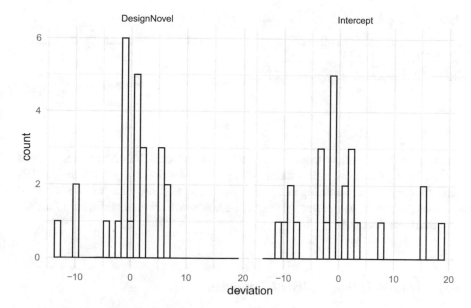

Fig. 6.8 Participant-level random effects in a CGM

Table 6.12 Coefficient estimates with 95% credibility limits

fixef	Center	Lower	Upper
Intercept	8.71	6.03	12.47
DesignNovel	6.02	2.98	9.82

have a left skew. As we will see in Chap. 7, this problem is not surprising and can be resolved. The distributions are also centered at zero, which is not a coincidence, but the way random effects are designed: deviations from the population mean. That opens up two interesting perspectives: first, random effects look a lot like residuals Sect. 4.1.2, and like those we can summarize a random effects vector by its *standard deviation*, using the grpef command from package Bayr (Table 6.12).

```
grpef(M_mlcgm)
```

Most design rescarch is located on the population level. We want to know how a design works, broadly. Sometimes, stratified samples are used to look for conditional effects in (still broad) subgroups. Reporting individual differences makes little sense in such situations. The standard deviation summarizes individual differences and can be interpreted the *degree of diversity*. The command bayr::fixef_ml is implementing this by simply attaching the standard deviation center estimates to the respective population-level effect (Table 6.13). As coefficients and standard deviations are on the same scale, they can be compared. Roughly speaking, a two-thirds of the population is contained in an interval *twice as large* as the SD.

Table 6.13 Population-level coefficients with random effects standard deviations

fixef	Center	Lower	Upper	SD_Part
Intercept	27.6	23.7	31.54	8.71
DesignNovel	−11.7	−15.3	−8.05	6.02

```
fixef_ml(M_mlcgm)
```

That having said, I believe that more researchers should watch their participant levels more closely. Later, we will look at two specific situations: psychometric models have the purpose of measuring individuals Sect. 6.8 and those who propose universal theories (i.e., about people *per se*) must also show that their predictions hold for each and everyone Sect. 6.4.

6.4 Testing Universality of Theories

Often, the applied researcher is primarily interested in a population-level effect, as this shows the *average* expected benefit. If you run a webshop, your returns are exchangeable. One customer lost can be compensated by gaining a new one. In such cases, it suffices to report the random effects standard deviation. If user performance varies strongly, this can readily be seen in this one number.

In at least two research situations, going for the average is just not enough: when testing hazardous equipment and when testing theories. In safety critical research, such as a medical infusion pump, the rules are different than for a webshop. The rules are non-compensatory, as the benefit of extreme high performance on one patient cannot compensate the costs associated with a single fatal error on another patient. For this asymmetry, the design of such a system must enforce a *robust* performance, with no catastrophes. The multi-level analysis of the infusion pumps in Sect. 6.3 is an example. It demonstrated that practically all nurses will have a benefit from the novel design.

The other area where on-average is not enough, is theory-driven experimental research. Fundamental behavioural researchers are routinely putting together theories on The Human Mind and try to challenge these theories. For example the Uncanny Valley effect Sect. 5.5: one social psychologist's theory could be that the Uncanny Valley effect is caused by religious belief, whereas a cognitive psychologist could suggest that the effect is caused by a category confusion on a fundamental processing level (seeing faces). Both theories make universal statements, about all human beings. *Universal statements* can never be proven, but can only be hardened. However, once a counter-example is found, the theory needs to be abandonded. If there is one participant who is provenly non-religious, but falls into the Uncanny Valley, our social psychologist would be proven wrong. If there is a single participant in the world, who is robvust against the Uncanny Valley, the cognitive psychologist was wrong.

Obviously, this counter-evidence can only be found on participant level. In some way, the situation is analog to robustness. The logic of universal statements is that they are false if there is one participant who breaks the pattern, and there is no compensation possible. Unfortunately, the majority of fundamental behavioural researchers, have ignored this simple logic and still report population-level estimates when testing universal theories. In my opinion, all these studies should not be trusted, before a multi-level analysis shows that the pattern exists on participant level.

In Sect. 5.5, the Uncanny Valley effect has been demonstrated on population level. This is good enough, if we just want to confirm the Uncanny Valley effect as an observation, something that frequently happens, but not necessarily for everyone. The sample in our study consisted of mainly students and their closer social network. It is almost certain, that many of the tested persons were religious and others were atheists. If the religious-attitude theory is correct, we would expect to see the Uncanny Valley in several participants, but not in all. If the category confusion theory is correct, we would expect all participants to fall into the valley. The following model performs the polynomial analysis as before Sect. 5.5, but multi-level:

```
attach(Uncanny)

M_poly_3_ml <-
  RK_1 %>%
  brm(response ~ 1 + huMech1 + huMech2 + huMech3 +
    (1 + huMech1 + huMech2 + huMech3 | Part),
  data = ., iter = 2500
  )

P_poly_3_ml <- posterior(M_poly_3_ml)

PP_poly_3_ml <- post_pred(M_poly_3_ml, thin = 5)
```

One method for testing universality is to extract the fitted responses (`predict`) and perform a visual examination: can we see a valley for every participant?

```
T_pred <-
  RK_1 %>%
  mutate(M_poly_3_ml = predict(PP_poly_3_ml)$center)

T_pred %>%
  ggplot(aes(x = huMech, y = M_poly_3_ml, group = Part)) +
  geom_smooth(se = F, size = .5) +
  labs(x = "human likeness", y = "fitted emotional response")
```

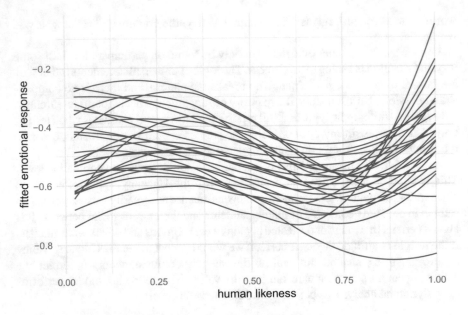

Fig. 6.9 Participant-level associations between human likeness and

The spaghetti plot in Fig. 6.9 broadly confirms, that all participants experience the Uncanny Valley. For a more detailed analysis, a facetted plot would be better suited, allowing to inspect the curves case-by-case.

We proceed directly to a more formal method of testing universality: In Sect. 5.5.1 we have seen how the posterior distributions of shoulder and trough can be first derived and then used to give a more definitive answer on the shape of the polynomial. It was argued that the unique pattern of the Uncanny Valley is to have a shoulder left of a trough. These two properties can be checked by identifying the stationary points. The proportion of MCMC iterations that fulfill these properties can is evidence that the effect exists.

For testing universality of the effect, we just have to run the same analysis on participant-level. Since the participant-level effects are deviations from the population-level effect, we first have to add the population level effect to the random effects (using the Bayr command `re_scores`), which creates absolute polynomial coefficients. The two commands `trough` and `shoulder` from package Uncanny require a matrix of coefficients, which is done by spreading out the posterior distribution table. Then all the characteristics of the polynomial are checked, that define the Uncanny Valley phenomenon:

- a trough
- a shoulder
- the shoulder is left of the trough

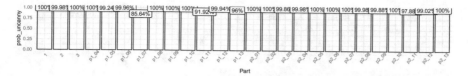

Fig. 6.10 Participant-level certainty that the Uncanny Valley phenomenon happened

```
# devtools::install_github("schmettow/uncanny")

library(uncanny)

P_univ_uncanny <-
  P_poly_3_ml %>%
  re_scores() %>%
  select(iter, Part = re_entity, fixef, value) %>%
  tidyr::spread(key = "fixef", value = "value") %>%
  select(iter, Part, huMech0 = Intercept, huMech1:huMech3) %>%
  mutate(
    trough = trough(select(., huMech0:huMech3)),
    shoulder = shoulder(select(., huMech0:huMech3)),
    has_trough = !is.na(trough),
    has_shoulder = !is.na(shoulder),
    shoulder_left = trough > shoulder,
    is_uncanny = has_trough & has_shoulder & shoulder_left
  )
```

To produce Fig. 6.10, the probability that the participant experienced the Uncanny Valley is calculated as the proportion (mean) of MCMC samples that meet the criteria.

```
P_univ_uncanny %>%
  group_by(Part) %>%
  summarize(prob_uncanny = mean(is_uncanny)) %>%
  mutate(label = str_c(100 * round(prob_uncanny, 4), "%")) %>%
  ggplot(aes(x = Part, y = prob_uncanny)) +
  geom_col() +
  geom_label(aes(label = label)) +
  theme(axis.text.x = element_text(angle = 45))
```

Figure 6.10 gives strong support to the universality of the Uncanny Valley. What may raise suspicion is rather that for most participants the probability is 100%. If this is all based on a random walk, we should at least see a few deviations, shouldn't we. The reason for that is that MCMC samples approximate the posterior distribution by frequency. As their is a limited number of samples (here: 4000), the resolution is limited. If we increase the number of iterations enough, we would eventually see few "deviant" samples appear and measure the tiny chance that a participant does not fall for the Uncanny Valley.

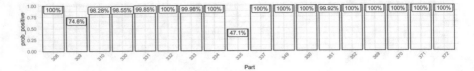

Fig. 6.11 Participant-level certainty that sleep deprivation causes delayed reactions

This is great news for all scientists who believe that the Uncanny Valley effect is an innate cognitive phenomenon (rather than cultural). The same technique can also be used for the identification of deviant participants, those few that are totally against the trend. We briefly re-visit case Sleepstudy, for which we have estimated a multi-level linear regression model to render individual increase of reaction time as result of sleep deprivation (Sect. 6.2). By visual inspection, we identified a single deviant participant who showed an improvement over time, rather than a decline. However, the fitted lines are based on point estimates, only (the median of the posterior). Using the same technique as above, we can calculate the participant-level probabilities for the slope being positive (Fig. 6.11).

```
attach(Sleepstudy)

P_scores <-
  posterior(M_slpsty_1) %>%
  re_scores() %>%
  mutate(Part = re_entity)

P_scores %>%
  filter(fixef == "days") %>%
  group_by(Part) %>%
  summarize(prob_positive = mean(value >= 0)) %>%
  mutate(label = str_c(100 * round(prob_positive, 4), "%")) %>%
  ggplot(aes(x = Part, y = prob_positive)) +
  geom_col() +
  geom_label(aes(label = label), vjust = 1) +
  theme(axis.text.x = element_text(angle = 45))
```

All, but participants 309 and 335, almost certainly have positive slopes. Participant 335 we had identified earlier by visual inspection. Now, that we account for the full posterior distribution, it seems less suspicious. There is almost a 50% chance that the participant is suffering from sleep deprivation, too. Figure 6.12 is an attempt at illustrating the uncertainty. It shows all the possible slopes the MCMC random walk has explored from (unsuspicious) participant 308 and participant 335. While

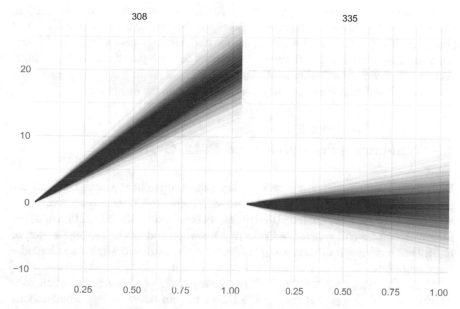

Fig. 6.12 Visualizing the uncertainty in Days for two participants

the latter has a distinctly different distribution, there is no compelling reason to get too excited and call 335 a true counter-example from the rule that sleep deprivation reduces cognitive performance.

```
P_scores %>%
  filter(Part %in% c(308, 335), fixef == "days") %>%
  ggplot() +
  xlim(0.05, 1) +
  ylim(-10, 25) +
  geom_abline(aes(intercept = 0, slope = value),
    alpha = .01
  ) +
  facet_grid(. ~ Part)
```

In turn, the method of posterior-based test statistics can also be used for *analysis of existence*. In the Sleepstudy case a hypothetical question of existence would be that there exist persons who are completely insensitive to sleep deprivation. Why not? Recently, I saw a documentary about a guy who could touch charged electric wires, because due to a rare genetic deviation, his skin had no sweat glands. Whereas universal statements can only be falsified by a counter-example, statements of existence can be proven by just a single case. For example, in the 1980 dyslexia became more widely recognized as a defined condition. Many parents finally got an explanation for the problems their kids experienced in school. Many teachers complained that many parents would just seek cheap excuses for their lesser gifted offsprings. And some people argued that dyslexia does not exist and that the disability to read is just a manifestation of lower intelligence. According to the logic of existence, a single person with a well functioning intellect, but hampered reading suffices to proof the existence of dyslexia. These people have been found in the meantime.

6.5   Non-human Populations and Cross-Overs

With multi-level models design researchers can examine how a design affects the population of users as a whole, as well as on individual level. If there is little variation between users, it can be concluded that the effect is uniform in the population of users. In this section we will generalize the term *population* and extend the application of multi-level modeling to other types of research entities, such as designs, questionnaire items and tasks.

Many studies in, what one could call *fundamental design research* seek to uncover general laws of design that may guide future system development. Fundamental design research is not concerned with choosing between individual designs, whether they are good enough or not, but with separating the population of possible designs into good ones and bad ones by universal statements, such as "For informational websites, broad navigation structures are better than deep ones". Note how this statement speaks of designs (not users) in an unspecified plural. It is framed as a universal law for the population of designs.

Comparative evaluation studies, such as the IPump case, are not adequate to answer such questions, simply because you cannot generalize to the population from a sample of two. This is only possible under strict constraints, namely that the two designs under investigation only differ in one design property. For example two versions of a website present the same web content in a deep versus a wide hierarchy, but layout, functionality are held constant. And even then, we should be very careful with conclusions, because there can be interaction effects. For example, the rules could be different for a website used by expert users.

If the research question is universal, i.e. aiming at general conclusions on all designs (of a class), it is inevitable to see designs as a population from which we collect a sample. The term population suggests a larger set of entities, and in fact many application domains have an abundance of existing designs and a universe of possible designs. Just to name a few: there exist dozens of note taking apps for mobile devices and hundreds of different jump'n run games. Several classes of websites count in the ten thousands, such as webshops, municipal websites or intranets.

We can define classes of objects in any way we want, but the term population, has a stronger meaning than just a collection. A population contains individuals of the same kind and these individuals vary, but only to some extent. At the same time, it is implied that we can identify some sort of typical value for a population, such that most individuals are clumped around this typical value. Essentially, if it looks similar to one of the basic statistical distributions Sect. 3.5.2, we can call it a population.

To illustrate that not every class is a population, take vehicles. Vehicles are a class of objects that transport people or goods. This broad definition covers many types of vehicles, including bicycles, rikshas, cars, buses, trucks and container vessels. If the attribut under question is the weight, we will see a distribution spreading from a 10 kg up to 100 tons (without freight). That is a a scale of 1:10.000 and the distribution would spread out like butter on a warm toast. Formally, we can calculate the average weight of a all vehicles, but that would in no way represent a typical value.

In design research the most compelling populations are *users* and *designs*. Besides that research objects exist that we can also call members of a population, such as *tasks*, *situations* and *questionnaire items*.

Tasks: Modern informational websites contain thousands of information pieces and finding every one of those can be considered a task. At the same time, it is impossible to cover them all in one study, such that sampling a few is inevitable. We will never be able to tell the performance of every task, but using random effects it is possible to estimate the variance of tasks. Is that valuable information? Probably it is in many cases, as we would not easily accept a design that prioritizes on a few items at the expense of many others, which are extremely hard to find.

Situations: With the emerge of the web, practically everyone started using computers to find information. With the more recent breakthrough in mobile computing, everyone is doing everything using a computer in almost every situation. People chat, listen to music and play games during meals, classes and while watching television. They let themselves being lulled into sleep, which is tracked and interrupted by smart alarms. Smartphones are being used on trains, while driving cars and bikes, however dangerous that might be, and not even the most private situations are spared. If you want to evaluate the usability of any mobile messaging, navigation and e-commerce app, you should test it in all these situations. A study to examine performance across situations needs a sample from a population of situations.

Questionnaire items: Most design researchers cannot refrain from using questionnaires to evaluate certain elucive aspects of their designs. A well constructed rating scale consists of a set of items that trigger similar responses. At the same time, it is desireable that items are unsimilar to a degree, as that establishes good discrimination across a wide range. In ability tests, for example to assess people's intelligence or math skills, test items are constructed to vary in difficulty. The more ability a person has, the more likely will a very difficult item be solved correctly. In design research, rating scales cover concepts such as perceived mental workload, perceived usability, beauty or trustworthiness. Items of such scales differ in how extreme the proposition is, like the following three items that could belong to a scale for aesthetic perception:

1. The design is not particularly ugly.
2. The design is pretty.
3. The design is a piece of art.

For any design it is rather difficult to get a positive response on item 3, whereas item 1 is a small hurdle. So, if one thinks of all possible propositions about beauty, any scale is composed of a sample from the population of beauty propositions.

If we look beyond design research, an abundance of non-human populations can be found in other research disciplines, such as:

- products in consumer research
- phonemes in psycholinguistics
- test items in psychometrics
- pictures of faces in face recognition research
- patches of land in agricultural studies
- households in socio-economic studies

In all these cases it is useful (if not inevitable) to ask multi-level questions not just on the human population, but on the encounter of multiple populations. In research on a single or few designs, such as in A/B testing, designs are usually thought of (and modeled) as common fixed-effects factors. However, when the research question is more fundamental, such that it regards a whole class of designs, it is more useful to think of designs as a population and draw a sample. In the next section we will see an example, where a sample of users encounters a sample of designs and tasks.

In experimental design research, the research question often regards a whole class of designs and it is almost inevitable to view designs as a population. As we usually want to generalize across users, that is another sample. A basic experimental setup would be to have every user rate (or do a task) on every design, which is called a complete (experimental) design, but I prefer to think of it as a complete *encounter*.

Every measure is an encounter of one participant and one design. But, if a multi-item rating scale is used, measures are an encounter between three populations. Every measure combines the impact from three members from these populations. With a single measure, the impact factors are inseparable. But if we have repeated measures on all populations, we can apply a *cross-classified multi-level model* (CRMM). An intercept-only CRMM just adds intercept random effects for every population.

In the following case Egan, the question is a comparison of diversity across populations. Three decades ago, [1] published one of the first papers on individual differences in computer systems design and made the following claim:

> differences among people usually account for much more variability in performance than differences in system designs

What is interesting about this research question is that it does not speak about effects, but about *variability of effects* and seeks to compare variability of two totally different populations. In the following we will see how this claim can be tested by measuring multiple encounters between populations

Egan's claim has been cited in many papers that regarded individual differences and we were wondering how it would turn out in the third millennium, with the probably most abundant of all application domains: informational websites. For the convenience, we chose the user population of student users, with ten university

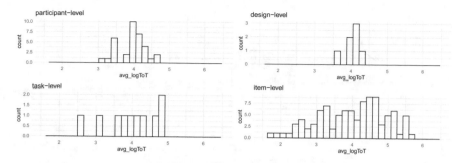

Fig. 6.13 Distribution of human and non-human populations in the Egan experiment (scale log(ToT))

websites as our design sample. Furthermore, ten representative tasks on such websites were selected, which is another population. During the experiment, all 41 participants completed 10 information search items such as:

On website [utwente.nl] find the [program schedule Biology].

```
attach(Egan)
```

Note that ToT is log-transformed for compliance with the assumptions of Linear Models. Generally, the advice is to use a Generalized Linear Model instead Sect. 7.3.2. Egan's claim is a two-way encounter to which we added the tasks, which makes it three-way. However, our data seemed to require a fourth random effect, which essentially is a conditional effect between tasks and websites, which we call an item. Figure 6.13 shows a grid of histogram with the marginal distributions of human and non-human populations. The individual plots were created using the following code template:

```
D_egan %>%
  group_by(Part) %>%
  summarize(avg_logToT = mean(logToT)) %>%
  ggplot(aes(x = avg_logToT)) +
  geom_histogram() +
  labs(title = "participant-level average log-times") +
  xlim(1.5, 6.5)
```

There seems to be substantial variation between participants, tasks and items, but very little variation in designs. We build a GMM for the encounter of the four populations.

```
M_1 <-
  brm(logToT ~ 1 +
    (1 | Part) + (1 | Design) + (1 | Task) + (1 | Design:Task),
  data = D_egan
  )
P_1 <- posterior(M_1)
```

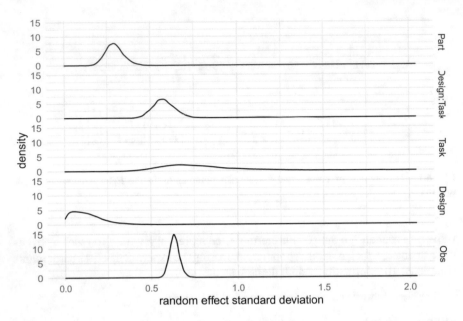

Fig. 6.14 Density plot of random effects standard deviations

A Bayesian multi-level model estimates the standard deviation alongside with coefficients, such that we can compare magnitude and certainty of variability. In addition, we include the standard error as an observation-level effect (Obs) for comparison (Fig. 6.14).

```
library(mascutils) # reorder-levels
P_1 %>%
  filter(type == "grpef" | type == "disp") %>%
  mutate(
    re_factor = if_else(type == "disp",
      "Obs", re_factor
    ),
    re_factor = reorder_levels(
      re_factor,
      c(4, 2, 5, 3, 1)
    )
  ) %>%
  ggplot(aes(x = value)) +
  geom_density() +
  labs(x = "random effect standard deviation") +
  facet_grid(re_factor ~ .)
```

The outcomes of our study are indecisive regarding Egan's claim. Variance of participants is stronger than variance of designs, but the posterior distributions overlap a

Table 6.14 The probability that Egan's claim is right derived from MCMC samples

prob_Egan_is_right
0.928

good deal. Both factors also produce much less variability in measures than does the remaining noise. Tasks seem to have the overall strongest effect, but this comes with huge uncertainty. The strongest variability is found in the sample of items (Design × Task), which is an interesting observation. How easy a task is, largely depends on the website where it is carried out. That makes sense, as all pieces of information somehow compete for space. For example, one university website could present the library on the homepage, whereas another websites hides it deep in its navigation structure.

A secondary observation on the posterior plot is that some effects are rather certain, such as Obs and Design:Task, whereas others are extremely uncertain, especially Task. There is a partial explanation for this: the variation is estimated from the "heads" in the human or non-human population. It therefore strongly depends on respective sample size. Design and Task have a meager $N = 10$, which is why the estimate are so uncertain. With $N = 41$ the participant level estimate has more data and reaches better certainty, same for the pairs ($N = 100$). The observations level can employ to all 410 observations, resulting in a highly certain estimate.

Still, Egan's claim is out in the world and requires an answer. To reduce the quantitative findings to a Yes/No variable, we use the same technique as in Sects. 5.5.1 and 6.4. What is the probability, that Egan is right? We create a Boolean variable and summarize the proportion of MCMC draws, where $\sigma_{Part} > \sigma_{Design}$ holds (Table 6.14).

```
P_1 %>%
  filter(type == "grpef", re_factor %in% c("Part", "Design")) %>%
  select(chain, iter, re_factor, value) %>%
  spread(re_factor, value) %>%
  summarize(prob_Egan_is_right = mean(Part > Design))
```

Such a chance can count as good evidence in favor of Egan's claim, although it certainly does not match the "much more" in the original quote. However, if we take the strong and certain Item effect (Design × Task) into account, the claim could even be reversed. Apparently, the difficulty of a task depends on the design, that means, it depends on where this particular designer has placed an item in the navigation structure. These are clearly design choices and if we see it this way, evidence for Egan's claim is practically zero (0.0005, Table 6.15).

```
P_1 %>%
  filter(type == "grpef", re_factor %in% c("Part", "Design", "Design:Task")) %>%
  select(chain, iter, re_factor, value) %>%
  spread(re_factor, value) %>%
  mutate(Egan_is_right = Part > Design & Part > `Design:Task`) %>%
  summarize(prob_Egan_is_right = mean(Egan_is_right))
```

Table 6.15 The probability that Egan's claim is right, including the Item effects (Design × Task)

prob_Egan_is_right
5e-04

In this section we have seen that measures in design research happen in encounters between users, designs and several other non-human populations. Cross-classified random effects models capture these structures. When testing Egan's claim, we saw how an exotic hypothesis such as the difference in variance, can be answered probabilistically, because with Bayesian models, we get posterior distributions for all parameters in a model, not just coefficients.

6.6   Nested Random Effects

In some research designs, we are dealing with populations that have a hierarchical structure, where every member is itself composed of another population of entities. A classic example is from educational research: schools are a non-human population, underneath which we find a couple of other populations, classes and students. Like cross-classified models, nested models consist of multiple levels. The difference is that if one knows the lowest (or: a lower) level of an observation, the next higher level is unambiguous, like:

- every class is in exactly one school
- every student is in exactly one school (or class)

Nested random effects (NRE) represent nested sampling schemes. As we have seen above, cross-classified models play an important role in design research, due to the user/task/design encounter. NREs are more common in research disciplines where organisation structures or geography plays a role, such as education science (think of the international school comparison studies PISA and TIMMS), organisational psychology or political science.

One examples of a nested sampling structure in design research is the CUE8 study, which is the eighth instance of Comparative Usability Evaluation (CUE) studies by Rolf Molich [2]. Different to what the name might suggest, not designs are under investigation in CUE, but usability professionals. The over-arching question in the CUE series is the performance and reliability of usability professionals when evaluating designs. Earlier studies sometimes came to devastating results regarding consistency across professional groups when it comes to identifying and reporting usability problems. The CUE8 study lowered the bar, by asking if professionals can at least measure time in a comparable way.

Table 6.16 Data set with 8 variables, showing 8 of 2620 observations

Obs	Team	Part	Condition	SUS	Task	ToT	logToT
1113	L3	223	Remote	83.0	3	89	4.49
1169	L3	234	Remote	80.0	4	102	4.62
1264	L3	253	Remote	25.0	4	102	4.62
1589	L3	318	Remote	85.0	4	127	4.84
2052	L3	411	Remote	68.0	2	90	4.50
2135	L3	427	Remote	75.0	5	82	4.41
2390	M3	478	Remote	92.5	5	48	3.87
2569	O3	514	Moderated		4	707	6.56

The CUE8 study measured time-on-task in usability tests, which had been conducted by 14 different teams. The original research question was: How reliable are time-on-task measures across teams? All teams used the same website (a car rental company) and the same set of tasks. All teams did moderated or remote testing (or both) and recruited their own sample of participants (Table 6.16).

```
attach(CUE8)
```

```
D_cue8
```

An analysis can performed on three levels: the population level would tell us the average performance on this website. That could be interesting for the company running it. Below that are the teams and their variation is what the original research question is about. Participants make the third level for a nested multi-level model. It is nested, because every participant is assigned to exactly one team. If that weren't the case, say there is one sample of participants shared by the teams, that would be cross-classification.

As the original research question is on the consistency across teams, we can readily take the random effect variance as a measure for the opposite: when variance is high, consistency is low. But, how low is low? It is difficult to come up with an absolute standard for inter-team reliability. Because we also have the participant-level, we can resort to a relative standard: how does the variation between teams compare to variation between individual participants?

Under this perspective, we examine the data. This time, we have real time-on-task data and as so often, it is highly skewed. Again, we use the trick of logarithmic transformation to obtain a more symmetric distribution of residuals. The downside is that the outcome variable may not be zero. For time-on-task data this is not an issue. Before proceeding to the model, we explore the original variable ToT on the two levels (Participant and Team). In the following code the mean ToT is computed for the two levels of analysis, participants and teams and shown in ascending order (Fig. 6.15).

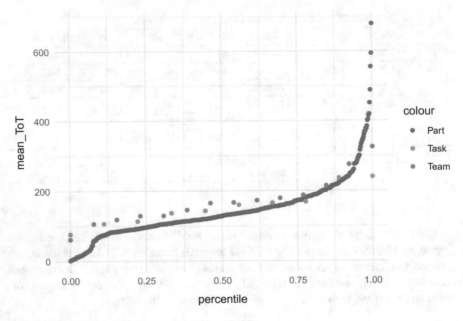

Fig. 6.15 Distribution of mean scores on three levels

It seems there is ample variation in ToT for participants, with mean ToT ranging from below 100 to almost 500 s. There also is considerable variation on team level, but the overall range seems to be a little smaller. Note, however, that the participant level contains all the variation that is due to teams. A model with nested random effects can separate the sources of variation. When two (or more) levels are nested, a special syntax applies for specifying nested random effects. `1 | Team/Part`.

```
M_1 <-
  D_cue8 %>%
  brm(logToT ~ Condition + (1 | Team / Part),
    data = .
  )
```

```
P_1 <- posterior(M_1)
```

Note that the model contains another feature of the CUE8 study, namely the effect of the testing condition, moderated or remote (Table 6.17). Why does this not have a participant-level effect? As participants are either moderated or remote, we simply don't get any data, on how the same participant behaved in the other condition.

```
P_1
```

The posterior object reveals two random factors, one for teams and one for participants. The interpretation is in no way different than cross-classified random effects.

Table 6.17 MCMC posterior with 4000 samples of 542 parameters in 1 model(s)

Model	Parameter	Type	fixef	re_factor	Count
M_1		ranef	Intercept	Team	14
M_1		ranef	Intercept	Team:Part	523
M_1	b_Conditionmoderated	fixef	Conditionmoderated		1
M_1	b_Intercept	fixef	Intercept		1
M_1	Sigma	disp			
M_1	sd_Team:Part__Intercept	grpef	Intercept		
M_1	sd_Team__Intercept	grpef	Intercept		

Table 6.18 Data set with 8 variables, showing 8 of 2620 observations

Obs	Part	Team	Condition	SUS	Task	ToT	logToT
568	H3_114	H3	Remote		3	49	3.89
977	K3_196	K3	Moderated	67.5	2	92	4.52
1152	L3_231	L3	Remote	50.0	2	329	5.80
1442	L3_289	L3	Remote	100.0	2	148	5.00
2144	L3_429	L3	Remote	100.0	4	157	5.06
2260	L3_452	L3	Remote	90.0	5	59	4.08
2520	N3_504	N3	Moderated	33.3	5	220	5.39
2543	N3_509	N3	Moderated	53.3	3	230	5.44

In both cases, the absolute group mean for a certain participant is obtained by adding up all two coefficients.

The syntax really is just a safe way to deal with nested samples, where participant identifiers could be re-used. If participant identifiers were unique (Table 6.18), a cross-classified model with the formula `logToT ~ Condition + (1|Part) + (1|Team)` would produce the exact same results.

```
D_cue8_x <-
  D_cue8 %>%
  unite(Part, Team:Part, remove = F) %>%
  as_tbl_obs()
```

```
D_cue8_x
```

Let's take a closer look at the results regarding consistency of ToT measures across teams (Table 6.19). We would always expect participants to show variation, but if team averages show strong variation, then we can suspect that there are biases. It turns out that the variation by team is by a factor of 1.5 larger than individual differences. And it is on par with the measurement error (sigma).

Table 6.19 Parameter estimates with 95% credibility limits

Parameter	fixef	re_factor	Center	Lower	Upper
b_Intercept	Intercept		4.629	4.062	5.19
b_Conditionmoderated	Conditionmoderated		0.326	−0.393	1.12
sd_Team__Intercept	Intercept	Team	0.619	0.417	1.01
sd_Team:Part__Intercept	Intercept	Team:Part	0.428	0.390	0.47

```
P_1 %>%
  filter(type %in% c("fixef", "grpef")) %>%
  clu()
```

It is not surprising to see the test users vary greatly in performance. What is concerning is that the discordance between professional teams. Note that this is the net variance after controlling for the condition, remote or moderated. Surprisingly, evidence for just that difference rather low and highly uncertain $(0.33[-0.39, 1.12]_{CI95})$.

In this section we introduced a new perspective on multi-level models. Here, the question was to quantify and compare samples (rather than conditions) as sources of variation. With multi-level models, we can separate sources of variation. This builds on how random effects are constructed, as factor levels drawn from a Gaussian distribution. In the following section, we will delve deeper into the matter of random effects.

6.7　What Are Random Effects? On Pooling and Shrinkage

At least half a dozen of definitions exist for the term random effect. This is so confusing that some authors refrain to use the term altogether. In addition, the very terms *random effect* and *random factor* are highly misleading, as there is nothing more or less random in a random factors as compared to fixed factors. Here, the definition of a random effects is conceptually based on the idea of a population, and implemented as a factor, where levels are assumed to follow a Gaussian distribution.

A Gaussian distribution extends in both directions infinitely, but the extreme tails are becoming very thin. The low assigned probability of extreme events acts on the estimate, by correcting extreme estimates towards the mean, which is called shrinkage.

When a data set contains a factor that we may wish to add to the model, the question is: fixed effect or random effect? In Sect. 6.5, I have introduced the heuristic of populations. If one can conceive tasks, designs, or whatever set of items as a population, there is clumping to some degree, but also variation. The more clumping there is, the better is the guess for unobserved members by observing some members.

Obviously, we would never speak of a population, when the objects of interest are from different classes. Entities gathering on super market parking lots, like persons, cars, baskets and and dropped brochures, we would never see as a population. People, we would generally see as a population, as long as what we want to observe is somewhat comparable between members. When the question is, how fast persons can do a 2000 m run at the Olympic games, we would certainly want one population per discipline (swimming, running, etc). Why is that so? It is because we expect members of a population to have some similarity, with the consequence that, if you already have observed some members of the population, this tells you something about any unobserved members.

Reconsider the Bayesian principle of prior knowledge by an experiment of thought: Consider, a UX expert with experience in e-commerce is asked to estimate how long it takes users to do the checkout, but without showing the expert the actual system. The expert will probably hesitate briefly, and then come up with an estimate of, let's say, 45 s. Without any data, the expert made some reasonable assumptions, e.g. that a disciplined design process has been followed, and then relies on experience. The experts personal experience has formed prior to the study by observing many other cases. Now, we confront the expert with an even more bizzare situation: guess the time-on-task for an unknown task with an unseen system of unknown type! The expert will probably refuse to give an answer, arguing that some systems have tasks in the second range (e.g. starting a car), whereas other processes easily run for hours or days (e.g. writing a report). This is a good point and the expert is provided, not with knoeledge of the system, but with average ToT of four other tasks within the same system:

$$ToT_{1-4} = 23, 45, 66, 54$$

Now, the expert is confident that ToT be around 50 s and that is probably a good guess. What has happened is that prior belief about the unkown task parameter has been formed not externally, but *by data* as it arrived. The likely value of one unit has been learned from the other units and this appears pretty reasonable. The same principle applies when visually identifying outliers in a boxplot or scatterplot. First, the mind of the observer forms a gestalt that covers the salient features of data, for example: almost all points are located in the range 100–500. Once this pattern has formed, deviant points stand out.

However, the salience of the gestalt may vary. Consider a situation where ToT has been measured by the same procedure, but using five different stop watches. Stop watches are so incredibly accurate that if you know one measure, you basically know them all. What many researchers do with repeated measures data, is take the average. This is the one extreme called *total pooling*. In the stopwatch case the average of the five measures would be so highly representative, that total pooling is a reasonable thing to do.

In other cases, the levels of a factor are more or less independent, for example tasks in a complex system, where procedure duration ranges from seconds to hours. Guessing the duration of one task from a set of others is highly susceptible and the average duration across tasks is not representative at all. The best choice then is to see tasks as factor levels, that are independent. This extreme of *no pooling* is exactly represented by fixed effect factors as they have been introduced in Chap. 4.

Random effects sit right between these two extremes of no and total pooling and implement *partial pooling*: the more the group mean is representative for the units of the group, the more it is taken into account. By this we can also see, why a multi-level model must estimate alle levels simultaneously. The best thing about partial pooling is that, unlike real priors, there is not even the need to determine the amount of pooling in advance. The variation of entities has been observed. The stronger the enities vary, the less can be learned from the group level. The variation is precisely the group-level standard deviation of the random effect.

How are random effects implemented to draw on both sources? Obviously, the procedure must be more refined than just adding participant-level dummy variables into the structural part of the model. In the Bayesian framework a remarkably simple trick suffices, and it is even a familiar one. By the concept of prior distributions, we already know a way to restrict the range of an effect based on prior knowledge. For example, intelligence test results have the prior distribution IQ Gaus(100, 15), just because they have been empirically calibrated this way. In most other cases, we do have rough ideas about the expected magnitude and range in the population, say: healthy human adults will finish a 2000 m run in the range of 5–12 min.

As prior knowledge is external to the data, it often lacks systematic evidence, with the exception of a meta analyses. This is why we tend to use weak informative priors. Like priors, random effects take into account knowledge external to the entity under question. But, they draw this knowledge from the data, which is more convincing after all. The basic trick to establish the cross-talk between random factor levels, is to *simultaneously estimate factor levels and random factor variation*. This has several consequences:

All random effects get a more or less subtle trend towards the population mean. As a side effect, the random factor variance is usually smaller than variance between fixed factors, or naive group means. This effect is called *shrinkage*. When the random factor variation is small, extreme factor levels are pulled stronger towards the population mean, resulting in stronger shrinkage. Or vice versa: When random variation is large, the factor levels stand more on their own.

The random factor variation is an estimate and as such it is certain only to a degree. As we have seen in Sect. 6.5, the more levels a random factor comprises, the more precise is the estimate of random factor variation. The strongest shrinkage occurs with few observations per factor levels and highly certain random factor variation.

Previously, I have stressed how important repeated measures design is, as the number of observations per entity plays a role, too. The more observations there are, the less is the group mean overruled by the population mean. Less shrinkage occurs. This is why multi-level models gracefully deal with imbalanced designs. Groups with more observations are just gradually more self-determined. Taking this to the opposite extreme: when a factor level contains no data at all, it will just be replaced by the population mean. This principle offers a very elegant solution to the problem of missing data. If you know nothing about a person, the best guess is the population mean.

Under the perspective of populations as a more or less similar set of entities, these principles seem to make sense. Within this framework, we can even define what fixed effects are:

> a fixed effect is a factor where levels are regarded so unsimilar, that the factor-level variance can be practically considered infinite.

The CUE8 study makes a case for seeing shrinkage in action: Teams of researchers were asked to conduct a performance evaluation on a website. Tasks and website were the same, but the teams followed their own routines. Some teams tested a few handful of participants, whereas others tested dozens remotely. Teams, as another non-human population (sic!) differ vastly in the number of observations they collected. We can expect differences in shrinkage.

To see the effect, we compare the team-level group means as fixed factor versus random factor. All teams have enough participants tested to estimate their mean with some certainty. At the same time, the group sizes vary so dramatically that there should be clear differences in adjustment towards the mean. However, in absolute terms, the sample sizes are very large. There is enough data to estimate team-level scores, and the shrinkage effect is barely visible. For the purpose of demonstration, we use a data set that is reduced to one tenth of the original. We estimate two models, a fixed effects model and a random effects model, from which we collect the (absolute) random effect scores.

```
attach(CUE8)

set.seed(42)
D_cue8_1 <-
  D_cue8 %>%
  sample_frac(.1)

M_2 <-
  D_cue8_1 %>%
  brm(logToT ~ Team - 1, data = .)

M_3 <-
  D_cue8_1 %>%
  brm(logToT ~ 1 + (1 | Team), data = .)

P_fixef <- posterior(M_2, type = "fixef")
P_ranef <- posterior(M_3) %>%
  bayr::re_scores()

T_shrinkage <-
  D_cue8_1 %>%
  group_by(Team) %>%
  summarize(N = n()) %>%
  mutate(
```

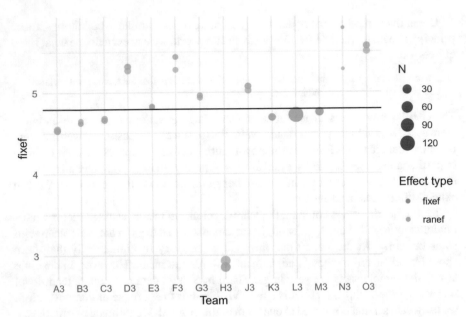

Fig. 6.16 Shrinkage shown as disparity of fixed effects and random effects

```
    fixef = fixef(P_fixef)$center,
    ranef = ranef(P_ranef)$center,
    shrinkage = fixef - ranef
)

T_shrinkage %>%
    ggplot(aes(x = Team, size = N)) +
    geom_point(aes(y = fixef, col = "fixef"), alpha = .5) +
    geom_point(aes(y = ranef, col = "ranef"), alpha = .5) +
    geom_hline(aes(yintercept = mean(ranef))) +
    labs(color = "Effect type")
```

Figure 6.16 shows how random effects are adjusted towards the grand mean. Groups that are distant (e.g. H, N and O) are more strongly pulled towards the mean. Also, when there is little data in a group, shrinkage is more pronounced (e.g. D, E and G).

In the case of full CUE8 data set, these correction are overall negligible, which is due to the fact that all teams gathered ample data. However, in all situations where there is little or unevenly distributed data, it makes sense to draw more information from the population mean and making inference from random effects is more accurate.

In conclusion, random effects are factors with the additional assumption of Gaussian distribution. When a multi-level model is estimated, the population level effect, the random effects levels and the variance of their distributions are estimated simultaneously. This creates two particular advantages of multi-level models with random effects:

1. In unbalanced research designs (with unequal number of observations per subject) small groups are corrected towards the population mean.
2. Strong outliers are corrected towards the population mean.

Classical techniques for repeated measures often require additional tweaks to work well with unbalanced designs and outliers. Multi-level models with random effects handle those situations gracefully.

6.8 Psychometrics and Design-o-Metric Models

Random effects apply to all factors, where the levels can be thought of as members of a population Sect. 6.5. Looking just at the variance inside the population is very common in experimental research, but we have already encountered situations, where analysis is based on individual random coefficients, for example when testing universality of an effect Sect. 6.4. Random coefficients can further be used to compare entities and rank them. If the entities are participants, this is called doing *psychometrics* and the individual scores represent a person's trait, like computer enthusiasm, or ability, like in a math test.

Traditionally, psychometrics deals with the valid and reliable measurement of personal characteristics, such as individual levels of performance, motivation, socio-cognitive attitude and the like. Advanced statistical models have been devised, such as factor analysis or item response models. The least to expect of a psychometric scale is that it can *order* persons by trait or ability.

In design research, multi-item validated scales are routinely used for one of two purposes:

1. A design-related research questions involve *traits or abilities of users*. For example: Do social network users with high Openness have more connections? A six-item test for Openness is used on every individual in the sample and the scores are compared the number of connections. In the following I will introduce how multi-level models can be used for basic *psychometric situations*, which is simply an *encounter of persons and items* and a cross-classified multi-level model applies.
2. In design research we frequently compare *quality of designs*, by using multi-item questionnaires. One example would be the comparison of user experience among a set of e-commerce homepages using scales such as the AttrakDiff (the hedonic dimension). Or, we want to rank a set of robot faces in how much they provoke eeriness.

When the aim is to rank designs by user responses (on some multi item scale), the study is an *encounter of users, items and designs*, resulting in *yet another multi-level model*. Such a model I call a *design-o-metric model* and will introduce you to how it works in Sect. 6.8.4.

We begin with the first case, standard psychometrics to assess user characteristics. For example, one could ask whether having a high visual-spatial ability helps in certain tasks, for example when a surgeon explores body cavities with an endoscope or an air traffic controller monitoring scattered displays. Visual-spatial ability could be a useful instrument to select good candidates. Let's assume for a moment there existed enough evidence to use such a test, how could this ability be measured?

Let's assume a simple experiment, such as mental rotation tasks, where reaction time is related to spatial processing speed. Reaction times are notoriously noisy and therefore a similar task is repeated ten times. Twenty participants solve such a sequence and reaction times are collected (Table 6.20).

```
set.seed(1317)
n_Part <- 10
n_Trial <- 20
n_Obs <- n_Part * n_Trial

D_Part <- tibble(
  Part = 1:n_Part,
  true_score = rnorm(n_Part, 900, 80)
)

D_Trial <- tibble(Trial = 1:n_Trial)

D_CTT <-
  mascutils::expand_grid(
    Part = D_Part$Part,
    Trial = D_Trial$Trial
  ) %>%
  left_join(D_Part) %>%
  mutate(RT = rnorm(n_Obs,
    mean = true_score,
    sd = 100
  )) %>%
  as_tbl_obs()
```

```
D_CTT
```

With that many measures at our hand, how can we arrive at a single score to compare participants. The approach known as *Classical Test Theory (CTT)* solves this by simply taking the average score as a measure for a person's processing speed (Table 6.21).

Table 6.20 Data set with 5 variables, showing 8 of 200 observations

Obs	Part	Trial	true_score	RT
1	1	1	899	952
182	2	19	984	853
93	3	10	985	1040
25	5	3	1021	1003
46	6	5	809	789
197	7	20	797	612
29	9	3	874	911
109	9	11	874	925

Table 6.21 CTT test scores for processing speed

Part	proc_speed
7	789
6	795
9	875
4	889
1	903
10	939
3	976
8	984
2	1018
5	1038

```
D_CTT %>%
  group_by(Part) %>%
  summarize(proc_speed = mean(RT)) %>%
  arrange(proc_speed)
```

The observed test score y_i for participant i is composed of the true score of participant i, μ_i, and a Gaussian measurement error ϵ_{ij}. By adding more (exchangeable) trials to the test, the measurement error can be reduced.

$$y_{ij} = \mu_i + \epsilon_{ij}$$

The following model implements CTT as a multi-level absolute group means model Sect. 4.3.4, with the only difference that the participant-level means are estimated as random effects, i.e. it assumes a Gaussian distribution of person scores (Table 6.22).

```
M_CTT <- brm(RT ~ 1 + (1 | Part), data = D_CTT)
```

Table 6.22 Coefficient estimates with 95% credibility limits

Part	Center	Lower	Upper
7	796	756	838
6	802	763	842
9	878	838	917
4	890	850	930
1	904	864	942
10	938	898	979
3	973	933	1013
8	980	939	1023
2	1013	974	1053
5	1032	991	1072

```
posterior(M_CTT) %>%
  re_scores() %>%
  ranef() %>%
  rename(Part = re_entity) %>%
  arrange(center)
```

What makes CTT models too simplistic, is that they assume items to be completely exchangeable. For a set of experimental RTs it only sometimes is true that they are exchangeable. Actually, for a mental rotation task, they usually are not, because trials differ by rotation angle. For all rating scales, item equality is rarely the case, and also not desired. Two items from the same scale can differ in several aspects, one of which is how hard (or strong) an item is. Consider the following two items from a fictional user experience scale; most likely, the second item would get lower ratings on average, because it is stronger ("awesome" compared to "nice"):

1. The user interface is nice.
2. The user interface is awesome.

One problem with CTT is that by averaging scores, the CTT swallows any information on item functioning. More advanced psychometric models are constructed based on either *Item Response Theory (IRT)* or *Factor Analysis (FA)*. With such models, different characteristics of items can be accounted for. As diverse and elaborated these models can be today, they all have in common, that items are modeled explicitly and get their own estimates. Discussing these models in more depth would require a separate book. Still, a simple item response model is nothing but an encounter of persons and test items, a simple two-way cross over (Sect. 6.5).

Some years ago, I proposed a novel personality construct, *geekism*, which states that users differ in how enthusiastic they are about tinkering with computers. The hope was that we could explain differences in user behavior by using this scale, such as how they react when having to learn a new software application. A qualitative study with self-proclaimed geeks and several psychometric studies resulted in rating scale

Table 6.23 Data set with 4 variables, showing 8 of 40 observations

Obs	Part	Item	Rating
33	1	5	−0.674
18	2	3	1.248
19	3	3	0.078
28	4	4	0.766
29	5	4	−0.495
6	6	1	−0.289
31	7	4	−0.133
39	7	5	−0.702

with 32 items. The Hugme case is one of the quantitative follow-up studies, where the Geekism scale was used together with the Need for Cognition scale (NCS), which assesses the tendency to enjoy intellectual puzzles in general. We were interested in

1. how the items function,
2. how reliable the scale is and
3. how Geekism correlates with Need-for-cognition.

```
attach(Hugme)
```

One important thing to note at this point is that psychometricians like to put things in participant-by-item matrices. And this is what most psychometric tools expect as input. For a multi-level model we need the long format, which can easily be accomplished by for the regression engine. Matrix form can be transformed into long form (Table 6.23) and vice versa (Table 6.24).

```
D_long <- expand_grid(
  Part = 1:8,
  Item = 1:5
) %>%
  mutate(rating = rnorm(40)) %>%
  mascutils::as_tbl_obs()
D_long

D_long %>%
  select(Part, Item, rating) %>%
  pivot_wider(
    names_from = Item,
    values_from = rating
  )
```

Psychometric programs often require matrix data, but for a multi-level models we need the long format. IRT models regard items as populations, too, and the basic IRT model is a cross-classified intercept-only model Sect. 6.5.

Table 6.24 Psychometric data often comes in matrix form

Part	1	2	3	4	5
1	0.851	0.526	−1.156	−0.642	−0.674
2	1.743	1.438	1.248	−0.535	−0.502
3	1.893	−0.713	0.078	0.184	0.881
4	−0.473	−0.275	−0.516	0.766	1.780
5	−0.267	−0.324	1.355	−0.495	−0.193
6	−0.289	0.262	−1.587	0.392	−0.487
7	1.800	−0.212	1.513	−0.133	−0.702
8	0.107	−1.188	−0.223	−0.912	0.888

```
D_psymx_1 <-
  D_quest %>%
  filter(Scale == "Geek", Session == 1)
```

```
M_psymx_1 <-
  D_psymx_1 %>%
  brm(rating ~ 1 + (1 | Part) + (1 | Item), data = .)
```

Once a rating scale instrument is ready to use, the researcher will ultimately be interested in the person scores. However, during the process of constructing a psychometric instrument, items scores play an important role. In the following I will demonstrate three psychometric evaluations, using multi-level models:

1. *Test coverage* of a scale can be assessed by comparing the distribution of item scores with the distribution of person scores
2. *Test reliability* can be estimated by comparing scores across two sessions of testing.
3. *Test validity* can be estimated as person score correlations between scales.

6.8.1   Coverage

Geekism was assumed to vary widely in the population of users and we wanted to be able to cover the whole range with good precision. In IRT models, items and persons are actually scored on the same scale. The person-level coefficients represent the persons' level of geekism. The item-level effects can best be called *item sensitivity*. A rule in the development of good psychometric instruments is that the range of interest has to be covered by items with a matching sensitivity. Any item with consistently high ratings is able to distinguish low levels of geekism, but is less useful for discriminating between high levels of geekism. Just think of how poorly a very simple arithmetic question, like "Which of the following numbers is divisible by 3? [2, 3, 5, 7, 9]" would be able to diagnose the math skills of you, the readers of this book. The inverse is also true: an item with a very strong proposition, like

> I always build my own computers

may be great to distinguish between amateur and pro level geekism, but most average and below average persons will just say No.

We have a linear model, where the rating is weighted sums of person tendency and item sensitivity. A high rating can mean two things (or both): coming from a very geek person, indeed, or it was a very sensitive item. For a good test coverage we need sensitive items for levels of low geekism and strong, i.e. *less* sensitive, items for the pros. Because random effects are centered at zero, we can simply reverse the scale with *item strength* being the negative sensitivity. Now we can compare the distributions of person and item scores side-by-side and check how the person tendencies are covered by item strength. *Note* that for obtaining the absolute scores, we can use the Bayr function `re_scores`, but for psychometric analysis, the deviation from the population average is sufficient, hence `ranef`.

```
P_psymx_1 <- posterior(M_psymx_1)

T_ranef <-
  ranef(P_psymx_1) %>%
  rename(geekism - center) %>%
  mutate(geekism = if_else(re_factor == "Item",
    geekism, geekism
  )) # reversing

T_ranef %>%
  ggplot(aes(
    x = re_factor,
    y = geekism,
    label = re_entity
  )) +
  geom_violin() +
  geom_jitter(width = .2) +
  ylim(-2, 2)
```

Figure 6.17 shows that the 32 items of the test cover the range of very low to moderately high geekism fairly well. The upper 20 percent are not represented so well, as it seems. If we were to use the scale to discriminate between geeks and super-geeks, more strong item should be added, such as: 'I rather express myself in a programming language, rather than natural language'.

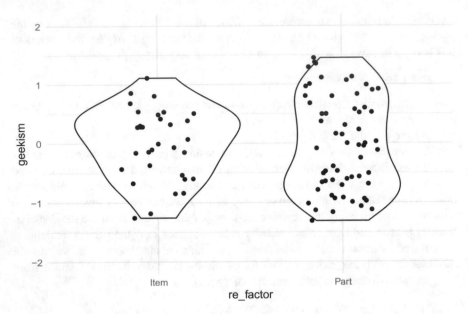

Fig. 6.17 Comparing distributions of item-level and participant-level scores

6.8.2 Reliability

Next, we examine the reliability of the Geekism scale. Reliability is originally a CTT concept and means that the measurement error is small. For example, a reliable personality scale produces almost exactly the same score when applied to a person on different occasions. Is the Geekism score reliable? In our study we asked participants to fill out the questionnaire twice, with an experimental session in-between. If reliability of Geekism is good, the correlation of scores between sessions should be very strong.

In order to obtain the scores per session, we add Session as a factor to the model. For reliability we are interested in correlation between person scores, so it would suffice to add the Session random effect to the participant level, only. However, the same model can be used to do assess *stability* of item scores, too. This is rarely practiced, but as we will see, there is an interesting pattern to observe.

```
D_psymx_2 <-
  D_quest %>% filter(Scale == "Geek")

M_psymx_2 <-
  brm(rating ~ 0 + Session +
    (0 + Session | Part) +
    (0 + Session | Item),
```

```
data = D_psymx_2
)
```

We extract the random effects and plot test-retest scores for participants and items (Fig. 6.18). The indicated line would be ideal stability for comparison.

```
T_ranef <-
  ranef(M_psymx_2) %>%
  select(re_factor, re_entity, Session = fixef, score = center) %>%
  pivot_wider(names_from = Session, values_from = "score")

T_ranef %>% sample_n(8)
```

re_factor	re_entity	Session1	Session2
Part	65	1.012	0.926
Part	64	−1.027	−0.904
Part	8	−1.007	−0.912
Item	Geek05	−0.444	−0.302
Item	Geek03	0.765	0.527
Item	Geek32	−0.688	−0.534
Part	66	−0.955	−0.840
Part	5	−1.119	−1.014

```
plot_stability <-
  function(ranef) {
    ranef %>%
      ggplot(aes(x = Session1, y = Session2)) +
      facet_grid(re_factor ~ .) +
      geom_point() +
      geom_smooth(aes(color = "observed"), se = F) +
      geom_abline(aes(
        intercept = 0, slope = 1,
        color = "ideal"
      )) +
      labs(x = "Stability")
  }
```

```
T_ranef %>% plot_stability()
```

The participant scores are highly correlated, indicating a very good reliability. If you measure the score of a person, you almost precisely know the result of another measure a few hours later. At least in short terms, the Geekism construct - whatever it truly is - can be measured with almost no error. Only ever so slightly is there a trend that lower scores get higher the second time and higher get lower, which could be called a trend towards the average. Perhaps, some experience during the experiment has led participants to report a more mediocre image of themselves.

In psychometric analysis it is common to assess participant-level test-retest reliability, but rarely is that done on items. This is, in fact, easy because the psychometric

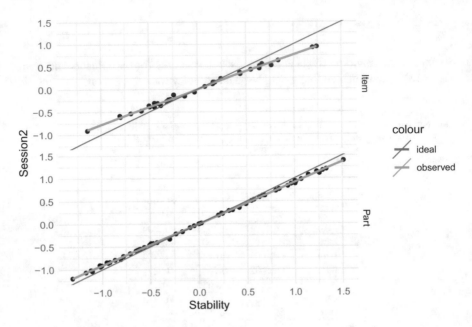

Fig. 6.18 Test-retest stability for item and participant scores

model contains intercept and slope random effects for items, and we can examine test-retest patterns in the same way. We see the same trend towards the average, but much stronger. In the present case, we see that this can be a mistake. Here it seems that the trend towards mediocrity does not produce a bias on the population mean, because it is bi-directional and the item and participant scores are nicely symmetric around the center of the scale. Not every test may have these properties and any asymmetric wear-off effect of items would produce more serious biases.

Another situation where item stability matters is when a person doing the test is actually learning from it. Usually, it is not desired that a test can be learned, because that means people can train for it. This is unlikely to occur in a regular math or intelligence test, but when the items are real-world tasks, like operating medical infusion pumps or driving a car, every test is an exercise and participants will learn.

The example of test-retest stability shows one more time, how useful plots are for discovering patterns in data. More formally, test-retest stability is reported as a correlation. We can produce a correlation estimate by using the standard cor command on the participant-level random effects (Table 6.25).

```
T_ranef %>%
  group_by(re_factor) %>%
  summarize(cor = cor(Session1, Session2))
```

Unfortunately, this lacks information about the degree of certainty. The better way is to let the regression engine estimate all correlations between random factors that are

Table 6.25   Correlation of scores between session 1 and 2 (point estimates)

re_factor	cor
Item	0.997
Part	1.000

Table 6.26   Random effects correlations with 95 percent credibility limits

re_factor	Between	And	Center	Lower	Upper
Item	Session1	Session2	0.983	0.913	0.999
Part	Session1	Session2	0.994	0.966	1.000

on the same level (Part, Item). The regression engine brm does that by default. The
following code extracts the posterior distributions of all correlations in the model
(Table 6.26).

```
clu_cor <-
  function(model) {
    model %>%
      posterior() %>%
      filter(type == "cor") %>%
      mutate(parameter = str_remove_all(parameter, "cor_")) %>%
      group_by(parameter) %>%
      summarize(
        center = median(value),
        lower = quantile(value, .025),
        upper = quantile(value, .975)
      ) %>%
      separate(parameter,
        into = c("re_factor", "between", "and"),
        sep = "__"
      )
  }
```

```
M_psymx_2 %>%
  clu_cor()
```

With random effects correlations assessing test-retest-stability is straight-forward.
If test and retest random effects correlate strongly, we can be sure that the error of
measurement is low and we can call it a reliable scale. Good reliability is necessary,
but not sufficient to also call a scale valid.

Table 6.27 Random effects correlations with 95 percent credibility limits

re_factor	Between	And	Center	Lower	Upper
Part	ScaleGeek	ScaleNCS	0.371	0.098	0.586

6.8.3   Validity

Reliability doesn't say anything about what the scale actually measures. In psychometric studies, *validity* of a scale is routinely evaluated by comparing the scores to external criteria. In a perfect world, it would be assessed how scores are related to relevant real-world behavior, such as:

1. Are high-Geek persons more enthusiastic to learn a programming language?
2. Do high-Geek persons perform better in computer jobs?
3. Are high-Geek persons more likely to buy robot toys for their offsprings?

In the real world, researchers in the field of personality are often content with relating a new rating scales to another, already validated personality scale. In the Hugme study, participants were also asked to rate themselves on the Need-for-Cognition scale (NCS). In very brief NCS measures how much a person enjoys intellectual puzzles. Since computers are intellectual puzzles, sometimes in a good way, often not, we thought that high-Geek persons must also score high on NCS. At the same time, a very strong correlation between Geek and NCS would indicate that the two scales render the same property, which would make one of them redundant, probably the newcomer. The following model estimates the person scores per scale and we can extract the correlations (Table 6.27).

```
M_psymx_3 <-
   D_quest %>%
   brm(rating ~ 0 + Scale + (0 + Scale | Part), data = .)

M_psymx_3 %>%
   clu_cor()
```

Table 6.27 shows a weakly positive association between Geek and NCS, just as was hoped for. The two constructs are related, but not quite the same.

6.8.4   Towards Design-o-Metrix

Psychometrics, as it was introduced above, deals with comparing human individuals. In Design Research, this may be of interest sometimes, but the real stake is to *compare designs*. As we will see in this section, psychometric concepts can well be transferred

Table 6.28 Data set with 6 variables, showing 8 of 7488 observations

Obs	Part	Item	Design	Session	Response
1242	p1_05	nE2	3	1	−0.967
4566	p2_03	nE6	71	3	−0.740
4589	p2_03	nE5	8	3	−0.258
5252	p2_06	nE4	72	1	−0.352
5362	p2_06	nE2	73	2	−0.705
6506	p2_10	nE2	46	2	−0.670
7035	p2_12	nE3	14	2	−0.567
7345	p2_13	nE1	69	2	−0.688

to *design-o-metric problems*. However, there is one twist, which has up til now been overlooked in most of Design Research: in design-o-metric studies the target population is designs, not humans. In a typical psychometric study, measurements are an encounter of humans with items, with the ultimate goal of measuring humans. A design-o-metric measurement is the encounter of three populations, humans, items and, ultimately, designs. Classic psychometric tools use a 2-dimensional matrix as input and cannot deal with a third dimension. Here it comes in very handy, that multi-level models use the long format, where more dimension can be added at will. All we have to do, is crossing in another non-human population Sect. 6.5.

We revisit the Uncanny Valley data set (Sects. 5.5 and 6.4). The experiment used eight items from the Eeriness scale [3] to ask the judgment of participants on 82 stimuli showing robot faces. In one of our experiments (RK_1), participants simply rated all robots face in three separate session. Since we are only interested in a design-o-metric analysis regarding the Eeriness scale, not the Uncanny Valley curve, we omit the human-likeness score (Table 6.28).

```
attach(Uncanny)

UV_dsgmx <-
  RK_1 %>%
  select(Part, Item, Design = Stimulus, Session, response) %>%
  as_tbl_obs()
UV_dsgmx
```

With this data we seem to be standing on familiar psychometric grounds: Persons encounter items and we have three measures over time. We can calculate test-retest stability of items and persons using a multi-level model. Voila! Here are your correlations, person and item stability - with credibility limits. But, wait a second! What is being measured here? Persons? No, robot faces. The original question was, how human-likeness of robot faces is related to perceived eeriness of robot faces and the Eeriness scale intended purpose is the comparison of designs, not persons. For example, it could be used by robot designers to check that a design does not trigger

Table 6.29 Random effects correlations of a design-o-metric model with 95 percent credibility limits

re_factor	Between	And	Center	Lower	Upper
Design	Session1	Session2	0.987	0.945	0.999
Design	Session1	Session3	0.987	0.946	0.999
Design	Session2	Session3	0.991	0.961	0.999
Item	Session1	Session2	0.849	0.228	0.989
Item	Session1	Session3	0.702	−0.066	0.958
Item	Session2	Session3	0.841	0.170	0.988
Part	Session1	Session2	0.816	0.557	0.950
Part	Session1	Session3	0.686	0.377	0.869
Part	Session2	Session3	0.815	0.570	0.930

undesirable emotional responses. Without knowing the human-likeness scores, robot faces become just a naked *population of designs* Sect. 6.5.

Measures in the Uncanny experiment are an encounter of three samples: Part, Item and Design, and designs is what we ultimately want to compare. That means we need a model that produces design-level scores. For the user of multi-level models that just means adding a Design random effect to the psychometric model (Part, Item). Models, where a design random factor sits on top of a psychometric model, I call *design-o-metric models*. The most basic design-o-metric model is a three-way cross-classified, intercept-only model, from which design scores can be extracted. By extending the test-retest psychometric model M_psymx_2, we can estimate design-o-metric test-retest stability. We only have to add the Design random factor to the model and extract the correlations, like in the psychometric applications.

```
M_dsgmx_1 <-
  brm(response ~ 0 + Session +
    (0 + Session | Part) +
    (0 + Session | Item) +
    (0 + Session | Design),
  data = UV_dsgmx
  )

M_dsgmx_1 %>%
  clu_cor()
```

Like in the psychometric situation, we extract the correlations Table 6.29. Since we have three sessions, we even get three stability scores. In addition, the design-o-metric model provides test-retest correlations for all three levels. The test-retest stability for designs is very reassuring. Ratings on the Eeriness scale are highly reproducible and the error will be very small. To a lesser, but still sufficient degree are person and item scores stable.

But, what does the person score (and its stability) actually mean? It describes the tendency of a person to give high ratings on Eeriness. Should a researcher want to assess how sensitive a person is to the Uncanny Valley effect, the Eeriness scale is also reliable for measuring persons. Many scales in design research lend themselves to be looked at from a design-o-metric and psychometric perspective. For example, a hypothetical scale to measure comfort of sitting can be used to evaluate seats, but can also be used to measure how comfortable a person is with sitting.

No seat fits every person, or put differently: the comfort of a seat depends on the person sitting in it. This points us at one of many possible extensions to carry out deeper design-o-metric analysis. If the difficulty of an item in a psychometric test depends on who is being tested, this is called *differential item functioning*. For example, the large international student evaluations PISA and TIMMS routinely check their test items for cultural differences. The aim is to formulate test questions in such a way that they are equally comprehensible with all cultural backgrounds. This is a desirable property for design-o-metric scales, too. In a multi-level design-o-metric model, this could be incorporated as an interaction effect between cultural background and item-level coefficients.

That all being said about design-o-metric models, my observation is that practically all published rating scales in design research have been validated under a psychometric perspective, rather than a design-o-metric. This is a mistake! If the purpose of the scale is to compare designs, the scale's reliability and validity must examined on the design level.

In many cases, a purportedly design o metric study has been conducted on a sample of participants and a sample of items, but only a single or a few designs. Isn't it obvious that a scale's capability to rank designs must be assessed on a sample of designs. This mindlessness in transfering psychometric concepts to design research is worrying and I call this the *psychometric fallacy*.

6.9 Further Readings

1. In psychometric models the population level is of lesser interest. One could build a single-level model, using fixed-effects factors for participants and items. Reference [4] show that random-effects models are superior, because they allow multiple pairwise comparisons, which is problematic with fixed effects. For psychometric situations, comparison of individuals is essential.
2. An introduction to planned missing data designs, as we used it in cases Egan and Uncanny, is given by [5].
3. Multi-level models for psycholinguistic studies have been used by [6].

4. In [7], we evaluated whether we can predict by the method of card sorting, how quickly users find a specific information on a website. A multi-level model showed that this is *not* so. This serves as an example, that you can prove the (practical) absence of effects with New Statistics, and publish.
5. Reference [3] is one of many examples of falling for the psychometric fallacy.

References

1. Egan D (1988) Individual differences in human-computer interaction. In: Helander M (ed) Handbook of Human Computer interaction. Elsevier Science Publishers, Amsterdam, The Netherlands, pp 543–568
2. Rolf M et al (2010) Rent a car in just 0, 60, 240 or 1,217 seconds? - comparative usability measurement, CUE-8. J Usability Stud 6(1):8–24
3. Ho CC, MacDorman KF (2017) Measuring the Uncanny Valley effect: refinements to indices for perceived humanness, attractiveness, and eeriness. Int J Soc Robot 9(1):129–139. ISSN: 1875-4805. https://doi.org/10.1007/s12369-016-0380-9
4. Gelman A, Hill J, Yajima M (2012) Why we (usually) don't have to worry about multiple comparisons. J Res Educ Eff 5(2):189–211. ISSN: 1934-5747. https://doi.org/10.1080/19345747.2011.618213
5. Graham JW et al (2006) Planned missing data designs in psychological research. Psychol Methods 11(4):323–343. ISSN: 1939-1463. https://doi.org/10.1037/1082-989X.11.4.323. http://doi.apa.org/getdoi.cfm?doi=10.1037/1082-989X.11.4.323
6. Baayen RH, Davidson DJ, Bates DM (2008) Mixed-effects modeling with crossed random effects for subjects and items. J Mem Lang 59(4):390–412. ISSN: 0749-596X. https://doi.org/10.1016/j.jml.2007.12.005. http://linkinghub.elsevier.com/retrieve/pii/S0749596X07001398
7. Schmettow M, Sommer J (2016) Linking card sorting to browsing performance - are congruent municipal websites more efficient to use? Behav Inf Technol 3001:1–19. ISSN: 0144-929X. https://doi.org/10.1080/0144929X.2016.1157207

Chapter 7
Generalized Linear Models

The preceding chapters introduced the Linear Model as an extremely flexible tool to represent associations between multiple predictors and the outcome variable. We saw how factors and covariates gracefully work together and how complex research designs can be captured by multi-level random effects. It was all about specifying an appropriate (and often sophisticated) right-hand side of the regression formula, the predictor term. In contrast, little space has been dedicated to the outcome variables, except that, sometimes we used log-transformed outcomes to accommodate the Gaussian error term. That is now going to change, and we will start by examining the assumptions that are associated with the outcome variable.

A particular question is probably lurking in the minds of readers with classic statistics training: What happened to the process of checking assumptions on ANOVA (and alike) and where are all the neat tests that supposedly check for Normality, constant variance and such? The Gaussian linear model, which we used throughout Chaps. 4 and 6, shares these assumptions, the three crucial assumptions being:

1. *Linearity* of the association between predictors and outcome variable.
2. *Gaussian distribution* of responses.
3. *constant variance* of response distribution.

In the next section, we will review these assumptions and lead them ad absurdum. Simply put, Gaussian distribution and linearity are mere approximations that actually never happen in the real world. Checking assumptions on a model that you know is inappropriate, seems a futile exercise, unless better alternatives are available, and that is the case: with *Generalized Linear Models* (GLMs) we extend our regression modeling framework once again, this time focusing on the outcome variables and their shape of randomness.

As we will see, GLMs solves some common problems with linearity and gives us more choices on the shape of randomness. To say that once and for all: What

© Springer Nature Switzerland AG 2021
M. Schmettow, *New Statistics for Design Researchers*,
Human–Computer Interaction Series,
https://doi.org/10.1007/978-3-030-46380-9_7

GLMs do not do is relax the assumptions of linear models. And because I have met at least one seasoned researcher who divided the world of data into two categories, "parametric data", that meets ANOVA assumptions, and "non-parametric data" that does not, let me get this perfectly straight: *data is neither parametric nor non-parametric*. Instead, data is the result of a process that distributes measures in some form and a good model aligns to this form. Second, a *model is parametric*, when the statistics it produces have a useful interpretations, like the intercept is the group mean of the reference group and the intercept random effect represents the variation between individuals. All models presented in this chapter (and this book) fulfill this requirement and *all are parametric*. There may be just one counter-example, which is polynomial regression Sect. 5.5, which we used for its ability to render non-monotonic curves. The polynomial coefficients have no interpretation in terms of the cognitive processes leading to the Uncanny Valley. However, as we have seen in Sect. 5.5.1, they can easily be used to derive meaningful parameters, such as the positions of shoulder and trough. A clear example of a non-parametric method is the Mann-Withney U-test, which compares the sums of ranks between groups, which typically has no useful interpretation.

The GLM framework rests on two extensions that bring us a huge step closer to our precious data. The first one is the *link function*, a mathematical trick that establishes linearity in many situations. The second is to select a *shape of randomness* that matches the type of outcome variable and removes the difficult assumption of constant variance. After we established the elements of the GLM framework Sect. 7.1, I will introduce a good dozen of model families that leaves little reason to ever fall back to the Gaussian distributions and data transformations, let alone unintelligible non-parametric procedures. As we will see, there almost always is a clear choice right at the beginning that largely depends on the properties of the response variable, for example:

- *Poisson LM* is the first choice for outcome variables that are counted (with no upper limit), like number of errors.

- *Binomial (aka logistic) LM* covers the case of successful task completion, where counts have an upper boundary.

These two GLM families have been around for many decades in statistical practice, and they just found a new home under the GLM umbrella. For some other types of outcome variables, good default models have been lacking, such as rating scale responses, time-on-task and reaction times. Luckily, with recent developments in Bayesian regression engines, the choice of random distributions has become much broader and now also covers distribution families that are suited for these very common types of measures. For RT and ToT, I will suggest exponentially-modified Gaussian *(ExGauss)* models or, to some extent, *Gamma* models. For rating scales, where responses fall into a few ordered categories, *ordinal logistic regression* is a generally accepted approach, but for (quasi) continuous rating scales, I will introduce a rather novel approach, *Beta regression*.

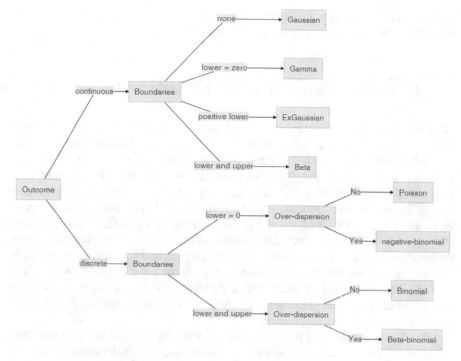

Fig. 7.1 Decision chart for Generalized Linear Models

Too many choices can be a burden, but as we will see, most of the time the appropriate model family is obvious. For the impatient readers, here is the recipe: Answer the following three questions about the outcome variable and follow (Fig. 7.1).

1. Is the outcome variable discrete or continuous?
2. What are the lower and upper boundaries of outcome measures?
3. Can we expect overdispersion?

To make it even easier, it is practically always adequate and safe to answer Yes to the third question (overdispersion). Based on these questions, the graph below identifies the correct distribution family and you can jump right to respective section, if you need a quick answer. In the following (Sect. 7.1), I will provide a general explanation of why GLMs are needed and how they are constructed by choosing a response distribution (Sect. 7.1.2) and a link function (Sect. 7.1.1). The remainder of the chapter is organized by *types of measures* that are typical for design research: count data (Sect. 7.2), duration measures (Sect. 7.3) and rating scales (Sect. 7.4). Together with Chap. 6, this introduces the family of models called *Generalized Multi-level Linear Models (GMLM)*, which covers a huge variety of research situations. The chapter closes with a brief introduction to an even mightier class of models: GMLMs still have certain limitations. One of them is that they are all about estimating average performance. *Distributional models* are one further step of abstraction and they apply when the research is concerned with variance actually (Sect. 7.5).

7.1 Elements of Generalized Linear Models

GLM is a *framework for modeling* that produces a *family of models* (Fig. 7.1). Every member of this family uses a specific *link functions* to establish linearity and a particular *distribution*, that has an adequate shape and mean-variance relationship.

Sometimes GLMs are mistaken as a way to relax assumptions of linear models, (or even called non-parametric). They are definitely not! Every member makes precise assumptions on the level of measurement and the shape of randomness. One can even argue that Poisson, Binomial and exponential regression are stricter than Gaussian, as they use only one parameter, with the consequence of a tight association between variance and mean. Several members, such as Poisson and logistic regression have routinely been used before they were united under the hood of GLM (in the early 1970s). These and a few others are called *canonical* GLMs, as they possess some convenient mathematical properties, that made efficient estimation possible, back in the days of limited computing power.

For a first understanding of Generalized Linear Models, you should know that linear models are one family of Generalized Linear Models, which we call a Gaussian linear model. The three crucial assumptions of Gaussian linear models are encoded in the model formula

$$\mu_i = \beta_0 + \beta_1 x_{1i} + \cdots + \beta_k x_{ki}$$
$$y_i \sim \text{Gaus}(\mu_i, \sigma)$$

The first term is a called the structural part as it represents the systematic quantitative relations between predictors and outcome variable. When it is a sum of products, like above, we call it linear. *Linearity* is a frequently under-regarded assumption of linear models and it is doomed to fail Sect. 7.1.1. The second term defines the pattern of randomness and it hosts two further assumptions: *Gaussian distribution* and *constant error variance* of the random component. The latter might not seem obvious, but is given by the fact that there is just a single value for the standard error σ.

In classic statistics education, the tendency is still to present these assumptions as preconditions for a successful ANOVA or linear regression. The very term *pre*condition suggest that they need to be checked upfront and the classic statisticians are used to deploy a zoo of null hypothesis tests for this purpose, although it is widely held among statisticians that this practice is illogical. If an assumptions seems to be violated, let's say Normality, researchers then often turn to non-parametric tests. Many also just continue with ANOVA and add some shameful statements to the discussion of results or humbly cite one research paper that claims ANOVAs robustness to this or that violation.

The parameters of a polynomial model usually don't have a direct interpretation. However, we saw that the useful parameters such as the minimum of the curve can be derived. Therefore, polynomial models are sometimes called *semiparametric*. As an example for a *non-parametric* test, the Mann-Whitney U statistic is composed of the number of times observations in group A are larger than in group B. The resulting sum U usually bears little relation to any real-world process or question. Strictly speaking, the label non-parametric has nothing to do with ANOVA assumptions. It refers to the usefulness of parameters. Research problems, where U has a useful interpretation, and hence can be called parametric, are hard to come by. A possible scenario would be a team competition in a dueling discipline, such as Fencing. If the competition is constructed such that every athlete from one team duels every member of the opponent team, the U statistic could be used to determine the winner team.

7.1.1 Re-linking Linearity

By linear relationship we mean that if the predictor changes by one unit, the outcome follows suit by a constant amount. In the chapter on Linear Models 4, we encountered several situations where linearity was violated.

- In 4.3.5 we saw that learning processes are not linear. The effect of one training unit is not constant, but diminishes with increase in practice. In effect, we used not an LRM, but ordered factors to estimate the learning curves.
- In 5.4.3, we saw that the effect of one intervention depends on the presence of another intervention (to cure headache). We used conditional effects when two or more interventions improve the same process in a non-linear way.
- and in 5.5 we used polynomials to estimate wildly curved relationships.

The case of Polynomial regression is special in two ways: first, the curvature itself is of theoretical interest (e.g. finding the "trough" of the Uncanny Valley effect). Second, a polynomial curve (of second degree or more) is no longer monotonously increasing (or decreasing). In contrast, learning curves and saturation effects have in common, that in both situations, outcome steadily increases (or decreases) when we add more to the predictor side. But, this effect diminishes with continued exposure and asymptotically approaches a limit (such as absence of headache).

For the learning process in the IPump study, we earlier used an OFM with stairways coding to account for this non-linearity (@ref(#ofm)) (Sect. 4.3.5), but that has one disadvantage. From a practical perspective, it would be interesting to know, how performance improves when practice continues. What would be performance in (hypothetical) sessions 4, 5 and 10. Because the OFM just makes up one estimate for every level, there is no way to get predictions beyond the observed range (Fig. 7.2).

With an LRM, the slope parameter applies to all steps, which gives us the possibility of deriving predictions beyond the observed range. To demonstrate this on the deviations from optimal path, the following code estimates a plain LRM and

Table 7.1 Virtual data for generating out-of-range predictions

Obs	Session	Range
1	0	Observed
2	1	Observed
3	2	Observed
4	3	Extrapolated
5	4	Extrapolated
6	5	Extrapolated
7	6	Extrapolated
8	7	Extrapolated
9	8	Extrapolated
10	9	Extrapolated

then injects some new (virtual) data to get *extrapolations* beyond the observed three tasks. Note that the virtual data comes without a response variable, as this is what the model provides (Table 7.1).

```
attach(IPump)

M_LRM_1 <- stan_glm(deviations ~ 1 + session,
  data = D_Novel
)

D_extra <-
  tibble(
    session = as.integer(c(0:9)),
    range = if_else(session < 3,
      "observed", "extrapolated"
    )
  ) %>%
  as_tbl_obs()
D_extra


predict(M_LRM_1,
  newdata = D_extra
) %>%
  left_join(D_extra) %>%
  ggplot(aes(
    x = session, y = center,
    ymin = lower, ymax = upper,
    color = range
  )) +
  geom_step() +
  geom_hline(aes(yintercept = 0, color = "impossible predictions below"), linetype = 2) +
  scale_x_continuous(breaks = 0:10) +
  ylim(-1, 1) +
  labs(y = "deviations", col = NULL)
```

If we use a continuous linear model to predict future outcomes of a learning curve, negative values are eventually produced, which is impossible. Non-linearity

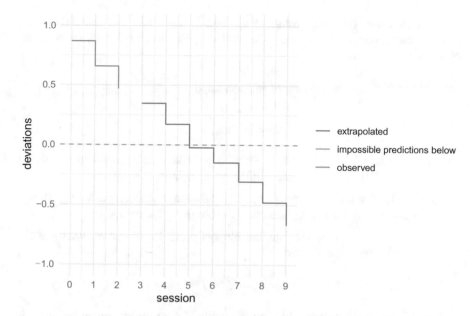

Fig. 7.2 Trying to predict future performance by a linear model produces inpossible predictions

is not just a problem with learning curves, but happens to all outcomes that have natural lower or upper boundaries. All known outcome variables in the universe have boundaries, just to mention velocity and temperature (on spacetime the jury is still out). It is inescapable that all measures in design research have boundaries and strictly cannot have linear associations:

- Errors and other countable incidences are bounded at zero.
- Rating scales are bounded at the lower and upper extreme item.
- Task completion has a lower bound of zero and the number of tasks as an upper bound.
- Temporal measures formally have lower bound of zero, but psychologically, the lower bound always is a positive number.

The strength of the linear term is its versatility in specifying multiple relations between predictor variables and outcome. It's Achilles heel is that it assumes measures without boundaries. Generalized linear models use a simple mathematical trick that keeps linear terms, but confines the fitted responses to the natural boundaries of the measures. In linear models, the linear term is mapped directly to fitted responses μ_i:

$$\mu_i = \beta_0 + x_{1i}\beta_1$$

In GLMs, an additional layer sits between the fitted response μ and the linear term: The *linear predictor* θ has the desired range of $[-\infty; \infty]$ and is linked directly to the linear term. In turn, we choose a *link function* ϕ that up-scales the bounded range of measures (μ). The inverse of the link function (ϕ^{-1}) is called the mean function and it does the opposite by down-scaling the linear predictor to the range of measures.

$$\theta_i \in [-\infty; \infty]$$
$$\theta_i = \beta_0 + x_{1i}\beta_1$$
$$\theta_i = \phi(\mu_i)$$
$$\mu_i = \phi^{-1}(\theta_i)$$

The question is: what mathematical function transforms a bounded space into an unbounded? A link function ϕ must fulfill two criteria:

1. mapping from the (linear) range $[-\infty; \infty]$ to the range of the response, e.g. $[0; \infty]$.
2. be monotonically increasing, such that the order is preserved

A monotonically increasing function always preserves the order, such that the following holds for a link function.

$$\theta_i > \theta_j \rightarrow \phi(\theta_i) > \phi(\theta_j) \rightarrow \mu_i > \mu_j$$

It would be devastating if a link function would not preserve order, but there is another useful side-effect of monotony: if a function ϕ is monotonous, then there exists an inverse function ϕ^{-1}, which is called the mean function, as it transforms back to the fitted responses μ_i. For example, x^2 is not monotonous and its inverse, $\sqrt{x}$, produces *two* results (e.g. $\sqrt{x} = [2, -2]$), and therefore, is not a even a function strictly speaking.

A typical case is count variables with a lower boundary of zero and no upper bound. The *logarithm* is a function that maps positive numbers to the linear range $[-\infty; \infty]$, in the way that numbers smaller than One become negative.

```
log(c(2, 1, .5))
```

```
## [1]  0.693  0.000 -0.693
```

The logarithm has the *exponential* function as a counterpart, which bends the linear range back into the boundaries. Other measures, like success rates or rating scales, have lower and upper boundaries. A suitable pair of functions is the *logit* link function and the *logistic* mean function (Fig. 7.3).

Using the link function comes at a cost: the linear coefficients β_i is losing its interpretation as increment-per-unit and no longer has a natural interpretation. Later, we will see that logarithmic and logit scales gain an intuitive interpretation when parameters are exponentiated, $\exp(\beta_i)$ (@ref(speaking-multipliers and 7.2.2.3).

Who needs a well-defined link between observations and fitted responses? Applied design researchers do when predictions are their business. In the IPump study it is compelling to ask: "how will the nurse perform in session 4?" or "When will he reach error-free operation?". In Sect. 7.2.1.2, we will see a non-linear learning process becoming an almost straight line on the logarithmic scale.

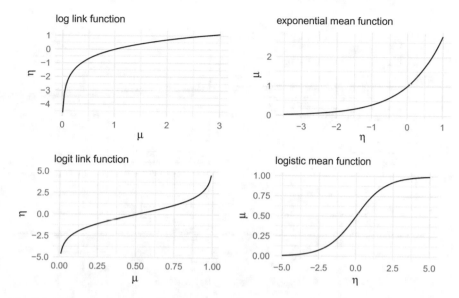

Fig. 7.3 Log and logit link functions expand the bounded range of measures. Mean functions do the reverse

7.1.2 Choosing Patterns of Randomness

The second term of a linear model, $y_i \sim Norm(\mu_i, \sigma)$ states that the observed values are drawn from Gaussian distributions (3.5.2.6). But Gaussian distributions have the same problem as the linearity assumption: the range is $[-\infty; \infty]$.

The problem can be demonstrated by simulating observations using a Gaussian pattern of randomness and see how this fails to produce realistic data. Imagine a study comparing a novel and a legacy interface design for medical infusion pumps. The researchers let trained nurses perform a single task on both devices and count the errors. Figure 7.4 shows a simulated data set with user errors. It was generated by a Gaussian factorial model with a standard error of $\sigma = .8$ and with two conditions: Legacy ($\mu = 3$) and Novel ($\mu = 1.2$).

```
set.seed(84)
N <- 80
D_pumps_sim <-
  tibble(
    Design = rep(c("L", "N"), N / 2),
    mu = if_else(Design == "L", 3, 1.2),
    errors = rnorm(N, mu, sd = 1)
  ) %>%
  as_tbl_obs()

D_pumps_sim %>%
  ggplot(aes(x = errors)) +
  facet_grid(~Design) +
  geom_histogram(bins = 20) +
  geom_vline(aes(xintercept = 0)) +
  coord_flip() +
  labs(color = "")
```

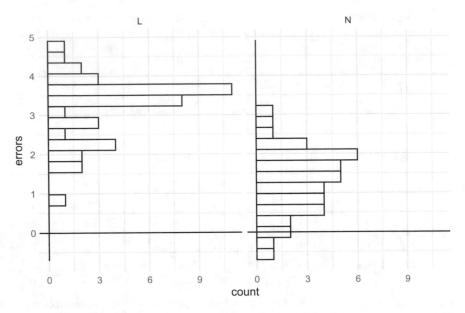

Fig. 7.4 Simulation with Gaussian error terms produces impossible values

We immediately see that simulation with Gaussian distributions is inappropriate: a substantial number of simulated observations is *negative*, which strictly makes no sense for error counts. The pragmatic and impatient reader may suggest to adjust the standard deviation (or move the averages up) to make negative values less unlikely. That would be a poor solution as Gaussian distributions support the full range of real numbers, no matter how small the variance is (but not zero). There is always a chance of negative simulations, as tiny as it may be. Repeatedly running the simulation until pumps contains exclusively positive numbers (and zero) would compromise the idea of random numbers itself. We can simply conclude that any model that assumes normally distributed errors must be wrong when the outcome is bounded below or above, which means: always.

Recall how linearity is gradually bent when a magnitude approaches its natural limit. A similar effect occurs for distributions. Distributions that respect a lower or upper limit get squeezed like chewing gum into a corner when approaching the boundaries. Review the sections on Binomial 3.5.2.3 and Poisson distributions 3.5.2.4 for illustrations. As a matter of fact, a lot of real data in design research is skewed that way, making Gaussian distributions a poor fit. The only situation where Gaussian distributions are reasonable approximations is when the outcomes are far off the boundaries. An example of that is the approximation of Binomial outcomes (lower and upper bound), when the probability of success is around 50%. That is also the only point, where a Binomial distribution is truly symmetric.

Table 7.2 Canonical probability distribution families by type of measures

Boundaries	Discrete	Continuous
Unbounded		Normal
Lower	Poisson	Exponential
Lower and upper	Binomial	Beta

In contrast, a common misconception is that the Gaussian distribution is getting better at approximation, when sample sizes are large. This is simply wrong. What really happens is that increasing the number of observations renders the true distribution more clearly.

In Sect. 3.5.2, a number of random distributions were introduced, together with conditions of when they arise. The major criteria were related to properties of the outcome measure: how it is bounded and whether it is discrete (countable) or continuous. Generalized Linear Models give the researcher a larger choice for modeling the random component and Table 7.2 lists some common candidates.

That is not to say that these five are the only possible choices. Many dozens of statistical distributions are known and these five are just making the least assumptions on the shape of randomness in their class (mathematicians call this *maximum entropy distributions*). In fact, we will soon discover that real data frequently violates principles of these distributions. For example, count measures in behavioral research typically show more error variance than is allowed by Poisson distributions. As we will see in Sect. 7.2.3, Poisson distribution can still be used in such cases with some additional tweaks borrowed from multi level modeling (observation-level random effects).

Response times in design research are particularly "misbehaved", as they do not have their lower boundary at zero, but at the lowest human possible time to solve the task. The complication arises that most continuous distributions have a lower boundary of exactly zero. In case of response times, we will take advantage of the fact, that modern Bayesian estimation engines support a larger range of distributions than ever seen before. The `stan_glm` regression engine has been designed with downwards compatibility in mind, which is why it does not include newer distributions. In contrast, the package `brms` is less hampered by legacy and gives many more choices, such as the Exponential-Gaussian distribution for ToT.

7.1.3 Mean-Variance Relationship

The third assumption of linear models is rooted in the random component term as well. Recall, that there is just one parameter σ for the dispersion of randomness and that any Gaussian distribution's dispersion is exclusively determined by σ. That is more of a problem as it may sound, at first. In most real data, the dispersion of randomness depends on the location, as can be illustrated by the following simulation.

Imagine a survey on commuter behavior that asks the following questions:

1. How long is your daily route?
2. How long does it *typically* take to go to work?
3. What are the maximum and minimum travel times you remember?

If we simulate such data from a linear model, the relationship between length of route and travel time would look like a evenly wide band, which is due to the constant variance (Fig. 7.5).

```
N <- 100
tibble(
  Obs = as.factor(1:N),
  km = runif(N, 2, 40),
  min = rnorm(N, km * 2, 10)
) %>%
  ggplot(aes(x = km, y = min)) +
  geom_point() +
  geom_quantile(quantiles = c(.25, .5, .75))
```

What is unrealistic is that persons who live right around the corner experience the same range of possible travel times than people who drive dozens of kilometers. That does not seem right.

Gaussian distributions are a special case, because most other distributions do not have constant variance. For example, a Gamma distribution takes two parameters,

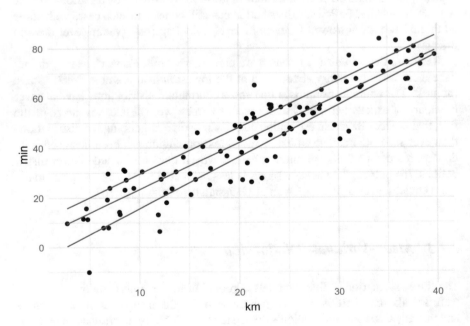

Fig. 7.5 A Gaussian linear simulation of travel times (min) depending on distance (km) results in an unrealistic mean-variance relationship

shape *alpha* and scale *tau*, and both of them influence mean and variance of the distribution, such that the error variance increases by the square of the mean (Fig. 7.6))

$$Y \sim \text{Gamma}(\alpha, \theta)$$
$$E(Y) = \alpha\theta$$
$$\text{Var}(Y) = \alpha\theta^2$$
$$\text{Var}(Y) = E(Y)\theta$$

```
tibble(
  km = runif(100, 2, 40),
  min = rgamma(100, shape = km * .5, scale = 4)
) %>%
  ggplot(aes(x = km, y = min)) +
  geom_point() +
  geom_quantile(quantiles = c(.25, .5, .75))
```

A similar situation arises for count data. When counting user errors, we would expect a larger variance for complex tasks and interfaces, e.g. writing an article in a word processor, as compared to the rather simple situation like operating a medical infusion pump. For count data, the Poisson distribution is often a starting point and for Poisson distributed variables, mean and variance are both exactly determined by the

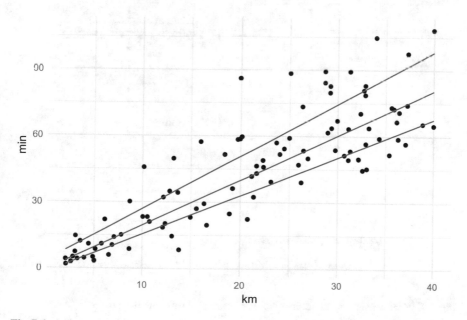

Fig. 7.6 A Gamma simulation of travel times (min) depending on distance (km) results in a realistic mean-variance relationship

Poisson rate parameter λ, and therefore, strictly connected to each other. Figure 7.7 shows hypothetical data from two tasks with very different error rates.

$$Y \sim \text{Poisson}(\lambda)$$
$$\text{Var}(Y) = E(Y) = \lambda$$

```
tibble(
  Task = rep(c("writing article", "using infusion pump"), 50),
  errors = rpois(100,
    lambda = if_else(Task == "writing article",
      200, 8
    )
  )
) %>%
  ggplot(aes(x = Task, y = errors)) +
  geom_boxplot() +
  geom_jitter()
```

Not by coincidence, practically all distributions with a lower boundary have variance increase with the mean. Distributions that have two boundaries, like binomial or beta distributions also have a mean-variance relationship, but a different one. For binomial distributed variables, mean and variance are determined as follows:

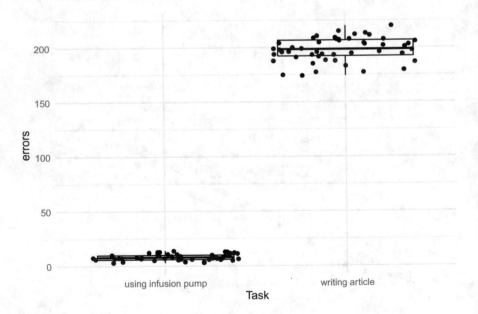

Fig. 7.7 Mean-variance relationship of Poisson distributed data with two groups

$$Y \sim \text{Binom}(p, k)$$
$$E(Y) = pk$$
$$\text{Var}(Y) = p(1 - p)k$$
$$\text{Var}(Y) = E(Y)(1 - p)$$

To see this, imagine a study that examines the relationship between user expertise (for the convenience on a scale of zero to one) and success rate on ten tasks. The result is a cigar-like shape, like in Fig. 7.8. For binomial distributions, variance gets largest, when the chance of success is centered at $p = .5$. This is very similar for other distributions with two boundaries such as beta and logit-Gaussian distributions.

```
tibble(
  expertise = runif(1000, 0, 1),
  successes = rbinom(1000, 25, expertise)
) %>%
  ggplot(aes(x = expertise, y = successes)) +
  geom_point()
```

In conclusion, real distributions are typically asymmetric and have mean and variance linked. Both phenomena are tightly linked to the presence of boundaries. Broadly, the deviation from symmetry gets worse when observations are close to the boundaries (e.g. low error rates), whereas differences in variance is more pronounced when the means are far apart from each other.

Still, using distributions that are not Gaussian sometimes carries minor complications. Gaussian distributions have the convenient property that the amount of

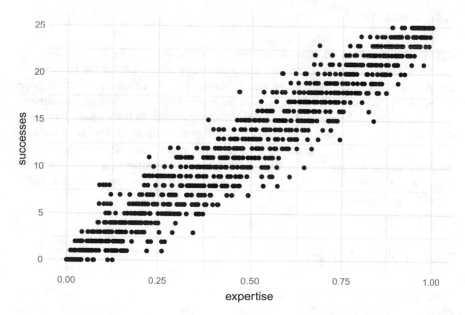

Fig. 7.8 Cigar shaped mean-variance relationship of Binomial data

randomness is directly expressed as the parameter σ. That allowed us to compare the fit of two models A and B by comparing σ_A and σ_B. In random distributions with just one parameter, the variance of randomness is fixed by the location (e.g. Poisson λ or Binomial p). For distributions with more than one parameter, dispersion of randomness typically is a function of two (or more) parameters, as can be seen in the formulas above. For example, Gamma distributions have two parameters, but both play a role in location and dispersion.

Using distributions with entanglement of location and dispersion seems to be a step back, but frequently it is necessary to render a realistic association between location of fitted responses and amount of absolute randomness. Most distributions with a lower bound (e.g. Poisson, exponential and Gamma) increase variance with mean, whereas double bounded distributions (beta and binomial) typically have maximum variance when the distribution is centered and symmetric. For the researcher, this all means that the choice of distribution family determines the shape of randomness *and* the relation between location and variance.

The following sections are organized by type of typical outcome variable (counts, durations and rating scales). Each section first introduces a one-parametric model (e.g. Poisson). A frequent problem with these models is that the location-variance relation is too strict. When errors are more widely dispersed than is allowed, this is called overdispersion and one can either use a trick borrowed from multi-level models, observation-level random effects @(olre) or select a two-parametric distribution class (e.g. Negative-Binomial).

7.2   Count Data

This chapter is about outcome measures that can count events of a certain type, and are therefore discrete. Examples are: number of errors, number of successfully completed tasks or the number of users. Naturally, count measures have a lower bound and sometimes this is zero (or can be made zero by simple transformations). A distinction has to be made, though, for the upper bound. In some cases, there is no well-defined upper bound, or it is very large (e.g. number of visitors on a website) and Poisson regression applies. In other cases, the upper bound is determined by the research design. A typical case in design research is the number of tasks in a usability study. When there is an upper bound, Binomial distributions apply, which is called logistic regression.

7.2.1   Poisson Regression

When the outcome variable is the result of a counting process with no obvious upper limit, Poisson regression applies. In brief, Poisson regression has the following attributes:

Table 7.3 Coefficient estimates with 95% credibility limits

Model	Type	Fixef	Center	Lower	Upper
Object	Fixef	Intercept	1.31	1.12	1.49

1. The outcome variable is bounded at zero (and that must be a possible outcome, indeed).
2. The linear predictor is on a logarithmic scale, with the exponential function being the inverse.
3. Randomness follows a Poisson distribution.
4. Variance of randomness increases linearly with the mean.

The link function is the logarithm, as it transforms from the non-negative range of numbers to real numbers (Sect. 7.1.1). For a start, we have a look at a Poisson GMM. Recall the smart smurfer game from Sect. 3.5.2.4. Imagine that in an advanced level of the game, items are well hidden from the player, and therefore, extremely difficult to catch. To compensate for the decreased visibility of items, every level carries an abundance of them. In fact, the goal of the designers is that visibility and abundance are so carefully balanced, that on average, a player finds three items. We simulate a data set for one player repeating the level 30 times (Fig. 7.9) and run our first Poisson model, which is a plain GMM (Tables 7.3 and 7.4).

```
set.seed(6)
D_Pois <-
  tibble(
    Obs = 1:30,
    items_found = rpois(30, lambda = 3.4)
  )

D_Pois %>%
  ggplot(aes(x = items_found)) +
  geom_histogram()


M_Pois <-
  stan_glm(items_found ~ 1,
    family = poisson,
    data = D_Pois
  )

fixef(M_Pois)
```

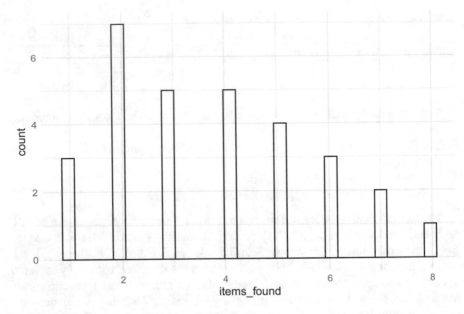

Fig. 7.9 Data sampled from a Poisson distribution

Table 7.4 Coefficient estimates with 95% credibility limits

Model	Type	Fixef	Center	Lower	Upper
Object	Fixef	Intercept	3.72	3.07	4.44

Poisson distributions have only one parameter λ (lambda), which has a direct interpretation as the expected mean and variance of the distribution. On the contrary, the regression coefficient is on a logarithmic scale to ensure it has no boundaries. To reverse to the scale of measurement, we use the exponential function as the *mean function* Sect. 7.1.1:

```
fixef(M_Pois, mean.func = exp)
```

The exponentiated coefficient can now be interpreted as the expected number of items found per session. Together with the credibility limits, it would allow the conclusion that the items are slightly easier to find than three per session. Before we move on to more complex Poisson models, let's take a look of the formalism of the Poisson GMM

$$\theta_i = \beta_0$$
$$\mu_i = \exp(\theta_i)$$
$$y_i \sim \text{Pois}(\mu_i)$$

In linear models, the first equation used to directly relate fitted responses μ_i to the linear term. As any linear term is allowed to have negative results, this could

Table 7.5 Coefficient estimates with 95% credibility limits

Fixef	Center	Lower	Upper
Intercept	0.831	0.244	1.406
DesignNovel	−1.555	−2.364	−0.785
Session	−0.234	−0.335	−0.133
DesignNovel:session	−0.074	−0.243	0.084

lead to problems in the last line, because Poisson λ is strictly non-negative. *Linear predictor* θ_i is taking those punches from the linear term and hands it over to the fitted responses μ_i via the exponential function. This function takes any number and returns a positive number, and that makes it safe for the last term that defines the pattern of randomness.

7.2.1.1 Speaking Multipliers

To demonstrate the interpretation of coefficients other than the intercept (or absolute group means), we turn to the more complex case of the infusion pump study. In this study, the deviations from a normative path were counted as a measure for error-proneness. In the following regression analysis, we examine the reduction of deviations by training sessions as well as the differences between the two devices. As we are interested in the improvement from first to second session and second to third, successive difference contrasts apply (Sect. 4.3.3).

```
attach(IPump)

M_dev <-
  stan_glmer(deviations ~ Design + session + session:Design +
    (1 + Design + session | Part) +
    (1 + Design | Task) +
    (1 | Obs), ## observation-level ramdom effect
  family = poisson,
  data = D_pumps
  )
```

Note that in order to account for overdispersion, observation-level random effect (1|Obs) has been used, see Sect. 7.2.3. For the current matter, we can leave that alone and inspect population-level coefficients (Table 7.5).

```
fixef(M_dev)
```

These coefficients are on a logarithmic scale and cannot be interpreted right away. By using the exponential mean function, we reverse the logarithm and obtain Table 7.6.

```
fixef(M_dev, mean.func = exp)
```

Table 7.6 Coefficient estimates with 95% credibility limits

Fixef	Center	Lower	Upper
Intercept	2.297	1.277	4.081
DesignNovel	0.211	0.094	0.456
Session	0.791	0.715	0.876
DesignNovel:session	0.928	0.784	1.087

Like in the GMM, the intercept now has the interpretation as the number of deviations with the legacy design in the first session. However, all the other coefficients are no longer summands, but *multiplicative*. It would, therefore, be incorrect to speak of them in terms of differences.

$$\mu_i = \exp(\beta_0 + x_1\beta_1 + x_2\beta_2)$$
$$= \exp(\beta_0)\exp(x_1\beta_1)\exp(x_2\beta_2)$$

Actually, it is rather unnatural to speak of error reduction in terms of differences as we did in the previous chapters. If we would say "With the novel interface 1.8 fewer errors are being made", that means nothing. 1.8 fewer than what? Instead, the following statements make perfect sense:

1. In the first session, the novel design produces 2.297 *times* the deviations than with the legacy design.
2. For the legacy design, every new training session reduces the number of deviations *by factor* 0.791.
3. The reduction rate per training session of the novel design is *92.843% as compared to the legacy design.

To summarize: reporting coefficients on the linearized scale is not useful. We are not tuned to think in logarithmic terms and any quantitative message would get lost. By applying the mean function, we get back to the original scale. As it turns out, what was a sum of linear terms, now becomes a multiplication. For this reason, Poisson regression has often been called a *multiplicative model*. Another name is *log-linear model*, which attests that, on the log scale the model is linear.

7.2.1.2   Linearizing Learning Curves

The Achilles heel of Gaussian linear models is the linearity assumption. All measures in this universe are finite, which means that all processes eventually hit a boundary. Linearity is an approximation that works well if you stay away from the boundaries. If you can't, saturation effects happen and that means you have to add interaction effects or ordered factors to your model. Unless, you go multiplicative.

Classic Mechanics assumes that the a space rocket accelerates linearly with the energy production by its thrusters. Every Joule you burn increases your current speed β_0 by β_1 km/h. The problem with this assumption is that when you are already close to speed of light and the next thrust pushes you beyond the border. In the real world, $E = Mc^2$ holds and every thrust increases the energy, and therefore, its drag β_0 is not constant. The advantage of the multiplicative model is that it does not cross the boundary between positive and negative.

In the *additive* linear model, the learning curve is non-linear and we had to use an ordered factor model. Learning curves are characterized by running against an asymptote, which is the level of maximum level of achievable performance.

As we will see now that the clumsy OFM (Sect. 4.3.5) can be replaced by a log-linear regression model with just one slope coefficient. The idea of replacing the OFM with a *linearized* regression model (LzRM), is attractive. The first advantage of such a model is that it can produce valid forecasts of the learning process. And second, the LzRM is more *parsimonous* Sect. 8.2.1. For any sequence length, an LzRM just needs two parameters: intercept and slope, whereas the OFM requires one coefficient per session.

As it happens, learning curves often follow the *exponential law of practice*. Basically, that means that the performance increase is defined as *rate*, rather than a difference. In a sentence that would be something like: Every training session reduces the number of errors by 20%. When initial errors are 100, then after n sessions it is
$$\text{ToT} = 100 \times .8^n$$

Exponential functions make pretty good learning curves and they happen to be the mean function of Poisson regression. This leads to the following simulation of a learning experiment. This simulation takes a constant step size of $\log(.8) = -0.223$ on the log-linearized scale, resulting in a reduction of 20% per session.

While the linear predictor scale is a straight line, the response scale clearly is a curve-of-diminishing returns (Fig. 7.10). This opens up the possibility that learning the novel pump design also has a constant difference on the linearized scale, which would mean a constant rate on the original scale. In the following, we estimate two Poisson models, one linearized OFM (OzFM) (with stairway dummies Sect. 4.3.5) and one LzRM. Then we will assess the model fit (using fitted responses). If the learning process is linear on the log scale, we can expect to see the following:

1. The two step coefficients of the OzFM become similar (they were wide apart for ToT).
2. The slope effect of the LzRM is the same as the step sizes.
3. Both models fit similar initial performance (intercepts)

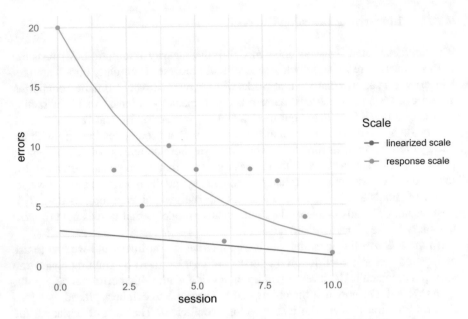

Fig. 7.10 Exponential learning curve becoming linear under the log link function

```
attach(IPump)

D_agg <-
  D_agg %>%
  mutate(
    Step_1 = as.integer(session >= 1),
    Step_2 = as.integer(session >= 2)
  )

## Ordered  regression model
M_pois_cozfm <-
  D_agg %>%
  brm(deviations ~ 0 + Design + Step_1:Design + Step_2:Design,
    family = "poisson", data = .
  )

## Linear regression model
M_pois_clzrm <-
  D_agg %>%
  brm(deviations ~ 0 + Design + session:Design, family = "poisson"
, data = .)
```

For the question of a constant rate of learning, we compare the one linear coefficient of the regression model with the two steps of the ordered factor model (Fig. 7.11):

```
T_fixef <-
  bind_rows(
    posterior(M_pois_cozfm),
    posterior(M_pois_clzrm)
  ) %>%
  fixef(mean.func = exp) %>%
  separate(fixef, into = c("Design", "Learning_unit"), sep = ":") %>%
```

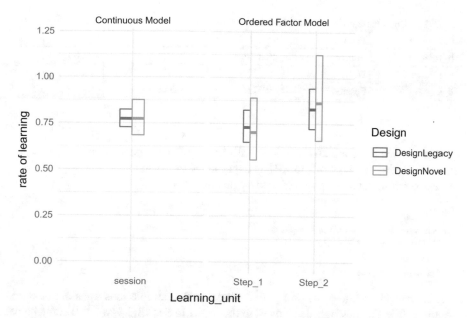

Fig. 7.11 Learning rate estimates from a log-linearized continuous model and an OFM

```
mutate(model = if_else(str_detect(model, "lz"),
   "Continuous Model", "Ordered Factor Model"
)) %>%
filter(!is.na(Learning_unit)) %>%
arrange(Design, Learning_unit, model) %>%
discard_redundant()

T_fixef %>%
  ggplot(aes(
   x = Learning_unit, y = center, col = Design,
   ymin = lower, ymax = upper
)) +
  geom_crossbar(position = "dodge", width = .2) +
  facet_wrap(. ~ model, scales = "free_x") +
  labs(y = "rate of learning", scales = "free_x") +
  ylim(0, 1.2)
```

With the Poisson OFM, the learning rates are very similar for both steps, which means the learning rate is almost constant and taking one learning step as a unit is justified. Furthermore, the learning rate appears to also be almost constant across designs. If that is true, one implication is that the novel design is superior in many aspects, accelerated learning may not be one of them. The other implication is that we no longer need two learning rate parameters (session). Since the two learning rates are so similar, we make them unconditional in our final model (Table 7.7). The results can be summarized in three simple sentences:

Table 7.7 Coefficient estimates with 95% credibility limits

Parameter	Fixef	Center	Lower	Upper
b_Intercept	Intercept	26.250	24.508	27.989
b_DesignNovel	DesignNovel	0.247	0.221	0.276
b_session	Session	0.773	0.731	0.815

1. On average there are 26 deviations with Legacy in the first session.
2. Novel reduces deviations to 25% at every stage of learning.
3. Per session, deviations are reduced by around 25%.

```
M_pois_lzrm <-
  D_agg %>%
  brm(deviations ~ 1 + Design + session,
    family = "poisson", data = .
  )
```

```
coef(M_pois_lzrm, mean.func = exp)
```

Another advantage of the simplified model is that simple messages are easy to report. But, is the message also closest to the truth? In Sect. 8.2.4, we will come back to this case and actually demonstrate that a unconditional model with two coefficients beats all the more complex models in predictive accuracy.

Normally, fitted responses are just retrospective. Here, we extrapolate the learning curve by fake data and obtain real *forecasts*. We can make more interesting comparison of the two devices. For example, notice that initial performance with Novel is around five deviations. With Legacy, this level is reached only in the seventh session. We can say that the Novel design is always seven sessions of training ahead of Legacy.

The conclusion is that log-linearized scales can reduce or even entirely remove saturation effects, such that we can go with a simpler models, that are easier to explain and potentially more useful. However, we cannot generally construct learning curves with log-linear models. The crucial property here is that the lower bound is Zero. Some measures have a positive lower bound, which is constant and known, and can be translated to a lower bound of Zero. For example, path length, the minimum number of steps to find something on the internet is One, Path length can be just shifted by One, e.g. `mutate(addional_steps = steps + 1)` to create a lower bound of Zero. This is different for Time-on-Task, which always has a strictly positive lower bound, which we don't know and which probably varies between individuals. Learning curves that approach strictly positive asymptotes have the following mathematical form:

```
# devtools::install_github("schmettow/asymptote")
asymptote::ARY
```

```
## perf ~ ampl * exp(-rate * trial) + asym
## <environment: namespace:asymptote>
```

The offset to Zero is in the summand `asym`, and because it is a summand, this term cannot be linearized in a straightforward manner. For general learning curves, a truly non-linear model is required, not just a linearized. This can be constructed with the Brm engine, but is beyond the scope of this book.

7.2.2 Logistic (aka Binomial) Regression

In the last section, we have seen how Poisson regression applies, when outcome variables are count numbers. More precisely, Poisson regression applies to count data, when there is no upper limit to counts (or if this limit is extremely large, as in the Smart Smurfer example). When the outcome variable is counts, but an upper limit exists and is known, *logistic regression* is an appropriate model. Such a situation often arises when the counts are successes in a fixed number of trials. Logistic regression has the following properties:

1. The outcome variable has a zero lower bound and a fixed upper bound, e.g. number of trials k.
2. The linear predictors are on a *logit scale*, also called *log-odds*, and can be reversed by a *logistic function*.
3. The random component follows a *binomial distribution*.
4. Due to the former, the variance of randomness is largest at $\mu = 0.5$ or $\eta = 1$ and declines towards both boundaries, taking a characteristic cigar shape.

Logistic regression applies for discrete outcomes, just like Poisson regression. The difference is that logistic regression has a finite number of possible outcomes, which is the number of trials plus one (no successes). In the following section, I will first introduce logistic regression for when there is only one trial per observation, with two possible outcomes. That is called *dichotomous outcomes*. Dichotomous outcomes are not limited to the Zero or One, Miss or Success, but apply to all outcomes that fall into two classes. In the subsequent section, we will look at logistic regression for when there is more than one trial. The most difficult part of logistic regression is to report the estimated coefficients in an intelligible manner, which will be covered in the final section.

7.2.2.1   Dichotomous Outcomes

The most simple form of successes-in-trials measure is when there is only one trial. This is called a dichtotomous variable:

- a user is successful at a task, or fails
- a visitor returns to a website or does not
- a usability problem is discovered or remains unseen
- a driver brakes just in time or crashes
- a customer recommends a product to a friend or does not
- a user starts searching on a website by keyword or by traversing links.

Often, dichotomous outcome variables have a quantitative notion in the sense of more or less desirable. When the outcome casts a positive light on the design, by convention it is coded as 1, otherwise 0. But, the dichotomy can also be two equal alternatives, such as whether a user starts a web inquiry by keyword search or by following a link. Let's take this as an example.

Research on search strategies of web users revealed that they are quite eclectic regarding their method to find a piece of information. In particular, most people use keyword search and link navigation at occasion. Web users are also known to be impatient companions, who build a first judgment very quickly and swiftly turn to a competitor's site, when the first impression leaves something to be desired. Therefore, it can be valuable to know what method the majority of users prefer initially.

For this purpose, we can classify users by what method they start with when given a search task during a usability study. As there exist only two options, keyword search or following links, we can capture the outcome in a dichotomous response variable. Below is the simulation of a small data set, where 40% of users initially prefer keyword search (Table 7.8).

```
set.seed(42)
D_web <-
  tibble(init_keyword = rbinom(100, 1, .4)) %>%
  as_tbl_obs()

D_web
```

For estimating the proportion of the two classes of users, we run a logistic regression grand mean model and inspect the coefficient table. Note that *logistic* regression is called so by its mean function (inverse link), not its shape of randomness. For counts with lower and upper border, the *binomial family* applies.

```
M_web <- stan_glm(init_keyword ~ 1,
  data = D_web,
  family = binomial
)

clu(M_web)
```

Clearly, the Intercept parameter is not a proportion, as that forbids negative values (Table 7.9). Like with Poisson regression, the coefficient is on a linearized scale with

Table 7.8 Data set with 2 variables, showing 8 of 100 observations

Obs	init_keyword
18	0
21	1
24	1
40	1
55	0
57	1
69	1
82	0

Table 7.9 Parameter estimates with 95% credibility limits

parameter	Fixef	Center	Lower	Upper
Intercept	Intercept	−0.167	−0.582	0.255

Table 7.10 Parameter estimates with 95% credibility limits

Parameter	Fixef	Center	Lower	Upper
Intercept	Intercept	0.458	0.359	0.563

infinite range. It is the *logit* functions that inflates the response range $\mu_i \in [0; 1]$ to the linear predictor *linear predictor* scale $\eta_i \in [-\infty; \infty]$.

$$\eta_i = \text{logit}(\mu_i) = \log \frac{\mu_i}{1 - \mu_i}$$

Note that the fraction $\frac{\mu_i}{1-\mu_i}$ is the proportion of keyword search divided by the proportion of the following links and is called an *odds*. The logit function is, therefore, often called *log-odds*. In Sect. 7.2.2.3, we will see how we can report logistic regression results as odds. In the case of our simple GMM, we can directly report the results as proportions, which requires to apply the *mean function*, which is the inverse of the logit, also known as the *logistic function*

$$\mu_i = \text{logit}^{-1}(\eta_i) = \frac{\exp \eta_1}{\exp \eta_i + 1}$$

In GMM, $\eta_i = \beta_0$ and we can directly obtain the estimated proportion by applying the logistic function to the Intercept. The `clu` command lets you pass on a mean function, resulting in Table 7.10.

```
posterior(M_web) %>% clu(mean.func = inv_logit)
```

From the GMM, we retrieve one estimate that reflects the *proportion* to start by keyword search. That works for absolute group mean, but most of the time, logistic regression coefficients are *exponentiated* and read as *odds* Sect. 7.2.2.3.

As a side note, proportions could also be called probabilities, like "with 40% probability a user starts by keyword search." However, I urge anyone to avoid speaking of logistic regression coefficients as probabilities. While mathematically this is correct, for the audience it can easily cause confusion with certainty or, beware of this, the p-value.

The apt reader may have noticed that the returners data set has been simulated with an exact return rate of 40%. Despite the sample size of 100, the center estimate seems rather off and hampered by considerable uncertainty. In computer science jargon, every dichotomous observation accounts to a *bit*, which is the smallest amount of information possible. Because the information of a single dichotomous observation is so sparse, large samples are important when dealing with dichotomous outcomes. Large samples can mean testing many users, or giving every user more than one trial.

7.2.2.2   Successes in a Number of Trials

If we repeatedly observe a dichotomous response, we can summarize the results as *successes-in trials*, like

```
responses <- c(0, 1, 1, 1, 0, 1)
cat(sum(responses), "successes in", length(responses), "trials")
```

```
## 4 successes in 6 trials
```

Imagine we had conducted an extended version of the previous experiment, where users get a set of ten tasks and we observe their initial behavior every time they open a new website. As such tasks sometimes take very long, it may also happen that a participant cannot finish all ten tasks within time. That means, we potentially have a different number of attempts per participant, which we simulate as Binomial random numbers (Table 7.11).

```
set.seed(42)
D_web_ex <-
  tibble(
    trials = round(runif(100, 7, 10), 0),
    init_keyword = rbinom(100, trials, .4),
    init_link = trials - init_keyword
  ) %>%
  mascutils::as_tbl_obs()

D_web_ex
```

In order to estimate a model on the proportion of successes in a number of trials, somehow this needs to be specified. That is done indirectly via the number of "failures", in this case, this is the number of times a link was followed, rather than a search query. The response side of the model formula takes this in as an array with two

Table 7.11 Data set with 4 variables, showing 8 of 100 observations

Obs	Trials	init_keyword	init_link
14	8	3	5
24	10	4	6
25	7	4	3
34	9	6	3
61	9	6	3
62	10	4	6
92	7	4	3
98	9	2	7

Table 7.12 Coefficient estimates with 95% credibility limits

Model	Type	Fixef	Center	Lower	Upper
Object	Fixef	Intercept	0.406	0.374	0.442

columns, which is generally constructed as cbind(successes, failures). We estimate a Binomial GMM and extract the coefficient as a proportion (Table 7.12)

```
M_web_ex <- stan_glm(cbind(init_keyword, init_link) ~ 1, # <--
  family = binomial,
  data = D_web_ex
)

fixef(M_web_ex,
  mean.func = inv_logit
)
```

With a ten-fold of data, as compared to the dichotomous model, the estimate is much closer to the real value and the credibility intervals tightened up too. By using the inverse logit, we can readily report the results as proportions. Again, make no mistake, this really only works for GMMs and AMMs. when effects come into play and additional coefficients are being estimated, reporting proportions does no longer work. Instead, we have to learn to talk odds.

Recall, how we characterized tasks as populations and introduced multi-level models with task-level coefficients (Sect. 6.5). It could appear as if a multiple-trials Binomial model is an alternative to multi-level modeling. It is not! First of all, there are no task-level estimates. In contrast, the above model assumes that chance of success is constant across tasks. If these are not simple experimental tasks, all quite the same, this assumption most is violated. More specifically, recall that the variance of Binomial distributions is fixed by the mean. If tasks vary, this will create *overdispersion* (Sect. 7.2.3).

7.2.2.3 Talking Odds

When presenting results of a statistical analysis, the linear predictor is likely to cause trouble, at least when the audience is interested in real quantities. Coefficients on a logit-linearized scale have only very general intuition:

- zero marks a 50% chance
- positive values increase the chance, negative decrease
- bigger effects have larger absolute values.

That is sufficient for purely ranking predictors by relative impact (if on a comparable scale of measurement), or plain hypothesis testing, but it does not connect well with quantities a decision maker is concerned with. Let's see this at the example of the infusion pump study, where some relevant questions for the evaluation of failures are:

1. What is the expected frequency of failure on first use?
2. The novel design reduces failures, but is it sufficient?
3. Is frequency of failures sufficiently reduced after two training sessions?

In the comparison of two medical infusion pumps (@ref(slope_RE)), 25 nurses completed a set of eight tasks repeatedly over three sessions. In @ref(slope_RE), a multi-level model was estimated on the workload outcome. It is tempting to apply the same structural model to success in task completion using binomial random patterns and logit links.

```
completion ~ Design*Session + (Design*Session|Part) +
(Design*Session|Task)
```

Such a model is practically impossible to estimate, because dichotomous variables are so scarce in information. Two populations encounter each other in the model: participants and tasks, with 6 observations per combination (6 bit). We should not expect to get reasonably certain estimates on that level and, in fact, the chains will not even mix well. The situation is a little better on the population level: every one of the six coefficients is estimated on 400 bit of raw information. We compromise here by estimating the full model on population level and do only intercept random effects to account for gross differences between participants and tasks (Table 7.13).

```
attach(IPump)

M_cmpl <-
  D_pumps %>%
  stan_glmer(completion ~ Design * Session +
    (1 | Part) + (1 | Task),
  family = binomial,
  data = .
  )

fixef(M_cmpl)
```

Table 7.13 Coefficient estimates with 95% credibility limits

Fixef	Center	Lower	Upper
Intercept	1.317	0.131	2.522
DesignNovel	0.403	0.080	0.719
Session2-1	0.692	0.138	1.237
Session3-2	−0.079	−0.635	0.457
DesignNovel:Session2-1	−0.301	−1.093	0.494
DesignNovel:Session3-2	0.286	−0.546	1.079

The result is one absolute group mean, the Intercept and five effects, which are mean differences on the logit-linearized scale η_i. If we want to report absolute group means, we can use the inverse logit function to obtain proportions, but for that we have to *first do the linear combination followed by the transformation*, for example:

- the completion rate in the first legacy session is 0.789
- in novel/session 1: `logist(Intercept + DesignNovel) = 0.848`
- in novel/session 2: `logist(Intercept + DesignNovel + Session2-1 + DesignNovel:Session2-1) = 0.892`
- in legacy/session 3: `logist(Intercept + DesignNovel + Session2-1) = 0.873`

Above we have used the inverse logit (aka logistic) mean function to elevate the absolute group means to proportions. This is an intuitive scale, but unfortunately, the mean function does not apply to individual effects. It is for example, *incorrect* to apply it like: "the novel pumps proportion of failures in the first session increases by `logist(DesignNovel) = 0.6`".

Log-odds are compound function. The inner part of the function, the *odds*, are the chance of success divided by the chance of failure. Especially in the anglo-american culture, odds are a rather common way to express ones chances in a game, say:

- odds are 1 against 1 that the coin flip produces Head. If you place €1 on Head, I put €1 on tail.
- odds are 1 against 12 that Santa wins the dog race. If you place 1€ on Santa, I place €12 against.
- 46% on Red. 54% on Blue

Reversing only the logarithm produces odds, as in Table 7.14

```
fixef(M_cmpl, mean.func = exp)
```

But is it legitimate to apply the transformation on individual coefficients in order to speak of changes of odds? The following arithmetic law tells that what is a sum on the log-odds scale is multiplication on the scale of odds

$$\exp(x + y) = \exp(x)\exp(y)$$

Table 7.14 Coefficient estimates with 95% credibility limits

Fixef	Center	Lower	Upper
Intercept	3.733	1.140	12.45
DesignNovel	1.497	1.083	2.05
Session2-1	1.999	1.148	3.44
Session3-2	0.924	0.530	1.58
DesignNovel:Session2-1	0.740	0.335	1.64
DesignNovel:Session3-2	1.331	0.579	2.94

Consequently, we may speak of changes of odds using *multiplicative language*:

- If you place €100 on failure in the next task with the legacy design in session 1, I place €373.303 on success.
- The odds of success with the novel design increase by *factor* 1.497. Now, I would place 373.303 × 1.497 = €558.835 on success.
- On success with the novel design in session 2, I would place 373.303 × 1.497 × 1.999 × 0.74 = €826.809 on success.

Once, we have transformed the coefficients to the odds scale, we can read coefficients as multipliers and speak of them in hard currency.

To summarize: Logistic regression applies when the basic observations falls into two classes. For any research design involving such outcomes, repetition is highly recommended, and outcomes can be summarized into successes-in-trials. Reporting coefficients on the logit scale is only useful when nobody is interested in intelligible effects sizes. How to report the results depends on the research question. If one is interested in proportions per group, the inverse logit applies to the absolute group means and this can be easily understood. If one wants to talk about effects or differences, such as the amount of improvement with a novel design, only the logarithm is reversed, and effects are reported as odds. Depending on the audience, this may be more or less intuitive, but it can always be embedded in a wager for illustration.

Logistic regression is known in many areas of application, as well as for some interesting extensions.

- In epidemiology research, logistic regression is the indispensable tool for several central outcomes, such as hospitalization, mortality, infection and recovery.
- In psychometrics, the famous Rasch model applies for measuring a persons ability by the number of correct answers in a test. A Rasch model is just a cross-classified multi-level logistic regression 6.8.4.
- If the outcome is a classification with more than two classes, *multi-nomial regression* is an extension of logistic regression.
- In section 4.3.5, we will encounter *ordinal logistic regression*, which applies for classifications with an order, such as responses on Likert scales.

One frequent problem when using logistic regression on successes-in-trials outcomes is that the assumption of a Binomial shape of randomness is violated by *overdispersion*. Like Poisson distributions, Binomial distributions have a variance tightly linked to the mean, but frequently there is more variance than allowed, for example, when tasks or test items vary in difficulty. In the following section, two solutions to the problem are introduced: *beta-binomial regression* and *observation-level random effects*.

7.2.3 Modeling Overdispersion

Poisson and binomial distributions are one-parameter distributions. As there is only one parameter, it is impossible to choose location and dispersion independently. In effect, both properties are tightly entangled. For Poisson distributions they are even the same.

$$Y \sim \text{Poisson}(\lambda)$$
$$\text{Var}(Y) = \text{Mean}(Y) = \lambda$$

For binomial distributions, mean and variance both depend on probability p and are entangled in cigar shaped form, as the dispersion shrinks when approaching the lower or upper boundaries. Binomial variance is also affected by the number of trials k, but that hardly matters as the value of k is usually not up for estimation, but known.

$$Y \sim \text{Binom}(p, k)$$
$$\text{Mean}(Y) = kp$$
$$\text{Var}(Y) = kp(1 - p)$$
$$= \text{Mean}(Y)(1 - p)$$

In real data, we often see similar relationships between variance and mean, except that variance is inflated by some additional positive factor, which is called *overdispersion*. Poisson or Binomial distribution cannot render inflated data, and using them on overdispersed data is a serious mistake. Fortunately, there exist two solutions to the problem, which I will introduce in the following three sections. In the first two sections, we will replace the one-parameter distribution with a *two-parameter distribution*, where the second parameter represents the variance inflation. The second method is to use *observation-level random effects*, which draws from the multi-level modeling toolbox.

Let me give you an example to illustrate the two methods. It is a common saying that some people attract mosquito bites more than others. But is that really true? A simple lab experiment could be done to test the "Sweet Blood" theory. A sample of

Table 7.15 Overdispersed counts can be sampled from a Negative-Binomial distribution

Mean(bites)	Var(bites)
6	19.2

participants are exposed to a pack of mosquitoes under carefully controlled conditions (time of day, environmental condition, hungriness of mosquitoes). We don't know the mechanisms that makes the blood sweeter, and hence cannot measure it. In the simulation below, it is just assumed that there is a such a property, but in a real study we would not know.

The following simulation function works by using a two-parameter distribution, that have the same properties as Poisson (or binomial) distributions. Negative-binomial distributions are discrete distributions with a lower bound of zero, just like Poisson distributions. They also have the same location parameter μ, but a new parameter size, which re-scales the scale of measurement. When the scale of measurement is down-scaled, the distribution becomes relatively wider. When size approaches infinity, we are left with a plain Poisson variance. The following data simulation samples Sweet-blood data from a negative-binomial distribution with a size of 3 (Table 7.15).

```
set.seed(42)
N <- 400
avg_sweet <- 6
size <- 3

Sweet_blood_nbin <- tibble(
  Method = "NegBinomial",
  bites = rnbinom(
    n = N,
    mu = avg_sweet,
    size = size
  )
)

Sweet_blood_nbin %>%
  summarize(mean(bites), var(bites))
```

The next simulation first creates an observation-level score for blood sweetness, which in real data would not be known to the researcher; it is, therefore, similar to a random effect. A property called Sweetness is first sampled from a Gaussian distribution. The result is exponentiated to achieve positive numbers and plugged into the Poisson random number generator. Table 7.16 shows how variance exceeds the mean of the so the produced responses (Fig. 7.12).

```
set.seed(42)
sd <- .5

Sweet_blood_olre <-
  tibble(
    Method = "OLRE",
    sweetness = rnorm(N, mean = log(avg_sweet), sd = sd),
    bites = rpois(N, lambda = exp(sweetness))
```

Table 7.16 Overdispersed counts can be sampled as Gaussian deviations on the linearized scalle, aka observation-level random effects

Mean(bites)	Var(bites)
6.67	20.3

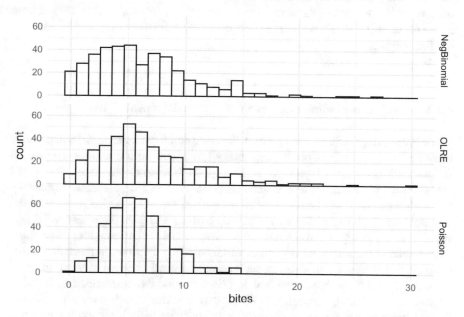

Fig. 7.12 Overdispersed samples (Negbinomial, OLRE) compared to Poisson samples of same average

```
)

Sweet_blood_olre %>%
  summarize(mean(bites), var(bites))


tibble(
  Method = "Poisson",
  bites = rpois(N, avg_sweet)
) %>%
  bind_rows(
    Sweet_blood_nbin,
    Sweet_blood_olre
  ) %>%
  ggplot(aes(x = bites)) +
  geom_histogram() +
  facet_grid(Method ~ .)
```

When building a model for overdispersed count data, the process of simulating it is simply reversed, for both methods. Either we choose a more flexible distribution, or we estimate the residuals on the linearized scale. The first method has the advantage of being leaner. Only one parameter is added, whereas OLRE results in one linearized residual for every observation. The advantage of OLRE is more of a conceptual kind. Not only is it appealing for researchers who are familiar with multi-level models, it also produces estimates similar to the well-known residuals. Furthermore, it also works with regression engines that do not cover the two-parameter distribution. In fact, the beta-binomial family is the matching two-parameter distribution for Binomial variables, but is not supported out-of-the-box by any regression engine I am aware of. In Sect. 7.2.3.2, we will see how user-defined distributions can be added to the Brm engine.

–>

7.2.3.1   Negative-Binomial Regression for Overdispersed Counts

When Poisson regression is used for overdispersed count data, the model will produce accurate center estimates, but the credibility limits will be too narrow. The model suggests better certainty than there is. To explain that in simple terms: The model "sees" the location of a measure, which makes it seek errors in a region with precisely that variance. There will be many measures outside the likely region, but the model will hold on tight, regard these as (gradual) outliers and give them less weight. A solution to the problem is using a matching response distribution with *two parameters*. A second parameter usually gives variance of the distribution more flexibility, although only Gaussian models can set it completely independent of location.

In Sect. 7.2.1.2, we have seen how log-linearization can accommodate learning curves, using a Poisson model. It is very likely that this data is overdispersed and that the Poisson model was not correct. To demonstrate overdispersion, we estimate the linearized learning curve one more time, with a negative-binomial pattern of randomness. Figure 7.13 shows the coefficient estimates next to coefficients from the Poisson model

```
attach(IPump)

M_negbin_lzrm <-
  brm(deviations ~ 1 + Design + session,
    data = D_agg,
    family = "negbinomial"
  )

bind_rows(
  posterior(M_pois_lzrm),
  posterior(M_negbin_lzrm)
) %>%
  filter(type == "fixef") %>%
  clu() %>%
  ggplot(aes(y = center, ymin = lower, ymax = upper, x = model)) +
  facet_wrap(~fixef, scales = "free_y") +
  geom_crossbar(position = "dodge")
```

We observe that the center estimates are precisely the same. Overdispersion usually does not bias the location of an estimate. But, credibility limits are much wider with an underlying negative-binomial distribution. A full parameter table would also

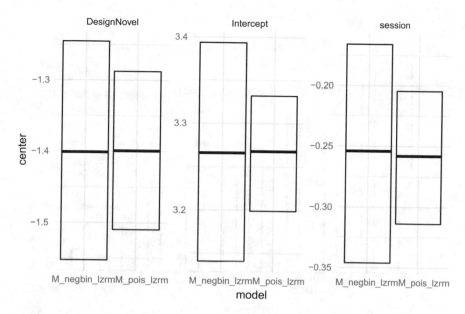

Fig. 7.13 Comparing credibility intervals of a Poisson and Neg-Binomial models

show the Neg-Binomial model additional parameter phi, controlling overdispersion relative to a Poisson distribution as

$$\text{Variance} := \mu + \mu^2/\phi$$

Due to the reciprocal term, the *smaller* ϕ gets, the *more* overdispersion had to be accounted for. From this formula alone, it may seem that neg-binomial distributions could also account for under-dispersion, when we allow negative values. But, in most implementations ϕ must be non-negative. That is rarely a problem, as under-dispersion only occurs under very special circumstances. Overdispersion in count variables in contrast, is very common, if not ubiquitous. Negative-binomial regression solves the problem with just one additional parameter, which typically need not be interpreted. Reporting on the coefficients that uses the same principle as in plain Poisson regression: inversion by exponentiation and speaking multiplicative.

7.2.3.2 Beta-Binomial Regression for Successes in Trials

Beta-binomial regression follows a similar pattern as negative-binomial. A two-parameter distribution allows to scale up the variance relative to a binomial model Sect. 7.2.2. A beta-binomial distribution is a mixed distribution, created by replacing binomial parameter p by a *beta distribution*, with parameters a and b (Fig. 7.14)

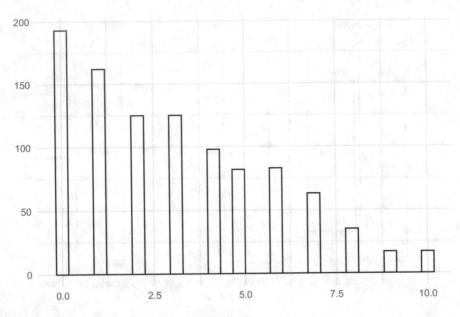

Fig. 7.14 Sampling from a beta-binomial distribution

```
rbetabinom <- function(n, size, a, b) {
  rbinom(n, size, rbeta(n, a, b))
}

rbetabinom(1000, 10, 1, 2) %>% qplot()
```

The Brms regression engine currently does not implement the beta-binomial family. That is a good opportunity to applaud the author of the Brms package for his ingenious architecture, which allows custom families to be defined by the user. The only requirement is that the distribution type is implemented in Stan [1], which is the underlying general-purpose engine behind Brms. The following code is taken directly from the Brms documentation and adds the beta-binomial family.

```
# define a custom beta-binomial family
beta_binomial2 <- custom_family(
  "beta_binomial2",
  dpars = c("mu", "phi"),
  links = c("logit", "log"), lb = c(NA, 0),
  type = "int", vars = "trials[n]"
)

# define custom stan functions
bb_stan_funs <- "
  real beta_binomial2_lpmf(int y, real mu, real phi, int N) {
    return beta_binomial_lpmf(y | N, mu * phi, (1 - mu) * phi);
  }
  int beta_binomial2_rng(real mu, real phi, int N) {
    return beta_binomial_rng(N, mu * phi, (1 - mu) * phi);
  }
"
```

Table 7.17 Parameter estimates with 95% credibility limits

Model	Parameter	Fixef	Center	Lower	Upper
M_betabin	b_Intercept	Intercept	0.104	0.093	0.116
M_betabin	phi		0.927	0.893	0.955
M_bin	b_Intercept	Intercept	0.103	0.097	0.110

Note that Beta-binomial distribution are usually parametrized with two shape paramneter *a* and *b*, which have a rather convoluted relationship with mean and variance. For a GLM, parametrization is required that has a mean parameter (for μ_i). Note, how the author of this code created a `beta_binomial2` distribution family, which takes μ and a scale parameter ϕ.

Defining the two functions is sufficient to estimate beta-binomial models with Brms. In the following, I simulate two outcomes from nine trials, `y` is sampled from a beta-binomial distribution, whereas `ybin` is from a Binomial distribution. Both have the same mean of .1 (10% correct). Subsequently, a beta-binomial and a binomial grand mean models are estimated. Note that the sampling function is taken from package VGAM, as this has the same parametrization.

```
set.seed(42)
D_betabin <- tibble(
  y = VGAM::rbetabinom(1000, 9, prob = .1, rho = .3),
  n = 9
) %>%
  as_tbl_obs()

M_betabin <-
  D_betabin %>%
  brm(y | trials(n) ~ 1,
    family = beta_binomial2,
    stan_funs = bb_stan_funs, data = .
  )

M_bin <- brm(y | trials(n) ~ 1, family = "binomial", data = D_betabin)
```

Table 7.17 collects the estimates from both models, the true beta-binomial and the binomial, which does not account for overdispersion in the data.

```
bind_rows(
  posterior(M_bin),
  posterior(M_betabin)
) %>%
  clu(mean.func = inv_logit)
```

When comparing the two intercept estimates, we notice that the center estimate is not affected by overdispersion. But, just like with Poisson models, the binomial model is too optimistic about the level of certainty.

To summarize: one-parameter distributions usually cannot be used to model count data due to extra variance. One solution to the problem is to switch to a family with a second parameter. These exist for the most common situations. When we turn to modeling durations, we will use the Gamma family to extend the Exponential distribution Sect. 7.3.1. Gamma distributions have another problem: while extra variance can be accounted by a scale parameter, we will see that another property of distribution families can be to rigid, the skew. The solution will be to switch to a three-parameter distribution family to gain more flexibility.

Another technique to model overdispersion does not require to find (or define) a two-parametric distribution. Instead, *observation-level random effects* borrow concepts from multi-level modeling and allow to keep the one-parameter distributions.

7.2.3.3   Using Observation-Level Random Effects

As we have seen in Chap. 6, random effects are often interpreted towards variance in a population, with a Gaussian distribution. On several occasions we used multi-level models to separate sources of variance, such as between teams and participants in CUE8 (@ref()). Observation-level random effect (OLRE) use the same approach by just calling the set of observation a population.

Using random effects with GLMs is straightforward, because random effects (or their dummy variable representation, to be precise), are part of the linear term, and undergo the log or logit linearization just like any other coefficient in the model.

For demonstration of the concept, we simulate from an overdispersed Poisson grand mean model with participant-level variation and observation-level variation.

```
sim_ovdsp <- function(
                       beta_0 = 2, # mu = 8
                       sd_Obs = .3,
                       sd_Part = .5,
                       N_Part = 30,
                       N_Rep = 20,
                       N_Obs = N_Part * N_Rep,
                       seed = 1) {
  set.seed(seed)
  Part <- tibble(
    Part = 1:N_Part,
    beta_0p = rnorm(N_Part, 0, sd_Part)
  ) ## participant-level RE
  D <- tibble(
    Obs = 1:N_Obs,
    Part = rep(1:N_Part, N_Rep),
    beta_0i = rnorm(N_Obs, 0, sd_Obs), ## observeration-level RE
    beta_0 = beta_0
  ) %>%
    left_join(Part) %>%
    mutate(
      theta_i = beta_0 + beta_0p + beta_0i,
      mu_i = exp(theta_i), ## inverse link function
      y_i = rpois(N_Obs, mu_i)
```

Table 7.18 Coefficient estimates with 95% credibility limits

re_factor	Center	Lower	Upper
Obs	0.330	0.289	0.373
Part	0.503	0.387	0.683

```
  )
  D %>% as_tbl_obs()
}

D_ovdsp <- sim_ovdsp()
```

The above code is instructive to how OLREs work:

1. A participant-level random effect is created as `beta_0p`. This random effect can be recovered, because we have repeated measures. This variation will not contaminate Poisson variance.
2. An observation-level random effect is created in a similar way.
3. Both random effects are on the linearized scale. The linear predictor `theta_i` is just the sum of random effects (and Intercept). It could take negative values, but ...
4. ... applying the inverse link function (`exp(theta_i)`) ensures that all responses are positive.

The extra variation comes from two sources: participant-level and observation-level. While participant levels, observations do not. How does come that we can estimate random effects on single measures? Recall that one-parameter distributions, such as Poissons, have their variance fully tied to the mean. At any position does the distribution "know" how much variance it is suppose to have, and therefore, the OLREs can be recovered. The following model contains an participant-level random effects and an OLRE. Table 7.18 recovers the two standard deviations.

```
M_ovdsp <-
  D_ovdsp %>%
  stan_glmer(y_i ~ 1 + (1 | Part) + (1 | Obs),
    data = .,
    family = poisson
  )

grpef(M_ovdsp)
```

Let's first take a look at the two random effect standard errors above. It seems that we got a fair recovery on the center estimates (for standard deviation). For the OLRE certainty is also good, even better than for the participant-level, which is simply due to the fact that there are more levels. Random effect variation is accurately recovered from the simulated data, but can we also recover the full vector of factor levels? In the following, I am extracting observation-level random effects and plot them against the simulated (linearized) coefficients.

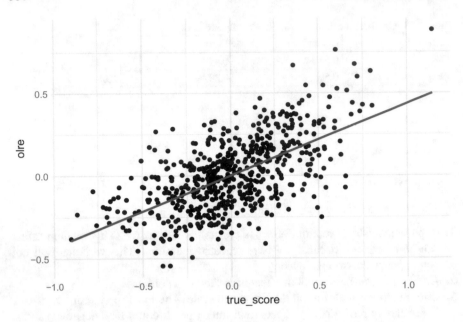

Fig. 7.15 Recovery of observation-level random effects

```
OLRE <-
  posterior(M_ovdsp) %>%
  filter(type == "ranef", re_factor == "Obs") %>%
  clu()

D_ovdsp %>%
  bind_cols(OLRE) %>%
  select(true_score = beta_0i, olre = center) %>%
  ggplot(aes(x = true_score, y = olre)) +
  geom_point() +
  geom_smooth(method = "lm", se = F)
```

Figure 7.15 shows that the observation-level deviations can be recovered not perfectly, but to some extent. An OLRE can be seen as generalized residual, or *linearized residuals*.

Linearized residuals can be used for different purposes, such as outlier detection or to compare sources of variation. Frequently, I reminded the reader to interpret parameters quantitatively by translating their magnitude to statements of practical relevance. For random effects variance, this is not always straightforward, especially when we are on a linearized scale. One way is to make comparative statements on the sources of variance, like "the variance due to individual differences exceeds the measurement error". OLREs are on the same scale as all other random effects in the model, which makes it a suitable reference source of variation.

```
## [1] "sim_ovdsp" "D_ovdsp"
```

7.3 Duration Measures

Time is a highly accessible measure, as clocks are all around us: on your wrist, in transport stations, in your computers and a very big (and accurate) one is hosted at the Physikalisch-Technischen Bundesanstalt in Braunschweig (Physical-technological federal institute in Braunschweig, Germany). Duration measures often carry useful information; especially, *Reaction time (RT)* measures are prime in experimental cognitive studies and have revealed fascinating phenomena of the human mind, such as the Stroop effect, memory priming, motor learning and the structure of attention.

In design research, reaction times are also sometimes used in experiments, but more common is *time-on-task (ToT)* as a measure of task efficiency. Formally, both outcome types measure a period of time. I am deliberately making a distinction between the two, because the data generating process of reacting to a simple task (like naming a color) may be different to a complex task, like finding information on a website. Also, RT and ToT usually are on different scales, with RT being typically in the fraction-of-seconds range and ToT in the minutes range.

Temporal variables are practically continuous (as long as one measures with sufficient precision), but always have lower bounds. First, I will introduce two families of zero-bounded model classes that use exponentially or Gamma distributed error terms. Modern Bayesian estimation engines offer an increasing variety of more exotic response distributions. Among those are Exgaussian response distributions, which works well when the lower bound is positive. Normally, this is more realistic for durations.

7.3.1 Exponential and Gamma Regression

Exponential distributions arise from basic random processes under some very idealized conditions. First, the lower boundary must be zero and second, the rate at which events happen is assumed to be constant rate, just like Poisson distributions assumes a constant λ.

Reconsider the subway smurfer example Sect. 3.5.2, where players collect items in a jump-and-run game. We have already seen how collection counts can be modeled using Poisson or binomial regression. Another way to look at it is the time between two events of item collection. For demonstration only, we assume such idealized conditions in the subway smurfer example and generate a data set. Exponential distributions are determined by one parameter, the *rate* parameter λ, which is strictly positive. The mean and variance of exponential distributions are as follows, and they are strictly tied to each other:

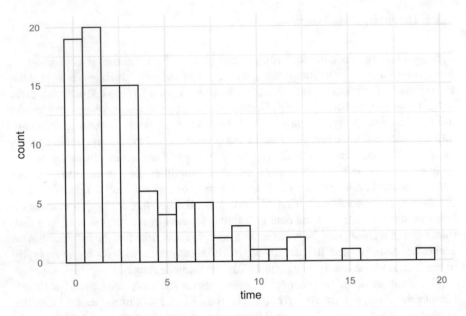

Fig. 7.16 Data sampled from an Exponential distribution

$$Y \sim \text{Exp}(\lambda)$$
$$\text{Mean}(Y) = 1/\lambda$$
$$\text{Var}(Y) = 1/\lambda^2$$
$$= 1/\lambda \times \text{Mean}(Y)$$

In the following, data is simulated from an exponential distribution (Fig. 7.16). Subsequently, the only parameter is recovered using an exponential GMM. Like for Poisson models, a log link function is reversed by exponentiation (Table 7.19).

```
set.seed(20)
D_exp <-
  tibble(
    Obs = 1:100,
    time = rexp(100, rate = 1 / 3)
  )

D_exp %>%
  ggplot(aes(x = time)) +
  geom_histogram(bins = 20)

M_exp <- brm(time ~ 1,
  family = "exponential",
  data = D_exp
)

clu(M_exp, mean.func = exp)
```

Exponential distribution are rarely used in practice for two shortcomings: first, the strict mean-variance relation makes it prone to overdispersion. This can be resolved

Table 7.19 Parameter estimates with 95% credibility limits

Parameter	Fixef	Center	Lower	Upper
b_Intercept	Intercept	1.19	1	1.38
lp__		−221.24	−223	−221.02

by using observation-level random effects Sect. 7.2.3.3 or using Gamma distributions, which accounts for extra variance by a second parameter. The second problem is the lower boundary of Zero, which will later be resolved by using Exgaussian error distributions Sect. 7.3.2.

Exponential regression has a single parameter and therefore has the same problem as seen with Poisson and binomial regression before. Only if all events have the same rate to occur, will an exponential distribution arise, which means for behavioral research: never. A general solution to the problem is introducing an observation-level random effect Sect. 7.2.3.3. Here, I will tackle the problem by using continuous, zero-bounded mixture distributions with two parameters, the Gamma family of distributions.

The canonical form of Gamma distribution uses two parameters rate and shape, which do not directly translate into location and dispersion. Still, the second parameter provides the extra degree of freedom to adjust variance. Albeit, the variance parameter is not set entirely loose, as with Gaussian distributions. Variance still rises with the mean, but as we have argued in 7.1.3, this is rather a desired feature than a problem. In the following, we simulate Gamma distributed observations (Fig. 7.17).

```
set.seed(20)
D_gam <-
  tibble(
    Obs = 1:100,
    time = rgamma(100, rate = 1 / 3, shape = 2)
  )

D_gam %>%
  ggplot(aes(x = time)) +
  geom_histogram(bins = 20)
```

In comparison to the exponential distribution (Fig. 7.16), a significant difference is that the mode of the gamma distribution (its peak) is not fixed at zero, but can move along the x-axis. That makes it appear a much more realistic choice for temporal data in behavioral research. We estimate a simple gamma GMM on the simulated data. For historical reasons, brm uses the inverse link function ($\theta = 1/\mu$) for Gamma regression per default, but that does not actually serve the purpose of link functions to stretch μ into the range of real numbers. Instead, we explicitly demand a log link, which creates a multiplicative model (Table 7.20).

```
M_gam <- brm(time ~ 1,
  family = Gamma(link = log),
  data = D_gam
)

clu(M_gam, mean.func = exp)
```

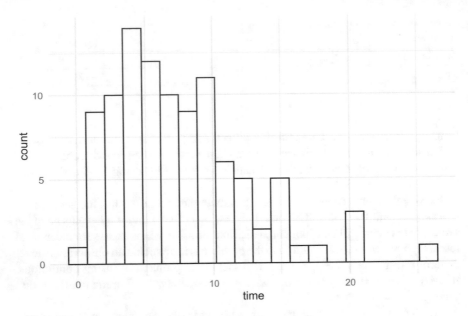

Fig. 7.17 Data sampled from a Gamma distribution

Table 7.20 Parameter estimates with 95% credibility limits

Parameter	Fixef	Center	Lower	Upper
b_Intercept	Intercept	2.03	1.90	2.17
Shape		2.25	1.73	2.85
lp__		−294.69	−297.65	−294.03

Both, Exponential and Gamma distributions support the range of real numbers including zero. The weak point of both models is that they have zero as their natural starting point. As we will see in the following section, this assumption is usually violated with RT and ToT data. So, what are they good for, after all? These two models are routinely used for the *time intervals (TI)* between events that are triggered independently. In nuclear physics the individual triggers are atoms, each one *deciding on their own* when to decay. If you measure the interval between two decays the time interval is exponentially distributed. (And if you count the neutrons per time interval, the result is a Poisson distribution).

Analog situations can be found in service design and logistics. Take the example of customer support systems. Customers are like atoms in that their decision to file a request is usually independent from each other. Just by chance it can truly happen that two customers call the service center practically in the same moment, so that the lower bound of Zero can actually be reached by some observations. Overwhelmed hotline queues do not make people happy. When planning a support system, the risk of angry customers has to be weighed against the costs of over-staffing. A good design would hit a certain sweet spot and in the ideal case there would be a predictive model of inflow rate of customers.

7.3.2 ExGaussian Regression

The problem with RT and ToT data is that Zero is not a possible outcome, as any task uses up a minimum time to complete. For example, Table 7.21 shows the minimum ToT for finding the academic calendar on ten university websites (case Egan). This varies a lot between designs, but is never even close to zero. The last column puts the minimum observed ToT in relation to the observed range. On two of the websites, the offset was even larger than the observed range itself, hence the problem of positive lower boundaries is real in user studies.

```
attach(Egan)

D_egan %>%
  filter(
    success,
    Task == "academic calendar"
  ) %>%
  group_by(Task, Design) %>%
  summarize(
    min_time = min(ToT),
    range = max(ToT) - min_time,
    min_time / range
```

Table 7.21 The lower boundaries of ToT are not Zero

Task	Design	min_time	range	min_time/range
Academic calendar	University of Antwerp	3	7	0.429
Academic calendar	UGent	8	70	0.114
Academic calendar	VU Brussel	21	130	0.162
Academic calendar	UHasselt	21	48	0.438
Academic calendar	University Tilburg	24	39	0.615
Academic calendar	KU Leuven	52	40	1.300
Academic calendar	RUG	119	132	0.902
Academic calendar	Leiden University	130	181	0.718
Academic calendar	VU Amsterdam	207	188	1.101

```
) %>%
arrange(min_time)
```

On the first glance, that does not seem to pose a major problem for Gamma distributions, as the left tail vanishes the more a Gamma distribution is shifted to the right, the impossible regions get smaller. However, Gamma distributions inevitably become more symmetric when moving away from the lower boundary. A Gamma distribution far to the right has almost symmetric tails and we may eventually use a Gaussian distribution for approximation. As there is no separate parameter controlling the skew of the curve, it may happen that the random component captures the amount of variance, but overdoes the left tail, which introduces a bias on the coefficients. Figure 7.18 illustrates the mean-variance-skew relationship on three Gamma distributions that move from left to right (M), keeping the variance constant (V)

```
M <- c(100, 200, 400)
V <- 8000

## gamma
rate <- M / V
shape <- rate^2 * V

ggplot(data.frame(x = c(0, 3000)), aes(x = x)) +
  stat_function(
    fun = dgamma,
    args = list(rate = rate[1], shape = shape[1])
  ) +
  stat_function(
```

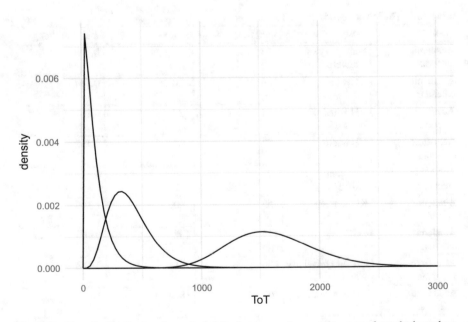

Fig. 7.18 Gamma distributions loose their left-skewness, when moving away from the boundary

```
  fun = dgamma,
  args = list(rate = rate[1], shape = shape[2])
) +
stat_function(
  fun = dgamma,
  args = list(rate = rate[1], shape = shape[3])
) +
labs(x = "ToT", y = "density")
```

So far in this chapter, we have seen that distributions with one parameter (Poisson, binomial, exponential) have a fixed relationship between mean and variance. In order to vary location and dispersion independently, a second parameter is needed (neg-binomial, beta-binomial, Gamma, Gaussian). However, only a three-parameter distributions can do the trick of setting skew separately. The so-called *exponentially-modified Gaussian* (Exgaussian) distributions are convolutions of a Gaussian distribution and exponential distribution and have three parameters, μ, σ (as usual) and rate β. Very roughly, the Gaussian component controls location and dispersion, whereas the exponential part adjusts the skew. When β is large in comparison to μ, the distribution is more left skewed. With this additional degree of freedom, we can simulate (and estimate) distributions that are far to the right, have strong dispersion *and* strong skew. Figure 7.19 shows Gamma, Gaussian and Exgaussian distributions with exact same mean and variance.

```
M <- 400
V <- 8000

## Exgaussian
mu <- M
```

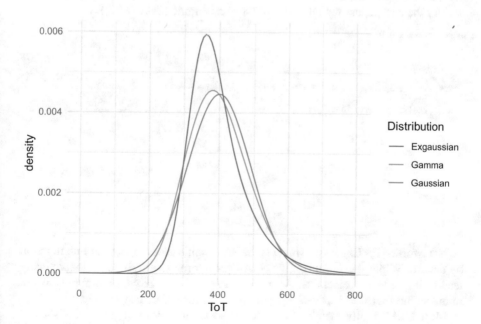

Fig. 7.19 Exgaussian distributions can be far from zero and still be left skewed

```
beta <- 80
sigma <- sqrt(V - beta^2)

## Gamma
rate <- M / V
shape <- rate^2 * V

ggplot(data.frame(x = c(0, 800)), aes(x = x)) +
  stat_function(
    fun = dgamma,
    args = list(rate = rate, shape = shape),
    mapping = aes(color = "Gamma")
  ) +
  stat_function(
    fun = dnorm,
    args = list(mean = M, sd = sqrt(V)),
    mapping = aes(color = "Gaussian")
  ) +
  stat_function(
    fun = brms::dexgaussian,
    args = list(
      mu = M,
      sigma = sigma,
      beta = beta
    ),
    mapping = aes(color = "Exgaussian")
  ) +
  labs(color = "Distribution", x = "ToT", y = "density")
```

The Gamma distribution in this example starts approaching a the perfect bell curve of the Gaussian distribution. In contrast, the Exgaussian distribution takes a steep left climb followed by a long right tail, which is caused by its pronounced exponential component. We do the usual exercise to simulate a grand mean model (Fig. 7.20) and recover the parameters with the help of the brm engine (Table 7.22)).

```
attach(Chapter_GLM)


set.seed(126)
D_exg <-
  tibble(Y = rexgaussian(100, mu = 100, sigma = 20, beta = 30))

qplot(D_exg$Y) + xlim(0, 300)


M_exg <- brm(Y ~ 1,
  family = exgaussian,
  data = D_exg
)

clu(M_exg)
```

Noteworthy, for Exgaussian models the brm engine uses the identity link function by default. While this is rather convenient for interpretation, it could theoretically lead to impossible predictions. As we will see later, the Exgaussian family is not immune, but *robust to impossible predictions* because of its tiny left tail.

Most GLM family members introduced so far are more or less established in the literature. The Exgaussian is a newcomer and it does not come with a clear cut

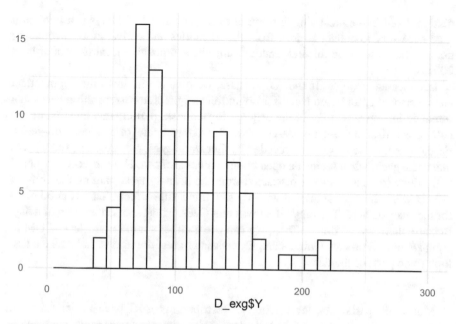

Fig. 7.20 Sampling from an Exgaussian distribution

Table 7.22 Parameter estimates with 95% credibility limits

parameter	Fixef	Center	Lower	Upper
b_Intercept	Intercept	99.4	92.9	106.6
Sigma		17.7	12.3	24.0
Beta		31.6	23.5	41.6
lp__		−500.1	−503.6	−499.0

data generation process and may, therefore, very well be considered just a hack. The following two sections examine Exgaussian models more closely and out them in competition against Gamma and Gaussian models. We will be using primarily graphical methods here, but will come back these cases in Sect. 8.2.5 with a more formal approach.

7.3.2.1 Reaction Times

In experimental studies, the *inertia of the nervous system* sets a limit larger than zero for reaction times. This is partly due to to some hard electrochemical and biomechanical limits of the peripheral systems. (Perhaps, octopuses with their long arms have decentralized nervous system for a reason!) Nerve cells and muscle fibers are slow working horses, adding to the time our minds need to process complex information. Even in the most simple priming experiments, there always is a minimum time necessary to collect an idea from the memories and activate the surrounding nodes. Therefore, experimental reaction times have a positive minimum of at least 200 ms.

Let's see an example: In the Hugme case, we tried to pin down the hypothetical Geek personality and used Need-for-cognition as a predictor for reaction times in a semantic Stroop task. Like in the original Stroop task, participants must name the color of words, but these are non-color words from two categories (geek/non-geek). Furthermore, these words are preceded by Geek/non-geek pictures. The theory was that a real geek, when seeing an open computer case followed by the word "explore" will briefly reminisce and be distracted from the primary task, naming the color. It did not work this way at all and we only saw minuscule effects. That is good news for the analysis here. The only effect was that Geek primes caused a minimal delay. Because there are no other effects, we can use a rather simple multi-level CGM to compare how Gaussian, Gamma and Exgaussian fit reaction times. Let's take a first look some parts of the data

```
attach(Hugme)
```

Most of the participant-level frequency distributions of RT have a clear cut-off at around .25 s. The steepness of the left climb varies between participants, but some at least are rather sharp, with a right tail that is leveling off slowly. When compared to the illustrations above, it seems that an Exgaussian model could accommodate this data well (Fig. 7.21).

```
D_hugme %>%
  filter(Part <= 6) %>%
  ggplot(aes(y = RT, x = PrimeGeek)) +
  facet_wrap(~Part, nrow = 2) +
  geom_violin()
```

Even the effect of geek primes is barely visible, but we clearly observe a left skew in most of the participants. In the following, we run three CGM models with Exgaussian, Gamma or Gaussian response distributions. For the subsequent analysis, multi-model posterior distributions and posterior predictive distributions are extracted and merged into one multi-model posterior object P_1.

```
memory.limit(16000)

F_1 <- formula(RT ~ 1 + PrimeGeek + (1 + PrimeGeek | Part))

M_1_gau <- D_hugme %>%
  brm(F_1,
      family = gaussian,
      data = .
  )

M_1_gam <- D_hugme %>%
  brm(F_1,
      family = Gamma(link = identity),
      data = .
  )

M_1_exg <- D_hugme %>%
```

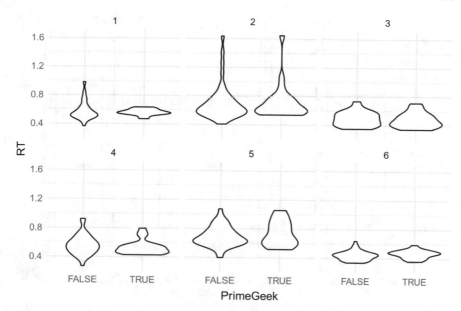

Fig. 7.21 Participant-level RT distributions

```
brm(F_1,
    family = exgaussian,
    data = .
  )

P_1 < bind_rows(
  posterior(M_1_gau),
  posterior(M_1_gam),
  posterior(M_1_exg).
)

T_1_predict <-
  bind_rows(
    post_pred(M_1_gau, thin = 5),
    post_pred(M_1_gam, thin = 5),
    post_pred(M_1_exg, thin = 5).
  ) %>%
  predict()
```

Note that the predictive posterior distributions runs over thousands of observation, which creates very large objects in your computer's RAM. To prevent running into a memory limit, you can crank up the memory limit (memory.limit) or thin out the number of posterior predictive samples by a factor, or do both.

The below plot shows the population-level effects for the three models. The center estimates are very close, which means that neither of the models has a significant bias. However, the Exgaussian model produces much tighter credibility intervals. We have seen such an effect before, when on overdispersed data, a Poisson model produced tighter intervals than the Negbinomial model. Here, it is the other way round: the model with more parameters produces better levels of certainty (Fig. 7.22).

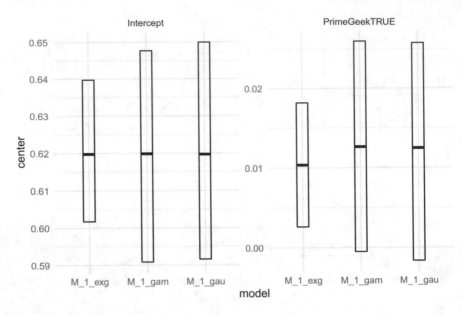

Fig. 7.22 Comparing CLU estimates of Exgaussian, Gamma and Gaussian models

```
fixef(P_1) %>%
  ggplot(aes(
    y = center, ymin = lower, ymax = upper,
    x = model
  )) +
  facet_wrap(~fixef, scales = "free") +
  geom_crossbar(width = .2, position = "dodge")
```

If the Exgaussian model has a better fit, we should primarily see that in how the residuals are shaped. The Exgaussian distribution has one more degree of freedom, which can be used to set an arbitrary skew. The following reveals that the extra flexibility of the Exgaussian has been employed. Both, Gaussian and Gamma are almost symmetric, whereas the Exgaussian takes a steeper left climb. The three distributions have almost the same right tail, but the left tail of the Exgaussian is consistently shorter (Fig. 7.23).

```
D_hugme <- D_hugme %>%
  left_join(T_1_predict) %>%
  mutate(resid = RT - center)

D_hugme %>%
  ggplot(aes(y = resid, x = PrimeGeek)) +
  facet_grid(. ~ model) +
  geom_violin()
```

We can carefully conclude that the Exgaussian may be very useful for analyzing psychological experiments as it seems to better accommodate reaction times. Given the novelty of Exgaussian models, it is recommended that researchers carry out a careful multi-model analysis. In Sect. 8.2.5, we will come back to this case with a

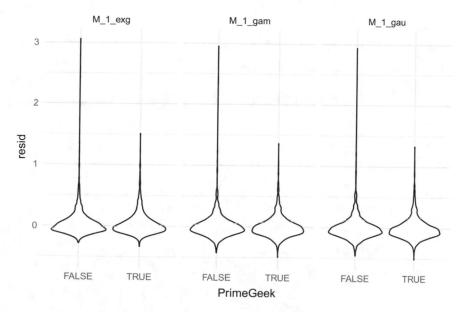

Fig. 7.23 Comparing residuals of Exgaussian, Gamma and Gaussian models

more formal approach and confirm that from the three response distributions, the Exgaussian has the best predictive accuracy.

7.3.2.2 Time-on-Task

Experimental psychologists call the Stroop task a complex one. But, essentially it is a decision between three colors and minimal processing time is rather short. Compared to tasks in usability studies, such as finding information on websites, this is almost trivial. Also, the dynamics of complex tasks can be rather different. For example, a single user error at the beginning of a task sequence can have dramatic consequences, such as getting totally lost. While ToT data also has a strictly positive lower boundary (the fastest way of achieving the goal), it often has a much wider spread than RT data. In the following, we will repeat the informal model comparison from the last section for ToT data.

We compare the three patterns of randomness on the CUE8 data set, which contains ToT measures on five tasks on a car rental website. In this study, 14 professional teams took part with two conditions: remote and moderated sessions. As data from the remote condition is contaminated with cheaters, we only use the moderated sessions. In order to compare the impact of the chosen distribution on the coefficient estimates, we examine the estimation of the five tasks (as an AGM).

```
attach(CUE8)

D_cue8_mod <-
  D_cue8 %>%
  filter(Condition == "moderated", !is.na(ToT)) %>%
  as_tbl_obs()

F_4 <- formula(ToT ~ 0 + Task + (1 | Part))

M_4_gau <- D_cue8_mod %>%
  brm(F_4,
      family = gaussian(link = log),
      data = ., iter = 2000
  )

M_4_exg <- D_cue8_mod %>%
  brm(F_4,
      family = exgaussian(link = log),
      data = ., iter = 2000
  )

M_4_gam <- D_cue8_mod %>%
  brm(F_4,
      family = Gamma(link = log),
      data = ., iter = 2000
  )

P_4 <- bind_rows(
  posterior(M_4_gau),
  posterior(M_4_gam) %>% mutate(value = if_else(value %in%
c("fixef", "ranef"), exp(value), value)),
  posterior(M_4_exg)
)


T_4_predict <- bind_rows(
  post_pred(M_4_gau, thin = 5),
  post_pred(M_4_gam, thin = 5),
  post_pred(M_4_exg, thin = 5)
) %>%
  predict()
```

Note that the Gamma model caused trouble when estimated with an identity link. For this reason, all three models were estimated on a log-linearized scale. This makes the back-transformed coefficients multiplicative, which actually makes more sense, as we have seen in Sect. 7.2.1.1.

```
fixef(P_4, mean.func = exp) %>%
  ggplot(aes(
    y = center, ymin = lower, ymax = upper,
    x = model
  )) +
  facet_wrap(~fixef) +
  geom_crossbar(width = .2) +
  theme(axis.text.x = element_text(angle = 45, hjust = 1))
```

In the previous Sect. 7.3.2.1, we have seen for RT data, that the three models agreed on the center estimates. As shown in Fig. 7.24, for ToT data the three families produce rather different coefficients. It seems that the models disagree on all but Task 1. It is not more than an observation, but the Exgaussian model produces the smallest variance between tasks. A recurring observation is that Exgaussian regression also produced the tightest credibility intervals.

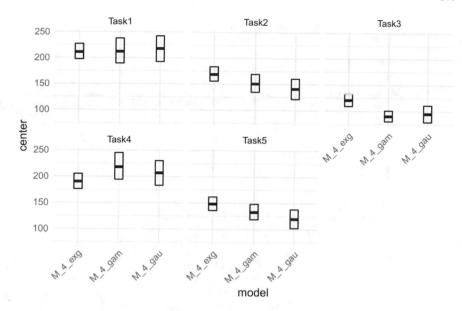

Fig. 7.24 Comparing CLU estimates of Exgaussian, Gamma and Gaussian models

Inspecting the residual distributions yields a similar pattern as with RT data: the Exgaussian model predicts a much sharper left raise than the other two (Fig. 7.25).

```
left_join(T_4_predict, D_cue8_mod, by = "Obs") %>%
  mutate(resid = ToT - center) %>%
  ggplot(aes(x = model, y = resid)) +
  facet_wrap(~Task, nrow = 2) +
  geom_violin() +
  theme(axis.text.x = element_text(angle = 45, hjust = 1))
```

In general, it seems that Exgaussian models for RT and ToT accommodates left skew better and produces estimates that are sharp and conservative. But, these are just informal comparisons. In Chap. 8, we will apply formal criteria for selecting between distributions. As will turn out, Gamma distribution is the preferred distribution for ToT in CUE8.

One last issue remains to get clarified: using the identity link for Exgaussian models is very convenient and is probably much safer as compared to Gaussian models with their fatter left tails. Still, impossible predictions can arise. But, how much of a risk is there? We can check this on the posterior predictive distributions of both studies, CUE8 and Hugme. Table 7.23 shows the proportion of observations, that get a negative 2.5% credibility limit assigned.

```
bind_rows(Hugme$T_1_predict, CUE8$T_4_predict) %>%
  group_by(model) %>%
  summarize(mean(lower < 0))
```

For the RT data (M_1), impossible predictions are not an issue with any of the models, as all 2.5% quantiles are positive. That is different for ToT (M_4): while the

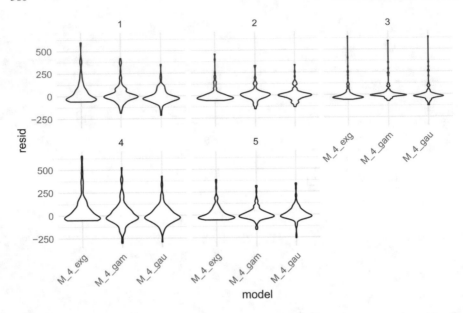

Fig. 7.25 Comparing residuals of Exgaussian, Gamma and Gaussian models

Table 7.23 Proportion of negative fitted responses per model

Model	Mean(lower < 0)
M_1_exg	0.000
M_1_gam	0.000
M_1_gau	0.000
M_4_exg	0.014
M_4_gam	0.000
M_4_gau	0.750

Gamma model is inherently immune to negative predictions, the Exgaussian model produced a few impossible lower 2.5% limits (around 3%). The Gaussian model is extremely off: more than 70% of all predictions have impossible lower 2.5% limits.

In the scientific literature, using the Gaussian model for RT and ToT is still the default. Probably, that is due to the lack of user-friendly engines supporting the more exotic GLM family members, Gamma or Exgaussian regression. The Brms engine covers a much broader set of distributions than any other implementation before and researchers have the choice. This chapter attempted to provide theoretical arguments as well as empirical indications that the Exgaussian regression can be a better choice than Gaussian and Gamma. First of all, it accommodates the strong left skew of RT and ToT much better than the Gamma, which takes a too symmetric form when far from the left boundary. Second, it is reasonably robust to impossible predictions, even when using the convenient identity link function. Third, and that is almost too good to be true, it strongly improves certainty in predictors. It seems that Exgaussian models are more efficient for carving out delicate effects in experimental studies.

However, as the discussion has just started, to declare it settled would be premature. In contrast, the aim of this section was to illustrate a semi-formal approach that researchers can follow to choose among the candidate models for their specific RT and ToT data. Data from other RT paradigms might take different shapes. For example, when measuring RT by events in EEG signals (rather than actual key presses), motor time plays a much smaller role, pushing RTs closer to the left boundary and the Gamma model would be in favor.

That being said, the brms engine offers even more opportunities. First, it supports two more distributions with an offset component: the shifted log-normal and the Wiener distribution. Interestingly, the latter grounds on one of the few formally specified cognitive process models, the diffusion model for simple choice tasks. All the four parameters of the Wiener distribution are directly linked to individual elements of the cognitive process. This brings us to another extension of Brms, which I will briefly cover in the last section of this chapter. *Distributional models* put linearized predictor terms not just on the distribution mean, but also on other parameters of a distribution family. It is thrilling to imagine what such models can do for experimental cognitive research.

7.4 Rating Scales

In classic design research of the last millennium, die-hard Human Factors researchers have mainly been asking objectively sounding questions, like:

- Can a user achieve accurate results with the system?
- Can they do so in less time?
- Is the number of errors reasonably confined?

For professional systems, these are still highly valid questions. For example, the purpose of a medical infusion pump is to improve the health status of a patient by accurately and reliably delivering medication into the bloodstream and the extent to which a nurse achieves this by correctly programming the device can be measured directly.

However, starting with the 1990s, wave after wave of novel electronic entertainment systems and digital gadgets rolled over the consumer market and user feelings got more into the focus. The purpose of a video recorder or a smartphone is to deliver joy. With the new millennium, design researchers began to recognize what consumer psychologists had discovered two decades earlier: users are not rational decision makers in a utilitarian sense, but are lead by their feelings. When people decide to adopt (or buy) a new system, this is only partly driven by their expectation of productivity. Such feelings come as a variety of different constructs:

- feeling of joy
- expression of self
- social connectedness
- aesthetic perception
- personal growth.

Whether or not these concepts are well-defined from a psychological point of view is beyond the scope of this book. What matters is that feelings are so elusive, that the most sincere researchers have not yet found objective criteria to measure them. Instead, almost everyone resorts to use of *self-report rating scales*, like this one

How beautiful do you perceive the user interface to be?

unattractive $1 - 2 - 3 - 4 - 5$ a piece of art

If you use a 5 point rating scale like this one to measure perceived beauty, it is the participants who convert their gut feeling into a number. This is a hidden and uncontrolled process, but it presumably involves the following three subprocesses:

1. anchoring
2. introspection
3. binning.

By *anchoring*, participants establish an idea of how ugly or beautiful something has be to get an extreme rating of 1 or 5. These imaginary endpoints define the *absolute range* of the rating scale. If an experiment is overtly about web design, then probably "very ugly" means the least attractive commercial website the participant can think of. However, participants old enough to remember web design in its infancy (say the early attempts of disney.com), may work with a lower anchor than today's kids. If not enough cues are given upfront, participants will make up their own minds (in an uncontrolled way) and at best adjust their anchors to the stimuli they see throughout the experiment. Probably, it will make a difference for what 1 or 5 mean, when the set of stimuli contain just websites, or websites *and* impressionist paintings *and* horrifying screenshots from splatter movies or brutal computer games.

By *introspection* participants intuitively assess the intensity of their *real feelings* as compared to the anchors. Reportedly, such feelings are influenced by:

1. visual simplicity
2. prototypicality
3. second exposure
4. Gestalt principles
5. fluency of processing
6. attribute substitution heuristics
7. color aesthetics
8. fashion
9. previous stimuli
10. current mood
11. a person's history
12. and cultural background.

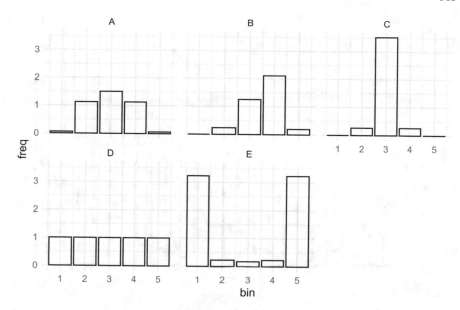

Fig. 7.26 Five participants with different response styles

Finally, by *binning*, the participant mentally divides the absolute range into five categories that are either fuzzy or defined by stereotypes, like "It must look at least as elegant as the Mapple website to get a 4."

As the outcome of anchoring, introspection and binning are not under the control of the researcher, the response patterns can vary between participants. Let's consider a few possible patterns of participants (and their dramatic stories, see Fig. 7.26):

1. A is indecisive and stays in the center region
2. B has a crush on the experimenter and always responds slightly more positive
3. C is Swedish and avoids extremes
4. D is a civil rights activist and habitually treats all bins equally.
5. E is annoyed by the experiment and falls into an almost dichotomous pattern

Many unknowns are in the game. Only one special case we can alleviate with the multi-level modeling tools in our hands. Anchoring can (but not necessarily does) result in a constant *shift* between participants. Compare participants A and B: A collects almost all stimuli in categories 2, 3 and 4, whereas B uses 3, 4 and 5. This is not much else than a participant-level intercept random effect. Unfortunately, the situation can be more difficult than that. When participants differ in how extreme they set their endpoints, like C and D, their responses will differ in variance. The maximum variance, however, will be found in participant D.

To speak of a real case: In the IPump study, a single-item rating scale was used to measure mental workload. The results suggest that all participants used the lower range of the scale, but differed vastly in where they set their upper point. Figure 7.27

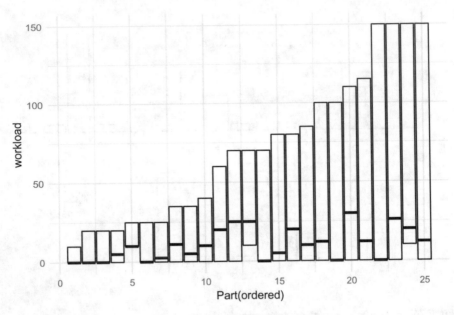

Fig. 7.27 In the IPump study participants vary greatly in how they exploit the range of a mental workload scale

orders participants by the maximum value they used. This is obviously related to variance, but seemingly not so much with location. It does not suffice to use a response distribution with mean-variance relationship, as we used to. All these issues make rating scales peculiar and we should not pretend they have the same neat arithmetic properties as objective measures.

```
attach(IPump)

D_pumps %>%
  group_by(Part) %>%
  summarize(
    min = min(workload),
    max = max(workload),
    median = median(workload)
  ) %>%
  mutate(Part_ord = rank(max, ties.method = "first")) %>%
  ggplot(aes(x = Part_ord, ymax = max, ymin = min, y = median)) +
  geom_crossbar() +
  labs(x = "Part(ordered)", y = "workload")
```

Setting the idiosyncratic rating scale responses aside, how does a common rating scale appear in our framework of link functions and patterns of randomness? Rating scales are bounded on two sides and we already know what that means: a suitable model for rating scales will likely contain a logit link function and a distribution of randomness that is bounded on two sides.

A real problem with rating scales is that they often are discrete. Most instruments force participants to give their answer as a choice between five or seven ordered levels. When the response variable has just a few levels, *ordinal regression* is a good choice, which is an extension of logistic regression.

However, most properly designed rating scales are composed of several items, because only that can sufficiently reduce measurement error and allow for in-depth psychometric assessments (Sect. 6.8). While from a psychometric perspective, single-item scales are susceptible, there can be situations where a researcher may use a validated single-item scale for pragmatic reasons. Especially, when measures happen in-situ, such as during a usability test or even a real operation, being brief and unobtrusive might be more important than perfecting the measures.

With multi-item rating scales, one also has the possibility to build a psychometric multi-level model, where items are considered a sample of a population of possible items. That is actually a very good idea, as the item-level random effects control for differences in item location. For example, the following item is likely to produce generally lower beauty ratings than the one shown earlier, because the anchors have been moved downwards

How beautiful do you perceive the user interface?
Like a screenshot from a splatter movie $1 - 2 - 3 - 4 - 5$ quite attractive.

Unless one builds such a psychometric multi-level model, ordinal regression is not very suitable for multi-item scales and here is why: The sum (or mean) score is still binned, but more finely grained. A sum score over three seven-binned items already has 21 bins, which would result in an inflation of number of parameters in ordinal regression.

As a rescue, one might well regard a measure with 21 bins as continuous . Furthermore, there actually is no strong reason to use binned rating scales at all. The so-called *visual analog scales* let participants make continuous choices by either drawing a cross on a line or move a slider control. For sum scores and visual analog scales, the problem of choice reduces to a logit link function (they still have two boundaries) and a continuous distribution bounded on both sides. That is precisely what is behind *beta regression* and, as we shall see, this distribution is flexible enough to smooth over several of the rating scale problems that were just discussed.

7.4.1 Ordered Logistic Regression

When the ordinal response has a low number of response categories (between 4 and 7), ordinal regression applies. Recall logistic regression: the response falls into one of two categories, which are coded as 0 and 1. Although not in a strict sense, the two categories can often be thought of as in an order: success is better than failure, presence more than absence and a return better than staying away. Instead of two categories, we can also conceive the situation as a *threshold* between the categories, that needs force to jump over it. Any positive impact factor x_i can then be thought of as such a force that pushes a response probability to the higher category, by the

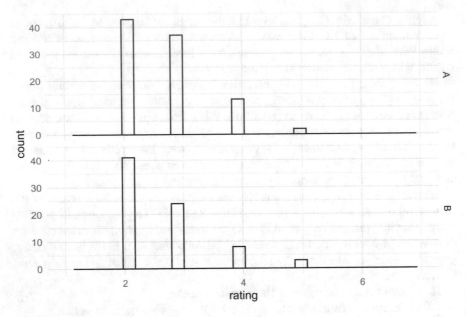

Fig. 7.28 Designs A and B rated on a sevel-point scale

amount β_i (on logit scale). At the same time, the intercept β_0 represents the basic log-odds of falling into category 1 in a default state, that is $x_i = 0$.

In ordinal regression, the idea of thresholds is extended more than two ordered response categories. The only arising complication is that with two categories, we have one threshold to overcome, whereas with three categories there are two thresholds and generally, with c categories, there are $c - 1$ thresholds. Ordinal regression deals with the problem by estimating $c - 1$ intercept estimates $\beta_{0[k]}$. Each threshold intercept $\beta_{0[k]}$ represents the probability (on logit scale) that the response falls into category k *or lower*, or formally

$$\text{logit}(P(y_i \leq k)) = \beta_{0[k]}$$

Let's see this at the example of the BrowsingAB case, first. User ratings have been simulated with seven levels (Fig. 7.28)

```
attach(BrowsingAB)

BAB1 %>%
  ggplot(aes(x = rating)) +
  facet_grid(Design ~ .) +
  geom_histogram() +
  xlim(1, 7)
```

Table 7.24 Coefficient estimates with 95% credibility limits

Fixef	Center	Lower	Upper
	−2.072	−2.557	−1.607
	−0.276	−0.633	0.075
	0.646	0.168	1.162
	1.205	0.320	2.274
DesignB	−0.543	−0.955	−0.122

The brms regression engine implements ordinal regression by the family `cratio` (cumulative odds ratio) with a default logit link function.

```
M_ord_1 <-
  BAB1 %>%
  brm(rating ~ Design,
    family = "cratio",
    data = .
  )

fixef(M_ord_1)
```

The four intercepts in Table 7.24 correspond with the thresholds of the four levels that have actually been observed (2–5). It is no coincidence that the intercept estimates increase by order, as they are cumulative (the "c" in cratio). The first intercept estimate represents (the logit of) the proportion of responses $y_i \leq 1$, the second $y_i \leq 2$, etc. The Design effect has the usual interpretation as compared to logistic regression, a change in odds. The only difference is that it now acts on all six reference points. The expected proportion of responses equal to or smaller than 2 for design A is

$$\pi(y_i \leq 2 \, A) = \text{logit}^{-1}(\beta_{0[2]}) \cdot$$
$$= \text{logit}^{-1}(-0.3) = 0.426$$

The expected proportion of responses equal to or smaller than 2 for design B we get by the usual linear combination

$$\pi(y_i \leq 2|B) = \text{logit}^{-1}(\beta_{0[2]} + \beta_1)$$
$$= \text{logit}^{-1}(NA) = NA$$

All coefficients are shifting all thresholds by the same amount (on the linear predictor scale). You can picture this as a single puppeteer controlling multiple puppets by just one stick, making them dance synchronously. That works well if the number of bins is small. Just imagine, you were estimating an ordinal multi-level model and all participant-level effects were five or seven-folded, too. However, the equidistancy of effects on bin thresholds is an assumption by itself, and in the presence of response styles on rating scales, it cannot be taken for granted.

Besides that, the ordinal model appears very snug to the structure of the data. It does not wipe over the fact that the response is discrete and the thresholds represent the order. Conveniently, effects are represented by a single estimate, which one can use to communicate direction and certainty of effects. On the downside, communicating absolute performance (that is, including the intercept) is more complicated. When presenting predictions from an ordinal model one actually has to present all thresholds, rather than a single mean. In practice that probably is less relevant than one might think at first, because predictions on self-report scales is less useful than metric performance data. Ordinal data also does not lend itself so much to further calculations. For example, you can use ToT measures on infusion pumps in calculating the required staffing of an intensive care unit, because seconds are metric and can be summed and divided. In contrast, it does not make sense to calculate the cognitive workload of a team of nurses by summing their self-report scores. The only possibility is to compare the strengths of predictors, but that does not require predictions.

7.4.2 Beta Regression

In my opinion, one of the most futile discussions in methodology research whether one should use a four, five or seven-binned Likert scale. From a pure measurement point of view, more bins give better resolution, the ultimate consequence being not to bin at all, that is using continuous rating scales. At the same time, many rating responses come from multiple item scales, which multiplies the number of bins. Speaking of ordinal regression, it seems reasonable to have seven intercepts for a single-item scale, but who would want 14 or 21 for a two or three-item scale? And most scales have even more items.

Psychometric research in the process of developing rating scales routinely uses a method called *confirmatory factor analysis*, which derives from the Gaussian linear model and inherits its assumptions. As always, Gaussian models are sometimes a reasonable approximation, but given the framework of GLM, it is unnecessary (to put it mildly) to go along with the Gaussian, violating the assumptions of normality and linearity. While the link function for a double bounded response variable is simply the logit, the only missing ingredient is a double bounded error distribution. Enter Beta distribution!

We demonstrate beta regression on rating scales at the example of the CUE8 study. This study aimed at assessing whether remote usability testing arrives at the same ToT measures as in moderated sessions. As we have seen in 6.6, the difference is marginal for ToT.

As rating scales are susceptible to all kinds of cognitive and social biases, a golden rule for user test moderators is to constantly remind participants to not blame themselves for errors. Reportedly, test moderators also do help participants (after counting to 10) in order to minimize frustration (and maximize information flow). What could the presence or absence of a moderator do to satisfaction ratings? Perhaps, remote participants feel the lack of assurance and support as higher levels of frustration. Furthermore, it is not unlikely that satisfaction ratings are sensitive to idiosyncrasies in the process of the user test, such that we could even expect differences between teams.

Before we build the model, there are two issues to regard: First, the boundaries of Beta distributions are 0 and 1, which requires a rescaling of responses into this interval. The SUS scores are on a scale from 0 to 100 and a divisor of 100 would produce the desired interval (Fig. 7.29). Second, the responses must actually lie *strictly between 0 and 1*, excluding the boundaries. On (quasi)continuous scales, it seems not very likely to have 0 or 1 as response, but it can happen. Indeed, participants in the CUE8 study have responded with a satisfaction rating of 100 quite often.

A practical solution is to scale the responses in such a way as to avoid the two boundaries, which is what the following hack does.

1. add a tiny value to all responses
2. create a divisor by adding twice that value to the maximum value the responses can take
3. divide all responses by that divisor

You may find it inappropriate to mangle a response variable in such an arbitrary way. However, keep in mind that the levels of ordinal responses are highly arbitrary. In terms of measurement theory, all transformations that maintain the order are permitted for ordinal scales. For the following analysis, the data set was further reduced by averaging the scores across tasks and excluding probable cheaters with a ToT < 30s.

```
attach(CUE8)

D_cue8_SUS <-
  D_cue8 %>%
  filter(!is.na(SUS)) %>%
  group_by(Part, Team, Condition) %>%
  dplyr::summarize(
    ToT = sum(ToT),
    SUS = mean(SUS)
  ) %>%
  ungroup() %>%
  filter(ToT > 30) %>%
  mutate(SUS = mascutils::rescale_unit(SUS)) %>%
  as_tbl_obs()

D_cue8_SUS %>%
  ggplot(aes(x = Team, y = SUS)) +
  facet_grid(~Condition) +
  geom_violin() +
  geom_count()
```

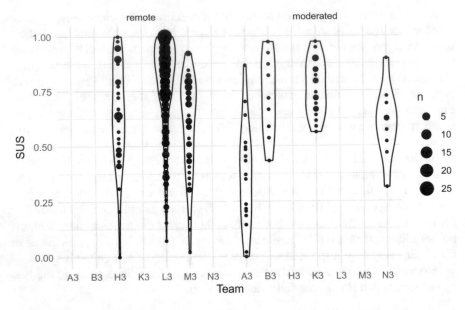

Fig. 7.29 Response distribution of SUS ratings across teams and conditions

Table 7.25 Population-level coefficients with random effects standard deviations

Fixef	Center	Lower	Upper	SD_Team
Intercept	0.771	−0.131	1.645	0.678
Conditionmoderated	−0.300	−1.572	0.958	

```
M_5_bet <-
  D_cue8_SUS %>%
  brm(SUS ~ Condition + (1 | Team),
    family = Beta(link = "logit"),
    data = .
  )

fixef_ml(M_5_bet)
```

Do participants in remote sessions feel less satisfied? There seems to be a slight disadvantage, but we cannot confirm this with sufficient certainty (Table 7.25). In contrast, the variation between teams is substantial, which indicates that SUS ratings are not independent of the particular setting. That is rather concerning for a widely used and allegedly validated rating scale.

7.5 Beyond Mean: Distributional Models

The framework of GLM, as flexible as it has proven to be up to this point, has one major limitation: it only renders the relationship between predictors and the mean of the distribution. We only think in terms of impact factors that improve (or damage) average response times, error rates, satisfaction ratings, etc. As we have seen multiple times in Chap. 6, variance matters too. With multi-level models we can estimate variance within a sample and even compare variance across samples, like in the CUE8 case, where more variance is due to teams rather than due to participants.

What cannot be done with plain multi-level models is estimate effects on variance, like: "Do teams in CUE8 differ in the variation of responses?". That brings me to the final feature of modern regression modeling in the scope of this book. With *distributional models*, we can put predictors on any distribution parameter that we want, not just location μ.

All but the one-parameter distributions come with additional parameters that allow to accommodate the dispersion of the error distribution, or even its skew in the case of Exgaussian models. In the following, I will present two application scenarios for distributional models. We start with a designometric problem when using bi-polar rating scales (see 7.4.) In the next section, I will illustrate the problem on simulated data from two items with different anchoring. Then, we will examine a real data set and we will see how differently participants exploit the range of a scale, which leads to another distributional model.

7.5.1 Item-Level Anchoring in Rating Scales

As a first illustration, imagine two versions of a continuous rating scale for visual beauty that differ in how their anchors are labeled. The first question is moderately labeled, the second is extreme.

1. like the ugliest website I have ever seen: 0 ——— 1 like the most beautiful website
2. distgusting as a screenshot from a splatter movie: 0 ——— 1 like the most beautiful impressionist painting.

For the sake of simplicity (not for a strong research design), let us assume that one participant has rated a sample of 400 websites in two conditions: moderate anchoring and extreme anchoring. The following simulates data such that both anchorings have the same location (mu), but the moderate anchoring condition produces a much more exploitation of the range. Note that Beta distribution's parameter phi does not increase variance, but just the opposite: the range of the scale is expanded, which lets the variance shrink. A comparable effect can be seen in a binomial process, where more trials lead to a more tightly shaped distribution (Fig. 7.30).

```
set.seed(42)

N <- 400
```

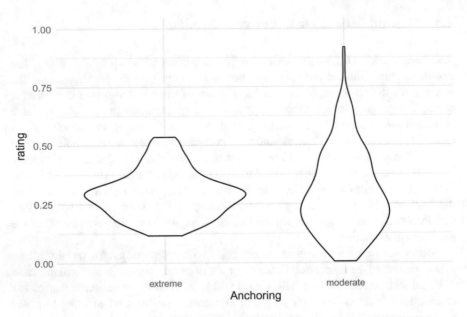

Fig. 7.30 Extreme and moderate anchoring produce differently varied response distributions

```
Conditions <-
  tribble(
    ~Anchoring, ~mu, ~phi,
    "extreme",  .3, 18,
    "moderate", .3, 6
  ) %>%
  mutate(
    a = mu * phi,
    b = phi - mu * phi
  )

D_Anchor <-
  tibble(
    Obs = 1:N,
    Anchoring = rep(c("extreme", "moderate"), N / 2)
  ) %>%
  left_join(Conditions) %>%
  mutate(rating = rbeta(N, a, b))

D_Anchor %>%
  ggplot(aes(x = Anchoring, y = rating)) +
  geom_violin() +
  ylim(0, 1)
```

Note that the `rbeta` command uses a different parametrization of beta distribution, with parameters `a` and `b`, which have are linked to the distribution mean and variance in rather convoluted ways.

Table 7.26 Parameter estimates with 95% credibility limits

Parameter	Fixef	Center	Lower	Upper
b_Anchoringextreme	Anchoringextreme	0.294	0.281	0.307
b_Anchoringmoderate	Anchoringmoderate	0.301	0.276	0.325
b_phi_Anchoringextreme		20.833	17.199	25.171
b_phi_Anchoringmoderate		5.717	4.701	6.842

The two response distributions have the same location, but the more narrow anchoring produces a wider dispersion of responses. How would we confirm this statistically? The Brms engine can link predictors to *any* other parameter of the response distribution, which the author of the package calls *distributional models*. They have an immense potential as they relax another assumption of GLM, namely that all variance parameters must strictly follow the mean-variance relationship demanded by a distribution family. As we have seen, one can easily create a case where this assumption is violated.

For Beta distributions, a large ϕ indicates less dispersion. Accordingly, when used in a distributional model, a positive effect decreases variance.

When estimating dispersion or scale parameters, we have to regard that these are positive, strictly. The Brms engine simply extends the principle of link functions to parameters other than the μ and sets a default log link for ϕ. In order to estimate the changes in μ and ϕ simultaneously, the brms engine receives two regression formulas. Having multiple formulas for a regression model is a notable extension of the R model specification language, which is why Brms brings its own command bf() to collect these. We run a distributional Beta regression on the simulated rating scale responses

```
M_beta <- brm(bf(
  rating ~ 0 + Anchoring,
  phi ~ 0 + Anchoring
),
family = Beta(),
data = D_Anchor
)
```

The parameter table below contains the two regular coefficients on location and, as expected, there is little difference. The intercept on scale parameter ϕ is the scale in the narrow condition (with wider variance). The treatment effect on ϕ is positive on the log scale, which means it deflates variance, just as expected (Table 7.26).

```
posterior(M_beta) %>%
  mutate(value = if_else(str_detect(parameter, "phi"),
    exp(value),
    inv_logit(value)
  )) %>%
  clu()
```

With such a distributional model, we can discover differences in anchoring. And, even better, we can account for it. It intuitively makes sense to mix items with extreme and modest anchoring. By merging a distributional model with a designometric multi-level model 6.8.4, we can evaluate and use such heterogeneous scales. The general concept is shown in the next section, where we account for participant-level employment of scale.

7.5.2   Participant-Level Employment of Scale

In the previous section, we have seen how to discover differences in anchoring of items. What is seen frequently in designometric studies is different response patterns in participants, in particular how much they tend to use the extremes. We can account for that by letting the variance parameter vary across participants. The following model comprises:

1. a structural part for the mean with a fixed-effects polynomial term and a participant-level random effect for the response curve.
2. a structural part for scale parameter `phi` with a participant-level random effect on the scale parameter `phi`
3. a Beta shape of randomness

```
attach(Uncanny)

RK_1 <-
  RK_1 %>%
  mutate(response_unit = mascutils::rescale_centered(response,
scale = .99) + 1)

M_poly_3_beta <-
  brm(
    formula = response_unit ~ 1 + huMech1 + huMech2 + huMech3 +
      (1 + huMech1 + huMech2 + huMech3 | Part),
    family = Beta(),
    data = RK_1,
    inits = 0
  )

M_poly_3_beta_dist <-
  brm(
    formula = bf(
      response_unit ~ 1 + huMech1 + huMech2 + huMech3 +
        (1 + huMech1 + huMech2 + huMech3 | Part),
      phi ~ 1 + (1 | Part)
    ),
    family = Beta(),
    data = RK_1,
    inits = 0
  )
```

Note that on such more exotic and complex models, the regression engine sometimes has difficulties in finding valid starting values for the MCMC walk. Like here, it often helps to fix all starting values to Zero. If participants show different employment of scale, we should see that on the participant-level standard deviation of `phi`.

```
ranef(M_poly_3_beta_dist) %>%
  filter(nonlin == "phi") %>%
```

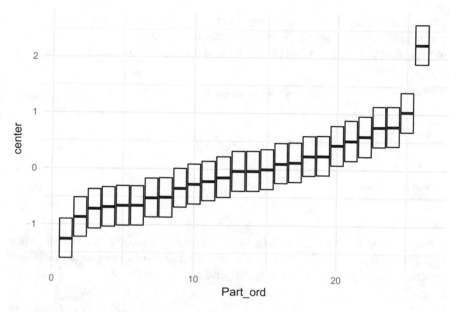

Fig. 7.31 Participant-level random effects for scale parameter phi

```
mutate(Part_ord = dense_rank(center)) %>%
ggplot(aes(x = Part_ord, y = center, ymin = lower, ymax = upper)) +
geom_crossbar()
```

Figure 7.31 shows (on the linearized scale) that participants vary considerably around the population-level value of phi ($\approx$ 1.4). While a regular Beta model adjusts the variance according to the usual mean-variance relationship, the distributional model also accounts for overall broader and narrower distributions. We would probably see some subtle adjustments in predictive plots, but this model is too complex for visual analysis (as every participant get their own phi). Therefore, we defer a deeper inspection to @ref(choos_resp), where we demonstrate the superiority of the distributional model using information criteria.

7.5.3 Participant-Level Skew in Reaction Times

In Sect. 7.3.2, the Exgaussian model seemed to sit well with reaction times, accommodating their left skew better than Gaussian or Gamma distributions. But if we review the participant-level plots carefully, we see that the shape of randomness differ between participants. There is visible differences in variance, as well as in skew.

The following distributional model estimates the same location effects (PrimeGeek), but granting all participants their own variance and skew. The maximum distributional model would estimate fully separate distributions per every participant and condition. But, since the two response distributions (Geek/nogeek) appear similar in the plots, a reduced predictor term is used, assuming that variance and shape are not affected by the experimental condition, but only the person doing the task. That is further justified by the fact that the effect of priming categories were meager at best.

```
attach(Hugme)

M_1_exg_dist <-
  brm(
    formula = bf(
      RT ~ 1 + PrimeGeek + (1 + PrimeGeek | Part),
      sigma ~ 1 + (1 | Part),
      beta ~ 1 + (1 | Part)
    ),
    family = exgaussian(),
    data = D_hugme,
    inits = 0
  )
```

First, we extract the fixed effects, as well as the group-level standard deviation from the posterior. If participants show different patterns of randomness, we should see that in participant-level variation of σ and β.

```
P_1_exg_dist <- posterior(M_1_exg_dist)

ranef(P_1_exg_dist) %>%
  filter(nonlin %in% c("sigma", "beta")) %>%
  group_by(nonlin) %>%
  mutate(Part_ord = dense_rank(center)) %>%
  ungroup() %>%
  ggplot(aes(x = Part_ord, y = center, ymin = lower, ymax = upper)) +
  facet_grid(~nonlin) +
  geom_crossbar()
```

Figure 7.32 confirms, that participants vary significantly in how there RTs are dispersed (`sigma`), as well as how skewed they are (`beta`). Finally, we can also examine whether there are any associations between location, variance and skew. Recall that parameter `beta` gives the model the flexibility to add extra skew for when the location is far from the left boundary. If that were the case, we would see a correlation between participant-level random effects between location and skew.

```
P_1_exg_dist %>%
  filter(type == "ranef" & fixef == "Intercept") %>%
  mutate(
    dist_par = str_match(parameter, "beta|sigma"),
    dist_par = if_else(is.na(dist_par), "mu", dist_par)
  ) %>%
  group_by(dist_par, re_entity) %>%
  summarize(center = median(value)) %>%
  ungroup() %>%
  spread(key = dist_par, value = center) %>%
  select(-re_entity) %>%
  corrr::correlate()
```

One could get excited about the strong correlation between `mu` and `beta` in Table 7.27, but recall that the amount of skew introduced by `beta` is proportional to the location. At the same time, we see a mild correlation between `mu` and `sigma`, which is just the usual mean-variance relationship, which most other distribution families have already factored in. In Chap. 8, we will learn how to compare models

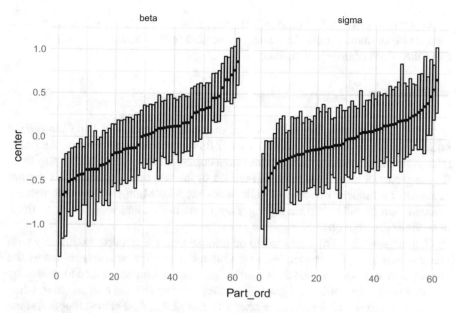

Fig. 7.32 Participant-level random effects for sigma in beta

Table 7.27 Correlations between individual location (mu), variance (sigma) and skewness (beta)

term	Beta	mu	Sigma
Beta		0.800	0.272
mu	0.800		0.463
Sigma	0.272	0.463	

by predictive accuracy. As it will turn out in 8.2.5, the distributional Beta model in the Hugme case has a better predictive accuracy than the location-only model.

Distributional models can do more than just better accommodate data. Applied researchers and experimentalists traditionally embrace on-average effects, but have been mostly blind to effects on variance. In safety relevant systems, strong variance can be a real problem, because this implies that extremely poor performance is becoming more likely, increasing the risk of hazard. For such systems, variance is a crucial parameter and the dispersion effects of design changes should be tracked carefully. For the readers interested in exercising this technique, several data sets from this book are candidates for such an analysis:

- CUE8: Do teams differ in the variance of ToT variance?
- Egan: What is the most robust web design (the one that reduces variance)?
- IPump: Does training (or the Novel design) reduce variance?

Experimentalists should scratch their heads too and take a fresh look at their theories. Systematic variation in variance can give further clues about what is going on in the minds of their participants.

In the last three chapters, we have met the family of models called *Generalized Multi-level Linear Models* (GLMM). Linear linear models mainly rest on the linear term, a simple mechanism that unfolds into a combinatoric explosion of possibilities for the predictor side. Groudning on the idea of factors, this is conceptually further expanded by random effects and multi-level models. Multi-level models redeem variance as a first-class citizen among model parameters, and we got used to think in terms of distributions.

Generalized Linear Models expand on that perspective and deal exclusively with the response side of a model. We saw that for all design research measures the Gaussian model is wrong and an (almost) right distribution can just be identified by just following a few rules. Is it just me, or does this feel like the sudden relief, when you untie a pair of bad fitting shoes after a full day hike. And almost literally, some real pain goes away, like ordered factors for a learning curve and saturation effects.

The recent past have seen many researchers beginning to see the beauty of the New Statistics approach. Suddenly, people start thinking of models, rather than arcane procedures, and start tinkering. Then their favorite regression engine gets a new feature, say distributional models, and it is always worth a try to improve a model.

Ironically, the abundance of possibilities leaves open the question of when to stop. How do we decide whether introducing, say distributional random effects, really improves the model? As we will see in the final chapter, there are two opposite forces at work, model complexity, which is to be avoided, and model fit. Let's tie our shoes one more time and get a good hold!

7.6 Further Readings

1. In [2], more variations of ordinal models are demonstrated using the Brms regression engine
2. The extended formula interface of package Brms is explained in [3], including distributional and even non-linear models.
3. The Rasch model is famous in psychometrics. It can be estimated as a logistic regression model with crossed random effects for persons and items [4].

References

1. Carpenter B et al (2017) Stan : a probabilistic programming language. J Stat Softw 76(1). ISSN: 1548-7660. https://doi.org/10.18637/jss.v076.i01
2. Bürkner P-C, Vuorre M (2019) Ordinal regression models in psychology: a tutorial. Adv Methods Pract Psychol Sci 2(1):77–101. ISSN: 2515-2459. https://doi.org/10.1177/2515245918823199
3. Bürkner P-C (2018) Advanced Bayesian multilevel modeling with the R package brms. In: The R Journal 10.1, pp. 395–411. ISSN: 2073-4859
4. Doran H et al (2007) Estimating the multilevel rasch model: with the lme4 package. J Stat Softw 20(2):1–18. ISSN: 1548-7660. http://www.jstatsoft.org/v20/i02

Chapter 8
Working with Models

In Chaps. 4 and 6, we have seen a marvelous variety of models spawning from just two basic principles, linear combination of multiple effects and Gaussian distribution. Chapter 7 further expanded the variety of models, letting us choose response distributions that sit snug on the outcome variable. This chapter is dedicated to methods that assess how snug a model is.

We begin with model criticsm Sect. 8.1, where we examine one model at a time and visually explore how well it fits our data. This section only refers to the Gaussian population-level linear models from Chap. 4, making it a good follow-up for readers who have just worked through that chapter. With linear models, we can combine and recombine any set of predictors in many ways. We saw examples, where the more simple of two model seemed to work better, but often it was the more complex conditional effects model that was closer to the data. We will use graphical methods to assess *goodness-of-fit*, which scrutinizes the structural part of linear models. The random part of linear models is fixed, in that errors follows Gaussian distribution, with a constant variance. Checking these assumptions is based on *residual analysis*.

In Sect. 8.2.4, we turn to the comparison of multiple models and we will see that the best model can be defined as the one that creates the most accurate *forecasts*. It turns out that goodness-of-fit is not sufficient for forecasting accuracy, but must be balanced by *model parsimony*. Leave-one-out cross validation Sect. 8.2.2 is a general technique for estimating forecasting accuracy, but is also very computing intensive. In many cases, *information criteria* approximate the relative accuracy of models well and are blazing fast. We will see that modern Bayesian information criteria, such as the WAIC, apply to a huge class of models, including all linear and linearized, multi-level and distributional models introduced throughout the book. We will revisit earlier cases and use model selection to justify choices between models we made earlier:

- The log-linearized Poisson model is a better approximation to teh learning curve, compared to the Gaussian ordered factor model Sect. 7.2.1.2.

© Springer Nature Switzerland AG 2021
M. Schmettow, *New Statistics for Design Researchers*,
Human–Computer Interaction Series,
https://doi.org/10.1007/978-3-030-46380-9_8

- The Exgaussian model for ToT and RT is compared to the Gamma and Gaussian models (Sect. 7.3.2).
- A multi-level distributional Beta model adjusts for different response styles when rating eeriness of robots faces (Sect. 7.5.2).

While the primary aim of model selection in New Statistics is drawing quantitative conclusions from data, in Sects. 8.2.6 and 8.2.7, I will show how model selection applies to statistical *hypothesis testing* and verify that the observations in the Uncanny Valley confirm predictions from theory.

8.1   Model Criticism

For a start, I would like to contrast the overall approach of model criticism to the work-flow frequently encountered in classic statistics. Boldly speaking, classically trained researchers often assume that the "assumptions of ANOVA" need to be checked beforehand. Often a process called *assumptions checking* is carried out before the researcher actually dares to hit the button labeled as *RUN ANOVA*. As we will see in this section, the order of actions is just the other way round. The straightforward way to check the integrity of a model is to first fit it and then examine it to find the flaws, which is called *model criticism.*

Another symptom of the classic workflow is the battery of arcane non-parametric tests that are often carried out. This practice has long been criticized in the statistical literature for its logical flaws and practical limitations. Here, I will fully abandon hypothesis tests for model criticism and demonstrate graphical methods, which are based on two additional types of estimates we can extract from linear models, next to coefficients:

1. with *residuals*, we test the assumptions on the shape of randomness
2. with *fitted responses*, we check the structural part of the model.

8.1.1   Residual Analysis

So far, it seems, linear models equip us well for a vast variety of research situations. We can produce continuous and factorial models, account for saturation effects, discover conditional effects and even do the weirdest curved forms, just by the magic of linear combination. However, Gaussian linear models make strict assumptions about the linear random term

$$y_i \sim N(\mu_i, \sigma_\epsilon)$$

In words, the random term says: *observed values y_i are drawn from a Gaussian distribution located at fitted response μ_i, having a fixed standard deviation σ_ϵ.*

In the notation displayed above, there are indeed as many distributions as there are observed values (due the subscript in μ_i). It appears impossible to evaluate not just one distribution, but many. However, an equivalent notation is routinely used for linear models, that specifies just one *residual distribution*. For the LRM, that is

$$\mu_i = \beta_0 + \beta_1 x_1$$
$$y_i = \mu_i + \epsilon_i$$
$$\epsilon_i \sim \text{Gaus}(0, \sigma_\epsilon)$$

In this notation, observed values y_i are decomposed into predicted values and *individual* residuals ϵ_i. These are frequently called *errors*, hence the greek symbol ϵ. The standard deviation of residuals σ_ϵ is called the *standard error*. The random pattern of the model can now be expressed as a single Gaussian distribution. Residual analysis looks at the pattern of randomness and whether it compares to the assumption of all linear models, *Gaussian distribution* with a*constant variance*. The reason why I did not use this notation routinely is that, it only works for linear models, but not for models with other random patterns. More specifically, Generalized Linear Models Chap. 7 cannot be specified that way.

As we have seen in Sect. 3.5.2, Gaussian distributions are one pattern of randomness among many and this choice may, therefore, be appropriate or not. As a heuristic, if observed values are located rather in the middle of the possible range of measurement (and avoid the edges), Gaussian distributions work well. But, like linearity is compromised by saturation, a distribution is affected when squeezed against a hard boundary, as has been discussed in Sect. 7.1.

Throughout the book, we have extracted fitted responses μ_i from estimated models. By plotting fitted responses, we can evaluate the structural part of the model, which typically carries the research question. By visual comparison of fitted responses and observations, we can determine whether the structural part has the right form.

8.1.1.1 Gaussian Residual Distribution

The first assumption of randomness underlying the linear model simply is that the distribution follows a Gaussian distribution. Visually, Gaussian distributions is characterized by

- one curved peak (unimodality)
- from which density smoothly declines towards both ends (smoothness)
- at same rates (symmetry)

For a rough evaluation of this assumption, it suffices to extract the residuals from the model at hand and plot it as a distribution. The `residuals` command returns a vector of residual values, exactly one per observation. With the vector of residuals at hand, we can evaluate this assumption by comparing the residual distribution to its theoretically expected form, a perfect bell curve. The following command chain extracts the residuals from the model and pipes them into the ggplot engine to create a histogram. With `stat_function` an overlay is created with the theoretical Gaussian distribution, which is centered at zero. The standard error σ_ϵ has been estimated alongside the coefficients and is extracted using the function `clu`.

```
attach(BrowsingAB)

tibble(resid = residuals(M_age_shft)) %>%
  ggplot(aes(x = resid)) +
  geom_histogram(aes(y = ..density..), bins = 15) +
  stat_function(
    fun = dnorm,
    args = c(
      mean = 0,
      sd = clu(M_age_shft,
        type = "disp"
      )$center
    ),
    color = "red"
  )
```

The match of residual distribution with the theoretical distribution is not perfect, but overall this model seems to sufficiently satisfy the normality assumption. To give a counter example, we estimate the same model using the outcome variable `returns`,

Table 8.1 Parameter estimates with 95% credibility limits

Parameter	Fixef	Center	Lower	Upper
Intercept	Intercept	0.921	0.527	1.313
age_shft	age_shft	0.012	0.000	0.023
sigma_resid		1.316	1.198	1.458

which captures the number of times a participant had (disparately) returned to the homepage (Table 8.1).

```
M_age_rtrn <-
  stan_glm(returns ~ 1 + age_shft, data = BAB1)
P_age_rtrn <- posterior(M_age_rtrn)

T_age_rtrn <- clu(P_age_rtrn)
T_age_rtrn
```

We now graphically compare the distribution of estimated residuals against the Gaussian distribution with the same standard error. The first chain in the code extracts the center estimate from the table of estimates. The command `stat_function` is plotting the Gaussian curve (Fig. 8.1).

```
C_age_rtrn_sd <-
  T_age_rtrn %>%
  filter(parameter == "sigma_resid") %>%
  select(center) %>%
  as.numeric()

tibble(resid = residuals(M_age_rtrn)) %>%
  ggplot(aes(x = resid)) +
  geom_histogram(aes(y = ..density..),
    bins = 20,
    color = "black",
    fill = "white"
  ) +
  stat_function(
    fun = dnorm,
    args = c(
      mean = 0,
      sd = C_age_rtrn_sd
    )
  ) +
  xlim(-5, 5)
```

The estimation produces the usual coefficients, as well as a standard error. However, the residuals do not even remotely resemble the theoretical curve, it rather is

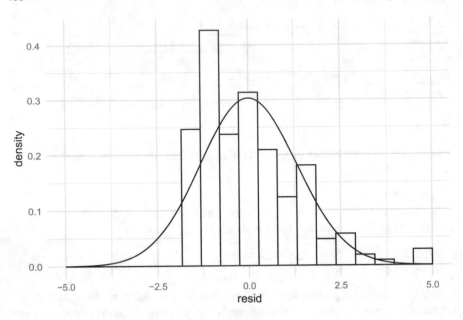

Fig. 8.1 Visual assessment of Gaussian distribution of errors

asymmetric, with a steep rise to the left and a long tail to the right. That is a typical outcome when count measures get too close to the left boundary.

How about unimodality? We have not discussed any multimodal theoretical distributions in Sect. 3.5.2, but one has been displayed in Sect. 2.1.3. In brief, a bimodal residual distribution can arise, when two groups exist in the data, which lay far apart. The following code illustrates the situation by simulating a simple data set with two groups, that is fed into a GMM. The result is a bimodal residual distribution, as in Fig. 8.2

```
attach(Chapter_LM)

set.seed(42)
D_bimod <-
  bind_rows(
    tibble(Group = "A", y = rnorm(50, 4, 1)),
    tibble(Group = "B", y = rnorm(50, 8, 1))
  )

M_bimod <- stan_glm(y ~ 1, data = D_bimod, iter = 500)

D_bimod %>%
  mutate(resid = residuals(M_bimod)) %>%
  ggplot(aes(x = resid)) +
  geom_histogram(aes(y = ..density..),
    bins = 20,
```

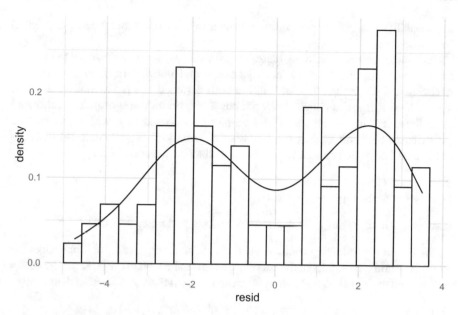

Fig. 8.2 A bimodal distribution indicates a strong unknown factor

```
        color = "black",
        fill = "white"
) +
geom_density()
```

These two deviations from Gaussian distribution have very different causes: asymmetry is caused by scales with boundaries. This is an often arising situation and it is gracefully solved by Generalized Linear Models Chap. 7.

Multimodality is caused by heterogeneous groups in the data like experimental conditions, design or type of user. For a grouping structure to cause distinguished multimodality, differences between groups have to be pronounced in relation to the standard error. It is often the case, that these variables are controlled conditions, such as in an AB test. It is also quite likely that strong grouping structures can be thought of beforehand and be recorded. For example, in usability tests with diverse user samples, it almost comes natural to distinguish between users who have used the design before and those who did not. If the grouping variable is recorded, the solution is group comparison models Sect. 4.3.1, already introduced.

Visual assessment of symmetry and unimodality is simple and effective in many cases. But, Gaussian distributions are not the only ones to have these properties. At least logistic distributions and t-distributions are unbounded and symmetric, too, with subtle differences in curvature. Gaussian and t-distributions differ in how quickly probability drops in the tails. Gaussian distributions drop much faster, meaning that extreme events are practically impossible. With t-distributions, extreme values drop in probability too, but the possibility of catastrophies (or wonders) stays substantial for a long time.

As a more advanced method, *quantile-quantile (qq) plots* can be used to evaluate subtle deviations in curvature (and symmetry and unimodality). In qq-plots, the observed and theoretical distributions are both flattened and put against each other. This is a powerful and concise method, but it is a bit hard to grasp. The following code illustrates the construction of a qq-plot that compares GMM residuals of a t-distributed measure against the Gaussian distribution. We simulate t-distributed data, run a GMM and extract residuals, as well as the standard error σ_ϵ.

```
set.seed(2)
D_t <- tibble(y = rt(200, 2))

M_t <- stan_glm(y ~ 1, data = D_t, iter = 500)
```

We obtain the following residual and theoretical distributions. It is approximately symmetric and unimodal, but the curvature seems to be a bit off (Fig. 8.3). The center is taller and extreme residuals seem far more frequent than by Gaussian distribution.

```
D_t <- mutate(D_t, resid = residuals(M_t))

C_sigma <- rstanarm::sigma(M_t)

D_t %>%
  ggplot(aes(x = resid)) +
  geom_histogram(aes(y = ..density..)) +
  stat_function(
    fun = dnorm,
    args = c(
      mean = 0,
      sd = C_sigma
    ),
    color = "red"
  )
```

The example shown in Fig. 8.3 is rather pronounced. More subtle deviations would be hard to spot in the histogram. For the qq-plot, we calculate the quantiles of observed and theoretical distributions. Quantiles are produced in fixed steps, say 1%, 2%, ... 99%%. Finally, theoretical and observed quantiles are put against each other in a scatterplot like Fig. 8.4.

```
D_QQ <- tibble(
  step = 0:100 / 100,
  quant_obs = quantile(D_t$resid, step),
  quant_theo = qnorm(step, 0, C_sigma)
)
```

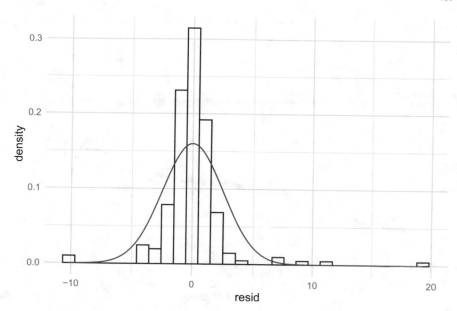

Fig. 8.3 Symmetric residual distribution with different curvature

```
D_QQ %>%
    ggplot(aes(x = quant_theo, y = quant_obs)) +
    geom_point() +
    geom_abline(slope = 1, intercept = 0, col = "red")
```

In the ideal case, they match perfectly and the quantiles are on a straight line. Instead, we see a rotated sigmoid shape and this is typical for fat-tailed distributions such as t. The shape is symmetric with turning points at around −4 and 4 on the theoretical scale. In the middle part, the relation is almost linear, however, not matching a 1-by-1. The t distribution loses probability mass rather quickly when moving from the center to the turning points. From these points, the theoretical quantiles start to lag behind. The lower and upper 1% sampled quantiles go to much more extreme values, ranging from −10 to almost 20, whereas the Gaussian distribution renders such events practically impossible. Generally, a rotated sigmoid shape is typical for fat-tailed distributions. The problem of misusing a Gaussian distribution is that it dramatically underestimates extreme events. Have you ever asked yourself, why in the1990s, the risk for a nuclear meltdown were estimated to be one in 10.000 years, in face of two such tragic events in the past 40 years? Rumor tells, researchers used the Gaussian distribution for the risk models, under-estimating the risk of extreme events.

Once mastered, the qq-plot is the swiss knife of distribution check. Next to the subtleties, we can also easily discover deviations from symmetry. Fortunately, we do not always have to do the quantile calculations, since the Ggplot package provides a

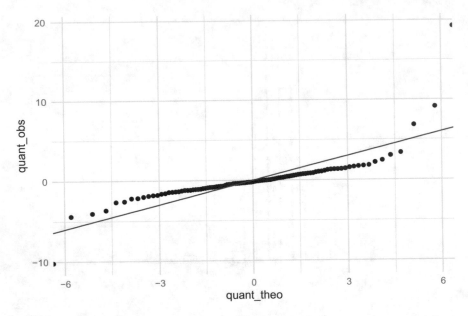

Fig. 8.4 A qq-plot reveals the heavier tails of the observed distribution

convenient geometry for the purpose, geom_qq. This command produces Fig. 8.5, showing how the residuals look like for the associations between age and returns-to-homepage events.

```
tibble(resid = residuals(BrowsingAB$M_age_rtrn)) %>%
  ggplot(aes(sample = resid)) +
  geom_qq(distribution = qnorm) +
  geom_abline(intercept = 0, slope = 1, col = "red")
```

To the left, extreme values have a lower probability than predicted by the Gaussian distribution, but the right tail is much fatter, once again. We also see how residuals are clumped, which is characteristic for discrete (as compared to continuous) outcome measures. This is poor behavior of the model and, generally, when a model is severely mis-specified, neither predictions nor estimates, nor certainty statements can be fully trusted. A model that frequently fits in case of count numbers is Poisson regression, which will enter the stage in Sect. 7.2.1.

8.1.1.2   Constant Variance

In Sect. 8.1.1.1, we assessed one assumption that underlies all linear models, namely Gaussian distribution of residuals. The second assumption underlying the linear model random (or residual) is that residual variance is constant, which means it does

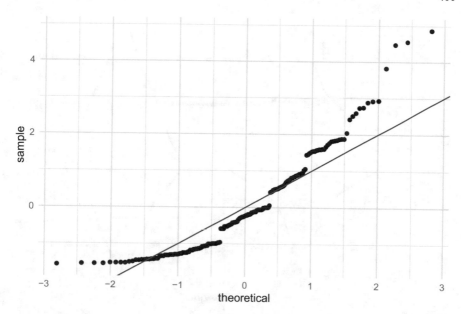

Fig. 8.5 Residual analysis with qq-plots

not change by any factor or across a scale. In the model notation, this is reflected by the fact that there is just a single σ_ϵ.

Before we dive into the matter of checking the assumption, let's do a brief reality check using common sense

1. Consider people's daily commute to work. Suppose you ask a few persons you know: "What is your typical way to work and what is the longest and the shortest duration you remember?". In statistical terms, you are asking for a center estimate and (informal) error dispersion. Is it plausible that a person with typical travel time of 5 minutes experienced the same variation as another person with a typical time of 50 min?
2. Consider an experiment to assess a typing training. Is it plausible that the dispersion of typing errors before the training is the same as after the training?

In both cases, we would rather not expect constant variance and it is actually quite difficult to think of a process, where a strong change in average performance is not associated with a change in dispersion. The constant variance assumption, like the normality assumption is a usual suspect when approximating with linear models. We will come back to that down below.

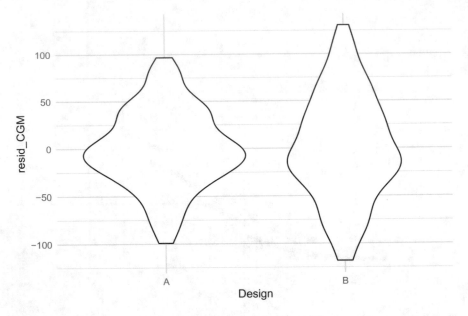

Fig. 8.6 Checking constant variance of residuals in factorial models

In a similar way, we can ask: can it be taken for granted that residual variance is constant when comparing two or more groups? Would you blindly assume that two rather different designs produce the same amount of spread around the average? It may be so, but one can easily think of reasons, why this might be different. We check the situation in the CGM of the BrowsingAB study. Do both design conditions have the same residual variance? Again, we extract the residuals, add them to the data set and produce a desnsity plot (Fig. 8.6).

```
attach(BrowsingAB)

BAB1 %>%
  mutate(resid_CGM = residuals(M_CGM)) %>%
  ggplot(aes(x = Design, y = resid_CGM)) +
  geom_violin()
```

Both sets of residuals are reasonably symmetric, but it appears that design B produces more widely spread residuals. Something in the design causes individual performance to vary stronger from the population mean. The cause of this effect has been disclosed in Sect. 5.4.2. (In essence, design B is rather efficient to use for younger users, whereas older users seem to have severe issues.)

Visual checks of constant variance for factors is straightforward using common boxplots. For continuous predictors, such as age, requires a more uncommon graphical representation known as *quantile plots* (Fig. 8.7).

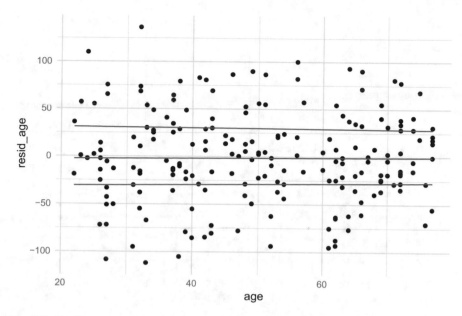

Fig. 8.7 Checking constant variance of residuals in continuous models

```
BAB1 %>%
  mutate(resid_age = residuals(M_age)) %>%
  ggplot(aes(x = age, y = resid_age)) +
  geom_point() +
  geom_quantile()
```

The quantile plot uses a smoothing algorithm to picture the trend of quantiles (25%, 50% and 75%). Here, the quantiles run almost horizontal and parallel, which confirms constant variance. Taking this as a starting point, we can evaluate more complex models, too. The grouped regression model on age and design just requires to create a grouped quantile plot. This looks best using faceting, rather than separating by color (Fig. 8.8):

```
BAB1 %>%
  mutate(resid_grm_1 = residuals(M_grm_1)) %>%
  ggplot(aes(x = age_shft, y = resid_grm_1)) +
  facet_grid(~Design) +
  geom_point() +
  geom_quantile()
```

This looks rather worrying. Especially with Design A, the residuals are not constant, but increase with age. In addition, we observe that residuals are not even centered at zero across the whole range. For design A, the residual distribution moves from positive centered to negative centered, design B vice versa. That also casts

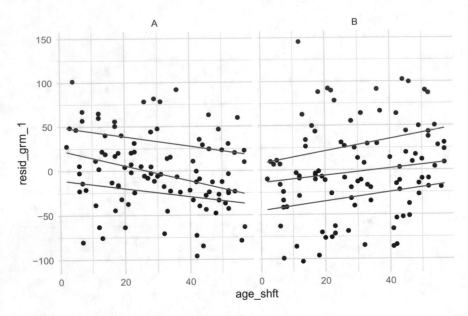

Fig. 8.8 Checking residuals in a grouped continuous model

doubts on the validity of the LRM on age: these contrariwise trends seem to mix into an almost even distribution. It seems that a lot more has been going on in this (simulated) study, than would be captured by any of these models.

Another model type we may want to check with quantile plots is the MRM. With two continuous predictors, one might be tempted to think of a three-dimensional quantile plot, but this is not recommended. Rather, we can use a generalization of quantile plots, where the x-axis is not mapped to the predictor directly, but the predicted values μ_i. We assess the residual variance on the MRM model on the AUP study, where resistance to fall for the active user paradox has been predicted by geekism tendencies and need-for-cognition (Fig. 8.9))

```
attach(AUP)

AUP_1 %>%
  mutate(
    resid_3 = residuals(M_3),
    mu_3 = predict(M_3)$center
  ) %>%
  ggplot(aes(x = mu_3, y = resid_3)) +
  geom_point() +
  geom_quantile()
```

We observe a clear trend in quantiles, with residual dispersion increasing with predicted values. Generally, plotting residuals against predicted values can be done

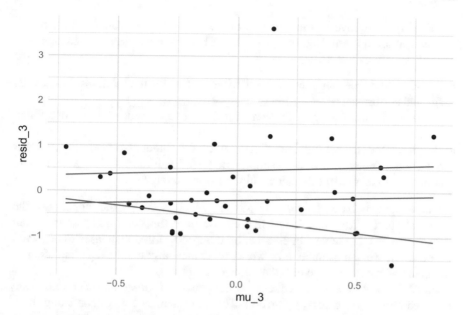

Fig. 8.9 Yet another violation of constant distribution

with any model, irrespective of the number and types of predictors. However, interpretation is more limited than when plotting them against predictors directly. In fact, interpretation boils down to the intuition we introduced at the beginning of the section, that larger outcomes typically have larger dispersion. This is almost always a compelling assumption, or even a matter of underlying physics and, once again, a linear model may or may not be a reasonable approximation. Fortunately, Generalized Linear Models Chap. 7, provide more reasonable defaults for the relationship between predicted values and dispersion. In contrast, residual variance per predictor allows to discover more surprising issues, such as conditional effects or heterogeneity in groups.

8.1.2 Fitted Responses Analysis

Frequently, the research question is how strong the effect of a predictor variable is on the response. This strength of effect is what coefficient table tell us. But, how do we know that the model actually fits the process under examination? We have seen several examples of models that do not align well with the observation, in particular, when plain MPM were used in the presence of conditional effect. Here, I will introduce a technique to assess whether the structural part of a model fits the data well.

The purpose of investigating model fit is to find structural features in the observations that are not rendered by the model at hand. We have already encountered multiple situations like this:

- BrowsingAB: Does an unconditional LRM suffice for the relationship between age and performance?
- IPump: Do both designs have the same learning progress, or do we need conditional effects?
- Uncanny: Does the cubic polynomial provide a right amount of flexibility (number of stationary points), or would a simpler model (a quadratic polynomial) or a more complex model render the relationship more accurately?

The method is based on *fitted responses*, which is the μ_i that appears in the structural üpart of the model. Just like coefficient estimates, fitted responses can be extracted as CLU tables. In essence, by comparing fitted responses to observed responses y_i, we can examine how well a model actually fits the data and identify find potential patterns in the data that the model ignores.

Fitted responses are more frequently called *predicted values*, and accordingly are extracted by the `predict()` function. This term is in two ways confusing: first, what values? Fair enough, but the second is more profound: The "predicted values" is suggesting that you can use them for forecasting future responses. Well, you can, but only after you tested forecasting accuracy. In Sect. 8.2.1, we will see that one can easily create a snug fitting model, without any value for forecasting. As [1] points out, one should rather call predicted values *retrodictions*. I believe the better term is fitted responses, because it reminds us that we are talking about *idealized responses under one model*. That should keep imaginations in check. The match between idealized responses and the *original* observations is called *model fit*. And that is *"fit" as in "fitted"* and not as in "fitness".

We can always compute fitted responses by placing the estimated coefficients into the model formula. A more convenient way is to use the standard command `predict()` on the model object. The package Bayr provides a tidy version, that produces tidy CLU tables (Table 8.2).

```
attach(BrowsingAB)

T_pred_age_shft <- predict(M_age_shft)
T_pred_age_shft
```

There will always be as many fitted responses as there are responses and they come in the same order. They can be attached to the original data, which is very useful for evaluating model fit.

```
BAB1 <- BAB1 %>%
  mutate(M_age_shft = T_pred_age_shft$center)
```

Note that here only the center estimate is extracted from the CLU table. Later, this will help to collect fitted responses from multiple models. The evaluation of model

Table 8.2 200 predictions (scale: resp) with 95% credibility limits (8 shown)

Obs	Center	Lower	Upper
23	116.2	21.92	210
35	84.5	−9.22	177
39	114.9	17.34	214
113	102.3	9.55	191
121	83.3	−12.14	175
172	98.3	4.43	196
191	82.1	−9.90	172
196	112.8	14.11	206

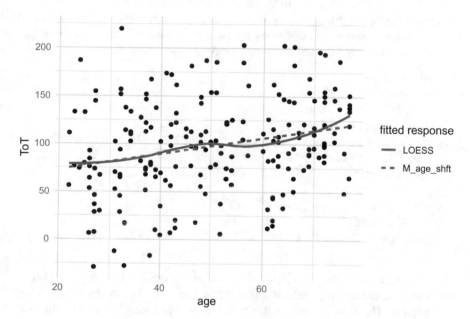

Fig. 8.10 A close match between the linear models predictions and LOESS indicates good linearity

fit is a visual task (at this stage). We start with a plot of the raw data, together with a LOESS (Fig. 8.10).

```
BAR1 %>%
  ggplot(aes(x = age, y = ToT)) +
  geom_point() +
  geom_smooth(aes(linetype =
"LOESS"), se = F) +
  geom_smooth(aes(y = M_age_shft, linetype = "M_age_shft"), se = F) +
  labs(linetype = "fitted response")
```

Note that the sequence of smooth geometries all use different sources for the y coordinate. The literal values for the color aesthetic produce the legend; the legend title is created by labs().

The only two features the LOESS smoother and the linear model have in common is their total upward trend and fitted responses at ages 20 and 50. The LOESS indicates some wobbliness in the response, with something that even could be a local maximum at around age 37. One has to be a little careful here, because LOESS is just another engine that produces a set of fitted responses. LOESS i a very flexible model, and as we will see in Sect. 8.2.1, flexible models tend to overfit, which means that they start to pull noise into the structural part. This results in less accurate forecasts.

In conclusion, LOESS and LRM tell different stories and we cannot tell which one is closer to the truth without further investigation. Conditional effects are always among the suspects, when in comes to non-linearity. The wobbly relationship could be the result of a mixture of conditions. By pulling the factor Design into the graph, we can assess how well the unconditional model fits both conditions.

```
G_Design_age <-
  BAB1 %>%
  ggplot(aes(x = age, y = ToT)) +
  facet_grid(~Design) +
  geom_smooth(aes(linetype = "LOESS"), se = F) +
  geom_point(size = 1) +
  labs(linetype = "fitted response")

G_Design_age + geom_smooth(aes(
  y = M_age_shft,
  linetype = "M_age_shft"
), se = F)
```

As Fig. 8.11 shows, once we look at two designs separately, the LRM fits poorly. For design A, the intercept estimate is too low and slope is too steep, vice versa for design B. The model clearly requires a conditional term, like in the following conditional GRM.

```
M_cgrm <- BAB1 %>%
  stan_glm(ToT ~ Design * age, data = .)

BAB1$M_cgrm <- predict(M_cgrm)$center

G_Design_age %+%
  BAB1 +
  geom_smooth(aes(y = M_cgrm, linetype = "M_cgrm"))
```

As Fig. 8.12 shows, the improved model now captures the overall increment by age in both conditions. Apart from the age-50 dip, the DesignA condition is reasonably fitted. The model also predicts a cross-over point at age of 73, where both designs are equal. In contrast, the model cannot adequately render the association in design

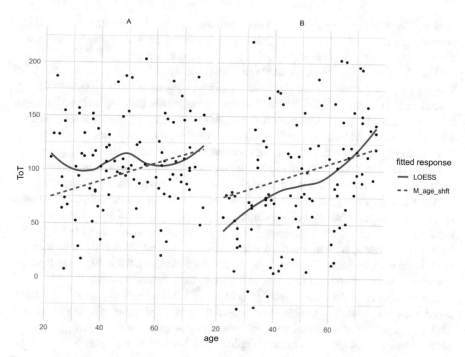

Fig. 8.11 Fitted response analysis per design reveals that the unconditional LRM fits poorly

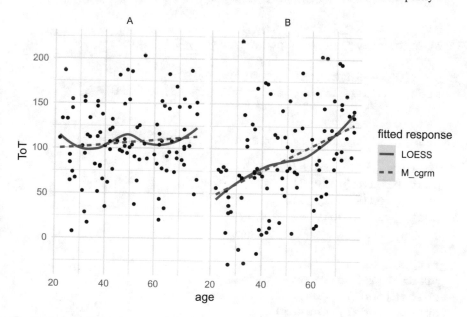

Fig. 8.12 A conditional regression model sitting snug on the LOESS

B, which appears inverse-sigmoid. These non-linear associations stem from a fancy psychological model I have put together over a long night and totally forgot how it went. Let us instead look at some wobbles that are eerily real.

The Uncanny Valley effect is all about non-linearity and we have seen in Sect. 5.5 how a complex curves can be captured by higher-degree polynomials. With every degree added to a polynomial, the model gets one more coefficient. It should be clear by now that models with more coefficients are more flexible. As another example, adding a conditional term to a multi-factorial model lets all group means move freely. The flexibility of a polynomial can be measured by how many stationary points are possible, shoulders and troughs. Higher degree polynomials can do even more tricks, such as saddle points, that have a local slope of zero without changing direction.

Mathur & Reichling identified a cubic polynomial as the lowest degree that would render the Uncanny Valley effect, which has at least one local maximum and one local minimum (both are stationary points). In fact, they also conducted a formal model comparison, which approved that adding higher degrees does not make the model better. Such a formal procedure is introduced in Sect. 8.2.6, whereas here we use visualizations of fitted responses to evaluate the possible models.

In the following, the cubic model is compared to the simpler quadratic model. It could be, after all, that a parable is sufficient to render the valley. On the other side of things, a polynomial model with the ridiculous degree 9 is estimated, just to see whether there is any chance a more complex model would sit more snug on the data.

```
attach(Uncanny)

M_poly_2 <- RK_2 %>%
  stan_glm(avg_like ~ poly(huMech, 2), data = .)

M_poly_3 <- RK_2 %>%
  stan_glm(avg_like ~ poly(huMech, 3), data = .)

M_poly_9 <- RK_2 %>%
  stan_glm(avg_like ~ poly(huMech, 9), data = .)

PP_poly <- bind_rows(
  post_pred(M_poly_2),
  post_pred(M_poly_3),
  post_pred(M_poly_9)
)

T_fit_poly <-
  predict(PP_poly) %>%
  select(model, Obs, center) %>%
  spread(model, center)

RK_2 %>%
  bind_cols(T_fit_poly) %>%
```

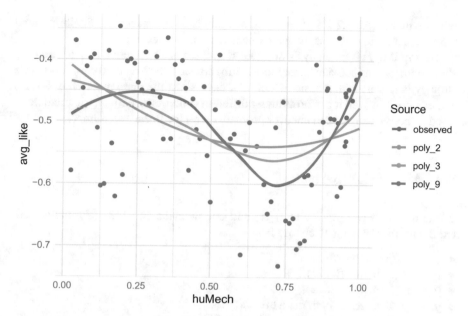

Fig. 8.13 Comparing fitted responses of three polynomial models of different degree

```
ggplot(aes(x = huMech)) +
geom_point(aes(y = avg_like, col = "observed")) +
geom_smooth(aes(y = avg_like, col = "observed"), se = F) +
geom_smooth(aes(y = M_poly_2, col = "poly_2"), se = F) +
geom_smooth(aes(y = M_poly_3, col = "poly_3"), se = F) +
geom_smooth(aes(y = M_poly_9, col = "poly_9"), se = F) +
labs(col = "Source")
```

Note that:

- all posterior predictive distributions (PPD) are collected into one multi-model posterior predictions object (class tbl_post_pred)
- from the PP, multi-model CLUs are then created at once and turned into a wide table using spread, which can be attached to the original data.

Figure 8.13 shows that the quadratic polynomial deviates strongly from the observed pattern. Describing a parable and one could expect it to fit the valley part somewhat, but it does not. The cubic polynomial curve seems better in place, whereas the 9-degree polynomial sits fully snug. However, recall that the 9-degree polynomial can take a ridiculous amount of shapes. But, instead of painting a totally different landscape, it merely pronounces the curvature of shoulder and valley.

These results confirm that [2] got it just right with using a cubic polynomial. This model captures the salient features of the data, not more, but also not less. One could argue, that since the 9-degree polynomial makes almost the same predictions as the cubic polynomial, it does no harm to always estimate a more flexible model. As we

will see in the Sect. 8.2.1, it does harm, as models with unnecessary flexibility tend
to see structure in the noise, which reduces forecasting accuracy.

To sum it up, visual analysis on fitted responses is an effective way to discover
shortcomings of a Gaussian linear model with respect to the structural part. A possible
strategy is to start with a basic model, that covers just the main research questions
and explore how well it performs under different conditions. With metric predictors,
fitted response analysis can uncover problems with the linearity assumption.

8.2 Model Comparison

If one measures two predictors x_1, x_2 and one outcome variable y, formally there
exist four linear models to choose from:

- y ~ 1 (grand mean)
- y ~ x_1 (main effect 1)
- y ~ x_2 (main effect 2)
- y ~ x_1 + x_2 (both main effects)
- y ~ x_1 * x_2 (both main effects and interaction)

For a data set with three predictors, the set of possible models is already 18.
This section deals with how to choose the right one. In Chap. 4, we have seen multiple times, how a model improves by adding another coefficient, for example a
missing conditional effect Sect. 5.4 can lead to severe biases. The opposite of such
under-specification is when a model carries unnecessary parameters, which causes
overfitting and reduces *predictive accuracy*. The subsequent sections accept predictive accuracy as a legitimate measure for model comparison and introduce methods
to measure predictive accuracy: simulation, cross validation, leave-one-out cross validation and information criteria. The final two sections show how model selection
can be used to test theories.

8.2.1 The Problem of Overfitting

In this chapter, we have seen multiple times how a model that is too simple fails to
align with the structure present in the data. For example, recall the IPump case, where
an ordinal model was much more accurate in rendering the learning process than the
simpler regression model. In several other cases, we have seen how introducing
conditional effects improves model fit. At these examples, it is easy to see how
omitting relevant predictors reduces the predictive accuracy of a model.

Too sparse models produce inferior predictions, but that is only one side of the
coin: Models that contain *irrelevant predictors* also produce inferior predictions.
This is called *overfitting* and can be understood better if we first recall, that a models
job is to divide our measures into the structural part and the random part Sect. 3.5.

Table 8.3 Coefficient estimates with 95% credibility limits

Model	Parameter	Fixef	Center	Lower	Upper
M_gmm	Intercept	Intercept	2.254	1.697	2.813
M_lrm	Intercept	Intercept	2.267	1.657	2.877
M_lrm	Pred	Pred	0.011	−0.659	0.651

The structural part is what all observations have in common, all future observations included. The structural part always is our best guess and the better a model separates structure from randomness, the more accurate our forecasts become.

The process of separation is imperfect to some degree. Irrelevant predictors usually get center estimates close to zero in a linear model, but their posterior distribution (or credibility intervals) usually has its probability mass spread out over a range of non-zero values. The irrelevant parameter adds a degree of freedom which introduces additional uncertainty. As an analogy, an irrelevant parameter is to a model, what a loose wheel is to a car. Even on a perfectly flat road it will cause a wobbly driving experience.

For further illustration, we simulate a small data set by drawing two variables from two Gaussian distributions. One variable is the (presumed) predictor, the other is the outcome and because they are completely unrelated, a GMM would be appropriate. But what happens if the researcher assumes that there is a linear relation and adds the irrelevant predictor to the model (Table 8.3)?

```
attach(Chapter_LM)

sim_overfit <- function(n - 10, seed = 1317) {
  set.seed(seed)
  tibble(
    pred = rnorm(n = 10, mean = 0, sd = 1),
    outcome = rnorm(n = 10, mean = 2, sd = 1)
  ) %>%
    as_tbl_obs()
}



D_overfit <- sim_overfit()

M_gmm <- stan_glm(outcome ~ 1,
  data = D_overfit, iter = 2000
)
M_lrm <- stan_glm(outcome ~ 1 + pred,
  data = D_overfit, iter = 2000
)
```

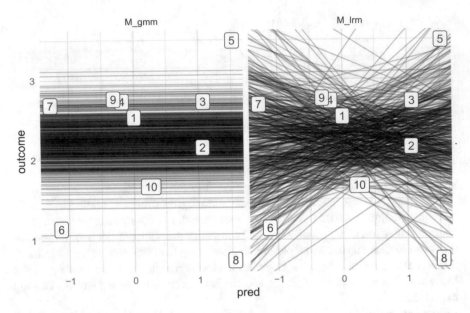

Fig. 8.14 Every line is one MCMC sample. The unneccessary slope parameter of the LRM model produces extra uncertainty

```
P_overfit <- bind_rows(
  posterior(M_gmm),
  posterior(M_lrm)
)
coef(P_overfit)
```

We first examine the coefficients. We observe that both models produce very close center estimates for the Intercept. At the same time, the slope coefficient (`pred`) is centered at a point very close to zero. Normally, irrelevant predictors do not add any biases. The credibility intervals are a different story. The most striking observation is that the LRM is very uncertain about the slope. The possibility of considerable positive or negative slopes is not excluded at all. Next to that, the intercept of the LRM is also less certain compared to the GMM.

Figure 8.14 illustrates the mechanism behind overfitting. It is created by extracting intercept and slope parameters from the posterior distributions and plotting them as a bunch of linear functions. For the GMM, all slopes are set to Zero, but we observe that the LRM has visited many rather strong slopes. These extreme slopes are mostly caused by the extreme observations Five, Six and Eight, which the LRM tries to reach, while the GMM stays relatively contained, assigning most of these extreme values to the random part. Finally, by the distribution of slopes, the distribution of left end-points is pulled apart and that is what we see as an extra uncertainty in the intercept.

```
P_overfit %>%
  filter(type == "fixef") %>%
  select(model, iter, parameter, value) %>%
  spread(key = parameter, value = value, fill = 0) %>%
  filter((iter %% 10) == 0) %>%
  ggplot() +
  facet_wrap(~model) +
  geom_abline(aes(intercept = Intercept, slope = pred), alpha = .2) +
  geom_point(aes(x = pred, y = outcome), data = D_overfit, col = "Red") +
  geom_label(aes(x = pred, y = outcome, label = Obs), data = D_overfit,
col = "Red")
```

Every parameter that is added to a model, adds to it some amount of flexibility. When this parameter is influential within the structure, the extra flexibility improves the fit. When it is not, the extra flexibility grabs on too much randomness, with the consequence of reduced forecasting accuracy. *Model pruning* is the process of discarding unnecessary parameters from a model until it reaches its maximum predictive accuracy. That is easy if you use simulated data, but in practice predictive accuracy can really only be estimated by throwing new data at an estimated model.

Nevertheless, unnecessary parameters in linear models can often sufficiently be identified by two simple rules (which actually are very similar to each other):

1. The center estimate is close to Zero.
2. If the parameter is removed, this causes little change in other parameters.

In the following, I will introduce formal methods to model pruning. These can be used in more complex situations, such as pruning multi-level models or selecting an appropriate error distribution type.

8.2.2 Cross Validation and LOO

Recall that coefficients are tied to fitted responses by the structural part. Consequently, stronger uncertainty in coefficients causes stronger uncertainty of predictions. Are the predictions of LRM inferior to the parsimonous GMM? Since we have simulated this data set, the true population mean is known ($\mu = 2$) and we can assess predictive accuracy by comparing the deviation of fitted responses to the true value. A standard way of summarizing the predictive accuracy of models is the *root mean square error* (RMSE), which we can compute from the *posterior predictive* distributions. As the following function definition shows, The RMSE can easily be computed (as long as the true values are known).

```
attach(Chapter_LM)

RMSE <- function(true, value) {
  se <- (true - value)^2
  mse <- mean(se)
  rmse <- sqrt(mse)
```

Table 8.4 Comparison of predictive accuracy by RMSE

Model	RMSE
M_gmm	0.996
M_lrm	1.124

```
    rmse
}

PP_overfit <-
  bind_rows(
    post_pred(M_gmm),
    post_pred(M_lrm)
  ) %>%
  left_join(D_overfit, by = "Obs")

PP_overfit %>%
  group_by(model) %>%
  summarize(RMSE = RMSE(true = 2, value))
```

As Table 8.4 shows, the LRM has a larger RMSE due to its irrelevant parameter. In contrast, the error of the GMM is close to One, which is almost precisely the standard deviation of the simulation function; the GMM has found just the right amount of randomness.

In practice, the central dilemma in evaluating predictive accuracy is that usually we do not know the real value. The best we can do, is use one data set to estimate the parameters and use a second data set to test how well the model predicts. This is called *cross validation* and it is the gold standard method for assessing predictive accuracy. Here, we can simulate the situation by using the simulation function one more time to produce future data, or more precisely: data new to the model.

```
D_new_data <- sim_overfit(n = 100, seed = 1318)

PP_cross_valid <-
  bind_rows(
    post_pred(M_gmm, newdata = D_new_data),
    post_pred(M_lrm, newdata = D_new_data)
  ) %>%
  left_join(D_new_data, by = "Obs")

PP_cross_valid %>%
  group_by(model) %>%
  summarize(RMSE = RMSE(value, outcome))
```

model	RMSE
M_gmm	1.12
M_lrm	1.23

Collecting new data before you can do model evaluation sounds awful, but new data is what cross validation requires. More precisely, cross validation only requires that the forecast data is not part of the sample you trained the model with. Psychometricians, for example, often use the split-half technique to assess the reliability of a test. The items of the test are split in half, one training set and one forecasting set. If the estimated participant scores correlate strongly, the test is called reliable.

Evaluating a model's forecasting accuracy can be done, by selecting one part of the data to train the model, and try to forecast the other part of the data. However, data is precious and spoiling half of it for forecasting is not very attractive. Fortunately, nobody actually said it has to be half the data. Another method of splitting has become common, *leave-one-out (LOO) cross validation* and the idea is simple:

1. Remove observation i from the data set.
2. Estimate the model $M_{/i}$.
3. Predict observation i with Model $M_{/i}$.
4. Measure the predictive accuracy for observation i.
5. Repeat steps 1 to 4 until all observations have been left out and forecast once.

The following code implements a generic function to run a LOO analysis using an arbitrary model.

```
do_loo <-
  function(data,
           F_fit,
           f_predict = function(fit, obs) {
             post_pred(fit, newdata = obs)
           }) {
    model_name <- as.character(substitute(F_fit))
    F_train_sample <- function(obs) {
      data %>% slice(-obs)
    } # Quosure
    F_test_obs <- function(obs) {
      data %>% slice(obs)
    } # Quosure
    F_post_pred <- function(model, model_name,
                            newdata, this_Obs) {
      post_pred(
        model = model,
        model_name = model_name,
        newdata = newdata
      ) %>%
        mutate(Obs = this_Obs)
```

```
  }

  out <- tibble(
    Obs = 1:nrow(data),
    Model = model_name,
    # training observations
    Train_sample = map(Obs, F_train_sample),
    # test observation
    Test_obs = map(Obs, F_test_obs),
    # model objects
    Fitted = map(Train_sample, F_fit)
  ) %>%
    mutate(Post_pred = pmap(list(
      model = Fitted,
      newdata = Test_obs,
      model_name = Model,
      this_Obs = Obs
    ), F_post_pred))
  return(out)
}
```

Before we put `do_loo` to use, some notes on the programming seem in order. Despite its brevity, the function is highly generic in that it can compute leave-one-out scores no matter what model you throw at it. This is mainly achieved by using advanced techniques from *functional programming*:

1. The argument `f_fit` takes an arbitrary function to estimate the model. This should work with all standard regression engines.
2. The argument `f_predict` takes a function as argument that produces the predicted values for the removed observations. The default is a function based on `predict` from the bayr package, but this can be adjusted.
3. The two functions that are defined inside `do_loo` are so-called *quosures*. Quosures are functions that bring their own copy of the data. They can be conceived as the functional programming counterpart to objects: Not the object brings the function, but the function brings its own data. The advantage is mostly computational as it prevents data to be copied every time the function is invoked.
4. `map` is a meta function from package purrr. It takes a list of objects and applies an arbitrary function, provided as the second argument.
5. `map2` takes two parallel input lists and applies a function. Here the forecast is created by matching observations with the model they had been excluded from.
6. The function output is created as a *tibble*, which is the tidy re-implementation of data frames. Different to original `data.frame` objects, tibbles can also store complex objects. Here, the outcome of LOO stores every single sample and estimated model, neatly aligned with its forecast value.
7. Other than one might expect, the function does not return a single score for predictive accuracy, but a dataframe with inidividual forecasts. This is on purpose

as there is more than one possible function to choose from for calculating a single accuracy score.

8. The function also makes use of what is called non-standard evaluation. This is a very advanced programming concept in R. Suffice it to say that `substitute()` captures an expression, here this is the fitting function argument, without executing it immediatly. Here the provided argument is converted to character and put as an identifier into the dataframe. That makes it very easy to use `do_loo` for multiple models, as we will see next.

Since we want to compare two models, we define two functions, invoke `do_loo` twice and bind the results in one data frame. As the model estimation is done per observation, I dialed down the number of MCMC iterations a little bit to speed up the process

```
fit_GMM <- function(sample) {
  stan_glm(outcome ~ 1,
    data = sample,
    iter = 500
  )
}
fit_LRM <- function(sample) {
  stan_glm(outcome ~ 1 + pred,
    data = sample,
    iter = 500
  )
}

Loo <- bind_rows(
  do_loo(D_overfit, fit_GMM),
  do_loo(D_overfit, fit_LRM)
)


Loo %>% sample_n(5)
```

This data frame `Loo` stores the rather large model objects that are produced. Doing a full LOO run is very computing expensive, and therefore, it makes a lot of sense to save all the models for potential later use.

Model comparison is based on the posterior predictive distribution. The following code merges all posterior predictions into one multi-model posterior prediction table and joins it with the the original observations. Now we can compute the RMSE and we even have the choice to do it on different levels. On a global level, the prediction errors of all observations are pooled (Table 8.5), but we can also summarize the prediction error on observations level (Table 8.6).

```
PP_Loo <-
  bind_rows(Loo$Post_pred) %>%
```

Table 8.5 Comparison of global RMSE scores

fit_GMM	fit_LRM	diff
1.34	1.55	0.217

Table 8.6 Comparison of observation-level RMSE scores

Obs	fit_GMM	fit_LRM	diff
1	1.17	1.21	0.032
2	1.07	1.23	0.150
3	1.18	1.27	0.084
4	1.12	1.21	0.088
5	1.64	1.95	0.305
6	1.54	1.89	0.344
7	1.15	1.48	0.322
8	1.88	2.33	0.454
9	1.15	1.24	0.087
10	1.19	1.27	0.083

```
    left_join(D_overfit) %>%
    rename(prediction = value)

PP_Loo %>%
    group_by(model) %>%
    summarize(RMSE = RMSE(prediction, outcome)) %>%
    spread(value = RMSE, key = model) %>%
    mutate(diff = fit_LRM - fit_GMM)

PP_Loo %>%
    group_by(model, Obs) %>%
    summarize(RMSE = RMSE(prediction, outcome)) %>%
    spread(value = RMSE, key = model) %>%
    mutate(diff = fit_LRM - fit_GMM)
```

8.2.3 Information Criteria

So far, we have seen that the right level of parsimony is essential for good predictive accuracy. While LOO can be considered gold standard for assessing predictive accuracy, it has a severe downside. Estimating Bayesian models with MCMC is very computing intensive and for some models in this book, doing a single run is in the range of dozens of minutes to more than an hour. With LOO this time is multiplied by the number of observations, which quickly becomes unbearable computing time for larger data sets.

Information criteria are efficient approximations of forecasting accuracy, accounting for goodness-of-fit, but also penalizing model complexity. The oldest of all IC is the *Akaike Information Criterion (AIC)*. Compared to its modern counter-parts, it is less broad, but its formula will be instructive to point out how goodness-of-fit and complexity are balanced within one formula. To represent goodness-of-fit, the AIC employs the *deviance*, which directly derives from the Likelihood (Sect. 3.4.3). Model complexity is accounted for by a penalty term that is two times the number of parameters k.

$$\text{Deviance} = -2\log(p(y|\hat{\theta}))$$
$$\text{Penality} = 2k$$
$$\text{AIC} = D + 2k$$

By these two simple terms, the AIC brings model fit and complexity into balance. Note that lower deviance is better and so is lower complexity. In effect, when comparing two models, the one with the *lower AIC wins*. As it grounds on the likelihood, it is routinely been used to compare models estimated by classic maximum likelihood estimation. The AIC formula is ridiculously simple and still has a solid foundation in mathematical information theory. It is easily computed, as model deviance is a by-product of parameter estimation. And if that was not enough, the *AIC is an approximation of LOO cross validation*, beating it in computational efficiency.

Still, the AIC has limitations. While it covers the full family of Generalized Linear Models Chap. 7, it is not suited for Multi-level Models Chap. 6. The reason is that in multi-level models the degree of freedom (its flexibility) is no longer proportional to the nominal number of parameters. Hence, the AIC penalty term is over-estimating complexity.

The *Deviance Information Criterion (DIC)* was the first generalization of the AIC to solve this problem by using an estimate for degrees of freedom. These ideas have more recently been refined into the *Widely Applicable Information Criterion (WAIC)*. Like DIC this involves estimating the penalty term p_{WAIC}. In addition, WAIC makes use of the full posterior predictive distribution, which is results in the *estimated log pointwise predictive density*, $\text{elpd}_{\text{WAIC}}$ as goodness-of-fit measure. The standard implementation of WAIC is provided by package Loo, and works with all models estimated with Rstanarm or Brms. When invoked on a model, it returns all three estimates:

```
attach(Chapter_LM)

loo::waic(M_gmm)
```

```
##
```

Table 8.7 Model ranking by predictive accuracy

Model	IC	Estimate	SE	diff_IC
M_gmm	looic	27.7	4.33	0.00
M_lrm	looic	31.5	5.37	3.76

```
## Computed from 4000 by 10 log-likelihood matrix
##
##              Estimate  SE
## elpd_waic    -13.8 2.1
## p_waic         1.5 0.6
## waic          27.6 4.2
##
## 1 (10.0%) p_waic estimates greater than 0.4.
We recommend trying loo instead.
```

Compared to LOO-CV, the WAIC is blazing fast. However, the WAIC has two major downsides: First, while the RMSE has a straightforward interpretation as the standard deviation of the expected error, WAICs are unintelligible by themselves. They only indicate relative predictive accuracy, when multiple models are compared. Second, WAIC as an approximation can be wrong. Fortunately, as can be seen from the warning above, the WAIC command performs an internal check on the integrity of the estimate. When in doubt, the function recommends to try another criterion, LOO-IC instead.

LO-IC is another approximation and not to be confused with the real LOO-CV method. LOO-IC is said to be a more reliable approximation of the real LOO-CV, than WAIC is. It is a tad slower than WAIC, but still has reasonable computation times. Again, the LOO-IC implementation features an extra safety feature, by checking the integrity of results and helping the user to fix problems.

```
Loo_gmm <- loo(M_gmm, cores = 1)
Loo_lrm <- loo(M_lrm, cores = 1)
```

Before we move on, a practical thing: the commands waic and loo (and kfold, see below), all create complex R objects. For loo, this object is of class "psis_loo". When you call the object in an interactive session, a predefined print method is invoked, but that does not look good in a statistical report. Function IC from package Bayr extracts estimates table from Loo objects as a tidy data frames. Command compare_IC creates an IC comparison table (Table 8.7).

With the tidy extraction of information criteria, we can start comparing models

```
compare_IC(list(Loo_gmm, Loo_lrm))
```

The interpretation of LOO-IC is the same as for all information criteria: the model with the smallest IC wins in predictive accuracy; here it is the GMM, once again.

What often confuses users of information criteria is when they see two ICs that are huge with only a tiny difference, like 1001317 and 1001320. Recall that information criteria all depend on the likelihood, but on a logarithmic scale. What is a difference on the logarithmic scale is a multiplier on the original scale of the likelihood, which is a product of probabilities. And a small difference on the log scale can be a respectable multiplicator

```
exp(1001320 - 1001317)
```

```
## [1] 20.1
```

8.2.4 Model Selection

ICs generally do not have an absolute meaning, but are always used to compare a set of models, relative to each other. Package Loo has the command `loo_compare` for this purpose. But, again, this is not tidy.

For a real application, we recollect the infusion pump case. We left it in Sect. 7.2.1.2, when comparing three Poisson models for the learning rate on path deviations:

- an ordered factor model with four learning rate coefficients (M_pois_cozfm)
- a Poisson model with two learning rate coefficients, one per design (M_pois_clzrm)
- a Poisson model with a universal learning rate (M pois_lzrm)

From the coefficients, it seemed that the leanest model M_pois_lzrm produced about the same predictions as the other two. We can confirm this by formal model selection (Table 8.8).

```
attach(IPump)

L_pois_cozfm <- loo(M_pois_cozfm)
L_pois_clzrm <- loo(M_pois_clzrm)
L_pois_lzrm <- loo(M_pois_lzrm)

list(
  L_pois_lzrm,
```

Table 8.8 Model ranking by predictive accuracy

Model	IC	Estimate	SE	diff_IC
M_pois_lzrm	looic	964	43.1	0.00
M_pois_clzrm	looic	967	43.3	3.00
M_pois_cozfm	looic	972	42.7	7.95

```
    L_pois_clzrm,
    L_pois_cozfm
)  %>%
    bayr::compare_IC()
```

Model comparison with LOO-IC points us at the unconditional LzRM as the preferred model, followed by the conditional LzRM. The conditional OFM goes in last. Model comparison confirms, that we may assume a learning rate that is approximately constant across the learning process *and* the designs.

8.2.5 *Comparing Response Distributions*

In model pruning, we compare the predictive accuracy of models that differ by their structural part. With modern evaluation criteria, there is more we can do to arrive at an optimal model. The methods for model comparison introduced so far also allow to compare different response distributions, i.e. the shape of randomness. As we have seen in Sect. 7.1, for many outcome variables, choosing an appropriate response distribution is a straightforward choice, based on just a few properties (continuous versus discrete, boundaries and overdispersion).

In Section 7.3.2, the properties of ToT and RT data suggested that Gaussian error terms are inappropriate, because the error distribution is highly skewed. While Gamma error distributions can accommodate some skew, this may not be sufficient, because the real lower boundary of measures is close to the measures. From an informal analysis of these three models, we concluded that the Exgaussian distribution is most suited for ToT outcomes, followed by Gamma, whereas the Gaussian showed a very poor fit. However, visual analysis of residuals on non-Gaussian models is difficult, due to the variance-mean relationship. With information criteria, we can easily select the response distribution with the best predictive accuracy.

This is one case, where *WAIC failed* to approximate predictive accuracy well, and we revert to the more robust LOO-IC. One advantage of LOO-IC over WAIC is that it produces observation-level estimates, which can be checked individually. Often LOO-IC also fails, but only on a few observations. The author of package Brms has added a practical fallback mechanism: by adding the argument `reloo = TRUE`, the problematic observations are refitted as real LOO-CVs (Table 8.9).

```
attach(Hugme)

Loo_1_gau <- loo(M_1_gau, reloo = TRUE)
Loo_1_gam <- loo(M_1_gam)
Loo_1_exg <- loo(M_1_exg, reloo = TRUE)

list(Loo_1_gau, Loo_1_gam, Loo_1_exg) %>%
    compare_IC()
```

Table 8.9 Model ranking by predictive accuracy

Model	IC	Estimate	SE	diff_IC
M_1_exg	looic	−4186	138	0
M_1_gam	looic	−3825	177	361
M_1_gau	looic	−2013	389	2173

Table 8.10 Model ranking by predictive accuracy

Model	IC	Estimate	SE	diff_IC
M_4_gam	kfoldic	6581	61.0	0
M_4_exg	kfoldic	6788	63.1	207
M_4_gau	kfoldic	7098	82.8	517

The comparison confirms that the Exgaussian response distribution is best suited for these reaction time data. It may also be better suited for reaction time experiments in more general, but this needs more proof by other data sets. For the time being, experimentalists are advised to estimate several response distributions (especially Exgaussian and Gamma) and select the best fitting distribution using the described method.

The other class of duration measures is ToT data, which is routinely collected in usability tests and other applied design research studies. Formally, it should have similar properties as RT data, but the underlying processes of data generation may still be very different. We investigate the CUE8 data using formal model selection on the same three response distributions.

In the previous analysis, LOO-IC was unreliable for a few observations and we refitted these. If more than just a few observations are unreliable, this can get too time expensive. In the worst case, we would be thrown back to the very inefficient LOO-CV method altogether. The authors of package Loo provide an alternative fallback to reloo-ing: In *k-fold cross validation*, a model is refit k times, always leaving out and predicting N/k observations. LOO cross validation actually is 1-fold cross validation, which results in fitting N models. 10-fold cross validation stands on middle ground by training the model ten times on a different 90% part of data and testing the model on the remaining 10% (Table 8.10)

```
attach(CUE8)

F10_4_gau <- kfold(M_4_gau, K = 10)
F10_4_gam <- kfold(M_4_gam, K = 10)
F10_4_exg <- kfold(M_4_exg, K = 10)

list(F10_4_gau, F10_4_gam, F10_4_exg) %>%
  compare_IC()
```

Table 8.11 Model ranking by predictive accuracy

Model	IC	Estimate	SE	diff_IC
M_poly_3_beta_dist	looic	−3738	108.9	0
M_poly_3_beta	looic	−1865	94.6	1872

In case of ToT data, the Gamma response distributions is favored over the Exgaussian. Again, this may or may not generalize to future data sets.

Obviously, predictive accuracy can also be used to check for overdispersion, just compare, for instance, a Poisson model to a Negbinomial model. However, overdispersion in count data is so common that model selection may be a waste of effort. In addition, should there really be no overdispersion, the Negbimomial model will behave almost exactly like a Poisson model and the costs (in terms of parsimony) are negligible.

Therefore, I close this section with a more interesting comparison: In Sect. 7.5, *distributional models* were introduced as a generalization of GLMs. Distributional models allow to also link predictors to variance and other shape parameters, such as the Gaussian σ, the Beta ρ and the two parameters of the Exgaussian distribution, σ for dispersion and β for skew.

A Beta model with two structural parts (mean and scale) was estimated on the eeriness ratings in the Uncanny study and their appeared to be significant variance in how participants employed the rating scale, i.e. the range of responses. However, by individual-level scale parameters add a good deal of complexity to the model. Is that for the good of predictive accuracy? Below, we use the LOO-IC estimate to compare the distributional model against a mean-only Beta regression (Table 8.11).

```
attach(Uncanny)

Loo_beta <- loo(M_poly_3_beta)
Loo_dist <- loo(M_poly_3_beta_dist)

list(Loo_beta, Loo_dist) %>%
  compare_IC()
```

Despite its opulence, the distributional model out-ranks the simpler model. It confirms that individual response patterns occur and by granting all participants their own scale, predictive accuracy improves.

8.2.6 Testing Hypotheses

For everyone who has to publish in Social Science journals, this book has so far left one question unanswered: What is the Bayesian method for testing null hypotheses? To give the short answer: There are no p-values in this statistical framework, but

Table 8.12 Model ranking by predictive accuracy

Model	IC	Estimate	SE	diff_IC
M_poly_3	looic	−169	10.5	0.0
M_poly_2	looic	−158	10.5	11.6

you can always use credibility limits to say "the effect is different from Zero with a certainty larger than 95%". If some pertinent reviewers want p-values, you can argue that a null hypothesis test is really just model selection, but unfortunately no p-value tests are available for the models that you are using, and then you introduce one of the methods based on predictive accuracy.

But, should you really do null hypothesis testing in design research? Well, if your research implies or even directly targets real costs, benefits and risks for real people, you should continue with quantifying impact factors. That can even go so far that an unnecessary predictor is left in the model, just to make its irrelevance transparent. Everyone whose final report draws any conclusion of how the results can be used for the better, must speak of quantities at some point.

Still, it could make sense to test theories by comparing predictive accuracy of models. Recall the uncanny valley phenomenon. In Sect. 5.5, the non-linear relationship between human likeness of robot faces and emotional response was modeled as a 3-degree polynomial, and we have derived some intersting statistics, such as the position of the trough. We encountered the case again for an examination of goodness-of-fit Sect. 8.1.2. Our plots of fitted responses suggested that the cubic polynomial fitted better than the simpler quadratic. A quadratic function produces a parable and can therefore also have a local minimum. But it cannot have the shoulder that makes the effect so abrupt. This abruptness is what has fascinated so many researchers, but is it real?

```
attach(Uncanny)

options(mc.cores = 1)
Loo_poly_2 <- loo(M_poly_2)
Loo_poly_3 <- loo(M_poly_3)

list(Loo_poly_2, Loo_poly_3) %>%
  compare_IC()
```

As shown in (Table 8.12), the cubic polynomial has the better predictive accuracy. It suggests that the Uncanny Valley effect is due to a disruptive cognitive change, like when you suddenly become aware that you have been fooled. This is not a direct test of a given theory, but it favors all theories that contain an abrupt process. One of the theories that does not contain a disruptive process goes that the UV effect is caused by religious beliefs. This theory is standing on shaky legs, whereas any theory explaining the effect as a the startling moment when the mind suddenly becomes aware of a deception is gaining ground.

8.2.7   A Note on Bayes Factor

Most Bayesian authors favor the interpretation of parameter estimates over null hypothesis testing. Reference [3] is an exception and targets an academic audience that is routinely concerned with hypothesis testing, rather than quantitative inference. Lee and Wagenmakers propose Bayes Factor as a solution. This approach is enthralling as it gives more intelligible answers than information criteria do. Bayes Factor of two models M_1 and M_2 is the ratio of their *marginal likelihood*

$$\text{BF}_{1,2} = \frac{P(D|M_1)}{P(D|M_0)}$$

If the result of the computation is, say 10, you can say that M_1 is 10 times more likely, given data D. Lee and Wagenmakers count this moderate evidence. One could say that Bayes Factor lets you directly make bets on models. If your opponent puts 1 Euro on M_0 (the effect does not exist), your rational counter would be 10 Euros. This is a wonderfully clear way of communicating level of certainty.

However, it has two downsides. The practical downside is that computation of Bayes Factor is not easy or even impossible for a wider range of models. The dogmatic downside is the same as for all null hypothesis testing. At least, when human behavior is involved, no condition can be said to have perfectly no effect. You may argue that this is not different to discard a predictor from a model using LOO-CV or information criteria, but there is a difference. With all methods based on predictive accuracy, predictors are discarded, because their presence does not assist in forecasting Sect. 8.2.1. This is a totally different thing to say than an impact factor to be totally absent.

8.3   Further Readings

1. [4, Chap. 6] illuminates the problem of overfitting. Next to LOO-CV and information criteria, a third approach is introduced to avoid overfitting: regularization with skeptical priors.
2. The same chapter is my best recommendation for readers longing for a deeper understanding of information criteria. Presumably, it is based on the [5].
3. Reference [6] is worth reading for two reasons: The selection process I presented is very basic, by just selecting *the* best model. Burnham and Andersen go further and present an approach to use multi models at once, for ultimate forecasting accuracy.
4. A huge book on response times in psychological research is [7].
5. Another in-depth analysis of reaction time distributions is [8].

References

1. Richard McElreath. Statistical Rethinking. Chapman and Hall/CRC, Jan. 3, 2018. DOI: https://doi.org/10.1201/9781315372495.
2. Mathur Maya B, Reichling David B (2016) Navigating a social world with robot partners: A quantitative cartography of the Uncanny Valley. Cognition 146:22–32. https://doi.org/10.1016/j.cognition.2015.09.008
3. Lee Michael D, Wagenmakers Eric-Jan (2009). Bayesian Cognitive Modeling Cambridge UNiversity Press. https://doi.org/10.1017/cbo9781139087759
4. Richard McElreath. "Statistical Rethinking". In: (2014)
5. Andrew Gelman, Jessica Hwang, and Aki Vehtari. "Understanding predictive information criteria for Bayesian models". In: Statistics and Computing 24.6 (2014), pp. 997-1016. ISSN: 1573-1375. https://doi.org/10.1007/s11222-013-9416-2. arXiv: 1307.5928
6. Kenneth P. Burnham and David R. Anderson. Model Selection and Multimodel Inference. A Practical Information-Theoretic Approach. Second. Springer-Verlag New York Berlin Heidelberg, 2002. ISBN: 0387953647
7. RD Luce. Response times: Their role in inferring elementary mental organization. 1991. URL: http://books.google.com/books?hl=en
8. Dora Matzke and Eric-Jan Wagenmakers. "Psychological interpretation of the ex-Gaussian and shifted Wald parameters: a diffusion model analysis." In: Psychonomic bulletin & review 16.5 (Oct. 2009), pp. 798-817. ISSN: 1531-5320. https://doi.org/10.3758/PBR.16.5.798.URL: http://www.ncbi.nlm.nih.gov/pubmed/19815782

Appendix
Cases

This book comes with eight research cases with real data and eight simulated cases. They will be provided as R environments saved as Rda files. To use these environments, you have to download the Rda file and load it

```
load("Cases/Uncanny.Rda")
```

The loading puts the environment into your R session and you can see the content using the Environment tab in Rstudio. Or you issue the `ls` command

```
ls(Uncanny)
```

```
##  [1] "D_UV"
##  [2] "DK_1"
##  [3] "Loo_beta"
##  [4] "Loo_dist"
##  [5] "Loo_poly_2"
##  [6] "Loo_poly_3"
##  [7] "M_dsgmx_1"
##  [8] "M_poly_2"
##  [9] "M_poly_3"
## [10] "M_poly_3_beta"
## [11] "M_poly_3_beta_dist"
## [12] "M_poly_3_ml"
## [13] "M_poly_9"
## [14] "P_poly_3"
## [15] "P_poly_3_ml"
## [16] "P_univ_uncanny"
## [17] "PP_poly_3_ml"
## [18] "PS_1"
## [19] "RK_1"
## [20] "RK_2"
```

© Springer Nature Switzerland AG 2021
M. Schmettow, *New Statistics for Design Researchers*,
Human–Computer Interaction Series,
https://doi.org/10.1007/978-3-030-46380-9

```
## [21] "trough"
## [22] "trough.data.frame"
## [23] "trough.matrix"
## [24] "trough.numeric"
## [25] "UV_1"
## [26] "UV_dsgmx"
```

In order to use the environment content in your R session, you have to attach it.

```
attach(Uncanny)
```

Real data cases contain one or more data sets as data frames (tibbles), such as

```
RK_1
```

Before switching to a different case environment, it is recommended to detach the present environment

Synthetic data cases contain a simulation function that precisely produces the data set as it has been used in this book. Sometimes, the simulation function also provides additional arguments to make changes to the data set.

```
load("Cases/AR_game.Rda")
attach(AR_game)
```

The following simulates the AR_game data set, exactly as it was used in section [amplification].

```
simulate() %>%
    ggplot(aes(x = technophile, color = sociophile, y = intention)) +
    geom_point() +
    geom_smooth()
```

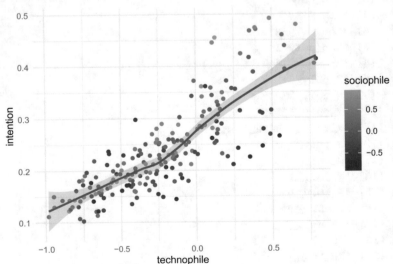

All simulation functions provide the argument seed, which sets the random number generator(s) to a specific value. Using a different seed value produces a data set with the same structure, but different values.

Table A.1 Data set with 18 variables, showing 8 of 7488 observations

Experiment	Obs	Part	Item	Scale	Stimulus	session	Session	Collection	Condition	presentation	response	RT	huMech	huMech0	huMech1	huMech2	huMech3
RK	70	1	nE6	nEeriness	65	0	1	MR	2	Inf	-0.832	2.00	0.812	1	0.812	0.660	0.536
RK	712	3	nE8	nEeriness	79	1	2	MR	2	Inf	-0.223	1.81	0.988	1	0.988	0.975	0.963
RK	1337	p1_05	nE1	nEeriness	60	1	2	MR	2	Inf	-0.880	1.67	0.750	1	0.750	0.562	0.422
RK	3451	p1_12	nE3	nEeriness	61	2	3	MR	2	Inf	-0.008	4.20	0.762	1	0.762	0.581	0.443
RK	3585	p1_13	nE1	nEeriness	26	1	2	MR	2	Inf	-0.498	3.50	0.325	1	0.325	0.106	0.034
RK	3901	p2_01	nE5	nEeriness	34	1	2	MR	2	Inf	-0.672	2.72	0.425	1	0.425	0.181	0.077
RK	5982	p2_08	nE6	nEeriness	39	2	3	MR	2	Inf	-0.667	1.66	0.488	1	0.488	0.238	0.116
RK	6264	p2_09	nE8	nEeriness	57	2	3	MR	2	Inf	-0.380	1.94	0.713	1	0.713	0.508	0.362

```
simulate(seed = 1317) %>%
  ggplot(aes(x = technophile, color = sociophile, y = intention)) +
  geom_point() +
  geom_smooth()
```

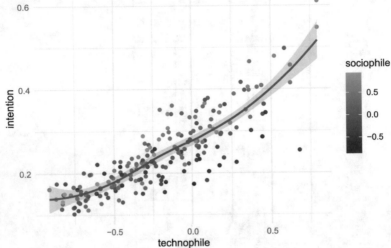

Additional arguments can be used to change the structure of the data set. In the present example, the amplification effect can be turned into a [saturation] effect, by changing the beta argument

```
simulate(beta = c(-1, 1, .4, -3)) %>%
  ggplot(aes(x = technophile, color = sociophile,
y = intention)) +
  geom_point() +
  geom_smooth()
```

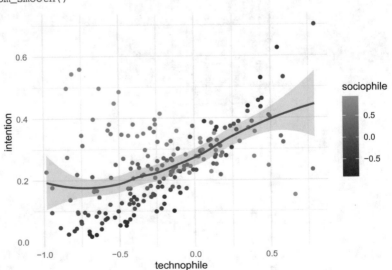

If you want to understand how a simulation function works and how it can be controlled, you can display the code of the function, just by calling it without parentheses

```
simulate
```

```
## function(N = 200,
##             beta = c(-1, 1, .4, .6),
##             sigma = .2,
##             seed = 42)
##    {
##      set.seed(seed)
##      out <-
##        tibble(Part = 1:N,
##                technophile = rbeta(N, 2, 3) * 2 - 1,
##                sociophile = rbeta(N, 2, 2) * 2 - 1) %>%
##        mutate( eta = beta[1] +
##                beta[2] * technophile +
##                beta[3] * sociophile +
##                beta[4] * technophile * sociophile,
##              intention = masculils::inv_logit(rnorm(N,  eta,
sigma))) %>%
##          as_tbl_obs()
##      #
##      # class(out) <- append(class(out), "sim_tbl")
##      # attr(out, "coef") <- list(beta = beta,
##      #                            sigma = sigma)
##      # attr(out, "seed") <- seed
##      #
##      out
##    }
## <bytecode: 0x00000000817b8f08>
## <environment: 0x0000000074dbb340>
```

Real and synthetic case environments provide all data used in this book, but also all models are included that have been estimated. When working through this book, this saves you the effort to run the models by yourself.

M_cmrm

```
## stan_glm
##  family:       gaussian [identity]
##  formula:      intention ~ 1 + sociophile + technophile + sociophile:technophile
##  observations: 40
##  predictors:   4
## ------
##                         Median MAD_SD
## (Intercept)             0.3    0.0
## sociophile              0.1    0.0
## technophile             0.2    0.0
## sociophile:technophile  0.2    0.0
##
## Auxiliary parameter(s):
##       Median MAD_SD
## sigma 0.0    0.0
##
## ------
## * For help interpreting the printed output see ?print.stanreg
## * For info on the priors used see ?prior_summary.stanreg
```

.1   Real Cases

A.1   Hugme

As swift and enthusiastic most people are with words, the more clumsy and desinterested many are with computers. Today's consumer computing devices are unmatched in usability and most people do not need to think harder than they like, when hunting for the best online prices, stream movies and enjoy their communications.

However, there is a minority of computer users, who call themselves the geeks. The hypothetical geek personality feels attracted to the inner workings of a computer system itself, rather than the applications and media entertainment it delivers. A geek person seeing a computer is more likely to have certain memories, for example, remembering how it was to build your first own computer, or the intellectual joy of learning a new programming language. If this personality type exists, we thought, then bringing up such thoughts should distract a geek in an experimental task, the Stroop task. This brief nostalgic would be measurable as a delayed response.

A.1.1   Measures

Before the experiment, participants filled out teh multi-item NCS and Geekism questionnaires. The geekism questionknaire was given a second time after the experiment, originally to assess test-retest reliability.

As response, we had chosen recation time in a Stroop task, where participants were first primed by a picture shown before the Stroop task. These pictures were from two conditions: either showing computers in a geekish way (for example, an open case or programming code on the screen) or as regular product images. Furthermore, we presumed that geeks like to think hard and used the need-for-cognition scale as a second predictor. It was expected that participants with high NCS scores would recognize computers as a source of delightful hard thinking, and hence have slower reaction times when priming image and target word are both from the category Geek.

A.1.2   Stimuli

Stimuli were composed of a priming picture and the word presented in the Stroop task, with prime/word pairs generated randomly for each observation.

Ninety words were selected, 30 for each of the following three categories and translated into English, German and Dutch:

1. hedonism (stylish, braging, wanting, …)
2. utilitarianism (useful, assisting, optimizing)
3. geekism (configuring, technology, exploring)

Seventy-two prime pictures were selected, with 24 for each of the following categories:

1. control (pictures unrelated to technology)
2. geek (pictures showing computers in a geekish setting, e.g. an open computer case or a terminal console).

A.1.3   Data Modeling in a Nutshell

The Hugme experiment is a multi-population study: participants, pictures, words and items (from two scales) all provide information that is relevant for the statistical model. For analyzing the relationship between geekism, NCS on te one hand and the difference in reaction times between word and picture categories, we need the table D_hugme, which provides the predictor data for every observation from the experiment. The way this table was constructed is an instructive example of how researchers can logically structure and efficiently transform data from complex studies.

The Table R_exp is the raw data that we got from the experiment. It contains the encounter of participants with primes and words, but misses the classification of words and primes, as well as participant-level variables. The classification of words and primes is stored separately in three *entity tables*: E_Words, E_Primes, whereas a E_part contains demographic data

```
load("Cases/Hugme.Rda")
attach(Hugme)

E_Part %>% sample_n(8)
```

Table A.2 Data set with 2 variables, showing 8 of 8 observations

Prime	PrimeCat
control03.jpg	Control
neutral03.jpg	Neutral
control11.jpg	Control
control04.jpg	Control
control24.jpg	Control
neutral23.jpg	Neutral
neutral13.jpg	Neutral
neutral12.jpg	Neutral

Part	gender	age
31	female	61
64	female	23
55	female	20
25	female	26
23	male	21
63	male	20
59	male	38
28	male	36

```
E_Words %>% sample_n(8)
```

Word	Word_DE	Word_NL	WordCat
wanting	wünschen	verlangen	hedo
assembling	einbauen	inbouwen	geek
usable	brauchbar	bruikbaar	util
useful	nützlich	nuttig	util
computing	berechnen	berekenen	util
manageable	handlich	handig	util
technology	Technologie	technologie	geek
cool	cool	cool	hedo

```
E_Primes %>% sample_n(8)
```

All entity tables capture the information in the sample of precisely one population, with one row per member and a unique identifier. This identifier is called a *key* and is crucial for putting all the information together, using *joins*. Any response measure, like RT, is something that happens at every encounter. More abstractly, we could say, that this encounter is a *relation* between participants, words and primes, and the response is an *attribute* of the relation. R_exp is a relationship table which stores responses together with the encounter.

Table A.3 Data set with 6 variables, showing 8 of 4027 observations

Obs	Part	Word	Prime	correct	RT
281	5	Skimping	geek08.jpg	TRUE	0.696
659	11	Applying	geek09.jpg	TRUE	0.540
923	15	Configuring	neutral18.jpg	TRUE	0.544
1194	19	Envying	neutral06.jpg	TRUE	0.655
1438	22	Admiring	neutral15.jpg	TRUE	0.543
2122	32	Assembling	neutral17.jpg	TRUE	0.567
2365	36	Pride	geek18.jpg	TRUE	0.365
2609	53	Admiring	control06.jpg	TRUE	0.751

In fact, the encounters between Part, Word and Prime can be called a key, because the combination truly identifies every observation

```
R_exp %>% as_tbl_obs()
```

```
cat(
  "The number of unique encounters is",
  nrow(distinct(R_exp, Part, Word, Prime))[1]
)
```

```
## The number of unique encounters is 4027
```

What is still missing in the table are all the variables that further describe or classify members of any of the three samples. Think of the püredictors you need for running group-means analysis or linear regression on the data. Table R_exp provides the scaffold and the other variables we can pull in from the entity tables by using *join* operations. A join always operates on two tables that share at least one key variable. The following code takes the R_exp the relationship table to the left and merges in additional data from the entity table, picking on the key variable. This works successively on the three entity tables

```
R_exp %>%
  left_join(E_Words, by = "Word") %>%
  left_join(E_Primes, by = "Prime") %>%
  left_join(E_Part, by = "Part") %>%
  as_tbl_obs()
```

Now you know how Entity Relationship Modeling works. This paradigm came up with the second generation of data base systems in the 1990s (The first generation used strictly hierarchical data structures) and has been fully adopted by the packages Dplyr and Tidyr from the Tidyverse.

Table A.4 Data set with 12 variables, showing 8 of 4198 observations

Obs	Part	Word	Prime	Correct	RT	Word_DE	Word_NL	WordCat	PrimeCat	Gender	Age
406	6	wanting	neutral09.jpg	TRUE	0.447	wünschen	verlangen	hedo	neutral	male	25
1040	16	appearance	neutral09.jpg	TRUE	0.856	Aussehen	uiterlijk	hedo	neutral	male	54
1096	16	mastering	neutral24.jpg	TRUE	0.575	meistern	behappen	geek	neutral	male	54
1115	17	calculating	geek17.jpg	TRUE	0.760	kalkulieren	calculeren	util	geek	female	24
1351	20	serving	control08.jpg	TRUE	0.824	bedienen	besturen	util	control	female	23
1399	21	serving	control20.jpg	TRUE	0.825	bedienen	besturen	util	control	female	22
1608	24	rebuild	neutral15.jpg	TRUE	0.420	umbauen	wijzigen	geek	neutral	male	22
3034	57	improving	neutral02.jpg	TRUE	0.666	verbessern	opkrikken	geek	neutral	male	24

Table A.5 Data set with 8 variables, showing 8 of 2620 observations

Obs	Team	Part	Condition	SUS	Task	ToT	logToT
185	C3	37	Moderated		5	74	4.30
213	C3	43	Moderated		3	64	4.16
586	H3	118	Remote	95.0	1	88	4.48
980	K3	196	Moderated	67.5	5	76	4.33
1373	L3	275	Remote	35.0	3	90	4.50
1687	L3	338	Remote	78.0	2	186	5.23
2143	L3	429	Remote	100.0	3	48	3.87
2219	L3	444	Remote	43.0	4	188	5.24

A.2   CUE8

CUE8 is one of the long series *Comparative Usability Evaluation* studies conducted by Rolf Molich CUE8. Previous studies had shown that usability experts differ a lot in identification and reporting of usability problems. In CUE8, Molich and colleagues put the bar much lower and asked, whether different professional teams would obtain consistent measures of time-on-task. Eight independent Teams were given the same test scenario, consisting of five user tasks on a car rental website. Teams were otherwise free to design the test. In particular, some teams conducted remote usability tests, whereas others did standard moderated testing.

A.2.1   Measures

Time-on-task was measured in seconds and are also provided on a logarithmic scale, because of violation of Gaussian distribution of errors. In addition, satisfaction has been measured using the Systems Usability Scale with the range of [0, 100].

```
load("Cases/CUE8.Rda")
attach(CUE8)
D_cue8
```

A.3   Uncanny Valley

The Uncanny Valley effect is an astonishing emotional anomaly in the cognitive processing of artificial faces, like ... robot faces. Intuitively, one would assume that people would always prefer faces that are more human-like. As it turns out, this is only up to a certain point, where increasing human-likeness causes a feeling of eerie.

For the first time, the UV effect could be rendered in an experiment by Mathur & Reichling. They measured the emotional response to pictures of robot faces using a simple rating scale (Likeability).

A.3.1 Experimental Design

In order to pursue deeper into the UV effect, two more experiments, PS and RK, have been conducted in our lab. Both experiments have in common that participants see a sequence of robot faces and give an emotional response. Experiments DK and PS aimed at identifying the cognitive level of processing that makes the UV occur and collected the responses under manipulation of presentation time. The presentation times were 50, 100, 200 and 2000ms. Experiment RK kept the presentation time constant at 2000ms, but presented all stimuli three times. This was to collect enough data for verifying that the UV phenomenon is universal, i.e. occurs for every participant. All three experiments used a full within-subject design. However, every trial presented just one item from the Eeriness scale.

A.3.2 Stimuli

The stimuli in the experiments are pictures of robot faces that vary from totally not human-like (like the casing of a robotic vacuum cleaner) to almost indistinguishable from human. Mathur and Reichling collected and tagged the major part of the set of stimuli. The two studies, PS [PS] and RK [RK], successively added stimuli to the set in order to increase the precision in the range where the effect occurs.

The central predictor in these experiments is the human-likeness of a robot face. Mathur & Reichling produced these measures by use of a rating scale, humano-mechanical scale (huMech). Stimuli that were added by PS and RK were rated by two experts, using MR collection as a a baseline. Variable huMech has been normalized to [0; 1].

A.3.3 Measures

The Eeriness scale of [1] has been used to measure the emotional response. This scale contains eight items and has specifically been designed to observe the UV effect. The scale was implemented as a visual analog scale. Because the Eeriness scales direction is reverse to the original Likeability scale of [2] , responses have been reversed (negative Eeriness) and normalized to the interval $[-1; 0]$. In addition, reaction times have been recorded.

```
load("Cases/Uncanny.Rda")
attach(Uncanny)
Uncanny$RK_2 %>%
  ggplot(aes(x = huMech, y = avg_like)) +
  geom_smooth() +
  geom_point()
```

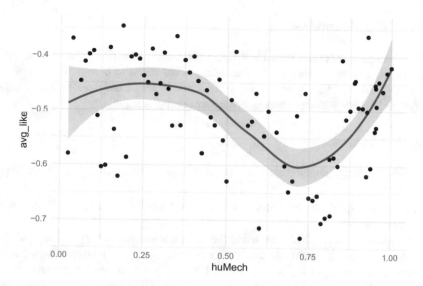

A.4   IPump

Medical infusion pumps are unsuspicious looking devices that are en-mass installed in surgery and intensive care. Their only purpose is controlled injection of medication in the blood stream of patients. Pumps are rather simple devices as infusion is not more than a function of volume and time. They are routinely used by trained staff, mostly anaesthesiologists and nurses. We should have great faith in safe operation under such conditions. The truth is, medical infusion pumps have reportedly killed dozens of people, thousands were harmed and an unknown number of nurses lost their jobs. The past generation of pumps is cursed with a chilling set of completely unnecessary design no-gos:

- tiny 3-row LCD displays
- flimsy foil buttons without haptic marking or feedback
- modes
- information hidden in menus

For fixing these issues, no additional research is needed, as the problems are pretty obvious to experienced user interface designers. What needs to be done, though, is proper validation testing of existing and novel interfaces, for example:

- is the interface safe to use?
- is it efficient to learn?
- is a novel interface better than a legacy design? And by how much?

We conducted such a study. A novel interface was developed after an extensive study of user requirements and design guidelines. As even the newest international standards for medical devices do not spell precise quantitative user requirements (such as, a nurse must be able to complete a standard task in t seconds and no more than e errors may occur), the novel interface was compared to a device with a legacy design.

A.4.1   Experimental Design

Eight successive user tasks were identified from training material and documentation. All participants were trained nurses and they were asked to complete the series of tasks with the devices. In order to capture learnability of the devices, every nurse completed the sequence of tasks in three consecutive sessions.

A.4.2   Measures

A number of performance measures were recorded to reflect safety and efficiency of operation:

1. *task completion*: for every task it was assessed whether the nurse had completed it successfully.
2. *deviations from optimal path*: using the device manual for every task the shortest sequence was identified that would successfully complete the task. The sequence was then broken down into individual operations that were compared to the observed sequence of operations. An algorithm called *Levenshtein distance* was used to count the number of deviations.
3. *time-on-task* was recorded as a measure for efficiency.
4. *mental workload* was recorded using a one-item rating scale.

Furthermore, several participant-level variables have been recorded:

1. professional group: general or intensive care
2. level of education (Dutch system): MBO, HBO and university
3. years of job experience as a nurse

```
load("Cases/IPump.Rda")
attach(IPump)
IPump$D_agg %>%
  ggplot(aes(x = Session, color = Design, y = ToT)) +
  geom_boxplot()
```

A.5 Case Sleepstudy

This data set ships with the lme4 package and has only been converted to the coding standards used throughout. Eighteen participants underwent sleep deprivation on ten successive days and the average reaction time on a set of tests has been recorded per day and participant. For further information on the data set, consult the documentation (?lme4::sleepstudy). Variable names have been changed to fit the naming scheme of this book.

```
load("Cases/Sleepstudy.Rda")
attach(Sleepstudy)
D_slpstd %>%
  ggplot(aes(x = days, y = RT)) +
  facet_wrap(~Part) +
  geom_point() +
  geom_smooth(se = F, aes(color = "LOESS")) +
  geom_smooth(se = F, method = "lm", aes(color = "lm")) +
  labs(color = "Smoothing function")
```

A.6 Egan

In the beginning of 1990s, Dennis Egan examined that the variability in performance is due to individual differences. He concluded that individual differences are the greater source of performance variance than design differences are. Twenty-five years later we have put this claim to a test.

A.6.1 Research Design

We selected ten university websites and identified ten typical information search tasks. Forty-one student users took part and performed the tasks. Our design is a full within-subject design, with *planned missing values*. Instead of all 100 possible combinations of websites and tasks, every participant got a set of trials, where websites and tasks were paired, such that every website and every task appeared *exactly once* per participant.

A.6.2 Measures

Four usability measures were taken per trial:

- task success
- number of clicks (clicks)
- number of tims user returns to homepage
- workload (measured by a one-item scale)

```
load("Cases/Egan.Rda")
attach(Egan)

plot_Egan <- function(Level) {
  level <- enquo(Level)
  out <-
    D_egan %>%
    group_by(!!level) %>%
    summarize(mean_ToT = mean(ToT)) %>%
    ggplot(aes(x = mean_ToT)) +
    geom_histogram() +
    labs(title = quo(!!level)) +
    xlim(0, 300)
}


grid.arrange(
  plot_Egan(Part),
  plot_Egan(Design),
  plot_Egan(Task),
  plot_Egan(Item)
)
```

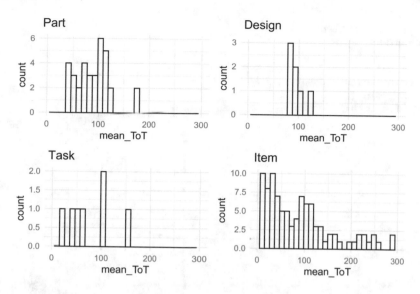

A.7 Case: Millers Magic Number

Miller's magic number says that the short term memory capacity is 7 ± 2. Later research by Baddeley & Hitch found that the so-called *working memory* is a multi-component system, that stores visual and verbal information separately. Following up on the experimental research by [Freudenthal], we were interested how differences in capacity of the verbal and visual subsystem explain performance differences in a real web search tasks.

A.7.1 Research Design

We selected five municipal websites and five search tasks. For creating the trials, websites and tasks were paired in ush c way, that all participants see every website and every task exactly once.

A.7.2 Measures

For visual working memory capacity, we used the Corsi block tapping task. For verbal capacity, the Ospan task was used and both scoring schemes, A and B, were applied. Number of clicks and time to completion were recorded as performance measures.

```
load("Cases/MMN.Rda")
attach(MMN)

MMN_2 %>%
  ggplot(aes(x = Ospan.A, y = time)) +
  geom_point() +
  geom_smooth()
```

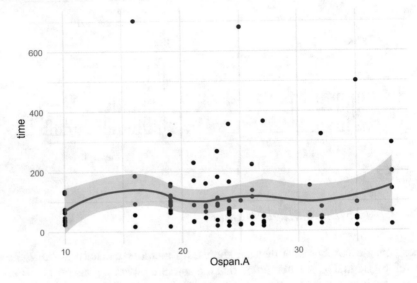

```
MMN_2 %>%
  ggplot(aes(x = as.factor(Corsi), y = time)) +
  geom_boxplot()
```

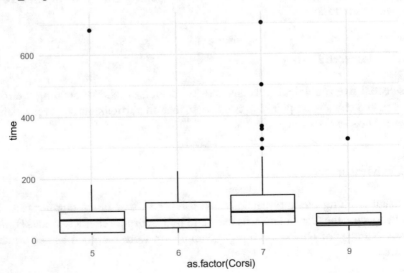

A.8 AUP

In their seminal article, [Carroll & Rosson] coin the term *Active User Paradox* for their observations, that users stick to their habits and are reluctant to put energy into learning a computer system. This seems irrational at first, as users miss a chance to increase their long-term efficiency. (Later research by [Fu & Gray] found that their is a hidden rationality to the AUP.) Still, there are users out there who are enthusiastic about computers and love to solve the intellectual puzzles they provide. We wanted to see whether people of that kind would be more likely to over-win the AUP.

A.8.1 Measures

For measuring the personality of users, we used

- the *need-for-cognition scale*

- the *Geekism (gex) scale*.
- a scale for *Computer Anxiety Scale*
- a scale for *Utilitarianism*

Users were given two complex tasks on a computer. Their behaviour was observed and events were coded, e.g. "User uses documentation of the system". Events were than rated, counted and aggregated into two scales:

- seeking challenges
- explorative behavior

By combining these two scales, we created a total score for *resistance to the AUP*, per participant.

```
load("Cases/AUP.Rda")
attach(AUP)

AUP_1 %>%
  ggplot(aes(x = zgex, y = zresistance)) +
  geom_point() +
  geom_smooth(aes(color = "Gex"), method = "lm", se = F) +
  geom_smooth(aes(x = zncs, color = "NCS"), method = "lm", se = F) +
  labs(color = "Trait")
```

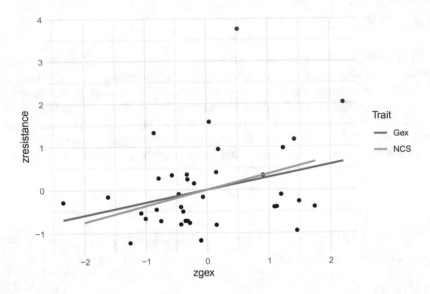

A.2   Synthetic Data Sets

A.1   *Rainfall*

We don't want to get wet, which is why we use the weather forecast. If we want to
make our own forecasts, we need data. This simulation records rainfall on 20 days.
On around 60% of these days, the sky was cloudy in the morning. With a blue sky
in the morning, the chance of rain is 30%. On cloudy days it is 60%.

```
## simulating the data set
Rainfall$simulate <-
  function(
          n_Days = 20,
          set.seed = 1,
          debug = F) {
    if (!is.na(set.seed)) set.seed()
    ## number of observations
    tibble(cloudy = rbinom(n_Days, 1, .6)) %>%
      mutate(rain = rbinom(20, 1, 0.3 + cloudy * 0.3)) %>%
      mutate(
        cloudy = as.logical(cloudy),
        rain = as.logical(rain)
      ) %>%
      as_tbl_obs()
  }
```

A.2   99 seconds

The maerketing department of a car rental website claims that "You can rent a car in 99 seconds." In this simulation, time-on-task measures are taken from 100 test users. These are Gaussian distributed with a mean of 105 and a standard error of 42. ToT also correlates with age, while there is no gender difference.

```
## simulating the data set
Sec99$simulate <-
  function(n_Part = 100,
           mu_ToT = 105,
           sigma_ToT = 30,
           set.seed = 42,
           debug = F) {
    if (!is.na(set.seed)) set.seed(set.seed)
    ## number of observations
    n_Obs <- n_Part

    ## OUT
    Sec99 <- tibble(
      Obs = 1:n_Part,
      Part = 1:n_Part,
      ToT = rnorm(n_Obs, mu_ToT, sigma_ToT)
    ) %>%
      ## dirty hack to create correlated age
      mutate(age = rpois(n_Part, rnorm(n_Part, 30 + ToT / 8, 2))) %>%
      mutate(Gender = if_else(rbinom(n_Part, 1, .4) == 1,
        "male", "female"
      ))
    Sec99 %>% as_tbl_obs()
  }

## missing values in age

Sec99$Ver20$age[c(6, 19, 73)] <- NA

load("Cases/Sec99.Rda")
attach(Sec99)
Ver20 %>%
  ggplot(aes(x = age, y = ToT)) +
  geom_point()
```

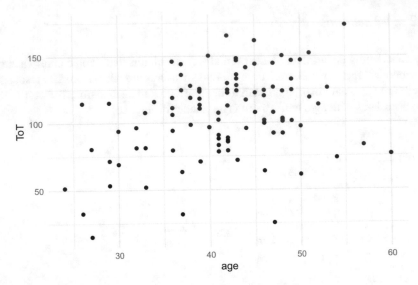

A.3 Rational

A project needs a predicted increase in revenue by a factor of 1.1 for management
to give green light. The simulation produces a between-subject comparison study,
where 50 users each see the current version of the website or the prototype. Revenue
in both groups is Gamma distributed with a mean of 100 for the current version and
a multiplyer of 1.1 for the prototype.

```
## simulating the data set
Rational$simulate <-
  function(n_Part = 100,
           mu_legacy = 50,
           eta_proto = 1.1,
           scale = 2,
           set.seed = 1,
           debug = F) {
    if (!is.na(set.seed)) set.seed(set.seed)

    RD <-
      tibble(
        Part = 1:n_Part,
        Design = rep(c("current", "proto"), n_Part / 2),
        mu = mu_legacy * ifelse(Design == "proto", eta_proto, 1),
        shape = mu / scale,
        scale = scale,
        Euro = rgamma(n_Part, shape = shape, scale = scale)
      ) %>%
      as_tbl_obs()
    RD
  }
```

A.4 BrowsingAB

```r
## simulating the data set
BrowsingAB$simulate <-
  function(
            n_Part = 100,
            n_Task = 5,
            ## within-subject design is default
            within_Part = T,
            ## Fixed effects
            # intercept
            beta_S0 = 120,
            # male
            beta_S1 = 2,
            # edu low
            beta_S2_1 = 20,
            # edu middle
            beta_S2_2 = 5,
            # age
            beta_S3 = .1,
            # age:edu low
            beta_S4_1 = .3,
            # age:edu middle
            beta_S4_2 = 0,
            # age:designB
            beta_S5 = .4,
            # designB
            beta_D1 = -60,

            ## Random effects
            # subject intercept
            sd_S0 = 20,
            # subject slope design
            sd_S1 = 10,
            # task intercept
            sd_T0 = 50,
            # Far_sightedness:Small_font
            lambda_SD1 = 60,
            # Residual
            sd_epsilon = 30,
            set.seed = 42,
            debug = F) {
    n_Design <- 2

    if (!is.na(set.seed)) set.seed(set.seed)
    ## number of observations
    n_Obs <- n_Part * n_Design * n_Task

    ## Subject frame
    Part <- tibble(
      Part = as.factor(1:n_Part),
      Gender = sample(c("F", "M"),
        size = n_Part, replace = T
```

```
  ),
  Education = sample(c("Low", "Middle", "High"),
    size = n_Part, replace = T
  ),
  theta_S0 = rnorm(n_Part, 0, sd_S0),
  theta_S1 = rnorm(n_Part, 0, sd_S1),
  age = as.integer(runif(n_Part, 20, 80))
) %>%
  # LVs
  # probability of far sightedness increases with age
  mutate(
    p_Far_sighted = age / 150
    # p_Far_sighted = plogis(mu_Far_sighted)
  ) %>%
  mutate(Far_sighted = as.logical(rbinom(n_Part, 1, p_Far_sighted)))

Task <-
  tibble(
    Task = as.factor(1:n_Task),
    theta_T0 = rnorm(n_Task, 0, sd_T0)
  )

Design <-
  tibble(Design = factor(c("A", "B"))) %>% ## LVs
  mutate(Small_font = (Design == "B"))

BrowsingAB <-
  ## creating a complete design
  expand_grid(
    Part = levels(Part$Part),
    Task = levels(Task$Task),
    Design = levels(Design$Design)
  ) %>%
  ## joining in the sample tables
  inner_join(Part) %>%
  inner_join(Design) %>%
  inner_join(Task) %>%
  ## latent variables
  # small font at website B
  mutate(lambda_SD1 * Small_font * Far_sighted) %>%
  ## dependent variable
  mutate(
    mu = beta_S0 +
      (Gender == "male") * beta_S1 +
      (Education == "Low") * beta_S2_1 +
      (Education == "Middle") * beta_S2_1 +
      age * beta_S3 +
      age * (Education == "Low") * beta_S4_1 +
      age * (Education == "Middle") * beta_S4_2 +
      age * (Design == "B") * beta_S5 +
      (Design == "B") * beta_D1 +
      theta_S0 +
      theta_S1 * (Design == "A") +
```

```
                    theta_T0 +
                    lambda_SD1 * Far_sighted * Small_font
            ) %>%
            mutate(
                ToT = rnorm(n_Obs, mu, sd_epsilon),
                clicks = rpois(n_Obs, mu / 20),
                returns = rpois(n_Obs, mu / 80),
                rating = ceiling(inv_logit((mu - 150) / 50) * 7)
            ) %>%
            select(
                Part, Task, Design,
                Gender, Education, age, Far_sighted, Small_font,
                ToT, clicks, returns, rating
            ) %>%
            as_tbl_obs()
    }
```

A.5   Headache

This simulation takes perceived headache measured on 16 participants before and
after an administration of headache pills. Participants either get both pills A and B,
only A, only B or no pill (placebo). Pill A and B are both effective on their own, but
there is a saturation effect, when both pills are taken. Baseline headache is generated
from Beta distributions. In order to avoid unplausible (i.e. negative) values, reduction
in headache involves a log transformation.

```
Headache$simulate <-
    function(N = 16,
             seed = 42) {
        set.seed(seed)
        tibble(
            before = round(rbeta(N, 3, 2) * 4 + 3),
            PillA = rep(c(TRUE, FALSE), N / 2),
            PillB = c(rep(TRUE, N / 2), rep(FALSE, N / 2))
        ) %>%
            mutate(reduction = rnorm(
                N,
                before / 7 * log(2 + 8 * PillA + 6 * PillB),
                0.5
            )) %>%
            mutate(
                PillA = as.factor(PillA),
                PillB = as.factor(PillB)
            ) %>%
            as_tbl_obs()
    }

load("Cases/Headache.Rda")
attach(Headache)
simulate() %>%
```

```
ggplot(aes(x = PillA, color = PillB, y = reduction)) +
geom_boxplot()
```

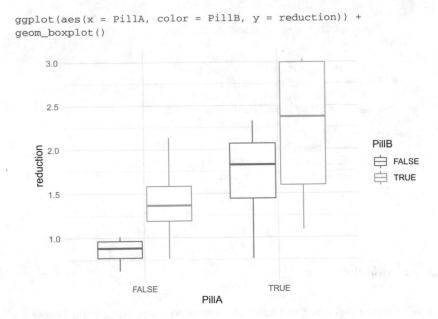

A.6   Reading Time

This simulation covers an experiment where participants got to read a text on screen and their reading time is recorded. Forty participants are divided over four experimental conditions, where the font size is either 10pt or 12pt and where the font color is either black (high contrast) or gray. Small and gray font results in an average reading time of 60 seconds. 12pt is read 12s faster and black font is read 10s faster. Due to a saturation effect, 12pt and black combined do not result in 22s, but only 14s. Reading time (ToT) is generated with Gaussian distribution.

```
Reading$simulate <-
  function(N = 40,
           beta = c(
             Intercpt = 60,
             fnt_size_12 = -12,
             fnt_color_blk = -10,
             ia_blk_12 = 8
           ),
           sigma = 5,
           seed = 42) {
    set.seed(seed)
    out <-
      tibble(
        Part = 1:N,
        font_size = factor(rep(c(1, 2), N / 2),
          levels = c(1, 2),
```

```
                  labels = c("10pt", "12pt")
              ),
              font_color = factor(c(rep(1, N / 2), rep(2, N / 2)),
                levels = c(1, 2),
                labels = c("gray", "black")
              )
          ) %>%
          mutate(
            mu = beta[1] +
              beta[2] * (font_size == "12pt") +
              beta[3] * (font_color == "black") +
              beta[4] *
    (font_color == "black") * (font_size == "12pt"),
              ToT = rnorm(N, mu, sigma)
          ) %>%
          as_tbl_obs()

        out
      }
load("Cases/Reading.Rda")
attach(Reading)
simulate() %>%
  ggplot(aes(
    col = font_color,
    x = font_size,
    y = ToT
  )) +
  geom_boxplot()
```

A.7 AR_game

A company seeks their customer profile for a novel Augmented Reality game. 200 participants rate how technophile or sociophile they are (generated from Beta distributions) and rate their intention to buy the product. The coefficients are set to create a slight benefit (for intention) of being sociophile or technophile and an amplification effect for participants that are both. Intention is sampled from a Gaussian distribution, but with an inverse logit transformation to create boundaries at [0; 1].

```
AR_game$simulate <-
  function(N = 200,
           beta = c(-1, 1, .4, .6),
           sigma = .2,
           seed = 42) {
    set.seed(seed)
    out <-
      tibble(
        Part = 1:N,
        technophile = rbeta(N, 2, 3) * 2 - 1,
        sociophile = rbeta(N, 2, 2) * 2 - 1
      ) %>%
      mutate(
        eta = beta[1] +
          beta[2] * technophile +
          beta[3] * sociophile +
          beta[4] * technophile * sociophile,
        intention = mascutils::inv_logit(rnorm(N, eta, sigma))
      ) %>%
      as_tbl_obs()

    # class(out) <- append(class(out), "sim_tbl")
    attr(out, "coef") <- list(
      beta = beta,
      sigma = sigma
    )
    attr(out, "seed") <- seed

    out %>% as_tbl_obs()
  }
load("Cases/AR_game.Rda")
attach(AR_game)
simulate() %>%
  mutate(
    technophile_grp = technophile > median(technophile),
    sociophile_grp = sociophile > median(sociophile)
  ) %>%
  ggplot(aes(
    x = sociophile_grp,
    color = technophile_grp,
    y = intention
  )) +
  geom_boxplot()
```

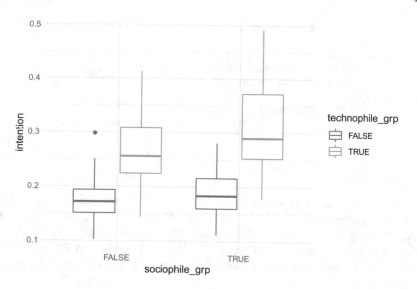

A.8   Sleep

This simulation is loosely modeled after an experiment Corcoran [%D. W. J. Corcoran (1962) Noise and loss of sleep, Quarterly Journal of Experimental Psychology, 14:3, 178-182, DOI: 10.1080/17470216208416533] who measured the combined effects of sleep deprivation and noisy environments. It turned out that noise and sleep deprivation both increase reaction times, but that noise helps when someone is very tired. Outcomes were simulated from Gaussian distributions.

```
Sleep$simulate <-
  function(N = 40,
          beta = c(
            Intcpt = 70,
            noisy = 8,
            deprived = 200,
            n_d = -100
          ),
          sigma = 50,
          seed = 42) {
  set.seed(seed)
  expand.grid(
    .N = 1:(N / 4),
    Environment = as.factor(c("Calm", "Noisy")),
    Sleep = as.factor(c("Rested", "Sleepy"))
  ) %>%
    select(-.N) %>%
    mutate(
      Part = 1:N,
      mu = beta[1] +
```

```
        beta[2] * (Environment == "Noisy") +
        beta[3] *
(Sleep == "Sleepy") +
        beta[4] * (Environment == "Noisy") * (Sleep == "Sleepy"),
     RT = rnorm(N, mu, sigma)
   ) %>%
   mutate(RT = ifelse(RT > 0, RT, NA)) %>%
   select(3, 1, 2, 4, 5) %>%
   as_tbl_obs()
 }

S <- simulate()
```

These results can be explained by the Yerkes-Dodson law, which states that performance on cognitive tasks is best under moderate arousal. It is assumed that arousal increases energy, but also causes loss of focus. These two counter-acting forces reach an optimal point somewhere in between. The two lines Energy and Focus have been produced by a logistic function, whereas Performance is the product of the two.

```
load("Cases/Sleep.Rda")
attach(Sleep)
simulate() %>%
  ggplot(aes(
    x = Environment,
    color = Sleep,
    y = RT
  )) +
  geom_boxplot()
```

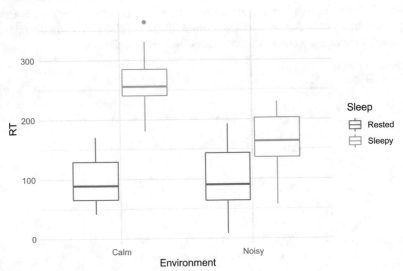

References

1. Ho CC, MacDorman KF Measuring the uncanny valley effect: refinements to indices for perceived humanness, attractiveness, and eeriness. Int J Soc Robot 9(1):129–139. https://doi.org/10.1007/s12369-016-0380-9 ISSN: 1875-4805
2. Mathur Maya B, Reichling David B (2016) Navigating a social world with robot partners: a quantitative cartography of the Uncanny Valley. Cognition 146:22–32. https://doi.org/10.1016/j.cognition.2015.09.008

Printed in the United States
by Baker & Taylor Publisher Services